Mentoring
in Health, Social Care
and
Beyond

A Handbook for Practice,
Training and Research

Edited by Sarajane Aris, Amra Rao,
Patrick Roycroft and David Clutterbuck

Mentoring in Health, Social Care and Beyond

© Pavilion Publishing & Media

The authors have asserted their rights in accordance with the Copyright, Designs and Patents Act (1988) to be identified as the authors of this work.

Published by:

Pavilion Publishing and Media Ltd
Blue Sky Offices
25 Cecil Pashley Way
Shoreham by Sea
West Sussex
BN43 5FF

Tel: +44 (0)1273 434943
Email: info@pavpub.com
Web: www.pavpub.com

Published 2024

A catalogue record for this book is available from the British Library.

ISBN: 978-1-803883-32-8

Pavilion Publishing and Media is a leading publisher of books, training materials and digital content in mental health, social care and allied fields. Pavilion and its imprints offer must-have knowledge and innovative learning solutions underpinned by sound research and professional values.

Editors: Sarajane Aris, Amra Rao, Patrick Roycroft and David Clutterbuck
Cover design: Phil Morash, Pavilion Publishing and Media Ltd
Page layout and typesetting: Tony Pitt, Pavilion Publishing and Media Ltd
Printing: Independent Publishers Group (IPG)

Contents

Foreword

Riza Kadilar

In an era marked by rapid advancements and unprecedented challenges in health and social care, the importance of effective mentoring has never been more pronounced. This book, a comprehensive exploration of mentoring practices and theories, and their transformative impact, serves as an essential guide for professionals dedicated to fostering growth, leadership, and innovation in their respective fields.

The roots of mentoring trace back to ancient times, reflecting a fundamental human need for reflection, guidance and support. In modern contexts, especially within health and social care, mentoring has evolved into a multifaceted tool that addresses complex professional and personal development needs. This evolution is meticulously charted in this volume, offering readers a thorough understanding of mentoring's historical foundations and its current applications.

Mentoring is defined here as a learning relationship, involving the sharing of skills, knowledge, and expertise between a mentor and mentee through developmental conversations, experience sharing, and role modelling. The relationship may cover a wide variety of contexts and is an inclusive two-way partnership for mutual learning that values differences. This definition, by EMCC Global, underscores the dynamic and reciprocal nature of mentoring, emphasizing its role in fostering mutual growth and understanding.

One of the book's greatest strengths is the diversity of its contributors. By bringing together esteemed scholars and practitioners from various disciplines and backgrounds, it offers a rich tapestry of perspectives and insights. This diversity not only enhances the depth and breadth of the content, but also reflects the inclusive nature of mentoring itself. Each contributor brings their unique experiences and expertise, shedding light on different facets of mentoring and its applications.

A mentor is defined as an individual who possesses a wealth of experiences, life lessons, and expertise – basically a contextual wisdom – in any given field. In the mentoring process, a mentor dispenses a meta wisdom acquired from their experiences to support the mentee's development. The dynamics between a mentor and a mentee are crafted through a dialogue rooted in mutual respect, devoid of judgment, where each party accepts the other as they are. This dialogue is not about debate, negotiation, or argument but focuses on unbiased, open communication. As a social equalizer, mentoring nurtures a transformative partnership that might otherwise not materialize, enabling both individuals to evolve and change through their interaction within a defined purpose.

The mentee, typically less experienced in the matters at hand, sets the agenda in the mentoring process. They grow and transform through the inspiration, courage, knowledge, and experience they absorb during this engagement. Mentoring is designed to facilitate a mentee's development across various subject areas via inspiring and horizon-expanding conversations. The mentor, acting as a role model, utilizes their wisdom and network to guide the mentee. This process promotes an almost utopian societal structure, free from prejudice, where each person's experience contributes to the development of others, preparing them for future challenges, empowering them, and aiding them in discovering and diversifying their own resources and capabilities.

At the corporate level, crafting a mentoring program stands as one of the most effective and efficient strategies. Mentoring, founded on unbiased dialogue, involves a knowledgeable individual using their life experiences to foster someone else's growth. This partnership emphasizes diversity and pursues mutual learning through role modelling and sharing of experiences, skills, expertise, and knowledge. As a tool for social equalization, mentoring enables a non-judgmental, empathetic dialogue, allowing two individuals who might not otherwise cross paths to engage in meaningful exchanges without bias, sympathy, or antipathy. In the realm of mentoring, the process is not about debating, negotiating, or arguing, but rather about embracing each other's perspectives as valid and engaging in a learning, evolving, and transformative partnership.

During the experience-sharing phase, mentors present their insights not as directives but as options for consideration, often concluding with a query like, "...what would you say if I said this?" This approach enhances awareness and empowers the mentee to discover their own truths and paths within a relationship underscored by privacy, respect, confidentiality, mutual trust, and a commitment to avoiding conflicts of interest. When effectively implemented, mentoring significantly contributes to fostering an inclusive culture within any organization or society where it is applied. It is crucial to pay attention to specific elements in the design and execution of mentoring programs to amplify the effectiveness of these individual mentoring interactions. In this context, I would strongly recommend the International Standards for Mentoring and Coaching Programs (ISMCP) framework provided by EMCC Global.

The book starts by laying down the groundwork by exploring past and current contexts, presenting models and research that have shaped mentoring practices. Here, as a reader, I truly enjoyed the discussions on the roots of mentoring, ethical issues, and the role of professional associations in fostering mentoring relationships. These foundational chapters are crucial for understanding how mentoring has evolved over time and the factors that continue to influence its practice today.

Then the focus shifts to initiatives and approaches in leadership and training. This section highlights innovative mentoring practices across different professions, including medicine, nursing, social work, and psychology. The chapters in this section showcase how mentoring can be tailored to meet the unique needs of diverse professional groups, emphasizing the importance of contextual understanding in mentoring. For instance, the discussion on mentoring skills for doctors and the interviews with nursing and social work professionals provide valuable real-world examples of mentoring in action.

In Section 3, the book addresses practical applications, emphasizing the development and diversity of mentoring services. From strategic approaches to mentoring within organizations to specialized programs for ethnic minorities and international contexts, these chapters offer valuable insights into implementing effective mentoring programs. The detailed accounts of programs like the National Institute for Health and Care Research Mentoring Programme and the Cherie Blair Foundation for Women's Mentoring Women in Business Programme illustrate how structured mentoring initiatives can lead to significant professional and personal development.

Finally, the book ends with various considerations about the future of mentoring. This forward-looking section encourages readers to think about the evolving nature of mentoring and its potential to address emerging challenges in health and social care. Topics such as spiritual mentoring, eco-systemic mentoring, and the boundary between coaching and mentoring are explored, providing a glimpse into the future of this critical practice. The interviews and personal reflections included in this section offer a visionary perspective on how mentoring can continue to evolve and adapt to meet future needs.

As we consider the future of mentoring, several reflective questions come to mind. Can the relatively recent growth of mentoring in health and social care spark new areas of research into the relational skills that enhance outcomes for mentees and mentors? Can the growth in mentoring training and programs lead to the development of more robust research and evaluation methods?

Professional bodies such as the EMCC Global (European Mentoring and Coaching Council) have the potential to draw together and integrate different strands of research in various contexts, supporting the accreditation of key skills common across different settings. Such actions could balance the diversity of mentoring approaches while enabling the evaluation of core skills and processes that different forms of mentoring share.

Moreover, mentoring is developing ways to integrate issues such as compassion, spirituality, and ecological factors into the framework of working. Each of these is a potential growth area for future practice and research. As mentoring evolves, can it maintain its generous and generative stance even as it moves towards more formal, and sometimes paid-for, programs? The growth of developmental relationships suggests a healthy future in which mentoring will continue to thrive.

As you embark on your journey through the pages of this book, I invite you to reflect on the profound impact that mentoring can have on individuals and organizations alike. Whether you are a seasoned mentor, a mentee, or someone new to the concept, this book offers a wealth of knowledge and inspiration to enhance your understanding and practice of mentoring. The diverse voices and insights presented here serve as a testament to the universal value of mentoring and its capacity to transform lives and communities.

In conclusion, this book is not just a collection of essays and studies; it is a beacon of wisdom for those committed to the noble endeavour of mentoring. It reminds us that mentoring is more than a professional obligation—it is a human connection that fosters growth, learning, and mutual respect. By embracing each other's perspectives as valid and engaging in a learning, evolving, and transformative partnership, mentoring becomes a tool for social equalization, enabling a non-judgmental, empathetic dialogue. As you delve into this book's chapters, may you find the guidance, inspiration, and tools you need to cultivate successful mentoring relationships in your own practice.

Dr. Riza Kadilar
President, EMCC Global

May 2024, Bennekom

About the editors

Sarajane Aris is a Consultant Clinical Psychologist, Associate Fellow of the British Psychological Society (BPS), Fellow of the Royal Society of Arts, and a mentor and coach. She has been involved in leading psychological services within the NHS for over forty years, including roles as Head of Adult Psychology Services for Derbyshire Healthcare Foundation Trust and Director of Policy for the BPS Division of Clinical Psychology. She has mentored women leaders and clinical psychologists for over twenty years. She set up and led the first national Senior Clinical Psychologists pilot mentoring scheme. She is the author or co-author of books including *Beyond Resilience: From Mastery to Mystery* and *Mental Health, Spirituality and Wellbeing*. Sarajane's life and work are informed by the principles of love, compassion, wisdom and truth, and a wish to serve and collaborate with whomever she connects with.

Amra Saleem Rao is a Consultant Clinical Psychologist and Organizational Coach and Trainer. She runs a Psychological Therapies and Organizational Consultancy in London, and she is attached to various educational and professional institutes nationally and internationally with a particular focus on leadership development, career coaching, group relations, power dynamics and therapeutic interventions. She is an Executive member of the British Psychological Society (BPS) Division of Clinical Psychology, and she chairs the BPS Leadership and Management Faculty and Faculties Network. She is involved in a number of projects in the UK in areas such as psychological practitioners' well-being, mentoring and supporting future leaders. Her specialist interest includes working with difference and power dynamics, intersectionality, spirituality, authority and leadership, and workplace well-being.

Patrick Roycroft is a Consultant Clinical Psychologist with more than twenty-five years of experience providing clinical services to people with complex mental health problems. As an Associate Director of Psychological Services within a large Mental Health Trust in the UK, he has experience of both providing and receiving mentoring. He was recently the lead for the national mentoring programme provided by the British Psychological Society (BPS), and he has been co-chair of the BPS Leadership and Management Faculty. He has published in the professional literature for clinical psychologists.

David Clutterbuck is a pioneer of developmental mentoring and the author or co-author of more than seventy-five books, including the classic *Everyone Needs a Mentor*. Published in 1985, this established key concepts of mentoring and has been revised multiple times. In 1991, David co-founded what was to become the European Mentoring and Coaching Council (EMCC), the key professional body in the field. He is practice lead at global educators Coaching and Mentoring International, and he holds a variety of academic posts internationally. His current projects include one to create five million school age coaches and mentors across the world.

Contributors

Amina Aitsi-Selmi is an award-winning leadership and career coach and author. Her clients include doctors, professionals and leaders working on global challenges who want to shift their career direction or grow their impact sustainably beyond the capitalist model of work. Prior to this, she was an academic clinician working for the UK Government on global policy including the United Nations Disaster Risk Reduction and Sustainable Development frameworks. She has co-authored more than forty peer-reviewed research papers and policy reports on health, inequality and the socioeconomic determinants of well-being, as well as the book *The Success Trap: Why Good People Stay in Jobs They Don't Like and How to Break Free*. She is the founder of the Royal Society of Arts (RSA) Coaching Network.

Nichola Ashby is Deputy Director of Nursing, Education, Research and Ethics at the Royal College of Nursing (RCN). She strategically leads organizational delivery of the RCN education, learning and development offer, research, International Diaspora and student membership across the UK. Nichola sits on the steering and advisory groups leading care audit and strategic planning, such as the National Clinical Enquiry of Outcome and Clinical Death. She influences through the development of global health policy and representing nursing and nurses from across the entire health and social care provision. As an active researcher, Nichola's PhD explored the stigmatising attitudes values and beliefs of healthcare workers towards iatrogenic infections, and she has developed a longitudinal educational model. She is a Senior Fellow of the Higher Education Academy and Honorary Associate Professor at Nottingham University. She continues to actively support research into student experiences of learning during COVID-19.

Clare Beckett-McInroy is a coach, mentor, SUPERvisor, researcher and psychometrist who has worked across sectors globally. She is a Certified Professional Co-Active Coach (CPCC) with Coaches Training Institute (CTI), and holds master coach qualifications with the International Coaching Federation (ICF), and the Association for Coaching International (AC). Described as 'The Mary Poppins of Coaching Cultures', Clare's company CoachME won the ICF Coaching Impact Award for 'Coach Education' 2023. She was awarded a special recognition in Team Coaching in 2022 from EMCC for trailblazing work supporting diversity and inclusion.

Leslie B. Brissett is Group Relations Programme Director and Company Secretary at the Tavistock Institute of Human Relations, London. Co-Director of the Dynamics at Board Level Programme, a world leading programme for those working in and with boards, Leslie co-edited the book *Dynamics at Boardroom Level: A Tavistock Primer for Leaders Coaches and Consultants*. He also directed the first group relations conference for Psychoanalysts and provides extensive consultancy to organizations, individuals and nations. He founded and co-ordinates the Global Group Relations Forum, and is a past member of the British Psychoanalytic Council's Independent Scrutiny and Advisory Committee.

Gill Buck is Associate Professor of Social Work at the University of Chester. She also co-directs the Prison Health research group at the University of Nottingham. Her research interests include peer approaches to criminal justice, lived experience-led research and practice, and the criminal justice voluntary sector. She is currently working on a large-scale research project which aims to reconceptualise prison regulation for safer societies, including the potential participatory roles of prisoners and the voluntary sector in prison regulation.

Angela Carter is an Occupational Psychologist who passionately applies the knowledge of psychology to our daily working lives. She has celebrated fifty years of working as a scientist and practitioner first in the health care sector, then in higher education and consultancy. She worked at the Institute of Work Psychology at the University of Sheffield for twenty-five years as a researcher and lecturer. She has published in a range of journals, and founded the European Association of Work and Organizational Psychology's journal *InPractice*. Latterly she has focused on youth employment, being struck by how few organizations employ young people under the age of twenty-four. Her book *Young People, Employment and Work Psychology: Interventions and Solutions* was published in 2019. Angela is involved in coaching interventions benefiting young peoples' school to work transitions in Devon.

Michelle Chan spent her first ten-year career in high-tech industry, and her second in the professional service industry. For the third ten years of her career, she has devoted herself to developing people and is one of the top executive mentors, coaches, team coaches and coaching supervisors in Asia. As a highly certified mindfulness teacher, she integrates mindfulness into her coaching and facilitation work where appropriate, coaching with exceptional presence. Michelle is currently a director and Head of the Chinese program of Transcend International, a coaching and leadership development firm, and a Faculty Member of the Global Team Coaching Institute. She also holds the position of Co-Country Director, China and Hong Kong, for Potential Project – the leading global mindfulness-based corporate training organization. She speaks native Mandarin and fluent English and Cantonese.

Paddy Cooney was, prior to his retirement in 2012, Director of the South West Development Centre of the National Institute for Mental Health In England. He was also Programme Lead for the Social Inclusion and Social Justice Programme within the National Mental Health Development Unit in DH. Prior to that, he was Chief Executive of the Somerset Partnership NHS and Social Care Trust, the first integrated mental health trust in Britain. A social worker by background, he worked in the mental health services in Nottingham and Sheffield and at the Centre for Mental Health Services Development in King's College London. Since 2012, Paddy has worked as a freelance consultant, including undertaking Interim Director of Mental Health Network with the NHS Confederation. He is also a Director of 121Support, a community interest company providing free mentoring to managers working in mental health services. Paddy has served on the board of Mental Health First Aid (England) and Second Step Housing, Bristol, and he chairs Irish Counselling & Psychotherapy (ICAP).

Tony Dickel is a seasoned and highly credentialed executive coach, team coach, coach trainer, and coaching and team coaching supervisor. As a coach, he has successfully helped leaders and teams grow in horizontal, skills-based leadership development as well as through catalysing vertical, capacity-building experiences which support individuals as they navigate the ever-increasing velocity of 'complexification'. Tony's expertise includes helping leaders and teams to develop exceptional individual and collective attentional, cognitive, motivational and emotional balance, discovering and working with limiting beliefs and biases through evidence-based interventions drawn from disciplines including mindfulness-based approaches, cognitive-behavioural approaches, positive psychology and neuroscience. He is passionate about and skilled in 'brain-based' leadership, coaching, mentoring and supervision.

Nora Dominguez is Director of the Mentoring Institute at the University of New Mexico (UNM), and President Emeritus of the International Mentoring Association (IMA). Nora has over thirty years of experience, holding academic and management positions in banking and higher education institutions and providing consulting and program evaluation services in the USA and Mexico. She is Chair of the American Educational Research Association (AERA) Mentoring and Mentorship Practices Special Interest Group and the UNM Annual Mentoring Conference. Nora sits on the Editorial Board of the *International Journal for Mentoring and Coaching*, is co-editor of the books *Making Connections: A Handbook for Effective Formal Mentoring Programs in Academia*, *Reciprocal Mentoring* and *The SAGE Handbook of Mentoring*, and Chief Editor of the online journal *The Chronicle of Mentoring and Coaching*.

Lillian Turner Eby is Distinguished Research Professor and a Faculty Member in the Industrial-Organisational Psychology Program at the University of Georgia. She is a Fellow of the American Psychological Association, the Association for Psychological Science, the Society for Industrial and Organisational Psychology, and the Academy of Management. Her research interests centre on relationships at work, factors that predict individual career success, worker well-being, and the intersection of work and family life. She has published over one hundred peer-reviewed articles in outlets such as *Journal of Applied Psychology, Personnel Psychology, Psychological Bulletin*, and *Journal of Vocational Behavior* among others. She is former Associate Editor of *Personnel Psychology* as well as the *Journal of Applied Psychology*. Currently she is the Editor in Chief of the *Journal of Applied Psychology*.

Lisa Fain is CEO of the Center for Mentoring Excellence, where she spends her time working with organisations across the globe to create more inclusive workplaces through mentoring. A global speaker, master facilitator, and executive coach, Lisa works with individuals and groups of all sizes to help them discover and create mentoring excellence. She formerly led the diversity and inclusion function at Outerwall Inc. and was an employment attorney at a multinational law firm for almost a decade. She lives in Seattle, where she loves to hike and enjoy the US Pacific North West with friends and family.

Tom Fairweather has worked for a UK Member of Parliament for fifteen years. He started work in Parliament as an intern in 2009, before becoming a caseworker, senior caseworker, and parliamentary assistant and finally running a Westminster office. He takes a particular interest in positive management practices, well-being at work, and making staff feel valued. In 2021 he co-authored a report with a cross-party group of Office Managers which highlighted concerns of unsustainable workloads in parliamentary offices and the associated impacts on well-being, retention rates and the democratic functions of Parliament. He currently co-runs the Wellness Working Group, a group set up to promote the betterment of the well-being of staff in parliamentary offices. More often than not, when he isn't working, Tom can either be found in the gym or unwinding by painting miniatures and playing board games.

Bob Garvey is Emeritus Professor at York St. John University, and an internationally known leading academic practitioner of mentoring and coaching. He is an experienced mentor/coach working with a range of people in a variety of contexts and subscribes to the 'repertoire' approach to mentoring and coaching. An active and widely published researcher, Bob is in demand as a keynote conference speaker, webinar facilitator and workshop leader. His latest book, with Paul Stokes, *Coaching and Mentoring: Theory and Practice* was published in 2022 as a fourth edition. He is a founding member of the EMCC and has been awarded the EMCC's Mentor award. In 2014 he received a Lifetime Achievement Award for contributions to mentoring. He is currently involved with the International Mentoring Institute by facilitating the 'Much Ado About Mentoring' series of webinars.

Dawn Gosden is a dual Chartered Coaching and Occupational Psychologist, an Associate Fellow of the British Psychological Society (BPS) and a Registered Psychologist with the Health and Care Professions Council (HCPC). She is also an Accredited Coach and Coach Supervisor with the International Society for Coaching Psychologists. Dawn has twenty-four years' experience of providing management consultancy services, with strategic level experience of leadership development and organisational change initiatives, including designing and implementing two organisational coaching strategies with the objective of improving leadership capability and bringing about organisational change through coaching. Since 2020, she has taken the lead on designing and implementing the BPS South West Branch Coaching and Mentoring Scheme. Throughout her career, Dawn has demonstrated a passion and commitment to working with individuals and groups, helping them to raise their self-awareness and confidence and to unblock any barriers to their careers.

Julie Haddock-Millar is Associate Professor of Human Resource Development at Middlesex University and Visiting Professor at the International University of Monaco. She is EMCC Global Work Group Lead for the International Standards for Mentoring and Coaching Programmes. Julie is an EMCC Global EIA Master Practitioner Coach and Mentor, Global IPMA Master Practitioner Coaching and Mentoring Programme Manager, and Global ITCA Practitioner Team Coach. She completed her Coach-Mentor Supervision training with the Tavistock Institute in Human Relations. Julie is an experienced consultant and researcher undertaking significant global programme impact evaluations with organizations such as Médecins Sans Frontières, Youth Business International and the Cherie Blair Foundation for Women.

Denise Harris has nearly forty years' experience of working in the NHS. She originally qualified as an Occupational Therapist, then moved to work within leadership and organizational development roles. Denise qualified as a coach in 2008 and as a coach supervisor in 2010. She has a particular interest in coaching and mentoring in the NHS and how these can be used to support, enable and develop staff. She is also interested in the impact that a coaching approach can have on the effectiveness of clinical interventions. The subject of her PhD thesis was 'Supervision in the NHS', a topic that she is passionate about. She continues to practice supervision, coaching and coaching supervision within her own organization across the Southeast region, and as an independent coach supervisor.

Lydia Hartland-Rowe is an Organizational Consultant in Tavistock Consulting, part of the Tavistock and Portman NHS Foundation Trust, working with people at all levels of organizations to support reflective capacity, skills and understanding. She is also a child and adolescent psychotherapist by background and has worked in a range of clinical CAMHS settings in the NHS and voluntary sector. She was Editor of the *Journal of Child Psychotherapy* between 2018 and 2021. She was a Cohort Director on the Elizabeth Garrett Anderson NHS Leadership Academy programme for senior leaders, and for over twenty years has taught and led a range of programmes focused on improving understanding of workplace dynamics at access, postgraduate and doctoral levels. She has been involved in Group Relations work, a transformational model for learning about organisational processes, since 2010. On behalf of the Association of Child Psychotherapists, she contributed to the development and delivery of the 'RISE' Mentoring training module, and as a Senior Fellow of the Higher Education (now Advance HE) she has mentored colleagues successfully to Fellowship and Senior Fellowship.

Peter Hawkins is Emeritus Professor of Leadership at Henley Business School, Chairman of Renewal Associates, and co-founder of the Global Team Coaching Institute. He is a global thought leader and a leading international consultant, coach, writer and researcher in systemic coaching, organizational strategy, leadership, culture change, team and board development, mentoring and coaching. He has coached more than a hundred boards and senior executive teams, enabling them to develop their purpose, vision, values, collective leadership and strategy in a wide range of companies, government departments, Health Trusts, professional services organizations and charities. Peter co-founded Bath Consultancy Group in 1986, was its chairman until the company was sold in 2010, and has chaired three other company boards as well as being a trustee director of several charities. He is the author of many best-selling books and papers in the fields of leadership, board and team coaching, systemic coaching, mentoring, supervision and organizational transformation.

Sarah Howarth joined the National Institute for Health and Care Research (NIHR) in 2021 as Development and Support Manager, with overall responsibility for the NIHR leadership and mentoring offer. Sarah gained her bachelor's degree in public relations from Exeter University. She recently co-authored a chapter for the book *Reciprocal Mentoring*, exploring the NIHR postdoctoral Academy Members mentoring programme. The programme supports postdoctoral researchers from a broad range of professional and disciplinary contexts across our diverse health and social care communities to mentor others and to seek a mentor. Sarah and her team adopted the EMCC Global International Standards in Mentoring and Coaching Programmes to provide structure, clarity, and rigour to the mentoring programme.

Sabinah Janally is a clinical psychologist in the NHS; she is also an EDI tutor on the Exeter Doctorate in Clinical Psychology, and a senior lecturer and academic lead on the Doctorate in Clinical Research at the University of Exeter. Her areas of specialism include trauma-informed anti-racism practice, occupational psychology, staff well-being, leadership and mentoring.

Paul Jenkins worked for more than thirty years in various health and care roles in Central Government, the voluntary sector and the NHS. He had a key role in the establishment of NHS Direct: at the time, the world's largest telephone and internet-based healthcare provider. For fifteen years, he worked as a Chief Executive in mental health in roles in the voluntary sector and the NHS.

Surinder Johore is a Principal/Lead Child and Adolescent Psychotherapist who has worked in NHS CAMHS services for twenty years. She is a Course Organiser and Tutor on the Tavistock and Portman NHS Trust MA course in Psychoanalytic Observational Studies, and is interested in applying psychoanalytic thinking in her clinical and teaching roles to further and deepen understanding to support work with children and families. Surinder has been a Service Supervisor to Trainee Child and Adolescent Psychotherapists working in CAMHS services. She also offers supervision and consultation to the MDT, and to other professionals working with infants, children and young people across the statutory and voluntary sector. She is a mentor on the HEE Rise mentoring scheme and is interested in issues around identity and diversity.

A. Maya Kaye is a neuroscience-informed, compassion-focused psychotherapist, researcher and professor. As a South Asian multilingual woman, she brings a unique perspective to her work, allowing her to connect with a diverse range of patients and colleagues. In her clinical work, she combines a variety of mind-body modalities that promote mind, brain, and body integration. Her professional and academic experiences have been diverse, with research playing a major role in her career. She is committed to contributing to scholarship involving the applications of compassion in psychotherapy, mentoring, and epilepsy care.

Neil Kaye is a Research Fellow at IOE, UCL's Faculty of Education and Society. He is an experienced researcher in the fields of social science, educational research and social policy evaluation, having worked on a wide range of local, national, European and international projects, evaluations and consultancies. His research interests include social inequalities, education policy, youth transitions, and the impact of mentoring and coaching. Neil has held research positions at the University of Cambridge and at UCL, as well as undertaking research consultancies in collaboration with Youth Business International, Médecins Sans Frontières (MSF) and the European Mentoring and Coaching Council (EMCC).

Kathy E. Kram is the R.C. Shipley Professor in Management Emerita at Boston University, USA. Her primary interests are in the areas of adult development and life transitions, relational learning, mentoring and developmental networks, gender and leadership development, and change processes in organizations. In addition to her book *Mentoring at Work*, she has co-authored *Strategic Relationships at Work: Creating your Circle of Mentors, Sponsors and Peers for Success in Business and Life* and *Peer Coaching at Work: Principles and Practices* and has co-edited *The Handbook of Mentoring at Work: Theory, Research and Practice*. In addition, she has published in many academic and practitioner journals. She is a founding member of the Center for Research on Emotional Intelligence in Organizations (CREIO), served as a member of the Center for Creative Leadership (CCL) Board of Governors from 2002 to 2009, and is currently a Principal in the ICW Consulting Group. Her current project, with a team of five retired colleagues, is a study of the transition into retirement.

Charmaine Kwame is Director of the Leadership Lounge and has been an executive coach for fifteen years. She has a breadth of knowledge across industries including healthcare, finance and pharma, and her work has included enabling high quality healthcare leadership development as National Lead for Coaching and Mentoring at NHS England and working with global executive leaders as Director of Coaching Services at CoachSource LLC. Charmaine was instrumental in the design and delivery of ground-breaking coaching and mentoring programs within the NHS, applying these to some of the most challenging issues faced by the system including equality, diversity and inclusion, ethical decision making and pandemic recovery and reset. She led on the amalgamation and expansion of coaching and mentoring registers across NHS England through delivery of a national digital platform, and commissioned research to understand and take action on systemic barriers to access.

Kelly Laham is an assistant professor at the University of North Carolina Wilmington (UNCW) School of Nursing. As an Adult Nurse Practitioner, she has practiced in both cardiology and rural primary care, which led to her rural health research focus. Kelly entered academia in 1998 and has taught across associate, baccalaureate, masters, and doctoral nursing degree programs. In working with students, she has served as a mentor for over twenty-five years, both formally and informally. As the former Doctor of Nursing Practice coordinator, she collaborated in establishing the DNP Mentoring Program. She continues to be a mentor in the community through the arts community and a tiny home village for those experiencing homelessness. She was honoured for her work in the community by receiving the YWCA Woman of Achievement Award in Health and Wellness in 2010.

Lise Lewis is the founder of Bluesky International, immediate Past President and Special Ambassador of EMCC Global, and an EMCC Global accredited coach, mentor, mentor supervisor and master coach. Lisa is a practicing Executive Coach and Mentor, working at a senior level supporting individuals to excel as team and relational leaders. She is a global keynote speaker and contributor of coaching, mentoring and supervision related webinars including AI, Ethics, EQ/SQ, Why Supervision Makes Sense, Leadership Development and Relational Feedback. A volunteer with EMCC Global for more than twenty years, Lise has initiated and contributed to the creation of professional standards in coaching, mentoring and supervision. She is a winner of the EMCC Global Supervisor Award and has been Highly Recommended for the Coaching at Work Contributions to Coaching Supervision Award and the Coaching at Work External Coaching Mentoring Champion Award.

Laura Lunsford is Professor of Psychology and Assistant Dean in the School of Education and Human Sciences at Campbell University, North Carolina. She consults with organizations on effective mentoring and coaching, and she is an expert in mentoring and leadership. A US Fulbright Scholar (Germany), she has written over fifty peer-reviewed articles, case studies and chapters on leadership and mentoring. She wrote the definitive guide for mentoring programs *The Mentor's Guide: Five Steps to Build a Successful Mentor Program*, now in its second edition, co-edited *The SAGE Handbook of Mentoring*, and co-authored *Faculty Development in Liberal Arts Colleges*. She received the International Mentoring Association's Hope dissertation award. Laura work has been funded by, among others, the National Science Foundation, the Institute for Decision Sciences, and the Department of Education.

Steph McTighe is an English-qualified solicitor, CEDR accredited mediator and former office manager to a Member of Parliament. Specialising in commercial and civil disputes, she has a keen interest in the concept of 'access to justice'. Having temporarily left behind her legal career, she is interested in 'how' things are done in the workplace and not just what is achieved. She values the need for role models to relate to and sees the importance of mentoring – especially in typically hierarchal structures. Whilst working in Westminster she collaborated in establishing a well-being group for the benefit of MPs' staff UK-wide. She also co-authored a 2019 report recommending additional supports for UK families bereaved by murder or suspicious death overseas. Having worked in London, Dubai and New York, she has returned to Edinburgh where she works as a solicitor for international law firm CMS.

Stephen Murgatroyd is a former Dean of the Faculty of Business at Athabasca University, Canada, and founder of the world's first fully online MBA. He has been an innovative pioneer of technology-enabled, flexible learning since he began his career at The Open University, UK. Since leaving a full-time university post, Stephen has worked extensively in the private sector as CEO of a large UK human resource consultancy and then, back in Canada, as an entrepreneur leading consulting, technology, and publishing companies. He has consulted for governments across Canada and worldwide on technology innovation, higher education, organizational change, and transformation. He is CEO of the Collaborative Media Group Inc., and he is an in-demand keynote speaker. He has published more than forty books and over four hundred papers, articles, and book chapters.

Efe Olokpa is a passionate advocate for women's empowerment and community development. She joined the Cherie Blair Foundation for Women in 2019 after working as a Programme Manager with Ambition Institute, leading their Governance Leadership Programme in partnership with the Confederation of School Trusts. Prior to that, Efe devoted herself to causes supporting trafficked women and human rights activists. At the Foundation, Efe manages the Mentoring Women in Business Programme across sixty low and middle-income countries. Her role involves overseeing day-to-day delivery and account management of successful partnerships with institutional partners like USAID as well as private sector partners like Bank of America, PayPal and Blackstone. She also handles program monitoring, evaluation, and develops tailored service offerings for partners.

Jonathan Passmore is Professor of Coaching and Behavioural Change at Henley Business School, and Senior Vice President at EZRA Coaching. Prior to this, he worked in a number of senior roles and held executive and non-executive posts in local government, the commercial sector and a national mental health charity. He has published widely over the past twenty-five years, with more than forty books and over two hundred and fifty scientific papers and book chapters, making him one of the most published writers in the field of coaching His recent titles include *Becoming a Coach: The Essential ICF Guide, Third Wave Cognitive-Behavioural Coaching* and *The Coaches' Handbook'*. His work has been recognised by awards from the BPS, ABP and EMCC, and he is listed on the Global Gurus List as one of the top executive coaches in their world.

Agnese Pinto works for Doctors Without Borders (Médecins Sans Frontières), holding the position of Programme Manager for the internal Individual Coaching Programme within the Mentoring and Coaching Hub (MCHub). She is based in Oslo, Norway, and has worked in the humanitarian sector for almost twenty years, with various NGOs and with the United Nations. She has been a coach since 2018 and has been influential in promoting quality standards and research evaluations of the services provided by the MCHub. She is passionate about exploring the ethical aspects of coaching practice and its function within the organization, promoting ongoing reflection and learning opportunities around it. She is accredited with the EMCC as both a coach (EIA) and a programme manager (PMQA).

Helen Pote is Professor of Clinical Psychology and Director of Clinical Programmes for Psychological Practitioners at Royal Holloway, University of London. She has over twenty-five years' experience of developing clinical training programmes and working with children and families across a variety of health and education services, both in person and online. Helen and Dr Jenny Taylor led the development of National and London Regional mentoring schemes for Clinical Psychologists for the British Psychological Society (BPS) Division of Clinical Psychology and Health Education England.

Cathy Presland is an experienced coach and facilitator. She is a former economist and worked for fifteen years in senior policy and strategy roles with the UK government. Prior to that, she worked on institutional reform with Central European Governments, and spent a number of years in Southern Africa working with NGO's, think tanks and international organisations on poverty alleviation. She primarily works with people in leadership roles in the social and international sectors seeking deeper contemplation of their role and how to create impact with what they do. As a volunteer, she has been a co-lead of the RSA coaching network for the past five years, coordinating a series of events on which her chapter is partly based.

Colleen Qvist is Director of CQ Associates. She works with individuals and groups and hosts Healthcare Hour on Vuka Online Radio. She is a Master Coach, Master Mentor and trained facilitator who partners professionally with her clients to discover who they are at a human level. Titles can obscure reality and often, especially in healthcare, the professional can be perceived as non-human. Colleen creates a space for people to be vulnerable and to feel non-judged as they come to terms with unlearning, learning, change, growth, connection, managing their stress, achieving BIG goals and finding the meaning in their lives. She also partners with other stakeholders to make a bigger difference in the world.

Masuma Rahim is a clinical psychologist, neuropsychologist, systemic practitioner, and expert witness specialising in brain injury and mental capacity. In 2019 she was appointed Special Medical Visitor to the Court of Protection and the Office of the Public Guardian by the Lord Chancellor. She is presently Director of Professional Ethics and Standards for the Association of Clinical Psychologists (UK). She is a member of the Committee on Training in Clinical Psychology, the national clinical psychology accreditation board, as well as a Visiting Lecturer at the University of Hertfordshire and an External Examiner for the Clinical Psychology Doctoral Programmes at the Universities of Karachi and Bahria.

Paula Reid is Associate Professor at the University of North Carolina Wilmington (UNCW) School of Nursing, where she founded the mentoring program with Kelly Laham and Laura Lunsford. Prior to this, she spent more than twenty years as a Women's Healthcare Nurse Practitioner. A large portion of her clinical practice and expertise included the care of a very diverse patient population at the nationally known Parkland Hospital in Dallas, Texas. This is where she developed a passion for caring for women living with HIV, and it flourished over to her PhD dissertation, research, scholarship, and publications with The International Nursing Network for HIV Research. She has mentored many healthcare professionals and students in clinical and academic areas over her professional career of almost forty years.

Melissa Richardson had a two-decade corporate career before moving into executive coaching and mentoring consultancy in 2003. Until 2022, she was CEO at Art of Mentoring, a mentoring software and services company she co-founded, and led the company's research initiatives, product development, as well as creation of an extensive training curriculum for mentors, mentees and mentoring program managers. Melissa is a member of the global assessment team for the European Mentoring and Coaching Council's ISMCP Award (International Standards for Mentoring and Coaching Programs). She has postgraduate qualifications in organisational coaching, counselling and marketing strategy. She current provides coaching and mentoring through her company, Horizons Unlimited in Australia.

Anne Rolfe is a UK-born Australian, living on the coast of New South Wales. Now retired, Ann Rolfe was a trainer, consultant, and coach. Prior to 2022, she spent over thirty years helping organizations to set up and run mentoring programs, train mentors and mentees and provide career development. She continues to make her life's work in mentoring, career, and strengths-based development accessible through her books and free webinars. She is the author of *Mentoring Mindset Skills and Tools, The Mentors Toolkit for Career Conversations*, and *Advanced Mentoring Skills: Taking Your Conversations to the Next Level*.

Chandana Sanyal is Associate Professor in Human Resource Management and Development at Middlesex University Business School, and EMCC Global Group Lead for European Individual Accreditation (EIA). Chandana is an EMCC Global EIA Master Practitioner Coach and Mentor and EMCC Global ITCA Practitioner Team Coach. She completed her Coach-Mentor Supervision training with the Tavistock Institute of Human Relations. She is a CIPD Academic Assessor and an external examiner for Ashridge Business School.

Rachel E. Scudamore holds the role of Head of QA and Standards at the British Psychological Society (BPS) and is responsible for the oversight of quality in the Society's educational offerings. Rachel has over twenty-five years' experience in academic development in higher education in Russell Group and post-92 inner city settings. She has focused on facilitating reflective practice and enabling university staff from all disciplines to find ways to address contemporary challenges including massification, internationalisation and commercialisation while retaining a student-centred approach. Her responsibilities have also included educational strategy development, managing student services and leading the implementation of innovative technical projects. At the BPS, Rachel has worked with a group of expert members to develop the Society's strategy and infrastructure for supporting members' mentoring programmes.

Nicki Seignot has more than thirty years' experience in the field of people management, leadership development and coaching. She has worked closely with senior leaders and executive board members across a wide range of organisations to design and implement mentoring and coaching programmes and lead flagship leadership and diversity programmes. Nicki is the founder of The Parent Mentor, an independent specialist consultancy which works within organisations to develop internal mentoring programmes in support of returning talent post parental leave. She is the co-author of the first business book on parental mentoring, *Mentoring New Parents at Work*.

Carolyn Smith qualified as a social worker in 2010 and has worked across a range of child protection settings. Since 2019, she has worked as an Advanced Social Work Practitioner within Wakefield Council's Learning Academy. The overarching remit of the Learning Academy is to work alongside practitioners to improve practice and create a resilient, confident, and research informed workforce. Carolyn has since progressed to be the Newly Qualified Social Worker and Student Social Worker lead, and she holds responsibility for nurturing their practice and supporting them to thrive in their role delivery. Across her role remits, Carolyn has supported, mentored and coached over fifty students, as well as over sixty NQSWs. Her passion and dedication to this work led to her being awarded 'Practice Educator of the Year' at the 2022 National Social Work Awards.

Akshay Sood is Distinguished Professor, Regents Professor, and the founding Miners' Colfax Medical Center Endowed Chair at the University of New Mexico's School of Medicine. Passionate about the role of mentoring junior faculty, he leads the UNM HSC Faculty Mentor Development Program, which has been adopted by thirteen institutions in seven states. He is Assistant Dean of Mentoring and Faculty Retention at the UNM School of Medicine Office of Faculty Affairs and Career Development, and past Associate Director of the Mentoring Core of the Mountain West-CTR-IN Professional Development Core. He is a national expert on faculty development and retention, with presentations at the UNM Mentoring Conference/AAMC. His work on faculty development has been published in *Academic Medicine, Journal of Continuing Education in the Health Professions*, and the *Chronicle of Mentoring and Coaching*. His current research interest is on the assessment of the institutional mentoring climate, strategies to improve URM faculty retention, and innovative mentor development initiatives.

Paul Stokes is Associate Professor of Coaching and Mentoring at Sheffield Business School, Sheffield Hallam University, UK. He is an EMCC Master Practitioner and an experienced consultant, researcher, coach, mentor and coach-supervisor. He has published many book chapters and peer reviewed journal articles on coaching and mentoring, and has co-written two books on coaching and mentoring: *Mentoring in Action* and *Coaching and Mentoring Theory and Practice*. In 2002, he co-founded one of the first Masters programmes in Coaching and Mentoring in the UK which is accredited at Master Practitioner level by the EMCC.

Rita Symons is a coach, mentor and leadership development specialist. She is passionate about supporting coaches and mentors at all stages of their development, being an accredited supervisor as well as a Senior Practitioner Coach. She was an internal coach in the NHS and held numerous posts, ten years of which were at Board level. She has lived experience of being a BAME Chief Officer. She has undertaken research commissioned to inform the national NHS Coaching strategy, a focus of which was looking at how coaching can be more inclusive, in terms of the diversity of coaches and individuals who access coaching. Rita also provided expert input co-leading the development of the Reciprocal Mentoring for Inclusion programme, and she works on inclusion programmes as well as senior leadership programmes. Until 2021, Rita was the President of EMCC UK.

Suzanne Triggs is a professional development coach, a registered social worker and a coaching trainer. She has spent almost thirty years in social work and has led many different projects in local authorities to improve social work practice. Her trailblazing doctoral research was the first globally to explore the use of coaching with social work practitioners and leaders. In 2021 she received Harvard's Institute of Coaching inaugural award for 'Coaching for the Social Good'. Suzanne runs a private coaching practice (coachdoctor.org), and during the pandemic she began offering free coaching to anyone in the social care professions via her Twitter account. She has since coached and trained more than three hundred social care staff, ranging from directors to students. She is a founder member of the 'Coaching for Social Impact' Community which aims to bring together anyone involved in coaching for the social good in a supportive and collaborative network.

Eve Turner has had multiple careers – in music, broadcasting and coaching, supervision, writing and research – and sees the connections through her interest in communication, collaboration and interrelationships. As a classical guitarist and occasional orchestral conductor, she understands how the whole can be more than the sum of the parts and how clarity of communication and relationships can affect outcomes. Eve was a journalist, senior leader and internal coach in the BBC before setting up her practice, winning many awards for her working and supervision. She co-founded the Climate Coaching Alliance, founded and co-leads the Global Supervisors' Network, and volunteers for APECS, the AC and the EMCC. Her writing includes co-editing or co-authoring *The Ethical Coaches Handbook, Ecological and Climate-Conscious Coaching: A Companion Guide to Evolving Coaching Practice, Systemic Coaching* and *The Heart of Coaching Supervision: Working with Reflection and Self-Care.*

Robyn Vesey is an Organisational Consultant and Leadership Coach. Originally trained as a clinical psychologist, after twenty years working in the NHS Robyn now consults to individuals and organisations from the Tavistock's systems psychodynamic model. She is Programme Director for Tavistock Consulting's Executive Coaching Programme, accredited at senior practitioner level by the EMCC. Robyn lectures, supervises and contributes to a number of other training programmes including at the Tavistock and Portman NHS Trust where she is a Visiting Lecturer on Professional Doctorate and Masters' programmes. She also works as a Group Relations Consultant and is Programme Director for the Advanced Personal Leadership Programme at Henley Business School.

Rebecca Viney founded, crafted and led the award-winning Coaching and Mentoring Service for doctors and dentists across London from 2008 until 2014. There were more than three thousand applications to be coached or mentored, and they trained over six hundred doctors substantively. In 2011, they won the National Leadership and Innovation Agency for Health Care Excellence in Human Resources award for their educational development strategy and enabling the concept to go viral. In 2012 Rebecca went on to pioneer the introduction of 'health coaching' training to the medical profession in the UK. During the COVID-19 pandemic, she co-founded the UK-wide 'Doctors' Mess', which celebrated diversity, inclusivity, kindness and self-compassion and became the 'caring for carers' charity. Rebecca has published and spoken extensively on coaching, mentoring and careers, both in the UK and internationally.

Trevor Waldock is a social entrepreneur, executive coach and mentor, who is especially committed to seeing the potential of young leaders liberated across the world. He created the for-profit company, The Executive Coach Ltd, with a blue-chip client list working across all sectors and developed the Integrated Global Leadership Model, a holistic framework used in corporate leadership development. In 2005, Trevor founded the international charity Emerging Leaders, a global non-profit that brings the best leadership development to the most vulnerable communities in the world. The Emerging Leaders programmes have impacted almost ninety thousand people in over twenty countries, with an indirect impact on over two and a half million people. Trevor has written and spoken on a wide range of leadership issues across three continents, and his nine books include *The 18 Challenges of Leadership* and *To Plant A Walnut Tree – The Legacy Beyond Leadership*.

Estelle Warhurst has eighteen years' experience of working as an Office Manager for a Member of Parliament. She joined the MPs Staff Wellness Working Group (WWG) as an Executive Committee Member in 2020, bringing to the role her passion for equality and access to mental health services for all. The WWG won the 'Outstanding Contribution Award' at the Parliamentary Staff Awards 2021 and the 'Your Parliamentary Community Award' at the 2021 Living Our Values Awards within Parliament Awards, jointly with the Members Services Team. Estelle is co-author of the WWG Reports 2021 and 2023; in her spare time, she volunteers for a well-being and mental health service hosted by the NHS.

Introduction

"Every great achiever is inspired by a mentor."

– Lailah Gifty Akita

'We are living in exceptional times.' This phrase, or one like it, must be uttered by every generation as it faces new and seemingly impossible challenges. With COVID-19 and the ensuing pandemic, we have recently navigated a global crisis of health and well-being that has left inequalities starkly exposed. As the Editors of this handbook, we are acutely aware of working against the backdrop of strongly polarised political upheaval across the world, events in Ukraine threatening a Third World War, socio-economic instability, cost of living crises and extremes of climate change – all of which could jeopardise our future survival.

Uncertainty looks us squarely in the face. No-one is unaffected in today's complex, volatile, often highly competitive, socio-technological globalised world. Never has there been a more appropriate time to consider creative possibilities for conversations, connections, and a collective 'lifting up' to face adversity. Hence the importance of mentoring in and for the world – for all people, across a range of sectors, organizations and life stages, to support and inspire them throughout the life cycle on their professional and personal journeys.

The social entrepreneur and thought leader Marc Freedman speaks about it eloquently:

"Mentoring brings us together – across generation, class, and often race – in a manner that forces us to acknowledge our interdependence, to appreciate, in Martin Luther King, Jr.'s words, that 'We are caught in an inescapable network of mutuality, tied to a single garment of destiny'."

Acknowledging the power of mutuality, mentoring can offer connections through conversations involving generational transmission of knowledge and experience. While it has existed for a long time, mentoring is increasingly being recognized as a method for achieving personal growth, professional and leadership development, well-being and workplace success. Mentoring relationships enable and nurture the qualities that make for exceptional leaders and performers in all walks of life, particularly within the public sector.

When designing this Handbook, we were mindful of the existence of a number of apparently similar works. As a result, we have chosen to build on what has gone before and to focus on the present context, current innovations and the future of mentoring, rather than to revisit detailed definitions, history, theoretical approaches, or methodological issues. These are dealt with extensively in other volumes; the uniqueness of this work lies in bringing together the experiences, perspectives and learning of a wide range of authors to open further space for discovery and growth in the field. Some chapter authors have chosen to include definitions, history or theories to set the scene for their contribution; however, the overarching ambition is to build on the existing knowledge base, to bring in new ideas for enriching practice, to explore cutting-edge innovations, and to examine mentoring from varied perspectives.

Whilst our primary focus is on health, social care and the public sector, we also cover other contexts and environments such as business, education and youth mentoring schemes – bringing together examples of applications informed by diverse theoretical perspectives. We feature initiatives that focus on particular areas of need – such as mentoring where careers intersect with parenthood, and mentoring to support leadership development for those from minority backgrounds. This breadth is intended to open up space for new ideas and learning. We also include fresh ideas such as spirituality, ecology, compassion, and attention to race and identity. By pushing boundaries in this way, and by widening the available space for innovative thinking, we hope that this Handbook will reinvigorate the mentoring field, opening new possibilities for further growth in areas where it has stalled somewhat.

We aim to offer an international flavour, considering a broad and rich variety of mentoring approaches and perspectives from well-known and less familiar authors. We also draw from a range of other sectors and schemes such as the Royal Society of Arts, the British Government and the Cherie Blair Foundation. Due to space restrictions, we have highlighted only a few mentoring initiatives from different countries. We are mindful that mentoring schemes and initiatives are developing elsewhere, such as in the Nordic countries, and these are referenced for the reader to follow up. We hope to ignite interest in looking at adaptations and innovations across cultures in our increasingly globalised world, and to add a valuable, forward-looking and complementary resource to those that have gone before.

This Handbook is divided into four sections:

- **Section One** includes chapters that explore the origins and development of mentoring, methodological issues in mentoring research and training, ethical and moral dilemmas, and the evolution of research in the mentoring field.

- **Section Two** is divided into three parts. The first part showcases examples of initiatives across a range of settings and professional groups such as medicine, nursing, social work, psychology, business, and law, demonstrating creativity and adaptation using a variety of theoretical frameworks, methodologies and approaches. The second part looks at approaches to mentoring for leadership development and legacy, offering perspectives to consider how mentoring can support leaders in a volatile, uncertain, complex, and ambiguous (VUCA) world. Finally, the third part introduces a variety of other relevant themes – including power dynamics, identity, race, diversity and intersectionality.

- **Section Three** focuses on examples of innovation and growth in mentoring practice and training. A range of themes are covered, such as mentoring through informal networks, addressing diversity, inclusivity, and equality with attention to wider systemic factors through a developmental approach. Readers will note the rich landscape of settings, with a particular focus on innovation and addressing cutting edge issues.

- ■ **Section Four** includes chapters that speak specifically to emerging and 'cutting edge' horizons – such as mentoring and compassion, mentoring and spirituality, eco-systemic mentoring, coaching, and the future delivery of mentoring. A final interview with Professor Lillian Turner Eby connects the various strands of research in mentoring, providing a rich overview of what has changed and developed in terms of theory, research and practice over the last fifteen years. This theme links with our central aim to offer a diverse range of chapters that consider models, perspectives, approaches, and applications to further developments in the mentoring field.

In bringing together this Handbook, as an editorial team, we have been keen to gather diverse perspectives and examples of the application of mentoring in such a way as to inspire fresh ideas and pave the way for further advancement in the field. We acknowledge that mentoring unlocks potential through a spirit of inspiration and generosity of giving, which is also a hallmark of other approaches such as coaching. We have had many discussions about this, allowing us to share our individual perspectives and experiences of receiving and offering help in various roles. We particularly debated the two fields of coaching and mentoring; it has yet to be seen how the landscape and dance between these two will develop, but we hope that they will come to be seen as equal partners and support one another's developmental journey over the coming years. This direction seems to be emerging.

Although it was described as a formal mechanism only relatively recently, mentoring has been part of all our lives since life began, as a naturally occurring process in some relationships. It holds tremendous potential and a broad reach across the life cycle for individuals in almost all domains. It is fast developing across a variety of public and private organizations, businesses and institutions, charities, educational establishments and health and social care services. It is an ever evolving and developing landscape. We believe that it has tremendous potential to help us embrace new challenges in the onrushing era of artificial intelligence and social media, and in our increasingly conflictual and globalised world.

This Handbook, then, aims to share some of mentoring's journey, potential and future directions with you. As its Editors, we have ourselves experienced a mentoring journey during its creation – acting as informal mentors to each other and enjoying the privilege of feeling supported and encouraged. It has been tremendously important for us to bring together new voices and fresh ideas, and to work with some authors proactively and collaboratively. To all our authors, to the publishing team and to our own personal mentors, our heartfelt thanks. We hope that we have created a valuable resource for you as a reader, for mentoring practitioners in health and social care and beyond, and for trainers, managers, service development leads and academics – one that will foster cutting-edge dialogue, spark creativity and research, and generate new developments in the mentoring field as it evolves.

Sarajane Aris
Patrick Roycroft
Amra Rao
David Clutterbuck

Section 1:
Past and Current Context – Models and Research

Chapter 1
The Roots of Mentoring and a Route to Health and Social Care

Bob Garvey

A brief history of mentoring

The name *Mentor* comes from Homer's poem *'The Odyssey*. Mentor was a trusted friend and adviser to King Odysseus and was left to care for Odysseus' son, Telemachus, while he fought the Trojan wars. The prefix 'men' means, 'of the mind' or 'one who thinks' and the suffix 'tor' means 'male'. Therefore, Mentor is a man who thinks! The suffix 'trix' would have applied if the character was female. So, Mentrix would be the female equivalent of Mentor! Although the origins of the term *mentor* are in Ancient Greece this is where the resemblance to our modern understanding of mentoring ends!

There are countless interpretations in the modern mentoring literature that suggest that the relationship between Athene (who Zeus sent in the guise of Mentor because the real Mentor wasn't doing the job he was supposed to do!) and Telemachus was about care and support, nurturing behaviour, and learning and development. Garvey (2017) argues that these are false interpretations and that they attempt to give a modern spin on the events of the poem by invoking what he calls 'the old as the hills' argument. Here, mentoring is given historical credibility because of its ancient roots.

Garvey (2017) shows that the ancient poem is a story of violence and macho aggression. Even Athene, Zeus' daughter, as the goddess of wisdom and warfare, was created from Zeus' head and, it can be argued, is therefore the 'embodiment of male rationality' (Colley, 2002, p. 4).

Few authors mention that Mentor was a failure, which is why Athene had to take over, in the guise of Mentor, to toughen Telemachus up and prepare him for the violent denouement of the story. A translation from the Ancient Greek of 'Telemachus' is 'far from the battle' or 'the weak one', and the name suggests someone in need of protection.

The narrative of the caring mentor, as represented in so many modern texts, was not the case. Telemachus was mentored for vengeance and the preservation of the monarchy. The cruel violence in the story is not how we think about mentoring today!

Moving forward in time, another 'old as the hills' narrative appears and that is the association of mentoring with medieval times. Two analogies are made by many modern writers. The first is the knight and squire relationship, and the second is the craftsperson and apprentice arrangement.

Garvey (2017) argues that both these models are romanticised notions of the past. The medieval period was a brutal time of feudalism, exploitation, disease and famine. The knight was a mercenary (Jones, 2015) who basically ran protection rackets, and not the noble, chivalrous and gallant hero as depicted in Hollywood films about King Arthur.

Similarly, the apprentice was often subject to exploitation and abuse. They were legally tied to the craftsperson, who would often pass off their apprentice's work as their own. The system was a form of child labour, with those under twenty-one being imprisoned for refusing an apprenticeship, and a documented fifty per cent dropout rate – despite it being illegal to drop-out of an apprenticeship, apprentices were obviously not content with their indenture. Even so, there are modern writers who argue that this was the model upon which mentoring was based!

It is in eighteenth-century France that we see the development of a different model of mentoring. Here, the tutor to Louis XIV's grandson, Fénelon, interpreted the themes found in Homer in the way we would appreciate them today. Clarke (1984) argues that this was an educational treatise and that the name 'Mentor' entered into the French and English languages as a common noun in the early eighteenth century.

Fénelon's book, *Les Adventures de Telemaque*, (1808) is written in the style of the epic poem from Ancient Greece. In some ways, Fénelon's poem is a treatise on leadership development but he also sets out ways in which education should be conducted. These include: learning from practical experiences through discussion with a more experienced 'mentor'; using reflective questions and creating a supportive but challenging environment; removing the fear of failure by employing positive feedback; building confidence; and role modelling.

Fénelon's work was greatly admired by the educational philosopher, Rousseau, and is referred to in Rousseau's 1762 novel, *Emile*, which is about the development of the young man. The French philosopher, Montesquieu (1748), who argued for the separation of power between the executive vehicles of the state and the legal system, was also greatly influenced by the humanity in Fénelon's work.

Other writers were also influenced by Fénelon. For example, Caraccioli published the book *Veritable le Mentor ou l'education de la noblesse* in French in 1759 and it was translated into English in 1760 to become *The True Mentor, or, an Essay on the Education of Young People in Fashion*. This is a treatise on education and how to mentor and Caraccioli dedicates the work to Fénelon. The collection of three volumes called *The Female Mentor* by Honoria (1793; 1796), are also dedicated to Fénelon and are about group mentoring.

It would seem then that Fénelon's version of Telemachus is probably the source of our modern understanding of mentoring. The values attributed to Homer or the medieval period made by modern writers are on full display in Fénelon.

Les Adventures de Telemaque was translated into several European languages and became a best-selling book in the time of a developing education system throughout Europe. This was just as well for Louis XIV interpreted the work as an attack on the divine right of kings. In Louis' eyes, Fénelon was suggesting that kingship could be learned and developed. Additionally, Louis saw the book as an argument for a republic rather than a monarchy, and so Fénelon was stripped of his role as tutor and his pension and banished to Cambrai. For a full account see Garvey and Stokes (2022) and Garvey (2017).

With the introduction of the word mentor into the English and French languages, there are examples of the use of the term in other writings of the time. For example, in 1750 Lord Chesterfield, in a letter to his son, describes the developmental process as 'the friendly care and assistance of your mentor' (Chesterfield, 1838). Lord Byron (1821; 1829; 1843) used the term 'mentor' in some of his poems where mentor is described as 'tolerant', 'stern' and 'friendly'. By the nineteenth century, mentoring was established as an educational process for personalised learning and development.

There are some negative connotations for mentoring in a piece of literature published in 1894. In the novel *Trilby*, George du Maurier created an evil character known as Svengali. This character is an evil hypnotist with bad intent who manipulates people. This novel was very successful in that it became the subject of a number of silent films and later some early talking movies. The association with the dark side of mentoring is clear and the controlling, advising mentor is played out through Svengali.

In the US in 1912, *The Mentor Association* was formed. It was a think tank where men would share their knowledge. Their publication, *The Mentor*, was first published in 1913 and ran until 1931.

Also in the early 1900s, Ernest Coulter started the *Big Brothers* mentoring organization to support boys coming out of the justice system in the US. At around the same time *The Ladies of Charity* group was established to offer the same support to girls. In 1977, these groups joined together to create *Big Brothers, Big Sisters of America*.

Again, in the US, Levinson et al. (1978) published the results of their research on male development in a book called *The Seasons of a Man's Life*. The research showed that mentoring could accelerate learning and development, and this was quickly followed by the *Harvard Business Review* article of 1978 called 'Everyone Who Makes It Has a Mentor' (Collins, 1978). This article became the catalyst for extensive mentoring activity in commercial organisations.

In the book *Passages: Predictable Crises of Adult Life*, Gail Sheehy (1976), does not recognize mentoring in the context of women's lives. However, in her second edition, *New Passages: Mapping Your Life Across Time* (Sheehy, 1996), she notes that mentoring had become more common among women due to changes in social attitudes.

In the UK, David Clutterbuck (1985) published the book *Everyone Needs a Mentor*, and this signalled the start of mentoring within the UK. This was based on David's work as a journalist in the US. The European Mentoring Centre, now the European Mentoring and Coaching Council, was established in 1992.

Clutterbuck (2007) argues that there are two broad models of mentoring; the US model of career sponsorship and the European model of learning and development. This may have been the case, particularly in business organisations in the early 2000s, but now across the US in other sectors, such as health care, education and charities, the trend is towards developmental mentoring. In the UK, in the business sector there has been a growth in talent mentoring, where the focus is on career sponsorship, while the developmental focus has persisted in other sectors. Mentoring approaches appear to vary considerably around the world. For example, in China, mentoring is viewed as 'passing on wisdom'; and in Russia, it is loosely based upon the term 'nastavnichestvo' from the Soviet era, which means a young employee starting their career at a manufacturing or scientific enterprise is supervised by an expert who introduces them to practical work in the profession. In Australia, mentoring is mainly associated with learning and development and in Saudi Arabia, where oil companies operate, mentoring is based on the US model of career sponsorship. In Sri Lanka, mentoring, as a term, is not really used. However, the university system there has a process called 'Kuppiya'. The word means 'small lamp' and could be interpreted as providing a light to guide people. This is a voluntary system of support for either groups or individuals to assist with their learning.

These few examples may give some indication of the direction of travel for mentoring in the future. There is a strong emphasis on learning and development, and voluntarism but it is likely that a form of group mentoring will start to develop.

Mentoring and coaching

It is very common for people to raise the question of the similarities and differences between mentoring and coaching. Both mentoring and coaching are social constructions. This means that they are processes that have been developed by people for various purposes in various situations. As can be seen with the history of mentoring outlined above, mentoring has followed a range of routes to become what it is today. Without going into the history of coaching in the same detail (see Garvey and Stokes (2022) for details) coaching has gone through various iterations since the word first appeared in print in the nineteenth century. The word *coaching* was a slang term used at the University of Oxford for helping students to improve their examination performance. Today, mentoring and coaching share similar processes and skills. They are specifically defined according to the purpose to which they are put and the context in which they happen (Garvey & Stokes, 2022). In general terms, coaching tends to be a paid, short-term and performance-orientated activity.

The route to health and social care

Due to its educative nature, mentoring activity first appeared in health sector literature in the early- to mid-1990s, although the activity probably started slightly earlier in practice.

These publications come mainly from the US, UK and Australia and cover a wide range of applications of mentoring. These include mentor schemes for trainee nurses, doctors and other health care professionals. They also include mentoring activity aimed at leadership development among administrators, doctors and nurses. Some are focused on specific areas, for example, operating theatres, and others on executive development in the health sector.

In 2006 in the UK, the National Institute for Health and Care Research (NIHR) was established. This had the purpose of developing *'a health research system in which the NHS supports outstanding individuals, working in world-class facilities, conducting leading-edge research focused on the needs of patients and the public'* (www.nihr.ac.uk/about-us/who-we-are/ accessed 24 May 2024). The NIHR worked in partnership with universities, local government and other research funders, patients and members of the public to deliver on this objective. A key feature of the NIHR is a mentoring programme to support postdoctoral researchers. The mentor has several potential functions to help and support:

■ professional and academic work
■ career progression
■ career transition
■ developing an international profile
■ diversity and inclusion in research
■ leadership development
■ networks and relationships
■ research funding applications
■ research practice
■ work/life balance

The programme lasts for twelve months, and both parties receive initial orientation to mentoring and ongoing support for both mentors and mentees.

Another large mentoring programme within the UK's NHS is the London Deanery's programme. This started in 2008 to support doctors and dentists in their career and leadership development in times of change. The mentors are drawn mainly from the medical profession and receive high-quality training in mentoring skills. They are also required, as mentors, to engage in continuous professional development and supervision. Participants report positive outcomes including:

■ increased confidence
■ a sense of realism
■ improved decision-making
■ self-development
■ new learning
■ insights into the profession

Mentoring started to appear in the social care sector slightly after the health sector. Publications started to appear in the late 1990s. Publications exist, similarly to the health context, on a wide range of topics. For example, mentoring for social inclusion, mentoring in relation to poverty, parenting, foster care, and teenage mothers and their children.

One example of mentoring in the social care sector is a UK charity based in the city of York called The Island (https://www.theislandyork.org/ accessed 24 May 2024). The Island provides space and time for vulnerable children and young people by building confidence, self-esteem and unlocking their potential through positive mentoring support. In turn, this helps to reduce antisocial and criminal behaviour in their communities.

The mentors are adult volunteers. The Island carefully selects and supervises these volunteers and trains them to support a young person over a year. The volunteer mentors give their time freely and are provided with a small weekly budget to cover the costs of travel and other activities for their mentee. A recent evaluation report stated:

> There was a general consensus amongst parents of mentees that the mentoring their child has received had positively impacted in a range of ways. Improvements in self-esteem, co-operation and behaviour, respect, peace of mind, calmness and general happiness.

A child mentee said in the report:

> I hated going to school and got bullied and don't like literacy. Since I met my mentor I feel happy at school, pay more attention and don't get in trouble as much. And it's made my Mum happier.

Another example of mentoring in the social care system is the Skills for Care programme (www.skillsforcare.org.uk/about-us accessed 24 May 2024)

Skills for Care was established in 2001 to provide workforce development for adult social care in the UK. Their vision is for a fair and just society where people can access the advice, care and support that they need to live life to the full. Their mentoring arrangements are aimed at building confidence by engaging in discussions that support self-development. One mentee said:

> I requested a mentor to support me as we entered the pandemic. I was surprised at how easy the process was and how helpful the mentor was. It helped me pull together an action plan which informed the staff team, and it was good just to talk to someone who understood. It helped me and my colleagues put a folder together with practical information. I would recommend mentoring, it builds the skills of registered managers who need advice on a more personal level.

Bringing the threads together, designing a scheme and concluding

Mentoring has its roots in education, learning and development and is normally a dyadic relationship, although there are some forms of mentoring that work with groups. The earliest example of group mentoring can be found in the volumes of *The Female Mentor* by Honoria (1793; 1796).

Mentoring in a range of settings has some commonalities. These include it being largely a voluntary activity and that mentors give of their time freely. It is also noticeable that the majority of these schemes provide development support in various formats for their mentors. This support is often in the form of an initial workshop but there is also a recognition that mentors need some ongoing support. Most arrangements tend to last a year with regular mentoring sessions during that time. It is also common for mentors to contract for a further year, either with the same person or with someone new. In addition, it is clear that a common purpose of mentoring across health and social care is learning and development, confidence building and leadership development.

The design of the scheme plays an important part in its success and the successful outcomes for the mentee and mentor. In Clutterbuck et al. (2005) the authors present the principles of mentoring scheme design. These include:

- defining the purpose of the mentoring
- evaluation
- recruitment and selection
- training
- matching criteria
- troubleshooting and ongoing support

Defining the purpose of the mentoring

The needs of any specific group of people can vary. However, the examples in the section 'The route to health and social care' all have a clear purpose for their mentoring schemes. The purpose needs to be created with consideration of both the stakeholders and the scheme. The key questions are, 'what is it for?' and 'who is it for?'

Evaluation

All the schemes briefly described in the section 'The route to health and social care' had an evaluation process. The purpose of the evaluation, in the main, needs to be to help improve the scheme over time. An appreciative inquiry-type evaluation can be utilised, as one of many self-report and evaluation measures to improve a mentoring scheme. However, there may be a need to provide evaluation for funders or managers. If this is the case, it is best done in relation to the original purpose of the scheme.

Recruitment and selection

In all the cases in the section 'The route to health and social care', there is an element of voluntarism in the scheme. This is an important aspect. Mentoring is rarely a paid activity, unlike coaching, but, in some circumstances, it is important to consider the mentors eligibility, credibility, availability and motivations for taking part as well as what kind of recognition the mentor will receive for their voluntary contribution. However, Stelter (2019) argues that coaching and mentoring practices are beginning to merge and in Stelter's terms the helper becomes 'a facilitator of dialogue'. Whether this leads to 'professionalisation' of mentoring and the payment of mentors remains to be seen. The final selection of mentors and mentees must be related to the purpose of the scheme.

Training

In all the cases in the section 'The route to health and social care', the mentors are trained in mentoring skills. In some cases, the mentees receive some orientation to the scheme as well.

Matching criteria

Matching people can be a difficult job in any scheme. There are four main factors to consider when matching:

- criteria
- mentor and mentee rapport
- similarity and difference
- choice

Criteria

Criteria need to be made clear and to take into account the purpose of the scheme. Also, the criteria should take into account diversity issues, which may include race, age, sexual orientation or religion.

Mentor and mentee rapport

This may need to take into account personal styles, credibility and the 'chemistry' between people. Sometimes, an initial meeting to consider these issues might be helpful.

Similarity and difference

A degree of difference between the participants is desirable. This may include experience, position or knowledge.

Choice

The choice of mentor from the mentee's point of view can be desirable. Some schemes now use this approach rather than matching. However, consider the mentee's motives as well. If the mentee is seeking access to power, that might not be a good thing.
It may also be desirable to allow choice from both sides of the relationship. This is where an initial chemistry meeting could be helpful.

Troubleshooting and ongoing support

Sometimes, things can go wrong and one common reason for this can be time constraints. In all circumstances, develop a graceful exit by establishing some scheme guidelines around a minimum requirement to meet for three sessions. If the relationship is not working out, they may then conclude after a review in the third meeting.

Other potential problems may be rapport building, trust and the mentee not taking any action as a result of the discussions. Rapport and trust building can take time, and it is the responsibility of both parties to not only engage with the purpose of the mentoring but also to get to know each other through a certain amount of social conversation. Establishing ground rules at the start can be helpful here.

If the mentee does not act as a result of the conversations, in the first instance, it is important for the mentor to realise that they are not in a management position with their mentoring relationship. Instead, it can be helpful to approach the 'non-action' with a sense of curiosity and to treat it as an exploration into the mentee's thinking.

Conclusion

This chapter has covered the historical development of mentoring through to its use in the health and social care context. Mentoring is a helpful learning and development process that has stood the test of time. It is currently rapidly developing within the public sector as an effective approach across the life cycle.

The future direction of mentoring

As a 'social construction' mentoring is dynamic and shifts according to the purpose it is put to and the social settings in which it happens. Therefore, in the future, mentoring will take on different forms. A key differentiator is the role of experience in the conversation. In coaching, the more traditional literature says that the coach does not make use of their experience and that it is not relevant to the conversation – a coach is expert in coaching. In mentoring, the mentor may share experiences with their mentee to illustrate, provide data to be discussed, create empathy or to guide. In recent years, this aspect of mentoring has been finding its way into coaching literature. Experience can help to establish rapport, credibility and inform questions. Garvey and Stokes (2022) and Stelter (2019) argue that mentoring and coaching are beginning to merge into a hybrid helping activity. Another possible development may be the use of a mentoring approach in working with groups and, finally, there are the questions of professionalisation of mentoring and of payment. Personally, I support the idea of ongoing development for mentors but maintain that payment will move mentoring away from its historical roots into a place that may not be recognisable. Only the future can tell!

Reflective questions

- What is influencing your mentoring practice?
- What evidence have you encountered that mentoring and coaching practices are merging?
- Coaching is often a paid activity and mentoring is a voluntary one. What difference might payment make to the coaching or mentoring relationship?

References

Byron, Lord (1821). *The Curse of Minerva: A Poem* (**5th ed.**). Galignani.

Byron, Lord (1829). *Childe Harold's Pilgrimage*. Du Jardin-Sailly Brothers.

Byron, Lord (1843). T. Moore (Ed.), *The Works of Lord Byron in Four Volumes* (**Volume III**, p. 187). Carey and Hart.

Caraccioli, L. A. (1760). *The True Mentor, or, an Essay on the Education of Young People in Fashion*. J. Coote.

Chesterfield, P. D. S. (1838). *First Complete American Edition, the Works of Lord Chesterfield, Including Letters to His Son to Which Is Prefixed an Original Life of the Author* (p. 331). Harper and Brothers.

Clarke, P. P. (1984). *The metamorphoses of mentor: Fenelon to Balzac. The Romanic Review*, IV, 199–211.

Clutterbuck, D. (1985). *Everyone Needs a Mentor*. IPM.

Clutterbuck, D. (2007). An international perspective on mentoring. In B. R. Ragins & K. E. Kram (Eds.), Handbook on Mentoring at Work: Theory, Research and Practice (pp. 633–656). SAGE.

Clutterbuck, D., Megginson, D., Garvey, B., Stokes, P., & Garrett-Harris, R. (Eds.) (2005). Mentoring in Action. Kogan Page.

Colley, H. (2002). A 'Rough Guide' to the history of mentoring from a Marxist feminist perspective. Journal of Education for Teaching, 28(3), 247–263.

Collins, E. G. C. (Ed.) (1978). *Everyone who makes it has a mentor: Interviews with F. J. Lunding, G. L. Clements, D. S. Perkins. Harvard Business Review,* **July-August,** 89–101.

Du Maurier, G. (1894). Trilby. Osgood, McIlvaine.

Fénelon, F. S. de la M. (1808). The Adventures of Telemachus, Vols 1 and 2 (2nd ed. in English). J. Hawkesworth (Trans.). Union Printing Office.

Garvey, B. (2017). Philosophical origins of mentoring: The critical narrative analysis. In D. A. Clutterbuck, F. K. Kochan, L. G. Lunsford, B. Smith, N. Dominguez, & J. Haddock-Millar (Eds.) The SAGE Handbook of Mentoring (pp. 15–33). SAGE

Garvey, B., & Stokes, P. (2022). Coaching and Mentoring Theory and Practice (4th ed.). SAGE.

Honoria (1793). The Female Mentor or Select Conversations, vols 1 and 2. T. Cadell.

Honoria (1796). The Female Mentor or Select Conversations, vol. 3. T. Cadell.

Jones, T. (2015). Chaucer's Knight: The Portrait of a Medieval Mercenary. Methuen.

Levinson, D. J., Darrow, C. N., Klein, E. B., Levinson, M. H., & McKee, B. (1978). The Seasons of a Man's Life. Knopf.

Montesquieu, C. L. (1748). De L'Esprit des Loix. Chez Barrillot & Fils.

Rousseau, J. J. (1762). Emile; or, On Education. J.M. Dent & Sons.

Sheehy, G. (1976). Passages: Predictable Crises of Adult Life. E.P. Dutton.

Sheehy, G. (1996) New Passages: Mapping Your Life across Time, London: HarperCollins.

Stelter, R. (2019). The Art of Coaching Dialogue: Towards Transformative Exchange. Routledge.

Chapter 2
Methodological Issues in Mentoring Research and Training

David Clutterbuck

Mentoring is not the same everywhere

Mentoring means different things in different contexts and cultures. Even the name isn't consistent, with many references to mentorship. What mentors do and how they do it is not the same in the US as it is in Europe and neither is it equivalent to mentoring in the context of, say, the Islamic cultures of the Gulf states. This has implications for the design and implementation of both research and training.

What is consistent is the understanding that mentoring has at its core the concept that a mentor uses their wisdom to help another person become wiser. Even this distinction is under threat, however, with confusion between mentoring and what we can call *fast knowledge transfer* (FKT) – transactional short interventions where one person taps into the expertise of another. While mentoring has traditionally been between an older person and a younger person, it has evolved in recent decades to include learning in the opposite direction. Developmental mentoring focuses on co-learning, with less emphasis on the relative seniority or age of the learning partners.

How mentoring research has evolved

In most cases, the academic study of mentoring can be traced back to the doctoral research by Kathy Kram, based on interviews with eighteen informal mentoring pairs in North America. In 1985, Kram published her conclusions in *Mentoring at Work* (Kram, 1985). My own book, *Everyone Needs a Mentor* (Clutterbuck & Devine, 1985), based upon research in Europe, appeared by coincidence at the same time. My interest in the topic was stimulated by an interview with Kram a few years earlier. Kram selected her participants on the basis that they were able to name a person who was pivotal in supporting their career development. Her interviews looked at the relationship from the perspective of both people. She identified several mentoring 'functions', which she divided into two categories – career and psychosocial. It should be noted that these relationships were within a specific culture and context – informal, North American and within a hierarchy of senior to junior.

This was a small-scale, limited study of one category of informal relationships. In an ideal world, subsequent studies would have undertaken further validation of, for example:

- Did all the functions belong within one role or more than one?
- Were the functions the same in formal relationships as they were in informal?
- To what extent were the functions identified as culturally dependent?
- What assumptions were made about the direction of learning?

The failure of the research community to address these issues – taking Kram's results and models as universally applicable – has led to a great deal of subsequent confusion and invalidates a considerable proportion of mentoring research. It has also led, in part, to confusion between mentoring and the emerging profession of coaching, because sponsorship implies a degree of control and directiveness. Depicting mentoring as low-skill, directive advice-giving may have helped coaches carve out a professional niche, but it had no basis in history. In reality, the entire history of coaching from the 1850s, when the term first appeared, to the early 1980s was one of directive tutoring. Mentoring, on the other hand, has had three thousand years of history as a form of learning dialogue, developing wisdom through reflective conversations. Indeed, what was arguably the first leadership text in Europe (if you discount Machiavelli) was a continuation of the conversations between Athena the Goddess of Wisdom and Telemachus, the son of Odysseus (Fenelon, 1699).

Methodological problems

The definitional issue is one of the major reasons why so much research into mentoring is limited in value. Among the methodological problems in so much of the literature are:

- **Conflation of roles.** Many studies fail to distinguish between mentoring as a relationship between two people within a boss-subordinate role and mentoring outside of the formal hierarchy. There are at least three contexts here: boss-subordinate; senior to junior within the same organizational structure; and peer to peer outside the organization. The power dynamics of each of these relationships is radically different, so any data based on amalgamation of them is immediately suspect.

- **Conflation of formal and informal mentoring relationships.** The dynamics of these two contexts is sufficiently different that data needs to be analysed separately. Again, there are at least three scenarios: formal, where participants are trained and matched; informal, where they pick it up as they go; and semi-formal, where participants choose each other but can have the opportunity to be trained. Anecdotal evidence suggests that sufficient effective formal mentoring leads to more effective informal mentoring, but this hypothesis remains to be tested.

- **Conflation between sponsorship and mentoring.** Sponsorship emerged as one of Kram's functions, yet it has no historical basis as a part of mentoring and is a separate and distinct construct. (This emerged very clearly from the statistical data in my own PhD (Clutterbuck, 2007)). Kram's approach at that time was to ask her subjects who had provided significant career support for them and what those people did for them. She then interviewed those career supporters to expand upon and validate the responses. However, it does not necessarily follow that the functions all belong to the same role, in the same way that being a leader involves different roles according to circumstance. Sponsorship has little or no role to play in peer mentoring, reverse mentoring or reciprocal mentoring. It cannot therefore be a universal component of a mentoring relationship. Kram herself addresses some of these issues in this book (see Chapter 37).

- **Failure to see the mentoring relationship in the context of its systems.** Kram has also been highly instrumental in evolving the concept of mentoring from single relationships to constellations or networks of relationships. Reverse mentoring, where the mentor is hierarchically junior to the mentee, is influenced by the different contexts (relating to power, politics, culture and hierarchically derived assumptions, etc.) in which it takes place. Reciprocal mentoring goes further and engages the mentoring pairs collectively in achieving change in the systems that create and sustain inequality.

Another major issue in mentoring research was failure to make valid comparisons. In the 1990s, a rift appeared between North American researchers, who focused on quantitative studies based upon asking participants about their experiences of different mentors, and European researchers, who focused on organizational cases studies. The former studies appeared to show that informal mentoring was far more effective than formal; the latter exactly the opposite. Even a brief read of the quantitative studies reveals: a) that the definition of mentoring was insufficiently specific; and b) that it was heavily biased towards relationships that worked. You have to kiss a lot of frogs before you find a prince! Only a small proportion of formal mentoring relationships were unsatisfactory in the European cases, where participants were trained and matched. Notable programme failures included a US bank that paired up female talent with more senior executives but gave no training and no support. Less than 10% of relationships delivered any value! The arguments for a degree of formality include the impact on diversity. Left to their own devices, mentors and mentees will gravitate towards people like themselves, marginalizing minorities and other disadvantaged groups. Much of the controversy was settled by a seminal paper from Belle Rose Ragins (1999) and her colleagues, which demonstrated that how the relationship came about was largely irrelevant – it was the quality of the relationship that counted.

Research methodology: Lessons and ways forward

Some of the lessons relating to research methodology include:

- In any study measuring the complex patterns of a relationship, it is essential first to define both the phenomena and the contexts in which they exist, then to design survey questions to reflect that complexity.
- Over-reliance on one methodological approach tends to exacerbate biases. The tendency for social science researchers to replicate the methodologies of previous researchers is dangerous. It is analogous to the financial crash of the noughties, when all the banks and their traders were using the same or similar algorithms. There is a need for mixed methods that combine, say, quantitative, qualitative and interpretative phenomenological analysis (IPA) methods. There is also a severe lack of both longitudinal studies and studies that triangulate the experiences and perspectives of mentors, mentees and other stakeholders.

- Context is critical. For example, the format and effectiveness of mentoring may be affected by cultural norms – national or organizational – or by the developmental climate. It can be argued that a fear-based organizational culture will place more emphasis on managing reputation and politics and a more open culture will bias mentoring towards a more reflective agenda emphasizing authenticity.

- Quantitative studies need to reduce the range of variables as much as possible, to eliminate noise in the system. It can be useful to ask:

  - What is the specific transition that mentees are going through?

  - What are the similarities and differences between them? (e.g., age, gender, ethnicity.)

  - What are the similarities and differences between mentors? (e.g., same area of the business or another?)

  - If multiple organizations are involved, what are the similarities and differences between them?

The point here is that every additional variable makes comparison and analysis more complicated and potentially less valid, if the subsets become too small.

- Results relating to one context are only generalizable when they have been replicated in multiple contexts. This is of particular concern in the case of studies that conclude without evidence that their results are applicable in any culture.

My five tests of mentoring research quality are:

1. **Definition: Is it clear what kind of relationship is being measured?**

   To increase the validity of research in mentoring, it is necessary, in my view, to provide a precise definition of exactly what kind of relationship is being measured and to ensure that all the samples lie within that definition.

2. **Process: Is it clear how the mentoring relationship is conducted?**

   The medium (in person, virtual, email and so on) can have a significant impact on relationship dynamics. The quality and quantity of training may also be important. For example, have both mentors and mentees been educated in their roles? Are they supported throughout their relationship? Have these factors been included as key variables? In my own PhD study (Clutterbuck, 2007), there was a correlation between relationship efficacy and the perception by participants that the organization was investing in making their relationships work. Other informal, unpublished experiments suggest that having guidelines and other support processes is associated with positive outcomes for both parties. However, what constitutes an appropriate level of support and what becomes disruptive bureaucracy?

3. **Outcomes**

   Much of the research literature uses Kram's functions of a mentor (or the subsequent recasting of the functions by Noe (1988)) as measures of outcomes. This is a fundamental error. There is no evidence that the number of functions exhibited equates to relationship quality or outcomes. The functions are merely intervening variables that may or may not lead to outcomes valued by the mentee. For a validated model of outcomes, we must fall back (with due regard to the comments above relating to generalizability) on my doctoral research (Clutterbuck, 2007), which identified four categories of outcome:

- career progress
- learning
- enabling (e.g., having a better personal development plan)
- emotional (e.g., increased self-esteem or self-confidence).

4. **Systemic complexity**

Additionally, we must ask the question: *Outcomes for whom?* Most research in the field focuses on one party – usually the mentee, sometimes the mentor and less frequently the organization, in the context of formal programmes. However, the mentoring relationship is a complex, adaptive system. A relationship that benefits one party but not the others may be regarded as only a partial success. The issue of mentor/mentee/organization reciprocity is rarely addressed. Nor is mentoring explored as a complex, adaptive system nested within the complexities of other systems, such as the mentee's team or the boss-subordinate relationship.

5. **Relevance**

This is the 'so what' test. At least a third of the papers I review for the academic publications in this field fail in this respect. Critical questions to ask include:

- How will this make a practical difference to the design of mentoring initiatives or the conduct of mentoring relationships?
- Will mentoring participants or programme managers immediately see the relevance to what they do?
- What significant additional research can be built on this?

Mentor and mentee training

The nature and quality of training in mentoring varies extensively. Although good practice guidelines recommend training both mentors and mentees, many corporate and social programmes invest in only mentors, or neither. The International Standards for Mentoring and Coaching Programmes (ISMCP), now run by the European Mentoring and Coaching Council (EMCC), were set up as a benchmark for programme management. One of the six key elements of the standards is training.

Among lessons learned from hundreds of programmes across the world (see, for example: Megginson and Clutterbuck (1997); Clutterbuck and Ragins (2002); Klasen and Clutterbuck (2002); and Clutterbuck et al. (2012)) are that:

- Untrained mentors often gravitate towards non-mentoring roles, such as advising or instruction. These relationships become at best one-way learning.
- Whether to educate mentors and mentees together or separately depends on several factors. In particular:

- The hierarchy gap (the more levels between mentor and mentee, the more power dynamics may interfere and prevent people being authentic).
- The openness of the company culture (the less psychological safety, the more senior people will want to avoid looking dumb in front of juniors and vice versa).
- The purpose of the programme (e.g., in programmes aimed at diversity and inclusion, it is important to consider how early to expose people to deep challenge about their implicit biases).

- Measurement (in the form of surveys and/or brief check-ins with each pair) stimulates participants to review their relationships in a structured way and leads to better results at both individual and programme levels.
- Education delivery needs to be paced to the development of the mentoring relationship. Some initial training is essential at the start, to ensure everyone understands their role and what to expect of each other. Thereafter, check-ins and targeted additional training help to keep relationships on track, while expanding the range of tools and techniques available.
- Supervision for mentors is increasingly common and is important in identifying issues that might derail relationships or the programme before they become serious (Viney and Harris, 2011).
- The involvement of line managers can provide additional support, although it is not advised that line managers and mentors communicate about the mentee.
- The role of mentoring programme manager is vital and there now exists an accreditation route (through the EMCC). International networks of programme managers allow continuous benchmarking and exchange of good practice.
- Mentor accreditation is one way to ensure continued commitment to the programme. The EMCC offers four levels: Foundation, Practitioner, Senior Practitioner and Master Practitioner.
- Specialist mentoring roles, such as in maternity mentoring or ethical mentoring programmes, require additional training and support.

Not all mentors are part of formal mentoring programmes within organizations. There are many programmes by not-for-profits, such as those for entrepreneurs by The Human Edge (https://humanedge.org.uk/), Young President's Organization (https://www.ypo.org/about-ypo-mentoring/) and the Cherie Blair Foundation for Women (https://cherieblairfoundation.org/what-we-do/programmes/mentoring/). There is also a growing army of independent professional coaches, educated in mentoring academies and accredited comparably to professional coaches.

While the ISMCP provides a broad framework for mentor and mentee training, it does not offer a defined curriculum. However, in recent years an EMCC working party has added to the competency framework for coaches by establishing two additional areas relevant to mentor training:

1. **Being a role model:**

    Being intentional and conscious that one's own unique behaviour, style, experiences, choices, successes and vulnerabilities may have a considerable impact on a mentee's own life and career choices, reflections and thinking. Doing so by demonstrating authenticity and humility, and recognizing it is a two-way learning synergy and journey.

2. **Using my professional experience:**

   Professional experience includes professional savvy, professional acumen and wisdom. It incorporates understanding about the mentee's own context and thinking and appropriately sharing one's own wisdom, knowledge and experiences. This might include sharing how to succeed in a particular ecosystem, and everything impacting that system such as unconscious elements, culture, interconnections, unwritten rules and power dynamics.

Role modelling is an under-researched skill that is most effective when undertaken proactively rather than passively. Using professional experience is a very different role to advising or teaching. It comes into play when the mentee has exhausted their own thinking and needs additional contextual information to progress; in many cases, this context-giving comes in the shape of questions that draw upon the mentor's relevant knowledge or experience.

There are, as yet, no competency frameworks for mentees that might inform the design of training. Research into mentee competencies is very limited (Clutterbuck, 2005) and is urgently needed to provide an evidence base for training design.

Other significant issues for mentor and mentee training include:

- Cultural adaptation. Especially in a relationship that has people from different hierarchical levels, or different generations, what works in one culture may not be as effective in another (for example, Clutterbuck et al. (2017).

- Participants not only need to know how to start and maintain a relationship; they also need to know how to make the formal relationship end well (Clutterbuck and Megginson, 2004).

- The general shift of training from face-to-face to virtual delivery poses particular problems for conversation-based skills training. The learning from practicing mentoring dialogue and from observing others practicing it is perceived to be less intense, not least because there are fewer visual clues, maintaining silent pauses is harder and observers may be more distracted and less engaged.

There is therefore a strong case for increased research into training within mentoring for all participants – mentee, mentor, line manager and programme manager. Among topics of potential interest may be:

- To what extent is it effective to import simplistic models from coaching? For example, the GROW model (Goal, Reality, Options, Will) has limited application outside of skills training. It also assumes that the mentee begins with a clear goal, when in practice the mentoring relationship is more typically about creating and evolving career and developmental goals.

- What does 'good' look like in mentee education?

- How do the learning needs of participants in reverse and reciprocal mentoring relationships differ from those in more traditional hierarchical or peer relationships?

- What are the competencies of an effective mentoring trainer?
- What is core to mentoring training and what is contextual?
- How does supervision help to embed good practice in trained mentors and mentees?
- What outcomes can we expect from mentoring?

The quality of research informs the quality of training. This then impacts on the quality of mentoring itself. To date, most of the research into mentoring has ignored the impact of training on relationship and programme outcomes, and what literature exists (e.g., Freemyer (2000)) is culturally bounded. Detailed exploration of this interaction – especially in multiple contexts – would both improve training provision, establish an agenda for further research, and develop and improve mentoring outcomes.

References

Blackman, A., Kon, D., & Clutterbuck, D. (Eds.) (2017). *Coaching and Mentoring in the Asia Pacific.* Routledge.

Clutterbuck, D. (2005). Establishing and maintaining mentoring relationships: An overview of mentor and mentee competencies. SA Journal of Human Resource Management, 3(3), 2–9.

Clutterbuck, D. (2007). *A Longitudinal Study of the Effectiveness of Developmental Mentoring.* King's College London.

Clutterbuck, D., & Devine, D. (1985). *Everyone Needs a Mentor.* CIPD.

Clutterbuck, D., & Megginson, D. (2004). *All good things must come to an end: Winding up and winding down a mentoring relationship.* In D. Clutterbuck & G. Lane (Eds.), *The Situational Mentor* (pp. 178–193). Gower.

Clutterbuck, D., & Ragins, B. R. (2002). *Mentoring and Diversity.* Butterworth-Heinemann.

Clutterbuck, D., Poulsen, K., & Kochan, F. (2012). *Developing Successful Diversity Mentoring Programmes: An International Casebook.* McGraw Hill.

Fenelon, F. (1699). *Telemachus, Son of Ulysses.* Republished in translation, Cambridge University Press (1994).

Freemyer, J. (2000) Presentation: The Impact of Mentor Training on the Perceived Effectiveness of a Mentor Program. Mid-Western Educational Research Association Annual Conference, Chicago.

Klasen, N., & Clutterbuck, D. (2002). *Implementing Mentoring Schemes: A Practical Guide to Successful Programs.* Butterworth-Heinemann.

Kram, K. E. (1985). *Mentoring at Work: Developmental Relationships in Organizational Life.* Scott Foresman.

Megginson, D., & Clutterbuck, D. (1997). *Mentoring in Action: A Practical Guide for Managers.* Kogan Page.

Noe, R. A. (1988). *An investigation of the determinants of successful assigned mentoring relationships. Personnel Psychology,* **41**(3), 457–479.

Ragins, B. R., & Cotton, J. L. (1999). *Mentor functions and outcomes: A comparison of men and women in formal and informal relationships. Journal of Applied Psychology,* **84**(4), 529–550.

Viney, R., & Harris, D. (2011). *Mentoring supervision in the NHS.* In T. Bachkirova, P. Jackson, & D. Clutterbuck (Eds.), *Coaching and Mentoring Supervision: Theory and Practice* (pp. 251–257). McGraw Hill, Open University Press.

Chapter 3
Ethics and Mentoring

Paul Stokes

Discussion

Due to its focus on interpersonal relationships, ethics and ethical boundaries are core considerations within mentoring. Mentoring is defined by Clutterbuck and Megginson (1999, p. 2) as being *'offline help by one person to another in making significant transitions in knowledge, work or thinking'*. While there are numerous definitions of mentoring, the 'offline' aspect of this definition is often seen as important from an ethical perspective due to the power imbalance that can exist between people who have a line management relationship – I shall explore more about power later in this chapter. However, as McAuley (2003) has argued, in his analysis of the psychodynamics of mentoring relationships, mentoring can offer several power-related ethical traps in terms of transference and countertransference between a mentoring pair. These include:

- the mentor being flattered by being asked to help and wanting to perpetuate the feeling by extending the relationship, even if the mentee no longer needs the support;
- the mentee being overawed by the mentor's perceived competence and developing a dependence on the mentor's help;
- the mentee 'sucking the mentor dry' in terms of their knowledge and expertise and then complaining about their incompetence; and
- victimizing the mentee in the session and, possibly, outside also.

Mentoring undertaken in health, social care and educational settings can be particularly susceptible to these dynamics. This is because health and social care and education professionals are often required to take up roles where service users or clients 'transfer' feelings onto them from previous relationships – often parent–child ones. By this I mean that such professionals may take up a professional 'persona' that is rather like a benevolent parent authority figure towards the client, who, in psychological terms, is seen as 'the child' in these relationships. For example, a carer working in an old people's home may find it helpful to adopt a cheery, breezy disposition toward the clients in the home as this helps to contain the client and feel that they can trust the carer to look after them. However, this may be less helpful if they carry this persona through to their relationships with colleagues and, indeed, any mentees that they may have as part of their work. This may, in turn, elicit unhelpful responses from those colleagues, as suggested by McAuley (2003), where members of the organization 'transfer' feelings onto each other as though they were operating in different, past relationships. For instance, someone with a difficult relationship with an actual parent may, subconsciously, resent being placed in a parent–child-type relationship with a colleague and friction may then ensue. Exploring the psychological and ethical boundaries to mentoring relationships in such settings is, therefore, important.

Pause for reflection

In mentoring relationships that you are involved in, do you see any of these things taking place? If so, what have you done about this so far?

In terms of ethics and mentoring, it is important to recognize that there are several ways of judging the ethical behaviour of those who participate in it. This is because there are different ethical theories which have different and competing criteria for deciding what is ethical and what is not. Passmore (2011, p. 147) has argued that there are three main categories of ethical theory to consider:

Consequentialist or Teleological – actions themselves are ethically neutral and it is their consequences that matter both in terms of right or wrong, and in terms of the greatest good for the greatest number of people.

Dutiful or De-ontological – some actions are intrinsically good, and some actions are intrinsically bad. Good ones might include telling the truth, being just and keeping promises; bad ones might include committing crimes, lying or breaking promises.

Pluralist – balancing the above perspectives. For example, if keeping a promise would harm others, what is the most important consideration?

As these are quite abstract theoretical constructs, it may be helpful to explore them using a short scenario case study illustration:

Case study illustration 1

You have been asked to mentor someone in your workplace by a senior colleague. Following your first couple of sessions, your senior colleague starts to press you to disclose the content of the conversations, despite the fact you have agreed with all parties that the conversations are confidential. They seem particularly keen to understand what your mentee is taking from the sessions and what they are putting into practice. You have reiterated your understanding of the confidentiality arrangements that have been put in place, but they persist.

Questions for the reader

How do you feel this should this be dealt with?

What important elements are there to consider here?

In Case study illustration 1, it could be argued that adhering to the confidentiality agreement is a moral, ethical duty and that divulging any content to the senior colleague would be unethical. On the other hand, it could be argued that the senior colleague's questions are legitimate. In the context of monitoring the performance and impact of the mentee, it could be said that sharing their progress may be ethically appropriate in terms of the consequences of doing so in relation to organizational performance. In other words, the senior colleague may become more confident in the mentee which may, in turn result in improved performance by the mentee, hence resulting in the greatest good for the greatest number of people.

While this chapter is not the place to explore differences between mentoring and coaching (see Garvey and Stokes (2022) for an exploration of this), it is sufficient to say that the skills and ethical issues faced by both coaching and mentoring pairs are quite similar. In their work on leaders as coaches (rather than mentors), Milner et al. (2022, p. 7) identify seven ethical traps facing leaders who wish to operate as coaches, which I have paraphrased below:

- *definition ambiguity* – lack of clarity about a specific skill set required and being unable to deliver it.
- *conflict of interest* – competing agendas between being a coach and being a manager.
- *confidentiality* – the use of coaching content to fulfil a coach's agenda.
- *power imbalance* – the coachee is intimidated by the coach's positional power.
- *freedom to participate* – the coachee not feeling free to fully participate.
- *boundaries* – the coach being asked to work beyond their personal/professional boundaries.
- *favouritism* – the coach selecting 'favourite' coachees to work with.

As argued above, all of these can be applied as equally to the organizational mentoring process as they can to the coaching process. In fact, in some cases, falling into these traps as a mentoring pair is arguably more likely. For instance, traditional mentoring relationships are often set up between a more experienced, more senior person (the mentor) and someone less senior and less experienced (the mentee). In these cases, it can be assumed that, because the mentor has the requisite experience, they are able to 'pass this on' to the mentee without incident, or, possibly that the mentee is skilled enough to 'extract' this experience from the mentor. If this is the case, there is a risk that untrained mentors and mentees may damage each other due to their mutual lack of understanding as to what skills and behaviours are appropriate to the mentoring relationship. Following this through, this makes it more likely that there may be breaches in the relationship due to poor contracting and lack of discussion about boundaries and expectations on the part of both. If this is also combined with a lack of clarity about the ethical positions of both parties in Passmore's (2011) three categories, then the possibilities for misunderstanding/misinterpretation are increased.

Pause for reflection

How important is it that mentors and mentees are aware of the ethical issues which surround their mentoring work together?

As well as a conflict of interest and agenda between mentor and mentee, there is also the possibility of a clash of ethical values, which raises an additional dilemma. This is briefly illustrated in the Case study illustration 2:

Case study illustration 2

Halfway through the second of six contracted mentoring sessions, you recognize a real clash of personal values between you and the mentee. For instance, the mentee makes remarks which you consider to be examples of racist microaggressions and unpleasant sexual innuendoes about colleagues (some of whom you are working with). You develop a strong dislike for the client and are finding it difficult to be fully present with them in the session.

Questions for the reader

How should this be dealt with?

To what extent is it appropriate to challenge the mentee on these microaggressions?

What might the consequences of a challenge be for your relationship with them?

The example in Case study illustration 2 raises the issue of a perceived clash of values between the mentor and mentee. The questions raise the possibility of different ways of addressing this ethical dilemma. The racial issues are particularly pertinent at the moment. Issues of racial intolerance and prejudice are regularly present in the news and often dominate the headlines. Applying the ethical positions (Passmore, 2011), raised above, to Case study illustration 2, it could be argued that such microaggressions should always be called out by the mentor. This would be to invoke the idea that challenging racist behaviour is a moral imperative. The mentor may even decide that to continue with the relationship is ethically inappropriate given that their personal values seem to clash with that of the mentee. On the other hand, it could be argued that the mentoring relationship may be the best channel through which to influence the behaviour of the mentee – particularly in relation to the greatest good for the greatest number – and that the ethical thing to do would be to stay and persist with the mentoring relationship. Clearly, this dilemma raises some challenging issues for the mentor, which may be best worked through as part of a mentoring supervision process.

As argued earlier, power is a critical ethical issue in mentoring. As Milner et al. (2022) argue, a power imbalance in a relationship can serve to inhibit a mentoring relationship as well as proving an unwanted burden on a mentor (and also on the mentee) as Case study illustration 3 shows.

Case study illustration 3

A managing director (MD) in privately owned manufacturing firm is a big advocate for mentoring within his organization. He has been the main sponsor for it and has engaged specialist mentoring scheme consultants to design, deliver and evaluate the programme. Because he is such a keen advocate, he wants to act as a participant in the programme, as a mentor. In doing so, he wants to be treated 'just like everyone else'. However, his experience of doing this suggests that the mentees (who also work for him) cannot put aside the fact that he is the MD of his organization. They engage with him very much as the MD and they seem to constantly be finding subtle ways to ask him to use his status as MD to make changes that they would like to see in the organization. As he puts it, they will not let him 'remove his cloak of power' and work with them as any other mentor would do within the organization. This proves to be a real dilemma for him as, on the one hand, he is pleased that so many people want to engage with him as a mentor (and he has invested much in the programme being a success) but on the other hand, he feels 'played' by his mentees in terms of their engagement with him and is not convinced that they are truly using the sessions to focus on themselves and their development.

Questions for the reader

What should the MD do in this situation?

What ethical theories/frameworks are most useful here?

As Kram (1985) argued many years ago, one of the possible functions of mentoring is that of career progression. This has led to mentoring, particularly in the US, being associated with the idea of sponsorship. Sponsorship mentoring is where the principal purpose of the mentoring is to enable career progression. In the Case study illustration 3, it seems that there is a mismatch of expectations between what the mentor and the mentees wish to get out of the relationship. In ethical theory terms, the behaviour of the mentees in this scenario might indicate that they hold an internal ethical framework that is closer to egoism (Rothstein, 2022) where behaviour is judged to be ethical where all individuals act in their own self-interest. The mentees' behaviour is to some extent explained in Case study illustration 3. In other words, why would they not use an intimate (but platonic) relationship with their MD to enhance their own position within their organization? Unfortunately for the mentor, they seem to be operating from a position of moral duty where mentoring others is an intrinsically 'good' act in itself. Hence, in their terms, they are not acting in their own self-interest but doing what they believe in. In my experience of mentoring scheme design (see Garvey and Stokes (2022) for some examples of this), it is often the mentors who say they wish to 'give something back' who can make the most ineffective mentors. This is because they may be more interested in telling the mentee what they should do, based on their own experience, as opposed to listening carefully to what the mentee wants and needs, and seeking to create value from the relationship. Paradoxically, therefore, mentors who are more overtly 'selfish' in terms of getting something out of the relationship for themselves (e.g., challenge to their own thinking, enhanced networks, development of their helping skills) tend to be more effective as mentors because, to get what they want out of the relationship, they must engage with the mentee in terms of focusing on the mentee's agenda (Garvey & Stokes, 2022).

Expert power and ethics in mentoring

Many years ago, French and Raven (1959) introduced the notion of bases of power in social relations. As well as legitimate, positional power in organizations, they pointed to the importance of expert power in relationships, where power is exerted by the individual perceived to have the most knowledge and expertise within the relationship. As I pointed out at the beginning of the chapter, in McAuley's (2003) work, one of the ethical risks in mentoring relationships is that the mentee may, at the beginning of the relationship, perceive the mentor to be an expert but, as time goes on and the mentee 'sucks the mentor dry' of their experience, the mentee can become dissatisfied with the mentor (see Beech and Brockbank (1999) for a good example of this in a UK National Health Service (NHS) context). As a result, the mentor can feel disempowered and deskilled, and the mentee can feel disappointed and cheated. In particular, this can happen if there is a mismatch in understanding of expertise within the relationship. This is shown in the following brief example:

Expert patient mentoring programme

An early pilot scheme was set up in 2005 to build on the Expert Patient scheme within the NHS in the UK. This involved patients, who were successfully self-managing long-term health conditions, acting as mentors to health care professionals (the mentees) to help them identify ways in which the health system could be changed to better serve these patients. What this meant was that there was a clash of different notions of expertise. On the one hand, health care professionals had the technical expertise and wider research experience of working with these conditions; on the other hand, the patients had the expertise that comes from direct personal experience of living and working with the conditions and relating to the NHS system. In some of the mentoring relationships, there were tensions due to the previously held notions of role and expertise that each party had; health care professionals were prone to wanting to help the patients clinically and, hence, take back their expert role within the normal patient relationship, while the patients, as mentors, were sometimes drawn back into their roles as passive recipients of health care. This created some ethical dilemmas for the scheme organizers in terms of the intentions of the scheme and the resulting power dynamics that played out.

As the above example illustrates, power and ethics are often interconnected within mentoring relationships. Clearly, the intent was to subvert the normal power relations that tend to exist within health care relations, so as to make systemic changes that would result in the greatest good for greatest number of people. However, as the report (see Garrett, 2006) suggests, this was only partly successful for a number of reasons.

Pause for reflection

What similar dynamics do you experience in your particular context?
What can be done about these?

Conclusion

In conclusion, I have sought, in this chapter, to explore some of the practical ethical dilemmas that can come up in mentoring relationships. As Passmore (2011) argued, there may be no neat way of resolving these dilemmas that is universally ethically applicable. However, it is clear that some awareness of what might be happening in mentoring relationships in ethical terms is helpful in deciding what choices can be made within them. Without this awareness, mentors and mentees run the risk of falling foul of these ethical traps within such relationships and, also, of doing damage to each other as a result. Furthermore, I suggest that those who are responsible for training and developing mentors within mentoring programmes need to consider how they might enhance the ethical education of their participants so that it is possible to move toward greater ethical maturity within mentoring. Finally, it is also worth reiterating that having ongoing reflexive processes – such as mentoring supervision, action learning sets or 'buddying' with other mentors – are effective ways of preventing possible ethical dilemmas escalating into ethical traps. Building in regular reviews of mentoring relationships with mentees also means that there is ample opportunity to identify what is working/not working in the relationships and that any ethical tensions can be identified and resolved. Engaging in these processes also has the added benefit of providing an additional vehicle for personal and professional development.

References

Beech, N., & Brockbank, A. (1999). *Power/knowledge and psychosocial dynamics in mentoring. Management Learning*, **30**(1), 7–25. https://doi.org/10.1177/1350507699301002

Clutterbuck, D., & Megginson, D. (1999). *Mentoring Executives and Directors*. Butterworth-Heinemann.

French, J. R. P. Jr., & Raven, B. (1959). *The bases of social power*. In D. Cartwright (Ed.) *Studies in Social Power* (pp. 150–167). Institute for Social Research, University of Michigan.

Garrett, R. (2006). Expert Patient Mentoring Evaluation Report , NHSU. https://scottishmentoringnetwork.co.uk/assets/downloads/resources/NHSExpertPatientMentoring.pdf, accessed 18/1/24

Garvey, B., & Stokes, P. (2022). *Coaching and Mentoring: Theory and Practice* (**4th ed.**). SAGE.

Kram, K. E. (1985). *Mentoring at Work: Developmental Relationships in Organizational Life*. Scott Foresman.

McAuley, J. (2003). *Transference, countertransference and mentoring: The ghost in the process. British Journal of Guidance & Counselling*, **31**(1), 11–23.

Milner, J., Milner, T., McCarthy, G., & da Motta Veiga, S. (2022). *Leaders as coaches: Towards a code of ethics. The Journal of Applied Behavioral Science*, **59**(3), 448–472. https://doi.org/10.1177/00218863211069408

Passmore, J. (Ed.). (2011). *Supervision in Coaching: Supervision, Ethics and Continuous Professional Development*. Kogan Page.

Rothstein, J. K., (2022). *Egoism and the limits of ethics. Journal of Mental Health and Social Behaviour*, **4**(1), 161. https://doi.org/10.33790/jmhsb1100161

Chapter 4
Mentoring in Professional Associations

Melissa Richardson

> **Note:** Art of Mentoring is a specialist mentoring firm based in Australia. While the company works across corporate, government and associations, it has had a long and special relationship with professional associations in Australia, working for over a decade with groups like the Australian Veterinary Association, the Association of School Business Administrators, the Australian HR Institute, the Australian Institute of Project Management and more. Much of the content in this chapter is based on the company's extensive experience working on the ground with professional associations.

Introduction

Being a 'professional' is no longer exclusively the domain of doctors, lawyers and accountants. Industry associations are becoming increasingly 'professionalized', moving from organizations that simply represent the interests of an industry or occupation to associations that exist to define and raise professional standards and foster a sense of professional identity.

In Australia, for example, the Australian HR Institute (AHRI) was once simply a membership organization for human resource managers but now has membership levels and requires accreditation and continuing education to maintain and advance one's membership level and recognition as a certified HR professional.

A significant proportion of white-collar jobs now have professional associations that represent their interests and provide resources, support and ongoing training. At the same time, the economic and employment conditions are fundamentally changing. As white-collar occupations increasingly 'professionalize' and establish stronger ties with their profession, the bond between worker and employer is weakening. Where employers could once be expected to provide career guidance and development, employees must increasingly look to outside relationships to foster their personal and professional growth.

The need for 'outside' mentoring relationships

Since 2000, mentoring research has refocused from a view of mentoring as a single dyadic relationship between a senior individual and a protégé within a single organization, to one of 'developmental networks'. Starting with Higgins and Kram (2001), much has been written on the importance of mentoring being a multirelationship phenomenon, with career success improved when developmental relationships are formed both in and out of one's organization of employment (Dobrow & Higgins, 2005).

Changes to the economic and employment landscape this century have made 'outside' mentoring increasingly critical to career learning and development.

Fast-shifting economic conditions have fundamentally changed the psychological contract between individuals and the employer (Rousseau, 1995). The increasing need for firms to be flexible in order to be successful has weakened the bond between employer and employee. Careers that once might have been guided by a single employer, are now operating in a 'boundaryless' model (Schalk & Rousseau, 2009). Individuals have greater freedom to move across the boundaries of separate employers, but equally can no longer expect those employers to be the primary anchor for their career and psychosocial support.

Add to this the increasing trend toward virtual work, which has been accelerated by the COVID-19 pandemic. Even within their organizations of employment, individuals are increasingly working in relative isolation, requiring them to look beyond intraorganizational support networks for learning and development.

The trend toward a 'gig economy' further weakens the relationship between individual and employer. The many workers now employed on a contract basis cannot rely on their employer for support in personal or career development. Where employers do run developmental programmes, in our experience these are frequently not open to contract workers.

As the employment landscape evolves, work and industry associations of all kinds must step up to play a key role in providing 'outside' mentoring programmes to enable members to establish the development networks needed to succeed in the new world for work.

Professional associations and professional identity

Professional associations have a unique responsibility to provide 'outside' mentoring programmes, as they are uniquely placed to build 'professional identity'. The concept of being a 'professional' is value-laden and aspirational (Bellis, 2000). In an increasingly untethered world of work, identifying as a professional gives a sense of belonging and self-confidence that is critical to psychosocial well-being and success in a boundaryless workforce.

The professional association is central to the concept of 'professional identity'. Without an association to bind professionals together, Bellis argues it is hard for an occupation to even be seen as professional. We would argue that associations have a unique responsibility to foster professional identity among their members.

Mentoring has been shown, across a range of professions, to be critical to embedding a sense of professional identity (Bellis, 2000; Matsuyama et al., 2020; Nganga et al., 2020; Bettin, 2021; Mantzourani et al., 2022). It is critical that professional associations offer mentoring programmes to build the 'outside' developmental networks and sense of professional identity that will benefit members and drive their careers forward.

Professional association mentoring: Advantages to members and associations

A well-designed and managed mentoring programme benefits both the professional association and its members.

Where corporate mentoring focuses on advancing an individual's progress within an organization, professional association mentoring programmes advance a member's standing in their profession. For younger, less experienced professionals, it is an opportunity to embed a sense of professional identity and belonging that will serve them throughout their career. For more experienced professionals, the opportunity to mentor is a chance to 'give back' to the profession, reinforcing professional identity and self-esteem.

Associations need compelling reasons for members to join and stay. Mentoring programmes that build a sense of professional identity not only benefit the members, but also bind them more strongly to the association representing that profession. Ritchie and Genoni (1999) note that mentoring programmes facilitate attraction and retention of association members.

As associations 'professionalize', setting professional standards and requiring continuing education, the bond between association and professional member becomes stronger as accreditation becomes a 'must have' designation (Peacock, 2010). Mentoring programmes can play an integral role in continuing education and also assist in building awareness of professional standards and professional values.

Finally, associations must cultivate their own leaders if they are to remain strong, a need identified by Zabel (2008). Mentoring programmes enable associations to foster both engagement and leadership skills that can be leveraged to keep association management fresh and capable.

The unique characteristics of professional association mentoring programmes

Having established that mentoring programmes are beneficial to both members and associations, we now explore some of the unique aspects of mentoring programmes run through professional associations. Art of Mentoring have been helping to design and manage mentoring programmes with professional associations for over a decade. We have had an opportunity to observe at first hand the unique advantages and challenges of professional association mentoring programmes.

Association mentoring: Opportunities for reciprocal learning and vulnerability

Professional association mentoring programmes usually match entry-level or junior professionals with more experienced people in the same profession. These relationships offer two distinct advantages when compared to mentoring relationships in corporate programmes:

1. Pairs are drawn from different cultures and industries, offering greater potential for reciprocal learning. Both mentor and mentee can learn from the sharing of information, processes and ideas from their partner's divergent industry experience.

2. Participants, and particularly mentors, are more willing to be vulnerable in 'outside' mentoring relationships. With professional association mentoring programmes mentors feel freer to step away from the role and responsibility of their company hierarchical position and be vulnerable enough to learn and share with someone junior. Mentees feel less pressure to impress their employer and are more willing to admit their fears and weaknesses.

Mentor motivation and commitment

As previously stated, professional association mentoring programmes represent an opportunity for more senior professionals to 'give back' to their profession. This added 'moral' motivation often makes it easier to recruit mentors to professional association programmes rather than to corporate programmes. In our observation, mentors are also far more likely to participate repeatedly, mentoring multiple people over a number of years. We rarely see this level of commitment in corporate programmes.

The commitment of mentors and experience gained through multiple mentorships improves the value of the programme for mentees and prepares mentors for leadership roles within their profession and the association itself.

Structural politics: The possibility of programme sabotage

In our experience the structure of professional associations can present unique political challenges to establishing a strong mentoring programme. Many associations operate on a federated basis, with state or regional chapters linked (sometimes loosely) through a national association. When power is disseminated among a number of chapters, it is critical to have all chapters onside before launching any national programme. We have literally seen national mentoring programmes sabotaged by state chapters that had not 'bought in' to the programme design.

Association vs employer: Conflict of interest?

Professional association mentoring programmes are by definition cross-company. Employers may have a genuine concern that participants will be poached by other employers and/or that confidential company information may be shared with competitors. Associations have to pay particular attention to ensure the design and governance of their mentoring programme protects the interests and confidentiality of participants and their employers. Having a clear code of conduct that must be read and accepted prior to participation is one measure that protects all parties and simply makes good sense.

CPD points: The impact on recruitment and engagement

As stated above, professional associations increasingly offer levels of membership and professional certification. Accreditation generally relies on the accrual of continuing professional development (CPD) points.

Attaching CPD points to participation in association mentoring programmes has both pros and cons. On the plus side, the opportunity to earn CPD points makes recruitment easier. It seems only fair that time spent providing or receiving mentorship should be counted as professional learning, in the same way that activities like conference attendance and completion of training courses accrue points.

However, we have observed that some people opt in to earn their points, but fail to truly engage in the programme. While this behaviour is observed in a minority of mentees and mentors, it can jeopardize the success of the programme overall. When mentees fail to engage, it makes it more difficult to encourage mentors to return for future programmes. When mentors fail to engage, their mentees gain less learning and professional confidence from the programme. And, of course, the less engagement in the programme the less opportunity to increase engagement with the association itself. Once a mentoring programme gains a reputation for having high dropout rates or numbers of pairs that do not complete the programme, it can be hard to keep key stakeholders enthusiastic and supportive. This is often when we see programme funding withdrawn.

Some associations pre-empt this by ensuring that CPD points are earned only after proving participation in the programme, such as completion of mentoring training, attendance at group events and having a certain number of mentoring meetings, rather than just for signing up in the programme.

Programme funding: The impacts on programme focus

Unlike corporate programmes, which can be directly funded by the organization, professional association programmes generally rely on some form of outside funding. In our experience, programme funding generally comes from one or a mix of three sources:

- programme fees paid by mentees
- sponsorship by corporations
- government grants.

It is essential to carefully consider the impact that different funding models may have on the focus and success of the programmes.

Corporate sponsorships can risk the mentee-centric nature of professional association programmes. In some sponsorship models, corporate sponsors receive a number of mentor places as part of their sponsorship package. When the corporation selects participants to take up those programme places, those mentees may feel responsible for delivering against an agenda set by the sponsoring organization, rather than focusing on a more general exploration of their professional development.

Ironically, high programme fees paid directly by mentees can have the same result. If the cost to participate in professional association mentoring programmes is high, mentees may turn to their employer for funding assistance. This again increases the likelihood that mentees will feel an obligation to achieve employer-centric outcomes.

Be aware that there is no evidence that high programme fees secure high levels of commitment and motivation from mentees. At one time we posited that this would be the case. However, we have been constantly surprised by the number of mentees who have paid high fees to participate in a mentoring programme, yet fail to engage fully.

Government grants can risk incentivizing quantity over quality. To ensure that public funding is being well used, grants for mentoring programmes will likely require that a minimum number of people are put through the programme. This is understandable from a funding perspective, but it can force a situation where pairs are matched for the sake of achieving the numbers, without sufficient regard for the quality of the match. The result can be 100 weak pairs, where 50 strong pairs might have meant a better outcome for the profession overall.

Design implications for professional associations

Given the importance and unique characteristics of professional association mentoring programmes, we outline below a number of design implications that require special attention.

Programme funding

Before setting programme fees or approaching corporate sponsors or government for funding, ensure that you consider the potential impacts on the programme as a whole. Obviously, funding is required to operate a well-run formal mentoring programme and compromises may need to be made. But it is important to recognize the possible impacts and try to design around them.

Steering committee

We recommend a steering committee, or group responsible for design and oversight, for all mentoring programmes. However, the make-up of the steering committee is particularly important with professional association programmes.

Attention must be paid to the association structure, particularly in federated models. It is essential that members from all chapters and power bases are represented on the steering committee. At best, this ensures cross-chapter buy-in to the programme. At worst, it makes visible any possible efforts to sabotage the programme.

Given potential perceptions of conflict of interest for employers, it is important to include on the committee people who understand the competitive dynamics in their region.

The steering committee can often be helpful when it comes to matching, as committee members often know applicants personally and can provide important knowledge of, for example, potential competitive conflicts.

Code of conduct

As already noted, development of a clearly stated code of conduct for the mentoring programme is critical. Any likely perceptions of employer conflict of interest should be specifically dealt with in the code of conduct. So, for example, the code might specify that poaching is a no-go for participants, with membership or accreditation penalties to be applied.

The code of conduct should be widely distributed, available to employers and reinforced in mentor and mentee training sessions.

Programme marketing

Before any programme marketing commences, ensure that all chapters are supportive of the programme design. Also ensure that the code of conduct has been agreed and the protections against competitive threats are clearly spelled out in marketing materials.

When marketing a professional association mentoring programme be sure to leverage the concept of 'professional identity' and the opportunity to 'give back' to the profession. As outlined above, the professional community is increasingly important in the boundaryless workplace. Promoting these concepts will assist in recruitment, particularly of mentors.

Pair matching

Special attention must be paid to competitive sensitivities when matching mentoring pairs. Programme managers must work closely with those who are familiar with the competitive context.

Some competitive lines will be geographic. For example, matching two veterinarians in the same small town almost certainly runs the risk that they are competitors, and their relationship may feel threatening to their employers. In a post-COVID world, virtual mentoring relationships are much more acceptable, so matching people outside of their own geographic locations is one way to reduce competitive risk.

Other competitive lines are in areas of industry or professional employer segments. For example, in an accounting profession mentoring programme, a match can be made between, say, an in-house accountant mentee and a mentor from an accounting practice, to reduce the risk of competition. Of course, this will depend on the mentee's mentoring needs. Getting the balance right between avoidance of competitive sensitivities and meeting the requirements of the programme participants makes matching in association programmes particularly complex and therefore time-consuming.

Conclusion

As economic demands and employment changes continue to weaken the relationship between employer and employee, there is a growing need for workers to broaden their 'developmental networks', seeking career and psychosocial support beyond their employer. Professional associations are ideally positioned to provide 'outside' mentoring programmes that not only expand development networks, but also build the 'professional identity' that gives a sense of belonging to a boundaryless workforce untethered from their employer.

Designing an effective mentoring programme for a professional association must take into account the advantages and challenges as compared with corporate programmes. Professional association programme design requires an understanding of and careful attention to the political structure of the association and competitive sensitivities of industry employers. The demands to fund association mentoring programmes may require compromise between the source of funding and the integrity of the programme.

Designers should be aware of the risks and endeavour to maintain as mentee-centric a programme as possible. Designers should also be aware of the motivational power of 'professional identity' and CPD points, and the heightened willingness to be vulnerable and have reciprocal learning opportunities for both mentors and mentees partnered with someone outside their employer.

References

Bellis, C. (2000). *Professions in society. British Actuarial Journal,* **6**(2), 317–344.

Bettin, K. A. (2021). *The role of mentoring in the professional identity formation of medical students. Orthopedic Clinics of North America.* **52**(1), 61–68. https://www.sciencedirect.com/science/article/abs/pii/S0030589820301280?via%3Dihub

Dobrow, S. R., & Higgins, M. C. (2005). *Developmental networks and professional identity: a longitudinal study. Career Development International,* *10*(**6/7**), 567–583.

Higgins, M., & Kram, K. (2001). *Reconceptualizing mentoring at work: A developmental network perspective. Academy of Management Review,* **26**(2), 264–288.

Mantzourani, E., Chang, H., Desselle, S., Canedo, J., & Fleming, G. (2022). *Reflections of mentors and mentees on a national mentoring programme for pharmacists: An examination into relationships, personal and professional development. Research in Social and Administrative Pharmacy,* **18**(3), 2495–2504.

Matsuyama, Y., Okazaki, H., Kotani, K., Asada, Y., Ishikawa, S., Lebowitz, A., Leppink, J., & Van der Vleuten, C. (2021). *Professional identity formation-oriented mentoring technique as a method to improve self-regulated learning: A mixed-method study. The Asia Pacific Scholar,* **6**(4), 49–64.

Nganga, C., Bowne, M., & Stremmel, A. (2020). *Mentoring as a developmental identity process. Mentoring & Tutoring: Partnership in Learning,* **28**(3), 259–277.DOI: 10.1080/13611267.2020.1783498

Peacock, J. (2010). *Becoming a 'must-join' association for professionals.* Associations Forum. https://associations.net.au/resources/professions/becoming-a-must-join-association.html

Ritchie, A., & Genoni, P. (1999). Mentoring in professional associations: Continuing professional development for librarians. *Health Libraries Review,* **16**(4), 216–225.

Rousseau, D. (1995). *Psychological Contracts in Organizations: Understanding Written and Unwritten Agreements.* SAGE.

Schalk, R., & Rousseau, D. (2009). *Psychological contracts in employment.* In N. Anderson, D. S. Ones, H. K. Sinangil, & C. Viswesvaran (Eds.) *Handbook of Industrial, Work and Organizational Psychology: Volume 2 – Organizational Psychology* (pp. 133–142). SAGE.

Zabel, D. (2008*). The mentoring role of professional associations. Journal of Business & Finance Librarianship,* **13**(3), 349–361.

Chapter 5
Developmental Networks for Faculty Success at Health Sciences Centers

Akshay Sood & Nora Dominguez

Introduction

The faculty members at Health Sciences Centers (HSCs) in the US have complex careers. Newcomers and faculty in early career stages must learn to navigate the health care and academic system, understand and prepare for the promotion and tenure process (P&TP), and complete duties and responsibilities regarding funding, grant writing and research and publications, while fulfilling community service, and teaching and clinical responsibilities. At higher ranks, the job responsibilities increase to include leadership and administrative duties at the departmental and college levels and participation in professional organizations with national and international recognition. Historically, the multidomain and demanding nature of faculty careers at the HSCs has yielded high attrition rates due to the lack of institutional support, low career satisfaction rates and burnout (Straus & Sackett, 2014). Developmental networks that include high-quality mentoring relationships reduce attrition and promote faculty success at HSCs.

Mentoring and developmental networks

Mentoring is a relationship that implies a learning partnership. It depends on the context, the purpose of the relationship and the participants' values and competencies. It develops through several stages of initiation, negotiation, cultivation and the relationship's end (Dominguez, 2017). Effective mentoring relationships are associated with positive career outcomes such as increased productivity, accelerated promotion, higher retention rates, clarity of professional identity, greater self-efficacy and career satisfaction. Reciprocal mentoring benefits both the mentor and mentee and the organization sponsoring mentoring programmes (Straus & Sackett, 2014). While there is no universal definition of mentoring, it is recommended to have an operational definition to clarify the participants' expectations. Some of the most common ways to define mentoring are based on: a) the participants (mentor/mentee); b) the type of support provided (career, academic and psychosocial support, coaching, sponsorship, networking, modelling); and c) the purposes, outcomes and benefits of the relationship (Dominguez & Kochan, 2020).

Scholars claim that true mentors provide high amounts of career and psychosocial support. However, we recognize that individuals receive mentoring assistance from many people at any point in time, including assistance from senior colleagues, peers, family and community members. Also, the mentoring paradigm has shifted. The mentee has changed from being a passive receiver to becoming an active learner, the mentor role has evolved from being an authority to becoming a facilitator of learning, the learning process has changed from mentor-directed to self-directed, and from face-to-face to multiple and varied opportunities and configurations of engagement. The relationship's focus has changed from transferring information to creating knowledge through critical reflection (Dominguez & Kochan, 2020).

Given the complexity of the organizational environment, we acknowledge that a single mentor can only provide some of the guidance, exposure and opportunities essential to effectively managing current job and leadership challenges. Therefore, applying social network theory to the field of mentoring, Higgins & Kram (2001) created the concept of *developmental networks* (DNs). A developmental network is an egocentric network comprised of a set of people a mentee names as taking an interest and action to advance their career by providing developmental assistance. The critical distinction between an individual's social and developmental network is that the former includes all social ties. In contrast, the latter includes only those critical to career growth and personal learning (Higgins & Kram, 2001).

For decades, mentoring has been viewed as a hierarchical, one-to-one, long-term working relationship. This is in contrast to a developmental network, which is comprised of multiple work and non-work, short- or long-term relationships in one-to-one or group configurations with multiple people such as superiors, peers, subordinates, friends, allies, sponsors, coaches and mentors – all of them called 'developers' (Higgins & Kram, 2001).

Since a single mentor cannot be the only source of support, DNs are critical for career success. Studies have demonstrated that diversified DNs have positive results in critical measures such as enhanced employee engagement, faster cycle times in knowledge development, and employee retention and satisfaction. Appropriate DNs can result in greater productivity, adaptability and organizational loyalty. DNs promote enhanced learning, collaboration and reflection and enable individuals to learn how to create positive work relationships with individuals of different cultural backgrounds (Higgins & Kram, 2001).

There are two essential components of a DN. First, *Relationship Diversity* is defined by: the *size* or the number of developers; the *range* or the number of social systems represented in the network; the *diversity of the participants* in terms of gender, race, ethnicity, nationality and educational background; and the *density* or the extent to which developers know each other. Second, the network's *Content* is defined by the amount and *types of support* available and the *strength of ties* which represent the level of engagement in terms of frequency of contact and the degree of trust, intimacy and mutuality that increase the quality of the relationship (Dobrow et al., 2011).

From an individual's point of view, the appropriate DN should be grounded in what the individual is seeking to accomplish and the resources available in his or her network. A homogeneous network may bring loyalty, good performance and promotion within some organizations at specific career stages. In contrast, a more diverse network may bring about mobility and leadership development (Higgins & Kram, 2001).

The need for faculty mentoring and developmental networks at HSCs

The faculty members at HSCs encounter multiple barriers and challenges while working toward career milestones considered 'critical' for success. Their ability to achieve these critical career milestones impacts their productivity, satisfaction, career advancement and retention, mainly if they are women or racial/ethnic underrepresented minorities (URM). These barriers and challenges have increased multifold during the COVID-19 pandemic. In a small qualitative study on barriers and challenges encountered during the pandemic that included two south-western HSCs, semi-structured interviews were conducted with thirty-one junior faculty staff, including twenty women, seven Asian, two Hispanic and five multiracial (Soller et al., 2022a). Qualitative analysis using NVivo software identified five key themes that illustrated barriers and challenges encountered, including: 1) job and career development; 2) discrimination and lack of workplace diversity; 3) lack of interpersonal relationships and inadequate social support at the workplace; 4) personal and family matters; and 5) unique COVID-19-related issues. Junior faculty staff need effective mentoring and adequate DNs to address these complex barriers and challenges and advance their careers.

The theoretical basis for mentoring and developmental networks

The growing application of social network-based theories and methods (Burt et al., 2013) in scholarship on mentoring indicates that mentoring goes beyond dyadic relationships (Higgins & Kram, 2001). Theories of social capital offer insight into the significance of social networking for people seeking career advancement. While scholars disagree upon an exact definition of social capital, most concur that social capital refers to the resources embedded in one's social relationships (Portes, 1998; Small, 2010). Resources can include *the obligations that people who are connected may feel toward each other, the sense of solidarity they may call upon, the information they are willing to share, and the services they are willing to perform'* (Small, 2010). These social resources are temporary, borrowed from social connections, and people *must* mobilize them to achieve their goals – that is, simply having access to resourceful connections does not guarantee the use of those resources (Lin, 1999; 2001). As a result of access to and use of these resources, well-connected individuals benefit more than less well-connected individuals. Workers who leverage their network in career advancement benefit by gaining meaningful access to more significant and diverse resources.

Developmental networks

Given that a single, hierarchical mentoring relationship does not satisfy an individual's complex and varied needs (Kram, 1985; Murphy & Kram, 2010), it is necessary to seek formal and informal career and psychosocial support from multiple developers (i.e., mentors, sponsors, friends and allies) and from multiple social arenas (i.e., social and professional groups where individuals gain developers, such as the workplace, professional organizations, community) (Higgins & Kram, 2001). Thus, the fundamental nature of career development has recently been transformed from one-on-one hierarchical mentoring relationships to networks of developmental relationships with mentors, sponsors, friends and allies (see Figure 5.1). For individuals pursuing a career in the health sciences, developing networks involves looking more widely for career and psychosocial support beyond an assigned traditional mentor. In our recent survey of eighty-five newly hired faculty at the University of New Mexico (UNM) School of Medicine (SOM), only 4.7% said that they did not perceive a need for a DN (Sood et al., 2022).

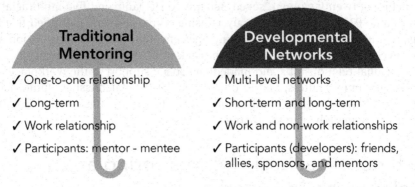

Figure 5.1: Comparison of traditional methods vs developmental networks (Kram & Higgins, 2009).

Developmental network (DN) building improves self-efficacy for academic success among mentees in a structured mentoring programme (Wingard et al., 2004). DeCastro et al. (2013) explored networks by interviewing one hundred mentee recipients of National Institutes of Health (NIH)-mentored career development awards and twenty-eight of their mentors, oversampling URM scientists. The study concluded that 'those who seek to promote the career of faculty in academic medicine should focus upon developing mentoring networks, rather than hierarchical mentoring dyads. The members of the mentoring team or network should reflect the mentee's individual needs and preferences, with special attention towards ensuring diversity in terms of area of expertise, academic rank, and gender', in response to both a shortage of available traditional mentors and to the challenges experienced by URM faculty scientists. These scientists 'often face social barriers that block access to effective mentoring relationships' (Ragins, 1997; Ragins & Scandura, 1997; Yip & Kram, 2017). Developmental networks (DNs) that involve relationships comprised of individuals who differ by race, gender, disability status, etc., may enrich career outcomes through increased access to knowledge, opportunities and other social resources that are potentially embedded in mentoring relationships (Ragins, 1997). However, a large body of literature demonstrates that social resources embedded in women's and URM social networks are less useful for career advancement than in the networks of white men (Braddock & McPartland, 1987; McGuire, 2000), indicating that network characteristics may be more important than having a network alone.

Network characteristics

Our team performed a preliminary study of DNs from eighty-one faculty members from UNM HSC and Oklahoma University (OU) HSC engaged in a mentoring intervention. The results of this study are summarized in Table 5.1. Faculty participants consisted of both mentees and mentors, and DNs were examined using an innovative online approach to the developmental network questionnaire (DNQ). The DNQ is an assessment questionnaire used in a business classroom setting – but never published in biomedical sciences – that collects information on network characteristics and can be used to identify areas of improvement. Leveraging the DNQ to assess the DNs of HSC faculty, we noted that participants received psychosocial and career support from an average of 4.9 current developers (4.8 and 5.1 for mentors and mentees, respectively). Developers came from 2.3 social arenas (2.2 and 2.4 arenas for mentors and mentees, respectively). While the most common social arena was the respondents' current job/position (62%, 64%, and 59% for all participants, mentors, and mentees, respectively), developers also came from other social arenas, including graduate school (11%, 6% and 17%), prior jobs/positions (13%, 16% and 9%) and family (8%, 5% and 11%). The relationship types in the DNs were mentors, friends, allies and sponsors, ranking in that order.

Network characteristics such as range and density are better understood by visualizing DNs. For example, Figure 5.2 depicts the DNs of two mentees (A and B) enrolled in our preliminary study. Developers are differentiated according to their relationship with the mentee (i.e., sponsor, friend, mentor, ally). The different social arenas where the mentee met the developers are differentiated by colour (see legend). The relationship ties between the mentee and developers are shown as solid lines, while the ties between individual developers are depicted using dotted lines. Figure 5.2A displays a network with two friends, two sponsors and no allies or mentors. Three developers are colleagues/collaborators in their current job, and one is a graduate school friend, which results in a range of 2. The network has a density of 0.33, given that only two of the six possible ties among developers are present. Figure 5.2B displays a network that includes three developers from graduate school and three developers from the current job, resulting in a range of 2. Half the developers are sponsors, one is a mentor, another is a friend and one is an ally. The network has a density score of 0.27, given that four of the possible fifteen ties among developers are present. As shown in Figure 5.2, all networks are not alike, and they can vary considerably in network characteristics such as size, range and density.

Table 5.1: Faculty developmental network characteristics (Soller et al., 2021).

Network characteristics (definitions provided in Table 6)	Mentors (n=44) Mean ± SD/%	Mentees (n=37) Mean ± SD/%
Network level measures		
Size	4.8 ± 1.4	5.1 ± 1.2
Range (number of social arenas)	2.2 ± 1.1	2.4 ± 1.2
Density (interconnectedness)	0.62 ± 0.32	0.65 ± 0.28
Social arena		
Childhood friends	0.9%	0.0%
Colleagues/collaborators	2.3%	1.0%
College friends	0.9%	1.5%
Current job or organization	64.4%	58.5%
Family	5.4%	11.0%
Graduate school friends	0.9%	6.0%
Graduate school professors	5.4%	10.5%
Other	0.5%	0.5%
Previous job or organization	15.8%	9.0%
Profession: Generic	1.8%	1.0%
Religious organization	0.5%	0.5%
Volunteering	1.4%	0.5%
Support		
Psychosocial support	24.6 ± 7.5	24.8 ± 7.5
Career support	20.1 ± 7.5	21.4 ± 7.9
Developer classification		
Mentor	36.0%	37.8%
Ally	20.2%	19.2%
Friend	31.5%	28.7%
Sponsor	12.3%	14.4%
Communication frequency	5.4 ± 1.8	5.5 ± 1.7
Emotional closeness	2.8 ± 0.9	2.9 ± 0.9

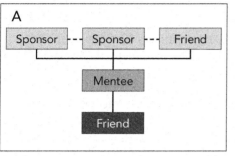 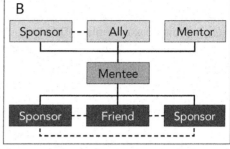

Legend:

Current Job ——— Ties from mentee to developers
Grad School ----- Ties between developers

Figure 5.2: Two examples of developmental networks.

In a small study from two south-western HSCs, we examined gender variation in social relationship dynamics that establishes the rationale for studying individual-level factors that may confound studies of DNs. Women comprise an increasing proportion of the workforce and yet report receiving less mentoring and lower career satisfaction, productivity and advancement than their male counterparts (Travis et al., 2013; Farkas et al., 2019). In our preliminary cross-sectional study, summarized in Table 5.2, we assessed gender differences in self-reported dimensions of ninety-two faculty members' DNs during the pandemic using multilevel regression, which accounts for the nested structure of our data and non-independence of observations within the respondents (Soller et al., 2022b). Study findings indicated that compared to their male counterparts, female faculty members reported receiving more psychosocial support (beta coefficient or $b = 0.418$, $p < 0.05$) but less career support ($b = -0.424$, $p < 0.05$) from their developers. Male and female respondents did not differ in network size, range or levels of communication frequency, or emotional closeness with developers after controlling for key confounders. Female faculty members reported greater gender diversity of developers. Female faculty members' developers were more often characterized as 'friends' and less often characterized as 'mentors' and 'sponsors' than male faculty, based on the relative levels of career and psychosocial support that individual developers provided (Table 5.2). The lower levels of career support and fewer mentors and sponsors for female faculty may have long-term implications for differential career advancement for women vs men.

Table 5.2: Comparison of developer types in male vs female faculty developmental networks.

Relationship type	Male (n=34) %	Female (n=58) %	p-value
Ally	23.0	17.4	
Friend	16.2	35.2	<0.001
Mentor	43.9	36.2	
Sponsor	16.9	11.3	

Additionally, research has linked network characteristics, such as range, density, emotional closeness and intensity (frequency of communication), to career outcomes such as professional identity (Dobrow et al., 2005), mutuality (Dobrow et al., 2011), career optimism (Higgins et al., 2010) and leadership development (Ghosh et al., 2013) in multiple settings (Murphy & Kram, 2010; Shen & Kram, 2011), professions (Higgins & Thomas, 2001; Higgins et al., 2008) and career stages (Chandler et al., 2005). However, the impact of these network characteristics on career outcome measures is inadequately studied in the health sciences.

Challenges to creating and cultivating networks

Despite the widely held belief that successful people are eager to ask for help, research in the business field suggests the opposite, citing 'egocentric bias' (Garvin & Margolis, 2015). Many refrain from seeking developmental help, citing no time or energy, being an introvert or having a shy personality, lack of knowledge on how to network, or finding it insincere, manipulative or unimportant (Ibarra & Hunter, 2007). We noted similar findings among newly hired clinicians at the UNM HSC who fail to engage others in developmental relationships (Sood et al., 2019). Individual-level factors that predict developmental help-seeking behaviours, which may impact network characteristics and career outcomes, are well-studied in the clinical context and business literature. However, they are inadequately studied in the DN context in the biomedical sciences.

In addition to differences in developmental help-seeking behaviours, additional challenges exist to creating and cultivating DNs. In a study at the UNM SOM, all newly hired faculty within their first year of hire (N = 131) were surveyed anonymously on their attitudes regarding mentorship and DNs. Newly hired faculty mentees reported that creating a DN was hampered by difficulties finding multiple mentors (55.3%), receiving conflicting advice from multiple mentors (22.4%) and gathering many mentors at the exact location at the same time (11.8%). Lack of clarity regarding faculty mentee needs (55.5%), mentors' unavailability (17.6%) and failure to find mentors (14.3%) were the most often mentioned difficulties during the initiation stage of the mentorship (Hitchcock et al., 1995). These findings are consistent with those reported in a recent literature review where the most cited institutional facilitator to mentoring in health-related research for new investigators, early-stage investigators and URM faculty was access to mentoring; conversely, the most cited institutional barrier was a lack of mentors (Ransdell et al., 2021). Especially lacking were mentors who matched the area of study, expertise, diversity or research deficits of the mentee. Mentors might be less willing to participate if they did not receive workload credit for mentoring or if the mentoring experiences were not mutually beneficial. Additionally, some institutions (e.g., predominately white institutions) and some academic disciplines lack diverse faculty to mentor (Coe et al., 2020; Zambrana et al., 2015).

The need for organizational interventions

Many HSC faculty are moving from a hierarchical dyadic mentoring relationship to a DN model, which should be welcome (Higgins & Kram, 2001; Carey & Weissman, 2010; Soller et al., 2021). However, for this move toward networks to become more commonly accepted, institutions should create a conducive climate and culture for DNs. Faculty should be taught how to network using a science-based curriculum. It may be reasonable to assign an organizational leader as a transitional mentor at the time of hire to help a new faculty mentee self-select a DN within their first year of hire (Sood et al., 2019). While providing different perspectives, multiple mentors in a DN may also provide conflicting advice to the mentee. The lead mentor in the DN should be trained to help the mentee negotiate these conflicts. An additional problem with a DN is logistical – trying to get multiple mentors simultaneously at the same place for a meeting. Organizations can help provide technological solutions for managing multiple online calendars and providing video-based meeting platforms. The organizational shortage of mentors will likely impact DNs more than dyadic mentoring relationships. Therefore, organizational strategies are needed to strengthen the organizational climate that values mentoring (Tigges et al., 2020) and the support networks of mentors, with some from outside one's organization and outside the work environment, including providing them with protected time, resources and training (Burnham et al., 2011). Faculty mentor development programmes effectively improve mentors' knowledge and competency, including those related to helping diverse mentees (Sood et al., 2020; Spencer et al., 2018). Institutions must identify and train mentors, incentivize and support mentorship, and encourage creating and maintaining self-selected DNs.

Conclusions

Diversified DNs provide access to information, resources and opportunities; however, the best network should fit the individual's needs, context, values, goals and career stage (Higgins, 2007). These ideas have several implications. Individuals need to look strategically for the support needed; organizations need to create a culture of learning and collaboration; faculty must recognize that assigning formal mentors to newcomers or junior faculty is insufficient. Instead, it is in everyone's best interests to create multiple opportunities for individuals to come together with their peers, juniors and seniors, internally and externally to the institution. More than ever, participants in a DN can learn from each other, creating complementary knowledge and skills to work together and solve shared challenges.

References

Braddock, J., & McPartland, J. (1987). *How minorities continue to be excluded from equal employment opportunities: Research on labor market and institutional barriers*. Journal of Social Issues, 43(1), 5–39.

Burnham, E. L., Schiro, S., & Fleming, M. (2011). *Mentoring K scholars: Strategies to support research mentors*. Clinical and Translational Science, 4(3), 199–203. https://doi.org/10.1111/j.1752-8062.2011.00286.x

Burt, R. S., Kilduff, M., & Tasselli, S. (2013). *Social network analysis: Foundations and frontiers on advantage*. Annual Review of Psychology, 64, 527–547. https://doi.org/10.1146/annurev-psych-113011-143828

Carey, E. C., & Weissman, D. E. (2010). *Understanding and finding mentorship: A review for junior faculty*. Journal of Palliative Medicine, 13(11), 1373–1379. https://doi.org/10.1089/jpm.2010.0091

Chandler, D. E., & Kram, K. E. (2005). *Applying an adult development perspective to developmental networks*. Career Development International, 10(6/7), 548–566. https://doi.org/10.1108/13620430510620610

Coe, C., Piggott, C., Davis, A., Hall, M. N., Goodell, K., Joo, P., & South-Paul, J. E. (2020). *Leadership pathways in academic family medicine: Focus on underrepresented minorities and women*. Family Medicine, 52(2), 104–111. https://doi.org/10.22454/FamMed.2020.545847

DeCastro, R., Sambuco, D., Ubel, P. A., Stewart, A., & Jagsi, R. (2013). *Mentor networks in academic medicine: Moving beyond a dyadic conception of mentoring for junior faculty researchers. Academic Medicine, 88*(**4**), 488–496. https://doi.org/10.1097/ACM.0b013e318285d302

Dobrow, S. R., & Higgins, M. C. (2005). *Developmental networks and professional identity: A longitudinal study. Career Development International, 10*(**6/7**), 567–583. https://doi.org/10.1108/13620430510620629

Dobrow, S. R., Chandler, D. E., Murphy, W. M., & Kram, K. E. (2011). *A review of developmental networks: Incorporating a mutuality perspective. Journal of Management, 38*(**1**), 210–242. https://doi.org/10.1177/0149206311415858

Dominguez, N. (2017). *A research analysis of the underpinnings, practice, and quality of mentoring programs and relationships.* In D. A. Clutterbuck, F. K. Kochan, L. Lunsford, N. Dominguez, & J. Haddock-Millar (Eds.), *The SAGE Handbook of Mentoring.* SAGE.

Dominguez, N., & Kochan, F. (2020). *Defining mentoring: An elusive search for meaning and a path for the future.* In B. J. Irby, J. N. Boswell, L. J. Searby, F. Kochan, R. Garza, & N. Abdelrahman (Eds.). *The Wiley International Handbook of Mentoring.* Wiley.

Farkas, A. H., Bonifacino, E., Turner, R., Tilstra, S. A., & Corbelli, J. A. (2019). *Mentorship of women in academic medicine: A systematic review. Journal of General Internal Medicine, 34*(**7**), 1322–1329. https://doi.org/10.1007/s11606-019-04955-2

Garvin, D. A., & Margolis, J. D. (2015). *The art of giving and receiving advice. Harvard Business Review,* (**Jan–Feb**).

Ghosh, R., Haynes, R. K., & Kram, K. E. (2013). *Developmental networks at work: Holding environments for leader development. Career Development International, 18*(**3**), 232–256. https://doi.org/10.1108/CDI-09-2012-0084

Higgins, M. C., & Kram, K. E. (2001). *Reconceptualizing mentoring at work: A developmental network perspective. The Academy of Management Review, 26*(**2**), 264–288.

Higgins, M. C., & Thomas, D. A. (2001). *Constellations and careers: Toward understanding the effects of multiple developmental relationships. Journal of Organizational Behavior, 22*(**3**), 223–247.

Higgins, M. (2007). A Contingency Perspective on Developmental Networks. In J. E. Dutton & B. R. Ragins (Eds.), Exploring positive relationships at work: Building a theoretical and research foundation (pp. 207–224). Lawrence Erlbaum Associates Publishers.

Higgins, M. C., Dobrow, S. R., & Chandler, D. E. (2008). *Never quite good enough: The paradox of sticky developmental relationships for elite university graduates. Journal of Vocational Behavior, 72*(**7**), 207–224.

Higgins, M., Dobrow, S. R., & Roloff, K. S. (2010). *Optimism and the boundaryless career: The role of developmental relationships. Journal of Organizational Behavior, 31*(**5**), 749–769.

Hitchcock, M. A., Bland, C. J., Hekelman, F. P., & Blumenthal, M. G. (1995). *Professional networks: The influence of colleagues on the academic success of faculty. Academic Medicine, 70*(**12**), 1108–1116.

Ibarra, H., & Hunter, M. (2007). *How leaders create and use networks. Harvard Business Review, 85*(**1**), 40–47.

Kram, K. E. (1985). *Mentoring at work: Developmental relationships in organizational life. Administration Science Quarterly, 30*(**3**), 454–456.

Kram, K. E., & Higgins, M. C. (2009). *A new mindset on mentoring: Creating developmental networks at work. MITSloan Management Review,* (**15 April**). https://www.bumc.bu.edu/facdev-medicine/files/2009/12/Kram-Higgins_A-New-Mindset-on-Mentoring.pdf

Lin, N. (1999). *Social networks and status attainment. Annual Review of Sociology, 25*, 467–487.

Lin, N. (2001). *Social Capital: A Theory of Social Structure and Action.* Cambridge University Press.

McGuire, G. (2000). *Gender, race, ethnicity, and networks: The factors affecting the status of employees' network members. Work and Occupations, 27*(**4**), 501–524.

Murphy, M. W., & Kram, K. E. (2010). *Understanding non-work relationships in developmental networks. Career Development International, 15*(**7**), 637–663. https://doi.org/10.1108/13620431011094069

Portes, A. (1998). *Social capital: Its origins and applications in modern sociology. Annual Review of Sociology, 24*, 1–24.

Ragins, B. R. (1997). *Diversified mentoring relationships in organizations: A power perspective. Academy of Management Review, 22*(**2**), 482–521.

Ragins, B. R., & Scandura, T. A. (1997). *The way we were: Gender and the termination of mentoring relationships. Journal of Applied Psychology, 82*(**6**), 945–953. https://www.ncbi.nlm.nih.gov/pubmed/9638090

Ransdell, L. B., Lane, T. S., Schwartz, A. L., Wayment, H. A., & Baldwin, J. A. (2021). *Mentoring new and early-stage investigators and underrepresented minority faculty for research success in health-related fields: An integrative literature review (2010–2020). International Journal of Environmental Research and Public Health, 18*(**2**), 432. https://doi.org/10.3390/ijerph18020432

Shen, Y., & Kram, K. E. (2011). *Expatriates' developmental networks: Network diversity, base, and support functions*. *Career Development International*, 16(**6**), 528–552. https://doi.org/10.1108/13620431111178317

Small, M. L. (2010). *Unanticipated Gains: Origins of Network Inequality in Everyday Life*. Oxford University Press.

Soller, B., Dominguez, N., Helitzer, D., Mickel, N., Myers, O., Tigges, B., & Sood, A. (2021). *Developmental network characteristics among mentors and mentees participating in a multi-site mentoring Intervention*. *Chronicles of Mentoring and Coaching*, 5(**Special Issue 14**), 375–382.

Soller, B., Martinez, J., Rishel Brakey, H., Dominguez, N., Tigges, B., & Sood, A. (2022a). *Barriers and challenges for career milestones among faculty mentees*. 2022 Annual UNM Mentoring Conference, Albuquerque, NM, US.

Soller, B., Shore, X. W., Myers, O., & Sood, A. (2022b). *Gender Differences in Self-reported Faculty Developmental Networks*. AAMC's Learn Serve Lead, Nashville, TN, US.

Sood, A., Sigl, D., Tigges, B., Myers, O., Greenberg, N., & Wilson, B. (2019). *Assigning mentors for new HSC faculty hires: A preliminary policy evaluation*. *Chronicles of Mentoring and Coaching*, 3(**Special Issue 12**), 427–432. https://www.ncbi.nlm.nih.gov/pubmed/32490172

Sood, A., Qualls, C., Tigges, B., Wilson, B., & Helitzer, D. (2020). *Effectiveness of a faculty mentor development program for scholarship at an academic health center*. *Journal of Continuing Education in the Health Professions*, 40(**1**), 58–65. https://doi.org/10.1097/CEH.0000000000000276

Sood, V., Wiggins, W., Rodriguez, A., & Sigl, D. (2022). *Attitudes of newly hired medicine faculty regarding mentorship and developmental networks*. *Chronicles of Mentoring and Coaching*. In Press, 6 (Special Issue 15), 624–629.

Spencer, K. C., McDaniels, M., Utzerath, E., Rogers, J. G., Sorkness, C. A., Asquith, P., & Pfund, C. (2018). *Building a sustainable national infrastructure to expand research mentor training*. *CBE—Life Sciences Education*, 17(**3**), ar48. https://doi.org/10.1187/cbe.18-03-0034

Straus, S. E., & Sackett, D. L. (2014). *Mentorship in Academic Medicine*. John Wiley & Sons, Ltd.

Tigges, B., Sood, A., Dominguez, N., Kurka, J. M., Myers, O. B., & Helitzer, D. (2020). *Measuring organizational mentoring climate: Importance and availability scales*. *Journal of Clinical and Translational Science*, 5(**1**), e53. https://doi.org/10.1017/cts.2020.547

Travis, E. L., Doty, L., & Helitzer, D. L. (2013). *Sponsorship: A path to the academic medicine C-suite for women faculty? Academic Medicine*, 88(**10**), 1414–1417. https://doi.org/10.1097/ACM.0b013e3182a35456

Wingard, D. L., Garman, K. A., & Reznik, V. (2004). *Facilitating faculty success: Outcomes and cost benefit of the UCSD National Center of Leadership in Academic Medicine. Academic Medicine*, 79(**10 Suppl.**), S9–11. https://doi.org/10.1097/00001888-200410001-00003

Yip, J., & Kram, K. E. (2017). *Developmental networks: Enhancing the science and practice of mentoring*. In D. A. Clutterbuck, F. K. Kochan, L. Lunsford, N. Dominguez, & J. Haddock-Millar (Eds.), *The SAGE Handbook of Mentoring*. SAGE.

Zambrana, R. E., Ray, R., Espino, M. M., Castro, C., Cohen, B. D., & Eliason, J. (2015). *'Don't leave us behind': The importance of mentoring for underrepresented minority faculty. American Educational Research Journal*, 52(**1**), 40–72.

Chapter 6
Mentor-Supervision is More than Mentoring the Mentor

Lise Lewis

Introduction

Mentoring, first mentioned some 3,000 years ago in Homer's *Odyssey*, has survived the apparent threat of coaching, that penetrated the business world when it exploded into the corporate environment in the 1990s. Mentoring seemed to retreat into the shadows as coaching became the more popular option, observed as creating kudos for the status of the client; replacing the opinion of it being a remedial measure to improving people development. What appeared to happen, for some, was a practice of retitling from mentor to coach, possibly to access the higher session rates paid by corporates, being early buyers in the executive coaching market. Despite this, mentoring survived – if it ever disappeared. Both practices have a foundation of common capabilities with mentoring continuing to be differentiated by taking a more holistic and extended developmental approach compared to the shorter–term goal-setting of coaching.

This chapter unfolds what mentoring is and its relevance in today's world of encouraging changes in methodology and expectations. Such change demands further change and creates expectations for the review of supplementary practices, such as supervision of mentors. These demands necessitate reaction and modification for supervision to be recognized as adding value to the practice of mentoring. Sponsors and practitioners increasingly recognize supervision as essential for the quality management, development and support of mentoring, coaching and supervision practices, enabled by the promotion of standards created by professional and qualification bodies and the increase in evidence-based literature.

The activity of mentor-supervision unfolds in this chapter, starting with a framework of definitions for coaching, mentoring and supervision, and followed by a typical mentor-supervision process organized under section headings and illustrated by scenarios from practice. The final section, 'Recommendations for further reading and resources', suggests topics for supervisors to be aware of when supporting mentors facing the rapid change prevailing in the workplace.

Framework for the mentor-supervision process

Definitions of coaching, mentoring and supervision are scene-setters and provide the framework for this chapter by offering practice differentiators and a foundation for promoting the merits of supervision as a value-added practice for mentors.

Universally agreed definitions for each practice are yet to be agreed as these disciplines remain unregulated. To offer guidance that encourages and promotes good practice for practitioners, clients and buyers operating in this environment, professional bodies provide definitions and design professional standards. Those available from European Mentoring and Coaching Council (EMCC Global) are offered as an exemplar:

Coaching

From the EMCC Global Glossary, last updated in April 2023:

> *A professional accredited coach (can be internal or external) is an expert in establishing a relationship with people in a series of conversations with the purpose of:*
>
> - *Serving the clients to improve their performance or enhance their personal development or both, choosing their own goals and ways of doing it.*
> - *Interacting with each person or group by applying one or more relevant methods, according to standards and ethical principles set up by EMCC Global and other professional associations.*

Mentoring

From the EMCC Global Glossary, last updated in April 2023:

> *Mentoring is a learning relationship, involving the sharing of skills, knowledge, and expertise between a mentor and a mentee through developmental conversations, experience sharing, and role modelling. The relationship may cover a wide variety of contexts, and is an inclusive two-way partnership for mutual learning that values differences.*

Supervision

From the EMCC Global Thought Leadership & Development web page, accessed on 24 May 2024:

> *A safe space for reflective dialogue with a practicing supervisor, supporting the supervisee's practice, development and well-being.*

It is worth mentioning here that for those wishing to gain recognition for personal practice 'a commitment to supervision is a requirement for accreditation as a practitioner'.

Reflections on the definitions informed by observations from coaching, mentoring and supervision practice:

Comparisons between coaching and mentoring

The distinction made between mentoring and coaching highlights the sharing of expertise between mentor and mentee that is not generally encouraged between coach and client. The concept that individuals are more likely to act upon self-discovered solutions suggests favouring a coaching approach in the first instance. Empowering the mentee to reflect on possibilities also encourages the mentor to suspend judgement and offering advice, to remain present and to actively listen. I notice when training and working with new mentors in supervision a tendency to 'overadvise'. The mentor offers this support with good intent and without meaning to potentially block the inherent wisdom of the mentee.

Let us also question the suggestion that coaches resist sharing experiences. Coaches without training may readily offer advice. Coaches with training are usually encouraged to be non-directive and use incisive questioning to support client development through self-discovery. Experienced, trained/ accredited coaches, displaying maturity in practice facilitated through reflective practice, will have progressed beyond this approach and, as with mentors, will share knowledge appropriately. The timing of when to offer relevant advice is a practice skill that avoids frustrating a client with overquestioning. Offering technical advice at any time is fundamental when contributing to learning.

The reference to 'two-way partnership' in the mentoring definition recognizes 'mutual learning' as endorsing the co-creative nature of mentoring, although it can have implications for the 'mentor–supervisor relationship' – more on this in the 'session content' section of this chapter. The practice of co-creative dialogue advocates personal and practice development through encouraging each to share thoughts, feelings, reflections and reactions that nurture new thinking and reciprocal learning. The result is reciprocity of learning for both the mentor and the supervisor.

Supervision

The definition offered by EMCC Global emphasizes the role of supervision as encouraging the shared practice of reflection as an aid to learning. The aim is to determine what is working well and how, through reviewing and evaluating alternative approaches, different results can be achieved that improve the mentor's offering and safeguards their well-being. 'Supporting the supervisee's practice' can be interpreted in the definition as encouraging mentors to work with professional standards as a benchmark for practice and continuing professional development to benefit the client. EMCC Global has a framework of performance indicators for both mentoring and coaching. More information about the framework indicators is available at: https:// www.emccglobal.org/leadership-development/leadership-development-mentoring/ – Thought Leadership and Development – Mentoring.

I believe that referencing the systemic nature of supervision will strengthen this definition by increasing the scope to include others (stakeholders) who may influence or be influenced by the topic of the mentor-supervision session and how this informs the supervision conversation.

The mentor-supervision process

A framework in preference to a prescriptive methodology is suggested as providing the flexibility that aligns with the flow and emergent nature of the mentor–supervisor conversation; with the recommendation that attention to relationship is critical from the start and throughout the mentor–supervisor programme. The relationship in coaching – and this suggests also in mentor-supervision – is an important one, explored from a wide variety of perspectives (O'Broin & Palmer, 2019).

Building the relationship: The supervisor and mentor creating the conditions for trust and safety

Creating the conditions for trust and safety as the basis for effective supervision evolves when both the mentor and supervisor have shared responsibility for developing and demonstrating qualities that achieve generative conversations:

- Attributes of a supervisee (mentor):
  - confident in the supervisor's intent to support and develop
  - comes to the conversation prepared with a topic/welcoming a practice review
  - has a desire for personal growth
  - wants to achieve professional goals
  - able to objectively reflect
  - is or is willing to raise emotional awareness
  - willingly accepts/offers transparent and honest feedback with care
  - open to different perspectives and options
  - able to self-evaluate realistically
  - takes responsibility for own learning.
- Profile for a supervisor:
  - offers sufficient self-disclosure to gain trust
  - instigates a working together conversation (contracting) that assures safety
  - comes with a growth mindset (Dweck, 2008)
  - strives to become a trusted critical friend and learning partner
  - encourages mentor learning through reflective practice
  - shares observations and reveals 'unlit corners' of self-awareness
  - challenges, supports and encourages openness through adapting style
  - willingly accepts/offers constructive and honest feedback in an appropriate style
  - has knowledge and concept of applying supervision models, theories, frameworks and ethical codes
  - supervisee leaves with heightened self-awareness/practice development. (Extract: Bluesky International, 2022)

The traditional perception of 'supervision' is having authority to review the work of others and holding a more senior position, and implies 'power over'. This directly opposes the nature of supervision for mentoring and I guess a different descriptor would more effectively define the intended purpose of the activity.

The power stance inferred by the perception of 'supervision' is resisted in the mentor–supervisor relationship, being instead one of working toward equality, inclusion and a learning partnership. Undoubtedly, adopting the practice from counselling and similar helping professions gave a practical 'short cut' and perhaps the title slipped under the wire of convenience without being questioned. The approach of mentor-supervision in this context – one of being 'power with the other' – differs from the general practice of supervision in counselling having a more directive impact on practitioners.

Emphasizing and agreeing how the relationship is intended to evolve is an essential element of the 'working together conversation' at the start of the mentor-supervision partnership. To maintain and sustain a relationship that creates the conditions of engagement it is essential to have this 'preparation' conversation that determines expectations and for each to agree the important boundaries to respect.

Revisiting this conversation is an opportunity for recontracting that reaffirms the supervisor role if a mentor unintentionally transfers power onto the supervisor. This happens when the mentor attributes characteristics of another, when the supervisor is a reminder of, say, an 'authority' supervisor such as a line manager or when the mentor has a perception of an embedded authority profile linked to the descriptor 'supervisor'.

The mentor–supervisor relationship seeks to learn through a systemic lens and is primarily one of reciprocal developmental mentoring; dialogue that discovers the nuances of ethical scenarios, discovers the meaning of practicing professionally and unfolds activities that are likely or are impacting on well-being. This approach to supervision closely follows the work of Hawkins and Smith (2013), that offers three elements of supervision: supportive–restorative–developmental, and is sometimes referred to as the 'three-legged stool' of supervision.

Creating the context: What might be the expectations of both the supervisor and the mentor

Preferably, the context for the mentoring relationship is initially established during the working together conversation (contracting) to determine from the start the expectations of each. These may change during the mentor-supervision programme and regular review is essential to maintain credibility in the relationship and to maintain mutual alignment.

This conversation is the bedrock for determining what each anticipates from the supervision and to be prepared for this to change and evolve over time when the dialogue informs topics. My experience is that mentors and their clients can be impatient to start their work together and may spend little, if any, time agreeing what is important to each at this contracting stage. Many, if not most, topics explored in the mentor-supervision conversation are ethical and boundary management dilemmas. Although contracting may not cover every occurrence – and recontracting is available – good practice at the start of the engagement often avoids challenging situations later. This good practice is to agree a 'chemistry' or 'getting to know you' meeting where both engage in light conversation that encourages rapport and establishes whether the relationship is likely to be a good fit. The 'working together' or contracting conversation agreeing logistics, such as when and where to meet and for how long, can be a useful entry into taking the conversation to the next level.

The next level includes although is not exclusive to:

- Preferences for goal setting on the continuum of:
  - *Setting immediately* --- *Giving time to emerge*

  Goals are not essential to define at the start of the mentor-supervision relationship although this is common practice. Sometimes the mentor needs to find clarity before determining the purpose of supervision. Occasionally, a supervisor is alerted to explore with the mentor a comment, use of language, tone or physicality observed in the belief that bringing this into the conversation will benefit the mentor. The terminology 'goal' is used here as a collective description of the various topics reviewed in supervision sessions.

- Who might be the stakeholders who have an interest in what is discussed and how might they be impacted? How do we include their voice in mentor-supervision conversations? I find that metaphorically engaging with possible stakeholders often identifies different perspectives for the mentor that reveal new possibilities for their clients. Suggestions for questions the mentor might ask their clients are:
  - Who else may have a view on this that will be helpful for you to know more about?
  - Who else might have an interest in knowing more about your intention?
  - Who else could help you to find more information?

- What does 'confidentiality' mean to each? The more I practice the greater is my preference for spending time to fully explore what this really means. Stating that 'everything will remain confidential between us' is insufficient to cover what may emerge:
  - safety of others
  - illegal practices
  - note taking possibly contravening the client's legal rights to data protection (EUR-Lex, 2016)
  - the mentor's view about the content of sessions possibly being shared with the supervisor's supervisor and how the supervisor feels about personal disclosure being shared outside the sessions.

  All are indicators of mutual engagement in the working agreement and what to clarify as a best fit for safeguarding future events.

  - How, and at what intervals, is the programme reviewed and evaluated?

Session content: Typical scenarios illustrating the purpose of mentor-supervision in supporting mentor and practice development, observing well-being and encouraging professional standards of practice

The quality of dialogue depends on the practice maturity of both practitioners. For practitioners to fulfil the guidelines within codes of practice, mentors and supervisors will have attended training accredited with a quality mark for professional practice and, ideally, have a similar personal recognition of practice. In an unregulated industry this is not mandatory and individuals are free to enter this open market without any formal evidence of training.

The scope of the mentor–supervisor relationship is consequently undefinable and is agreed during a conversation determining the working arrangement. This is where professional body guidance informs.

'Start-up' mentors may rely on career expertise influencing an advisory practice role and may not see the need for, or value of, supervision whereas experienced mentors lean into a desire for a peer-learning relationship. Mentors and supervisors are likely to develop and adapt alongside the clients they attract and vice versa.

An adaptive supervision conversation seeks to work with what is best to discuss within the scope of the mentor and their stakeholders (clients, sponsors, human resources, internal mentoring programme manager, those influenced or impacted by the mentor's practice) and what will take practice and self-awareness to the next level of maturity.

Developing practitioners: focusing on practice and practitioner

Developing maturity of practice depends on the individual's capacity, capability and propensity for learning. Describing the boundaries of the practice continuum offer typical scenarios:

Scenario 1: New to mentoring

A recent training with new mentors revealed supervision preferences for reviewing start-up arrangements and guidance on building a mentoring practice, what to include in the contracting conversation and how to establish trust and build rapport. This transactional approach is usual in helping new mentors to establish and grow practice.

Developing mentors are likely to benefit from more regular supervision at the start of practice with peer supervision, in the absence of working with a trained supervisor, preferential to no supervision.

Scenario 2: Maturity of practice

With maturity of practice, usually, comes a complexity in supervision topics attracting a deeper level of dialogue engaging 'use of self' as a resource for informing the conversation. The benefits of analysing ethical situations are more likely to be raised by experienced mentors having the ability to recognize when these events emerge.

Tools and techniques are usually favoured more by mentors new to practice with experienced mentors having synthesized learning, expertise and experience to form a personal model of practice.

We can all remember the 'comfort blanket' of relying on tools when starting out. A process model that practitioner feedback suggests is of benefit generally to practice development is the REFLECT framework (Lewis, 2019) in Figure 6.1.

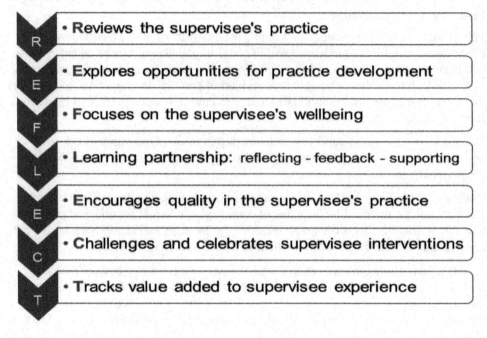

R • **Reviews the supervisee's practice**

E • **Explores opportunities for practice development**

F • **Focuses on the supervisee's wellbeing**

L • **Learning partnership:** reflecting – feedback – supporting

E • **Encourages quality in the supervisee's practice**

C • **Challenges and celebrates supervisee interventions**

T • **Tracks value added to supervisee experience**

©REFLECT Lise Lewis 2008 revised 2019 – all rights reserved worldwide

Figure 6.1: The REFLECT framework. © REFLECT Lise Lewis, 2008; revised 2019 – all rights reserved worldwide.

The supervisor chooses any section or sections from the process that are relevant to raising self-awareness and support the mentor's practice development including meeting professional standards. The framework also recommends eliciting feedback from the practitioner to act as a satisfaction benchmark and, importantly, if a change of direction or even change of supervisor will benefit mentor development.

Resourcing (replenishing) practitioners: focus on well-being

What sometimes surprises experienced mentors is to be asked 'How well are you taking care of your own well-being?'

Scenario 3: Shedding light on self-care

The practice of coaching attracts people who care about others and have a desire to help. These are healthy attributes as long as 'rescuing' clients is avoided and have the potential for the practitioner to demonstrate self-care. A vignette from practice illustrates how supervision helps to shed light on self-care when the mentor appears overattentive with their clients.

Vignette: Revealing a 'blind spot'

JC has been a mentor for twenty years. In fact, ever since retiring early on the grounds of ill health due to stress. Although JC was relieved to leave a highly pressurized role the thought of retiring was unwelcome. Reflecting on the obligatory exit interview JC recalled talking about transitioning from employment into retirement when a kindling of a thought, now remembered, ignited into a desire to 'give back'. The idea of retraining did not attract enthusiasm so the opportunity for mentoring suggested by a colleague greatly appealed. Before leaving, JC enquired through HR and was warmly welcomed into the mentoring programme. JC attended a brief introductory training before meeting with a client. JR's practice grew over the years as mentoring became a popular development opportunity. When the organization announced another restructuring aimed at reducing employees JC readily agreed to the offer of additional clients. Around this time, HR recruited a supervision service on the recommendation of their professional body as demonstrating good practice in supporting internal mentoring. JC decided to attend more out of curiosity. What JC was not prepared for was the emotional outpouring when asked the question 'you seem to have a large caseload of mentees during these disruptive times – how well are you taking care of your own well-being?' Once JC felt able to continue the conversation, the revelation of a repeated pattern of increasing workload, without consideration for self, stimulated JC into recognizing supervision was necessary and supportive in avoiding a repetition of stress induced by lack of self-care.

Maintaining and sustaining professional standards in mentor practice

A role of the supervisor is to encourage reflection on practice that enables the mentor to recognize whether they are practicing ethically and with the level of competence and capability that meets the needs of client development. Ideally, mentors engage with supervision accepting this as essential for raising self-awareness and developing and maintaining professional practice. Those with mature practices usually seek stimulation through dialogue with a supervisor, whereas new and developing mentors initially seek supervision for reassurance of practice development and help.

The following sample of scenarios from practice illustrate situations where mentor-supervision benefits professional practice.

Scenario 4: External/Internal Mentors

External mentors offer the benefit of bringing knowledge, experience, networking opportunities and multisector case studies. However, they can lack an understanding of the systemic issues and practices inherent to internal mentors. What each brings to supervision aligns with these differences. The external mentor may feel the pressure that can be attributed to those 'outside of the organization'. They can have the label of 'expert' transferred to them as a perception of anticipated capability and, if adopted, may feed the 'impostor syndrome' insecurities latent if not already present in those lacking self-confidence.

The internal practitioner may enter the trap of collusion when knowing the pressures faced by the mentee, who feels unable to cope with work pressure, and empathizes with them rather than facilitating a coping strategy. This is more likely to happen when the mentor also experiences a similar level of overwhelm when accommodating mentee requests into their own busy work schedule. Working within the same system as the mentee can lead to issues with objectivity – not able to see beyond or step outside of what is everyday practice.

Scenario 5: Reverse (reciprocal) mentoring

This practice is increasingly popular in organizations for 'levelling out' hierarchical structures and reacting to the expectations of younger employees, especially Generation Z having expectations of mentoring as part of the employment contract. The usual arrangement is for a 'junior' employee to enter a mentor arrangement with a 'senior' employee. Effective partnerships evolve when each gain. The 'junior' person has the benefit of learning from the more experienced employee who possibly also supports career progression. The 'senior' person learns more about what people at the grass roots in the organization are thinking and that shrinks the 'remoteness gap' of not having time or exposure to interact with others at all levels in the organization.

Vignette: Walking in each other's shoes

In this scenario the senior person is older and a different gender. A description of how each finds the relationship gradually reveals a level of both 'overcompensating'. The younger person was rightly proud of the effort made to be open about potential improvements involving junior employees and enthusiastically praised the more senior person to the point of 'hero worship'. As the conversation developed the 'senior' increasingly portrayed a parental posture. The combination seemed reminiscent of 'nurturing parent' and 'adaptive child' to use transactional analysis ego states (Berne, 1958).

Questions when reviewing this scenario are: What might be the parameters for the programme lifecycle?; and How does this hinder rather than develop both the mentor and client?

Scenario 6: Mentoring women

The growth in mentoring for women seeks to enhance opportunities for development that are fair and equitable and offer representation in organizations where women are less represented. Good intentions may sometimes confuse mentoring with 'rescuing'.

Successful mentoring recognizes capability by celebrating strengths, builds confidence by challenging limiting beliefs and facilitates routes to career development.

Scenario 7: Ethics

Mention of ethics in practice tends to arrive with the 'issue label'. Ethics does involve – although is not exclusive to – dilemmas waiting to be resolved. Experience from practice suggests that supervision topics that emerge as ethical dilemmas can often be resolved with strong contracting. There seems to be a tendency to avoid detailed contracting as it is perceived as being 'too formal' and counter-intuitive to the practice of mentoring. Contracting, or as I prefer the 'working together conversation', if approached as mutually beneficial, can aid initial relationship building and encourage recontracting when helpful or necessary at any stage in the programme.

The nature of ethical topics is that, usually, there is no one answer or solution given the complexity of human dynamics and world views. The best-fit solution is to explore all possibilities and consequences and arrive at what emerges as a way forward.

An ethical scenario is not exclusive to mentoring practice. A two-way learning or co-creative partnership assumed between mentor and supervisor has the potential for complications within the relationship. Creating rapport, sharing experiences and limited self-disclosure are essential elements within the relational activity of supervision.

Possible side effects of creating 'closeness' can foster dependency: likely to manifest as the mentor overly relying on the supervisor's advice or codependency when both perpetuate the relationship beyond its limits of objectively adding value to the mentor.

Scenario 8: Inclusivity and cultural awareness

Table 6.1 represents a supervision tool supporting mentor development to a further level of intelligence beyond emotional and social intelligence. The tool is particularly useful for mentors working with multicultural teams.

Table 6.1: Supervision tool supporting mentor development to a further level of intelligence beyond emotional and social intelligence.

Encouraging inclusivity	Cultural intelligence as a mentor
Builds cultural knowledge relating to race, customs, social class, gender balance, generational hierarchy	Evaluates influence of own ethnicity in creating judgements, bias and uninformed stereotyping; shows up as a human being
Develops awareness of culture-based values, beliefs, attitudes	Self-manages, where known, the impact of personal values, beliefs and attitudes accepting unconscious bias dwells within us all as a result of social conditioning
Contracting conversation determines boundaries / confidentiality / safe environment	Actively encourages relationship building with and works to the client and stakeholder agenda; engages the client in a transparent and open conversation about how differences may impact on and support the work
Is able to communicate in a shared language	Is alert to the propensity for using colloquialisms, metaphor and regional variations that may distort understanding
Researches corporate culture and organization norms of behaviour	Compares norms with own perception of corporate culture and assesses the potential influences on engagement with clients

Reflection and review: Eliciting perceptions of what has emerged in the mentor-supervision conversation

The aim of this part of the supervision process is to encourage reflection on the learning process as preparation for the evaluation of the session(s). Becoming a reflective practitioner enables us to learn by progressively reviewing events: explore the learning from an activity or event > review progress > identify what worked and what needs changing > implement the change and repeat the cycle.

How did each feel about how the session evolved and the direction of exploration? Was the pace and style of conversation conducive to encouraging a safe space? The practice of review also encourages mentor and supervisor to reflect on what has been shared during the session and also to share affirmations of what both appreciated about the other's contribution.

Evaluation and endings: The added value of supervision and achieving appropriate closure to the relationship

Here is the opportunity to share thoughts about how well the session has met the expectations agreed at the start based on the reflection and review cycle outlined in the previous section. How worthwhile has the session been in making a difference for the mentor? What was helpful and what wasn't and what could have been different? Encouraging the mentor to articulate the effectiveness of the session helps to further embed learning and also determines what the mentor will take away from the supervision experience. The supervisor learns what can be improved and how well the quality of the relationship is facilitating or hindering the dialogue. The key to evaluation is identifying the value added for the mentor and their practice.

Attention to timing and bringing the session to a natural close combine to gain a sense of completion; a sense that what needed to be heard and said had the space to emerge and evolve to at least a point of acceptable closure for the available time.

What is critical in the mentor-supervision relationship is knowing and agreeing when the end of the mentoring programme arrives. Mentoring programmes can cover extended periods and the role of both the mentor and the supervisor is to evaluate the benefits of continuing to work together.

Some questions to reflect upon are:

- Will the mentor benefit from working with another mentor?
- Has the mentoring relationship reached a natural ending?
- Are there any signs of codependency that can be explored in the supervision of supervision conversation?

In summary

The practice of mentor-supervision is vital for safeguarding, investing in and developing the professional practice and well-being of mentors.

The quality of the relationship cannot be underestimated in securing the benefits and success of mentor practice. Mentors have a safe haven to download any tensions culminating from practice and feeling secure with a supervisor is essential in providing the conditions for a willingness to disclose and have frank conversations about practice.

Taking time to include a contracting or 'working together conversation' enables both practitioners to create a productive environment. The mentor feels the supervisor is working in their best interests and the supervisor is confident that areas important to the success of the mentor-supervision arrangement are discussed and agreed. The conversation can be revisited and a review of whether the working agreement remains relevant is essential for demonstrating good practice.

The most productive mentor-supervision relationships are those where both prepare for each conversation and spend time to check-in at the start so that each is aware of anything that needs attention as impacting on the session. Preparation also makes sure that both feel relaxed about being transparent in the conversation and for the supervisor, especially, to be aware of the maturity of the mentor's practice. This helps to calibrate the conversation to meet expectations.

Checking in together during and at the end of sessions enables time to reflect on whether the conversation is moving in a productive direction and to make any helpful changes. Evaluating what has been discussed and how this benefits the mentor going forward is an important end of session discussion.

Important ingredients are also to enjoy the mentor-supervision experience and laughter when appropriate along the way certainly aids learning and reduces any tension that may be present when discussing challenging topics.

.... and finally – to revisit the title of this chapter. Supervision practice does involve a 'mentoring' role and may have the appearance of 'advice giver'. The aim of this chapter is to demonstrate that mentor-supervision has a wider scope in encouraging reflection on self and practice in a way that aids development, raises self-awareness and develops practice.

References:

Berne, E. (1958). *Transactional analysis: A new and effective method of group therapy*. American Journal of Psychotherapy, **12**(4), 735–743.

Bluesky International (2022). Diploma for Professional Coach/Mentor Supervision training programme. https://www.blueskyinternational.com/2023/01/19/diploma-for-coach-mentor-supervision-next-virtual-programme-starting-2-march-2023/

Dweck, C. S. (2008). *Mindset*. Ballantine Books.

EUR-Lex (2016). Regulation (EU) 2016/679 of the European Parliament and of the Council of 27 April 2016 on the protection of natural persons with regard to the processing of personal data and on the free movement of such data, and repealing Directive 95/46/EC (General Data Protection Regulation). European Parliament, Council of the European Union. https://eur-lex.europa.eu/eli/reg/2016/679/oj

Hawkins, P., & Smith, N. (2013). *Coaching, Mentoring and Organizational Consultancy: Supervision and Development* (**2nd ed**). McGraw Hill, Open University Press.

Lewis, L. (2019). *The REFLECT Framework: A Developmental, Resourcing and Qualitative Questioning Framework for Coach\Mentor Supervision*. **First edition 2008**.

O'Broin, A., & Palmer, S (2019). *The coaching relationship: A key role in coaching process and outcomes*. In S. Palmer, & A. Whybrow (Eds.) *Handbook of Coaching Psychology: A Guide for Practitioners* (**2nd ed.**, pp. 471–486). Routledge.

Recommendations for further reading and resources

As a supervisor acting in the best interests of clients, we can anticipate having to be aware of the rapid change prevailing in the workplace. We do not have to be experts; we do need to have an idea of where and when change is happening and how we might alert our clients or be able to reference guidance if issues are raised.

A question for us as practitioners is reflecting on what responsibility we have for acquainting ourselves with the topics listed below, offered as areas for further exploration:

■ Demographics: we have five generations in the workplace – how will each generation relate to each other?

- Post-COVID expectations for hybrid working: these are now becoming part of the employment contract with some employers and employees having mixed views about how to manage the challenge of 'who's in the workplace and when' and the loss of the social aspect of being in person with work colleagues.
- Diversity, equity and inclusion initiatives: these are important factors in recruiting and retaining talent.
- Climate change: the authenticity of organizational positions has become important, especially transparency about 'green' issues.
- Artificial intelligence (AI) is saturating the workplace: how is rapid technological change already impacting and likely to impact on clients and their clients?

For further information access: Kelly, J. (2023, March 1). *Can 5 generations coexist in the workplace? Forbes.* https://www.forbes.com/sites/jackkelly/2023/03/01/can-five-generations-coexist-in-the-workplace/?sh = 3dea159031f2

Section 2:
Perspectives on Mentoring – Initiatives and Approaches to Leadership and Training

Part 1:
Mentoring Initiatives

Chapter 7
Mentoring Skills: An Essential Part of the Armamentarium for Doctors

Denise Harris & Rebecca Viney

Introduction

The concept of mentoring, having access to a confidential, guiding relationship outside of any formal support arrangements, has been part of medical education for many years (McCrossan et al., 2020). Historically, doctors were allocated a named 'mentor' who was a senior clinician, usually from the same speciality. McCrossan et al. (2020) describe this traditional understanding of mentoring as a:

> ...*process whereby an experienced, highly regarded, empathic person (the mentor), guides another individual (the mentee) in the development and re-examination of their own ideas, learning and personal and professional development.*

> (Standing Committee on Postgraduate Medical and Dental Education (SCOPME), 1998, p.1)

In the past, the position of mentor was not usually accompanied by any preparation or training and was bestowed on a senior medic without consideration of their aptitude for such a role (Hutton-Taylor, 1999). The lack of training in educational principles and potential for mentoring to support more junior doctors in their development, meant that sometimes the approach was seen to be about imparting knowledge or visits to the 'pub'. This may have had some value in making the junior doctor feel welcome, but it did not help them to develop their potential or facilitate their learning. In this context, the mentor was seen as an 'imparter of wisdom' and the relationship more akin to 'patronage' (McCrossan et al., 2020, p. 405).

The approach to mentoring began to shift in the 1990s, with formal mentoring schemes and mentor development programmes being developed across the UK. An enquiry into mentoring for doctors and dentists conducted by the Standing Committee on Postgraduate Medical and Dental Education (SCOPME) (1998) identified a wide range of schemes that had been established. This was followed by the British Medical Association's (BMA) (2004) resource Exploring Mentoring and the Department of Health's (2004) guidance document which laid out the recommendations for mentoring schemes for doctors.

This chapter describes how mentoring has continued to develop for doctors and identifies the benefits of this, using examples from successful schemes that have been evaluated. It outlines some of the ongoing challenges faced when implementing mentoring for doctors and concludes with thoughts for the future.

Implementing mentoring for doctors

In their report Exploring Mentoring, the BMA (2004) highlighted the importance of mentoring throughout a doctor's career. There is recognition that the focus of mentoring will shift through the various stages of a doctor's career (SCOPME, 1998) and that it can fulfil a range of functions. For example, Viney and McKimm (2010) describe medical mentoring as 'maximising potential' and identify that it could cover:

- growing talent
- developing leadership skills
- managing change
- career decisions
- achieving work–life balance
- developing resilience in times of adversity.

(Viney & McKimm, 2010, p. 107)

However, the BMA (2004) report also identified the importance of ensuring there are sufficient resources and support systems in place and that without these the impact of mentoring is likely to be less effective.

In response to the SCOPME (1998) report, mentoring schemes began to be developed by some of the medical deaneries[1] across the country. An important feature of these programmes was the focus on training and ongoing professional and personal development for participants, both mentors and mentees (Connor et al., 2000). However, many of the schemes did not flourish as they suffered from underinvestment and lacked the robust processes needed to ensure mentoring is effective. They also continued to focus on mentoring as an intervention for 'doctors in difficulty', a point elaborated on later in the chapter.

Since then, the expansion of mentoring across specialties and for doctors at all stages of their career has been patchy. For example, Huline-Dickens (2021) reflects that in the field of psychiatry, mentoring has been acknowledged as an important support mechanism for newly appointed consultants, but other applications and benefits of having a mentor have not been so widely appreciated. She highlights the value of a mentoring approach in supporting learning and the potential for mentoring to contribute to development of leadership skills, concluding that skills associated with mentoring should be professionalized in psychiatry. The impact is also emphasized by Mohammed (2022, p.1) who cites mentoring as *one of the most effective approaches to developing your skills, knowledge, and insight around specific goals*. He describes how having a mentor expanded his perspective of the world of medicine and enabled him to advance his career. He also acknowledges the value of being challenged in mentoring and the opportunity to think more deeply about his values and decisions.

---

1 Deaneries were the regional organizations responsible for postgraduate medical and dental training in the UK until 2014, after which this was transferred to Health Education England (HEE).

Challenges

Mentoring is countercultural for doctors, both as a mentor and a mentee. One reason for this is that doctors are used to giving advice to patients and of being in the position of 'expert' (Department of Health, 2004; Taherian & Shekarchian, 2008; McCrossan et al., 2020). Whereas mentoring means shifting to view a mentee as a capable and resourceful individual who has the capacity to identify their own path (Viney & McKimm, 2010). One of the contributors to the Department of Health (2004, p. 25) best practice guidelines, commented that as a mentor, *'You have to learn to sit on your hands'*.

For potential mentees, accessing mentoring may be perceived as a weakness, making them more reluctant than other health care professionals to engage in schemes. This reluctance is linked to the culture of medical learning which does not encourage asking for help (Connor et al., 2000; BMA, 2004; Taherian & Shekarchian, 2008; Essuman & Smith, 2021). The SCOPME (1998) investigation into mentoring for doctors and dentists acknowledged that early papers aligned mentoring with addressing poor performance and, as mentioned in the previous section, there was an emphasis in some of the medical deanery schemes of the application of mentoring for 'doctors in difficulty' (BMA, 2004; Essuman & Smith, 2021). This compounds the view that accessing mentoring is an admission of weakness or failure and reinforces the perception of mentoring as a remedial intervention, rather than normalizing it as a development opportunity for doctors at all stages of their career (BMA, 2004; Viney & Harris, 2017; Huline-Dickens, 2021).

Other challenges are related to the different applications of mentoring and, in some instances, lack of clarity of what it might constitute. MacLeod (2007) discusses this and notes that lack of understanding of mentor and mentee roles and the informality of some arrangements can result in less helpful manifestations of mentoring. This is linked to the history of allocating mentors without adequate preparation or training and the tendency for doctors who are mentors to want to 'solve the problem' when presented with an issue, rather than supporting the mentee to identify their own solution (McCrossan et al., 2020).

Alongside these cultural issues, there are organizational challenges in terms of time, space to meet, availability of mentors and financial support for training and preparation. There are debates around the precise roles of mentors, such as whether a line manager can also be a mentor (Huline-Dickens, 2021). This is particularly relevant as mentees are looking for a confidential space, usually preferring to have mentoring from an external mentor. This can be challenging when mentoring schemes operate in a small community and relationships may overlap.

The impact of mentoring for doctors

Despite the challenges, there is a growing body of evidence of the potential for mentoring to have a beneficial impact for doctors. For example, a study by Ong et al. (2018) looked at the effect of mentoring on junior doctors and identified that there was a positive correlation between being mentored and achieving a pass in the Membership of the Royal Colleges of Physicians (MRCP) examinations. This was particularly dramatic for those doctors who had trained abroad.

Steven et al. (2008) conducted an extended qualitative analysis of a multisite interview study to explore benefits of mentoring. Their findings show that as well as providing personal benefit to mentees, the impact extended beyond this to their professional role. For example, participants cited instances of adopting *'a more egalitarian approach to patients'* (Steven et al., 2008, p. 554) following mentoring. They also found benefits extended to working relationships and teamwork, job satisfaction and an overall increase in confidence:

> *There appears to be a reciprocal relationship between professional practice and personal well-being; the perceived benefits of being involved in mentoring thus cut across the complex personal-professional interface of doctors' lives.*

(Steven et al., 2008, p. 555)

These examples of research illustrate the qualitative and quantitative benefits for doctors of being mentored. In addition to this, Taherian and Shekarchian (2008) recognize the impact of mentoring is not limited to the mentee, noting that mentors and the organization will also benefit. Examples of this include:

- Benefits for the mentee:
  - learning about the organization, environment, customs and priorities
  - supporting academic progress
  - gaining knowledge and skills
  - developing emotional intelligence
  - building resilience
  - learning the 'unwritten rules of the game' such as networking, negotiation and conflict management
  - developing relationships.
- Benefits for the mentor:
  - a sense of satisfaction when observing the mentee's development
  - the motivation to develop their own learning in order to share this with the mentee
  - being part of a community of practice of mentors and being helped themselves
  - a reduction in their own stress levels.
- Benefits for the organization:
  - improved quality of care for patients
  - contribution to clinical governance
  - opportunity to identify and address difficulties at an early stage.

(Taherian & Shekarchian, 2008, p. e96)

Alongside this evidence, the following examples demonstrate some of the different ways mentoring has been implemented for doctors.

London Deanery Coaching and Mentoring Service

Dr Rebecca Viney led the team that set up the London Deanery mentoring service in 2008 (later renamed 'Coaching and Mentoring Service'). The development of this programme is detailed in Viney and Paice (2010) and Viney and Harris (2017); significant aspects of the scheme included the principles of inclusivity and robust quality assurance processes that underpinned the approach. The London Deanery service was unique in training senior educationalists, who already had an appreciation of adult learning, to form the pool of mentors. This strategy, and attention to the quality of training provided, led to it being one of the largest schemes in the country. It also became apparent that the approach of starting with senior members of the community was a significant factor in the success of the scheme. These senior influencers helped to ensure the scheme became embedded in organizations (Viney & Harris, 2017).

Oxford Brookes University conducted an evaluation of the Coaching and Mentoring Service on behalf of the three London Local Education and Training Boards (LETBs) (Bachkirova et al., 2014). Their report highlighted that as well as the positive impact on mentors and mentees the scheme offered benefits to the wider system, including colleagues and patients:

- impact on self
  - improved confidence
  - better time management at work, leading to an improved work–life balance
  - improved capacity to solve problems and make decisions, including career decisions
  - better relationships with family members
  - decided to stay within the profession after seriously considering leaving the NHS.
- impact on colleagues
  - improved interactions and communication with colleagues
  - used coaching/mentoring techniques with colleagues.
- Impact on patients
  - improved interactions with patients
  - improved feedback from patients
  - used coaching/mentoring techniques with patients
  - changes in patients' behaviour, such as reduced dependency, better use of doctors' time.

General Practice Retention Intensive Support Sites (GPRISS) programme

In recent years, retention of doctors has become a major issue, particularly in General Practice (NHS England, 2016). In response to this, NHS England rolled out a programme in 2018 to support and improve GP retention in seven geographical areas facing the greatest challenges. The programme was designed to not only offer a swift response, but also to evaluate the most efficacious of eleven interventions, one of which was mentoring for GPs.

The first evaluation of this initiative (Berg et al., 2019) provided an indication that the programme had beneficial impact on practices. A follow up evaluation (Essuman & Smith, 2021) examined the more long-term effect of the various interventions. The results of the second evaluation showed that having mentoring was one of the most effective interventions and having access to a trained mentor had a long-lasting impact.

The skills acquired through mentoring were transferrable and participants were able to support others through change as well as apply the principles to the approach used in patient consultations. The evaluation highlighted the psychological benefits of mentoring, such as an improvement in confidence, resilience and morale, along with a deepened understanding of 'self'. This had a positive impact on relationships and on the quality of consultations with patients. Mentoring also helped with clarifying personal and professional issues and, in some cases, had a direct impact on a decision to remain in practice.

It is important to note that mentoring formed part of a suite of interventions in this scheme and the combination of these will have had an effect. However, mentoring was consistently identified by participants as having a most significant and positive impact.

City and Hackney GP Confederation mentoring scheme

In September 2018, the East London Health and Care Partnership provided each GP Federation in north-east London with funding to support work on GP retention. Led by Director of HR and Improvement Janet McMillan, City and Hackney GP Confederation used the funding to establish a GP mentoring programme. The response was positive and in 2019 they successfully bid for funding from City and Hackney Clinical Commissioning Group (CCG) to continue and expand the offer to include nurses, practice managers and receptionists, along with GPs, to train as mentors and access mentoring.

This scheme has not been formally evaluated but feedback from GP mentors illustrates the positive impact for mentors of participating in such a scheme:

I was concerned initially but it has been rewarding.
Personally, as I have given up training, I have enjoyed this role.

I find it a really fulfilling and rewarding experience and
believe my mentees really value it and have benefitted from
my support and signposting.

Rewarding for both parties.

I think the idea is excellent. I wish I'd had access to mentoring
when a young GP. Perhaps it should be available to all GPs
should they want it, at whatever stage in their career.

It's an amazing resource which City and Hackney are lucky
to have.

GP mentees were asked about what they have found helpful about having a GP mentor, and the feedback included the following reflections:

> *It is useful to have a place to talk about whatever I have been finding difficult. My mentor is an excellent listener and gave some great advice.*

> *My mentor has a wealth of experience that I could never imagine.*

> *Useful to talk about career planning and life as a GP in Hackney.*

> *It has helped me feel more focused about career plans and feel more confident in my decision making.*

> *Great to have an inspirational GP who is objective and keen to see me develop.*

These exemplars provide additional evidence of the potential for mentoring to have a positive impact on the medical profession, their practice and their organization. It is appropriate therefore to consider how to take this forward and present a vision for the future.

The future… and a call to action

There is a looming crisis for retention and recruitment of doctors in the UK that requires an urgent response. As discussed by Tilley (2021), doctors, and in particular general practitioners, are under increasing levels of stress and at risk of burnout. Evidence from the research studies, and evaluation of schemes outlined in the previous section, demonstrates that mentoring has significant potential to impact doctors' well-being, with a consequential positive impact on their ability to deliver quality care to patients (Essuman & Smith, 2021).

We believe providing access to robust, quality-assured mentoring programmes for doctors is critical to attract, retain and maintain the well-being and long-term development of doctors. This is also pertinent when considering the increasing numbers of doctors who are trained overseas and arrive in this country to work. Moving to a job in another health care system with a new peer group will be challenging. This is compounded by the different language, culture and clinical challenges these colleagues face (Jalal et al., 2019). When the needs of their families are also considered, this amounts to an unimaginably challenging transition. Overseas doctors clearly benefit from access to mentoring (Ong et al., 2018) so providing them with a mentor who meets them at the airport and greets them with thanks and a big welcome should be part of the offer.

There are several aspects of mentoring that present opportunities for more exploration and research. One of these is the impact of multiple and different 'types' of mentoring relationships across a mentee's career and how the focus for mentoring may shift in that time. Other areas include evidence of the short- and long-term effectiveness of mentoring in addressing the challenges outlined above, the impact of systemic support and the relationship between mentoring and job planning.

In this chapter, we have focused on mentoring for medical doctors, but our experience indicates that, as discussed by MacLeod (2007) and Bellman (2003), a multiprofessional approach has potential to multiply the benefits of mentoring. The evaluation of the GPRISS programme (Essuman & Smith, 2021) highlighted the benefit of mentoring to an entire system, in this case GP practices. The programme was designed to support GP retention but the inclusion of other clinical staff, such as nurses, pharmacists and practice managers, contributed to the success of the interventions. Newham in East London was one such area. They trained doctors, pharmacists and nurses, and set up a website so all primary care staff could access coaching or mentoring.

MacLeod (2007) suggests that drawing on the wider workforce to become mentors and offering mentoring across staff groups is important. She advocates that having mentoring from outside the profession has benefits, particularly as it can help to address the challenge outlined in the 'Challenges' section of providing safe and confidential mentoring within a small community. In an earlier paper, Bellman (2003) came to a similar conclusion when she evaluated a scheme that included different staff groups in a primary care setting. Participants noted that this approach contributed to improvements in multiprofessional and collaborative working as well as increasing engagement and strengthening relationships. This aspect of mentoring would also benefit from further development and research.

So, our call to action to all health service leaders is to ensure high-quality mentoring skills are 'a key part of the armamentarium of today's doctor' (De Souza & Viney, 2014). The core skills of quality mentoring and the personal qualities needed to be an excellent mentor need to be celebrated and recognized as contributing to positivity and compassion for the workforce.

> *There is a convincing evidence base for the beneficial effects of compassion on patient outcomes and the well-being of health and care professionals. Neglect, incivility, bullying and harassment of staff have quite opposite effects.*
>
> (West & Coia, 2019, p. 18)

The health of the nation requires we ensure we create workplaces that promote staff well-being and thereby the health of the population, our key aim as health care practitioners. The NHS should be a model for the world in creating and promoting staff well-being and the evidence in this chapter indicates the potential for mentoring to address the challenges faced by health care practitioners. However, there is also a note of caution that, to be effective, any system or initiative requires the 'wrap around' of high-quality training and preparation along with robust quality assurance processes (De Souza & Viney, 2014; McCrossan et al., 2020). In other words, it needs to be accompanied by sufficient resources in terms of time, finance and people.

References

Bachkirova, T., Arthur, L., & Reading, E. (2014). *Evaluation of the Professional Support Unit Coaching and Mentoring Service on Behalf of the Three London LETBs*. Unpublished report for the Professional Support Unit, Health Education England.

Bellman, L. (2003). *Evaluation of a multiprofessional mentoring scheme in primary health care. Journal of Interprofessional Care*, **17**(4), 402–403.

Berg, G., Essuman, J., Haining, S., Riding, R., & Smith, J. (2019). Independent Evaluation Report for the GP Retention Intensive Support Sites (GPRISS) Programme. NHS England. https://www.england.nhs.uk/publication/independent-evaluation-report-for-the-gp-retention-intensive-support-sites-gpriss-programme/

British Medical Association (2004). *Exploring Mentoring*. British Medical Association. https://scottishmentoringnetwork.co.uk/assets/downloads/resources/BMAexploringmentoringinhealthstudentsprofessions.pdf

Connor, M. P., Bynoe, A. G., Redfern, N., Pokora, J., & Clarke, J. (2000). *Developing senior doctors as mentors: A form of continuing professional development. Report of an initiative to develop a network of senior doctors as mentors: 1994–99. Medical Education*, **34**(9), 747–753.

Department of Health (2004) Mentoring for Doctors: Signposts to Current Practice for Career Grade Doctors. Guidance from the Doctor's Forum. http://bit.ly/1En75le

De Souza, B., & Viney, R. (2014). *Coaching and mentoring skills: Necessities for today's doctors. British Medical Journal*, **348**, g4244. https://doi.org/10.1136/bmj.g4244

Essuman, J., & Smith, J. (2021). *A follow-up evaluation the GP Retention Intensive Support Sites (GPRISS) programme*. Available on request from: necsu.websiteenquiries@nhs.net

Huline-Dickens, S. (2021). *Coaching and mentoring: An overview for trainers in psychiatry. British Journal of Psychiatric Advances*, **27**(4), 219–227. https://doi.org/10.1192/bja.2020.53

Hutton-Taylor, S. (1999). *Cultivating a coaching culture. British Medical Journal*, **318**(7188), S2–7188. https://doi.org/10.1136/bmj.318.7188.2

Jalal, M., Bardhan, K. D., Sanders, D., & Illing, J. (2019). *Overseas doctors of the NHS: Migration, transition, challenges and towards resolution. Future Healthcare Journal*, **6**(1) 76–81. https://doi.org/10.7861/futurehosp.6-1-76

MacLeod, S. (2007). *The challenge of providing mentorship in primary care. Postgraduate Medical Journal*, **83**(979), 317–319. https://doi.org/10.1136/pgmj.2006.054155

McCrossan, R., Swan, L., & Redfern, N. (2020). *Mentoring for doctors in the UK: What it can do for you, your colleagues, and your patients. British Journal of Anaesthesia Education*, **20**(12), 404–410. https://doi.org/10.1016/j.bjae.2020.07.005

Mohammed, R. (2022, February 25). *Mentoring: The key to growth and development*. Faculty of Medical Leadership and Management. https://www.fmlm.ac.uk/news-opinion/blog/mentoring-the-key-to-growth-and-development

NHS England (2016). *General Practice Forward View*. https://www.england.nhs.uk/gp/gpfv/

Ong, J., Swift, C., Magill, N., Ong, S., Day, A., Al-Naeeb, Y., & Shankar, A. (2018). *The association between mentoring and training outcomes in junior doctors in medicine: An observational study. BMJ Open*, **8**(8), e020721. https://doi.org/10.1136/bmjopen-2017-020721

Standing Committee on Postgraduate Medical and Dental Education (1998). *Supporting Doctors and Dentists at Work: An Enquiry into Mentoring*. Standing Committee on Postgraduate Medical and Dental Education (SCOPME).

Steven, A., Oxley, J., & Fleming, W. G. (2008). *Mentoring for NHS doctors: Perceived benefits across the personal–professional interface. Journal of the Royal Society of Medicine*, **101**(11), 552–557. https://doi.org/10.1258/jrsm.2008.080153

Taherian, K., & Shekarchian, M. (2008). *Mentoring for doctors. Do its benefits outweigh its disadvantages? Medical Teacher*, **30**(4) e95–e99. https://doi.org/10.1080/01421590801929968

Tilley, C. (2021, December 15). *GPs most likely to 'bear the brunt' of burnout, warns the GMC. Pulse*. https://www.pulsetoday.co.uk/news/regulation/gps-most-likely-to-bear-the-brunt-of-burnout-warns-the-gmc/

Viney, R., & Harris, D. (2017). *Coaching and mentoring doctors and dentists: A case study*. In D. A. Clutterbuck, F. K. Kochan, L. Lunsford, N. Dominguez, & J. Haddock-Millar (Eds.), *The SAGE Handbook of Mentoring* (pp. 595–599). SAGE.

Viney, R., & McKimm, J. (2010). *Mentoring. British Journal of Hospital Medicine*, **71**(2), 106–109.

Viney, R., & Paice, E. (2010). *The First Five Hundred: A Report on London Deanery's Coaching and Mentoring Service 2008–2010*. London Deanery.

West, M., & Coia, D. (2019). *Caring for doctors. Caring for patients*. General Medical Council. https://www.gmc-uk.org/-/media/documents/caring-for-doctors-caring-for-patients_pdf-80706341.pdf

Chapter 8
Mentoring in Nursing in the UK

Interview with Nichola Ashby

How has mentoring evolved in nursing in the UK?

Mentoring has been tightly bound up with the progression from pre-qualification to qualification, so that when you qualify you immediately get trained to mentor others and often forget about the possibility of further mentoring for yourself. We have changed the language around registration to that of assessors and supervisors rather than mentors, but we seem to be perpetuating the thinking that mentoring is predominantly for pre-qualification nursing students. The language has developed but is also muddied around roles, such as supervisor, assessor, mentor, coach and clinical supervisor. There has not been enough work done yet to really clarify these roles to the workforce. There is the opportunity for all these roles to fit together to support the nursing role, if we do clarify them. We also lean toward the idea that mentoring must always be from within the profession. As we move and evolve mentoring then interprofessional mentoring could evolve in the future, as well as flexibility across a lifespan approach, so that people can access leadership mentoring or systemic mentoring through different stages of their career. At the moment, mentoring is spreading across different areas and, in some ways, it is at an early stage of evolution.

Is it fair to say that mentoring has been a part of the evaluation process for nurses?

It has been used as an evaluative, performance-based relationship, but there is that developmental and supportive relationship that is supposed to be in there as well. So, for pre-registration nurses, the mentor has been the person who 'signs you off' –they are supposed to be teaching, assessing and approving your skills and values, and also supposed to be 'signing you off', so that does put the mentor in a potential position of power.

Packaging all of these different roles into the title of the mentor produces a lot of pressure on that mentor and that relationship. This has, in the past, been self-perpetuating and self-feeding, because as soon as the student passed their qualification they would be trained as a mentor to replicate the same role delivery method at times. However, some people would be best placed not to be mentors, because it is not what they are best at. Maybe, they don't have quite the right skill set, whereas other people are really good at it. Traditionally, we don't seek mentoring outside of the profession. Whereas now, with the supervisor and assessor roles, nurses can actively seek out supervisors who are doctors occupational therapists or physiotherapists, so long as they are registered health care professionals, which gives a more rounded experience. But so far, this doesn't happen right throughout the career – it doesn't continue after qualification.

What would you most like to share for this handbook in terms of your perspectives on mentoring?

I think that nursing considers itself as established in this journey when we are not. We have a lot more to learn, and we have a lot more defining to do around what those roles are and how we can grow those roles – what mentorship is about and what values it aligns with. We need to do work on looking at the power and hierarchy aspects of mentoring relationships, and also how mentoring can work throughout somebody's career, with people seeking their own mentors rather than being allocated them We need to establish the supportive space in nursing so that supervision, coaching and mentoring can all be different and complement each other to provide development opportunities throughout the nursing career. It should be something that we can dip in and out of during our careers, and at the moment we just use it at the start and maybe when we come into leadership roles but there is a whole group of people in the middle who don't access mentoring. Mentoring isn't currently supported with time – we have enough trouble getting clinical supervision embedded into work schedules. To have mentoring valued by your employers as a support for the workforce would be hugely important.

What would a mentoring programme in nursing look like?

They don't exist any more. When the Standards for Student Supervision and Assessment (SSSA) from the regulator, the Nursing and Midwifery Council (NMC), came in, mentoring programmes were no longer funded. We have a few small top-up programmes but the previous mentoring programme does not exist in its previous format. The mentorship programme was very much based around 'this is how you support and sign off pre-registration nurses', and now that has gone. There does seem to be more awareness of what mentoring opportunities could be like among mental health nurses with it being a more embedded approach. So, mentoring was a word that we had established in one particular sense, and it is a word we continue to use, but we don't really use it to describe a different relationship in a true sense. We have not really established a new role for mentoring across nursing. People still use the word, but it tends to be used interchangeably with supervisor.

The time pressures on nurses are such that we often don't allow time to focus on our development needs, we don't have an allocation for continuing professional development (CPD) time like some other professions do.

What are the key opportunities and threats in terms of mentoring for the nursing profession right now?

The big threat is staffing levels – we also have an ageing workforce and we will be losing a lot of expertise. The big opportunity is to begin learning from each other in lots of different ways – particularly in less hierarchical ways, and also in interprofessional ways. The language of coaching is an opportunity to look at mentoring in new ways too, rather than it just being seen as a part of the sign-off process for student nurses, and that it is not just a management tool. Nurses don't fully yet understand the difference between a coach and a mentor, and these roles serve different needs. It is also an opportunity to see mentoring as two-way – so that the mentor is learning as well as the mentee – and this can be seen most clearly in reverse and peer mentoring approaches. This sort of language is being used more and more in nursing, and I have been in the profession for nearly forty years but I could learn a lot from younger colleagues in a reverse mentoring relationship. This reverse mentoring is picking up momentum in nursing now and is being discussed strategically across organizations, which is how it should be.

So, the threats are staffing levels, allocated and protected time set aside for mentoring and shifting staff understanding that mentoring is of benefit throughout a career; we have a wide-ranging workforce with ages from seventeen to – would you believe it – ninety years old! So, shifting the culture and understanding around mentoring will take time. The opportunities are all about fresh understanding of mentoring as more than a management tool, that it is a powerful way of learning from each other and is a reciprocal process that can involve reverse mentoring.

I had a mentor as a student nurse, and I have a mentor now. But there is thirty years in the middle of that where I didn't have a mentor – and I would never have looked for one because I didn't understand the potential benefits. We should be getting in there a lot earlier and showing people how to develop their careers through mentorship relationships.

What do you think could make mentoring for nurses really groundbreaking?

To be groundbreaking we need to encourage a change in the way nursing sees itself so that mentoring it is an essential part of career and personal development. This is not about moving up the grades, it is about how to shape a career even if you want to stay at the grade that you are, which is OK. Also, there is a lot of excellent evidence out there around the impacts of mentoring, including the impacts of cross-professional mentoring, so how do we get that into play? Can we encourage staff to look around and spot the mentoring relationships they need to develop and to have confident conversations around what they need? For example, one of my mentors is a senior nurse leader, but my coach is someone with an economics background who works in business – so it is about what you need at different times in your career and being open to looking across at other professions. Mentoring has been helpful during COVID to support people's resilience, mental health and career development. To see mentoring as an essential for nursing would be groundbreaking really.

How could mentoring evolve in the future for nursing?

At the moment, nursing is moving away from the word 'mentor' toward the word 'supervisor' and we shouldn't; we should be having conversations about how mentoring and supervision can complement each other. We should be considering how mentoring can be a longitudinal offer across our career, and develop reverse mentorship. The Royal College of Nursing (RCN) has a role in engaging nurses in conversations about how mentoring can evolve in the ways listed above. It can operate as a think-tank resource with over half a million members, each with expertise in their particular areas. The RCN should be positioning itself as a place where you can seek that expertise at different stages in your career. We have lots of requests for the RCN to offer mentorship, so it is about how we do that and how we shift mindset and culture around what mentoring can be. There are always pockets of good practice in various NHS and social care providers now, but it could be time to consider the issue more widely. The RCN should facilitate mentorship from our UK nurses to international nurses, and vice versa, in the country, raising the voice of nursing.

I would also question how many medics and how many other professions come to a nurse to mentor them? Multidisciplinary mentoring could and should offer nurses as mentors, as well as mentees, to other professions. We see it informally when we see the newly qualified doctors coming in – they are often mentored by nurses through that initial period as they come through. This often happens but it is informal – there is no structure and no recognition around it. It would be groundbreaking to be recognized in this way because it would really recognize the nurses' expertise as mentors, as well as the needs nurses have to receive mentoring.

For this to happen, there would need to be true interdisciplinary learning with recognition of the different skill sets. So, while we all work together as a team, the skill sets are quite unique for each profession. I think we are on our way towards this but it is not there yet, it is very much a work in progress.

What are the key messages that you would like to get across to colleagues about nursing and mentoring?

First, the value of mentoring is not only the 'sign off' of students, it is also the development of skills and knowledge across a career. Second, by considering mentoring alongside coaching and supervision, initiatives like reverse mentoring can really become important, especially globally– we can look at aspects of mentoring through impact analysis rather than getting stuck with the current concepts about it. Third, we need to develop recognition that each member of a multidisciplinary team has the skill set to offer mentoring sharing their area of expertise. Mentoring needs to be seen not as an add-on, but as an essential, and needs to be embedded in a career framework right from the beginning – and this means time needs to be allocated and protected for it.

What needs to happen for mentoring to become more embedded?

Further understanding is the key to embedding mentoring and more collaborative research across multidisciplinary teams is needed around the impact of mentoring – this would, for example, highlight not only the mentoring given by nurses to junior doctors but also vice versa, with the mentoring received by nurses from medical colleagues. Also, strategic leaders such as the RCN could be much more active and vocal around this issue. We are starting to shape issues around priority areas of supervision and preceptorship, so it would also be helpful to become more vocal about mentoring in future to nurture and develop our workforce. This will help to retain the current and future workforce.

It is also important to cast our net more widely than just the UK when looking at mentoring. We now have a global workforce and, although there are similarities internationally, we do see sparks of different things that nobody else has looked at – so international research and evidence is also essential.

We have to take a three-pronged approach – we have to look at the evidence base, we also have to look at our employment terms and conditions and therefore our ability to deliver that evidence base, and we have to look at our strategic and political leverage point to support the initiative as a norm. You cannot change anything without the evidence base, but then strategy and policy move things forward by influencing what is done in reality. The RCN is both a union and a professional body, so it is well placed to leverage change in this way.

Now, our biggest opportunity is for nursing to own this, driving the change. We have got experts and researchers in this area who have done a lot of the evidence work, but we need to give them a platform for influencing and embedding approaches to mentoring, so we can explore the impacts for nurses and for patients. We need to be more flexible in accepting some changes in language and theory around mentoring, coaching and supervision. We also need to cohesively draw together the strands of evidence we have for mentoring and the RCN is well placed to facilitate this through the new Institute of Nursing Excellence and academies.

We recently went out on strike – not just about pay, but about terms and conditions, about career support and about identifying what nurses do, what their role is. So, there is now a chance for strategic influence to embed more access to clinical supervision and mentoring relationships during work time. We need to reach the point where you have the right to access mentoring whether you are heading for a senior position or maintaining your current position as a support worker. This is about empowering the workforce to articulate what they want, and build on that.

It would be great if we could reach the point where mentoring is linked directly to recruitment and retention and helps to demonstrate that as an employee you are valued by your organization, and that you have a right to access mentoring rather than having to fight for an hour a week to support your development needs.

Why aren't the various Royal Colleges and other professional organizations uniting their voices around issues like this? There is strength in the voices coming together, and while there will be different nuances for different professions, we are all delivering health care, and coming together to look at the pros and cons of mentoring would be helpful in embedding it as a collective – by uniting and by looking at individual case studies and evidence of how mentoring can be delivered.

You mentioned the pros and cons of mentoring – what might they be?

We have covered a lot of the pros already, the cons include that not everyone is a good mentor. We do not want to force people to do it, and a bad mentoring relationship can be just as damaging as not having one at all. If you look at the data on attrition in nurse courses, some of that is due to poor mentoring relationships.

Having competencies for mentoring can be part of the solution, but we have to be aware that competencies continue to grow and they are not just about ticking a box to say you have achieved that competence at that period in time. It is really essential that mentoring is a live and iterative process. My mentorship relationships are very different now to what they were in 1999 when I qualified as a mentor – my skills have changed. So, while I officially achieved a level of competence as a mentor in 1999, I haven't had further training and yet I wouldn't be an effective nurse mentor in today's environment if I hadn't chosen to continue to develop my skills. There is a change in culture needed to really support mentoring and the RCN is well placed to be a leading force in this change, working with our nurse experts.

In an ideal world, what would a mentoring programme look like for nursing?

Normality – it would be what you knew you needed to do and you would be able to develop that mentorship journey, as a mentee or as a mentor. It wouldn't be something you need to seek permission for. It would be something you naturally did and naturally progressed through, and it would be part of your career progression. If we could move from a position where a different kind of relationship to a number of mentors could develop over a career, then people would gain more from these sorts of relationships. It would also be that mentors see mentoring as something they are truly invested in to help the next generation to come through and provide a model for retention. So, time to deliver that, resources to deliver that, and an acceptance that it is normal. Each profession has come along a different path and each is at a different stage in that journey.

In an ideal world it would be empowering to nurses in their careers, and there would be a policy shift to ensure investment in mentoring and to see it as an essential, putting it at the top of the agenda. Getting clinical supervision to a healthy place, where it is at a high standard everywhere, is a start and then building out from there, looking at areas around it, such as mentoring, would be the way. Nurses still tend to put their own needs second to that of patient care, but if we can emphasize that we need the right people, at the right time, in the right place, to deliver the right care, we can see the value of investing in those people.

Empowering people would include helping them to choose when they need mentoring, how they need it and from whom rather than always making it compulsory. The value of mentoring across the career span could then be seen, and mentoring would not just be a way to get the next job, but for the sake of good, safe, effective care in whatever job you are in. A mentor can help mentees recognize that everything we do has the potential to be a learning experience, and mentors can always learn too from mentees – I've learnt something from every mentee that I've mentored.

Chapter 9
Implementing a Mentorship Programme for Online Doctoral Nursing Students: Lessons Learned

Kelly B. Laham, Paula Reid and Laura Lunsford

> *I never lose an opportunity of urging a practical beginning,*
> *however small, for it is wonderful how often in such matters*
> *the mustard-seed germinates and roots itself.*
>
> Florence Nightingale (Cook, 1942)

Introduction

Mentorship has been part of the nursing profession since Florence Nightingale, known as the mother of nursing (Karimi & Alavi, 2015). Nightingale was mentored by Sir Sidney Herbert during the Crimean War (1853–1856) and went on to emulate his hierarchical method in mentoring others (Jacobs, 2018). Mentorship in nursing has evolved from such a hierarchical model, where a senior person imparts knowledge to a less experienced person, toward reciprocal models, where there is a more reciprocal teaching and learning process between a mentor and mentee. Despite the emphasis on mentorship in the practice of preparing nurses, there is still no standard for effective mentorship in graduate nursing programmes (Jacobs, 2018). At the same time, the number of Doctor of Nursing Practice (DNP) programmes in the US continues to increase (McCauley et al., 2020), suggesting more attention is needed to understand how best to implement mentoring in the preparation of nurses.

There is also a need to diversify the nursing workforce, which is characterized by low participation of men, ethnic and racial minorities, and those who identify as LBGTQ (National League for Nursing [NLN], 2016). Educating and preparing a diverse nursing workforce is needed to better reflect the population nurses serve (AACN, 2020b). University admission practices, however, are often barriers to increasing diversity. *Holistic admission*, endorsed by the American Association of Colleges of Nursing (AACN), is a proven strategy to increase diversity in the profession (AACN, 2020b). The AACN defines holistic admission as a balanced process that considers students' unique experiences and backgrounds in addition to the traditional admission metrics of grades and coursework (AACN, 2020a). Enrolling more diverse students from varied backgrounds means they may need support to overcome barriers, such as scholarly writing, critical thinking and professional networking, that may otherwise jeopardize their academic success. The NLN proposes that nursing programmes establish mentorship initiatives to provide such support (NLN, 2016).

In summary, it is important to diversify the nursing profession in a climate where more nurses are needed. While mentoring has long been part of the preparation for nursing, there is little evidence or practice-based information about mentoring support for doctoral nursing students. Thus, in this chapter, we draw on literature and practice to describe the development of a mentorship programme for first-year online DNP students. The programme elements and participants are presented, followed by preliminary assessment data. We end with thoughts and suggestions for mentoring in the health professions.

Literature

Effective mentorship can create an environment where mentees and mentors may engage in open and non-judgemental communication. Psychological safety is a belief that participants can feel safe and comfortable sharing their ideas, feelings and problems without the fear of repercussions (Lyman et al., 2020). This sense of psychological safety has been found to enhance subjective well-being and may be related to the successful progression, retention and completion of mentees' academic programmes (Wen et al., 2019).

Yet, there is a dearth of evidence on mentorship, naturally occurring or in organized programmes, for doctoral nursing students. Related literature suggests what might be effective. For example, having a mentor improved the transition of undergraduate nursing students from school to practice through confidence building and camaraderie (Rush et al., 2013; Szalmasagi, 2018). Other researchers reported that mentorship reduced turnover intentions and increased retention among the nursing workforce (Brook et al., 2019). Wynn et al. (2021) call on the nursing profession to give more attention to the importance of mentorship as a knowledge transmission practice. They find that a lack of mentorship may be related to high attrition rates in the profession.

Doctoral students in other fields perceive mentoring as important and receive mentoring support both from their faculty advisors and peers (Lunsford, 2012; Baker et al., 2013). Scholars report that mentoring has the potential to contribute to graduate students' socialization and academic support, and satisfaction with the programme (Hadjioannou et al., 2007).

Rationale for mentorship

DNP faculty members in a public south-eastern university in the US adopted a holistic admissions process for new online DNP family nurse practitioner (FNP) and psychiatric mental health nurse practitioner (PMHNP) programmes. This change was designed to attract more diverse students and was related to diversity and inclusion programme goals (Bice et al., 2021). However, students would not experience formal clinical mentorship until after their first year of the programme. Thus, the faculty members and senior administrators felt that mentorship was needed in the first year.

Two volunteer faculty coordinators were charged with conducting a needs assessment for mentorship and consulting with experts. They first collected survey responses from first-year DNP students and faculty about mentoring experiences and needs. Almost all (97.5%) of students and faculty stated they would be somewhat or extremely likely to participate in a formal mentorship programme. One of the response items, presented below, illustrates the desire for mentorship.

> *Mentoring allows an outside perspective from someone knowledgeable about the topics/issues being experienced in real-time, and that would assist me in understanding processes, assignments, the DNP role, etc. while also allowing me a safe space to express my needs/concerns… this (mentoring) would hopefully help to alleviate some anxiety by offering clarity and firsthand knowledge.*
>
> (DNP student)

In consultation with a mentoring expert, the faculty coordinators reviewed the survey data and programme goals to identify two goals for the DNP mentorship program:

- to develop professional networks to enhance acclimation to the discipline and profession; and
- to gain professional knowledge to accelerate mentee career trajectories.

The faculty coordinators consulted with two out-of-state universities that offer graduate-level mentorship programmes. As a result, the faculty coordinators made four critical decisions to:

1. use an existing platform the faculty members and students used as their learning management system;
2. start the programme at the beginning of the fall semester;
3. provide evidence-based guidelines for mentors and mentees; and
4. adopt a group mentoring approach, with a faculty and a peer mentor, to require fewer mentors and to encourage networking and support among the DNP students.

Programme description

First, this section presents the main elements of the DNP mentorship programme. Subsequently, the programme participants are described.

Programme elements

The programme lasted for one academic year. It began in September 2021 and ended in May 2022. There were three programmatic elements: recruitment activities, onboarding activities and seven monthly mentoring sessions, along with assessment and evaluation of the programme (Figure 9.1).

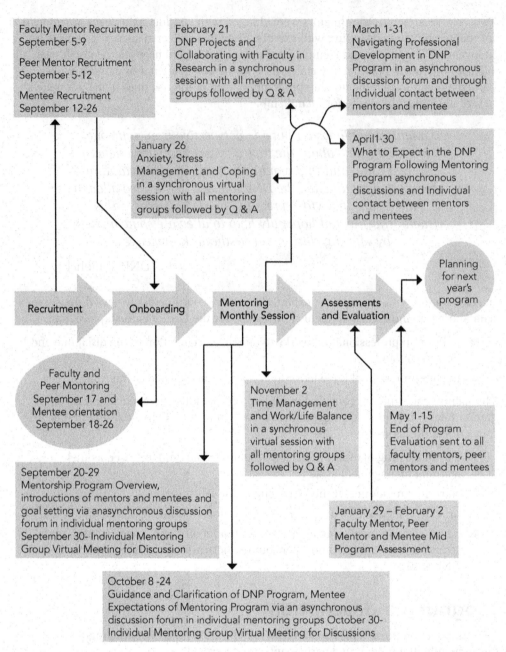

Figure 9.1: DNP mentoring programme timeline: September 2021–May 2022.

Recruitment activities

The recruitment activities involved faculty and peer mentor introductory videos. These videos were available to all first-year DNP students in the learning management system (LMS). Each video was three to five minutes long and presented the mentors' nursing experiences, research focus and reason for becoming a mentor. The students who were interested in participating in the programme viewed the videos and chose the faculty and peer mentor by whom they would like to be mentored. All preferences were honoured.

Onboarding activities

The onboarding period provided evidence-based mentoring guidelines to mentors and mentees. The faculty coordinators provided a 45-minute, live virtual training to review the programme expectations with faculty and peer mentors. Evidence-based mentoring guidelines were reviewed by both faculty and student mentors and guidelines were published in the LMS for mentees. These guidelines were provided to the mentees prior to the first session and reviewed in the September monthly session of the mentorship programme overview.

Monthly mentoring sessions

The mentoring groups of four to five mentees, a faculty mentor and peer mentor engaged monthly on topics that were identified in a student survey. Table 9.1 shows the topics discussed by month. The faculty coordinators drew on their experiences to organize the topics in a manner that reflected the timing of students' needs for this information.

To initiate the programme, eight 'course spaces' entitled 'DNP Mentoring Group #' were created in the LMS for groups to interact privately. Faculty mentors designed their own 'course spaces' incorporating the above monthly mentoring topics. The monthly asynchronous discussions were held in these group spaces and the synchronous sessions were held on Zoom with all mentoring groups invited. Synchronous sessions were recorded and faculty mentors posted the recording link in each of their 'course spaces', allowing mentees to view if unable to attend.

An asynchronous discussion forum was provided for mentees to discuss each month's topic. The discussion forum was informal and did not require students to use academic writing, but to communicate in an informal way to express themselves and their needs and experiences with both the mentors and other mentees in their groups. Also, the discussion forum was always open for any questions or comments following the large group presentations.

Students also had the opportunity to reach out to faculty and peer mentors privately if needed. Near the end of the pilot programme, private conversations with both faculty and peer mentors increased.

Table 9.1: Monthly topics for DNP mentorship programme.

Month	Topic	Discussion Content
September	Mentorship programme overview	Faculty and peer mentors lead asynchronous[2] introductions of all programme participants, mentorship programme guidelines, goal writing with the SMART goals template (Doran, 1981); mentorship programme's purpose and goals, roles of mentors vs faculty advisors.
October	Guidance and clarification about the DNP programme	Faculty and peer mentors lead asynchronous[3] discussions on expectations and responsibilities, role definition, course navigation and management.
November	Time management, work–life balance	A synchronous[3] session was presented by a content expert (a DNP-prepared community adult nurse practitioner) on self-care, home/family, and school and work balance. Open discussions followed presentation. Session was recorded for viewing by all mentees.
January	Anxiety, stress management and coping	A synchronous[4] session was presented by a content expert (a DNP-prepared psychiatric mental health nurse practitioner faculty) on stress management. Open discussions followed presentation. Session was recorded for viewing by all mentees.
February	Collaboration with faculty in research	A synchronous[4] session was presented by a content expert (a DNP- and Ph.D.-prepared nurse practitioner faculty) on quality improvement project brainstorming. Open discussions followed presentation. Session was recorded for viewing by all mentees.
March	Navigating professional development in the DNP programme	Faculty and peer mentors led asynchronous[3] discussions on membership in professional organizations, networking and taking on leadership roles.
April	Next steps: What to expect from the mentor DNP, second and third years of the programme and DNP role development	Faculty and peer mentors led asynchronous[3] discussions on what to expect beyond the first year of the DNP programme as well as opportunities to enhance the NP role. A mentee survey on the DNP mentorship programme was distributed by mentorship coordinators.

Programme participants

The programme took a group mentoring approach with a faculty mentor and a peer mentor, who was a DNP student in the second year of the programme, paired with four to five mentees in a group. There were eight mentoring groups in the pilot programme. The role of the peer mentor was to work alongside the faculty mentor in each group by attending synchronous sessions, participate in the asynchronous discussions, and to reach out individually to mentees.

2   Asynchronous sessions were when individuals participated at their convenience during a specified period.

3   Synchronous sessions were scheduled for and held at a specified date and time.

Mentees

The first-year DNP students were introduced to the DNP mentorship programme at their on-campus orientation. An announcement was posted in the LMS for the DNP students to recruit them. Thirty-seven mentees signed up to participate in the programme, which included 35 female mentees and two male mentees, of 16.2% African–American, 0.3% Asian and 83.6% Caucasian ethnicity.

Mentors

The mentorship programme was announced to faculty members and interested doctoral-prepared faculty members were asked to contact the DNP mentorship coordinators. An invitation for peer mentors from the second-year DNP cohort was posted in the LMS and interested students also contacted the programme coordinators. Peer mentors were asked to write a paragraph about why they would like to serve as a mentor. Eight faculty mentors and eight second-year DNP student mentors were recruited through this process. The DNP programme coordinator randomly assigned peer mentors to faculty mentors.

There were eight female faculty mentors, six female peer mentors and two male peer mentors. Among the faculty mentors, one was African–American and seven were Caucasian, one with an Eastern European background. Of the peer mentors, one female was African–American and the rest were Caucasian, with one Eastern European native. In the nursing field, males are considered a minority; therefore, having two male mentors diversified the mentoring groups.

Programme assessment

The assessment is ongoing as the second year of the programme recently concluded. This section presents formative and summative data about the programme's effectiveness.

Monthly topics were facilitated by experts in the School of Nursing and the local community of nurse practitioners. Mentees were actively engaged in the synchronous sessions and the online discussion forums in the first two months of the programme; however, as the first semester progressed and students became more involved in course assignments, participation waned.

An assessment was administered in January following the end of the autumn term, to better understand possible reasons for a decline in engagement. Twenty-one of the mentees and mentors responded to the survey. The assessment showed that 76% of the respondents plan to continue in the mentorship programme, with 15% stating they do not wish to continue and 9% unsure if they wish to continue. There were no significant changes to the remaining monthly session topics or new topics suggested. One respondent commented that the programme 'seemed like another class'. Most of the mentees felt the mentorship programme was beneficial to them (Figure 9.2).

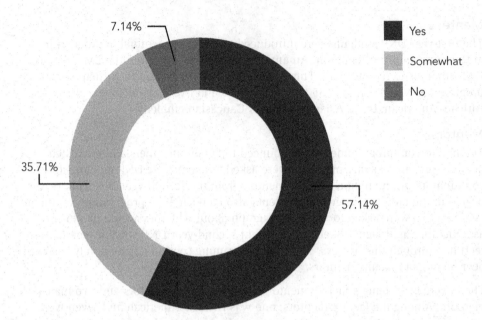

Figure 9.2: Mentee and mentor responses at mid-year of the first year when asked whether they felt the mentorship programme was beneficial to them.

A formative assessment was collected at the end of the first academic year with 63% of faculty and peer mentors responding and 14% of mentees responding. There was a concern about the low mentee response rate. However, there was a better response the second year with 78% of faculty and peer mentors and 35% of mentees responding. The responses provided important information to improve the DNP mentorship programme. Programme participants were asked to reflect on their experience in the mentorship programme and share what did and did not work for them. The main theme was a sense of disconnection in the online environment.

Disconnected

For example, one faculty member noted the LMS felt too much like a class rather than promoting warm relationships. This observation was also reflected in mentee comments.

> ...perhaps not using (the LMS) for the mentoring. It felt a bit too academic to me.
>
> (Faculty Mentor)

> The Zoom option is nice, but it seems to me that mentoring truly requires a face-to-face opportunity. I know that this is nearly impossible because of distance learning and the nature of our programs.
>
> (Faculty Mentor)

I come from education via a brick-and-mortar university. The online advance environs feels very foreign. The lack of human interaction affected me in ways I did not anticipate.

(Mentee)

In our first semester we uploaded video responses to each other. When we started to only talk to each other in writing it lost the personalization. We feel cold and disconnected.

(Mentee)

Connection and role modelling

The two programme goals focused on developing a professional network and professional knowledge. There is evidence these goals were achieved for some participants as some mentees felt a sense of connection from their participation. For example, one peer mentor felt the interactions provided a place for 'camaraderie, *mutual respect, and to provide a space that was inclusive and conducive to professional and personal growth*'. Another peer mentor seemed to overcome the disconnection in the LMS by connecting outside of it.

...much of my time spent mentoring was outside the (LMS) course. I would receive emails and requests for my opinion and insight from mentees. Those interactions seemed much more organic and reinforced my preference for a more fluid approach to mentorship.

(Peer Mentor)

Mentees also noted a sense of camaraderie. One noted that,

the mentorship program allowed me to make contact with my fellow students who I would not have the opportunity to speak with otherwise.

(Mentee)

Another mentee noted the importance of connections:

through these connections, I feel this program has aided in my success.

Another one wrote that,

honestly, just knowing we were all in it together and could relate to others was huge!

Finally, one peer mentor observed the importance of role modelling. They wrote:

> *Realizing one is not alone and having the support system*
> *of a small group of other students and one faculty mentor*
> *seemed valuable in completing a successful semester overall.*
> *Furthermore, speaking with someone who has successfully*
> *completed the first year is essentially 'proof' that it can be*
> *done, which I also felt was a sign of encouragement.*

(Peer Mentor)

Based on observations from faculty mentors, it was found that minority students, both racially and gender diverse, were well engaged in the mentorship programme.

Lessons learned

We know the importance of mentorship in nursing education. We drew on the scholarly and practice literature to develop an effective mentorship experience for first-year nursing students in a DNP program. Our evaluation of this initial effort suggests five points for others to consider for mentorship in graduate health care education. However, based on the participants' formative assessment responses demonstrating 'Connection and Role Modelling', we can see how this type of mentoring programme can also be transferred to a broader health care view. For example, institutions can develop a programme for health care professionals just entering the workforce or transitioning to another area following the core principles of the five points that are outlined below.

First, it is important that a mentorship programme be different from another 'course'. Many participants felt a part of a mentoring community. As new graduate students, having mentors relieved stressors and helped mentees to focus with less fear and uncertainty as they progressed through their first year. The programme allowed mentees to have a support group of peers and faculty, and a comfortable space to ask questions and seek advice. Mentees felt they had the opportunity to have an 'inside perspective' on different topics pertinent to their courses. Mentees noted that the topics presented were relevant and interesting and that the content experts were engaging and gave practical advice to help them succeed in the programme and beyond. Participants also valued the small group setting. Mentees enjoyed the peer–mentor relationship, often connecting outside of the LMS platform.

However, other mentees did not feel this sense of camaraderie and community and perceived the programme as more academic work. Further, the discussion board format seemed ineffective as mentors contacted students via email, text messaging or phone call to form a better rapport with mentees. Mentees recommended more personal communication rather than announcements in the LMS. Group or personal texting, along with positive messages and images, were suggestions for building a mentee–mentor relationship. Mentees also desired more social events in the future to engage face-to-face. In addition, mentees and peer mentors recommended having more structured and frequent check-ins for mentoring.

Second, time constraints also present a challenge that might be addressed by setting out dates at the start of the programme. Mentors noted that finding scheduled time with mentees in the second semester was difficult due to faculty schedules. The COVID-19 pandemic also created additional time burdens for participants.

Third, the importance of peer mentorship emerged. Peer mentorship might also reduce the time constraints for a faculty mentor-led experience. Peer mentorship provided mentees with a more comfortable setting to discuss personal and professional issues. An additional benefit is that mentoring may help prepare effective future mentors in the nursing workforce.

Fourth, it is important to develop and provide resources for mentorship education. We provided information on mentoring to the participants but more attention to quality mentorship education is needed. Faculty mentors had mentored students informally. However, there was mixed participation among the faculty mentors in a more structured experience, with some being fully engaged and others only minimally engaged. Some mentors felt ill-prepared with an open forum, and no script or repository of resources provided. Providing mentoring training and certification for mentors both recognizes that mentoring is a skill to be developed and highlights those who improve their mentorship. In the second year, we added formal mentor training by a national consultant as a result of the lessons learned in the first year.

Fifth, the sustainability and alignment of the programme to institutional goals is critical. The programme is working to create a better mentorship culture across the college. For example, a DNP mentor programme was planned for second- and third-year students through an ancillary department. However, that department could not locate any nurse practitioner mentors, meaning work needs to be done to create opportunities for formal mentorship beyond the first year of graduate school. Relatedly, during the second semester of the programme, there were administrative changes that required additional work for faculty members, who needed to take over duties left by vacant positions. It will be important to educate new administrative leaders on how the DNP mentorship programme is aligned with the college's strategic priorities. Having a designated mentorship programme coordinator in a paid position, or with an assigned workload, is important to provide participants with the support they need.

Overall, mentees met the programme goals by beginning to develop professional networks within the nurse practitioner field. This occurred through mentorship with nurse practitioner faculty mentors, as well as community nurse practitioner experts who presented topics to the mentees. Mentees also developed relationships with peer mentors, who are also DNP/NP students further along in the programme. Mentees and peer mentors both expressed better acclimation to the programme through the use of peer mentors. Mentees expressed knowledge gained to accelerate their careers and transition from a nurse to an advanced practice nurse. In addition, mentees felt more comfortable in their roles as advanced practice nursing students than prior to the mentoring experience.

It is the hope of the faculty coordinators and mentors that the mentorship programme will improve racial and gender diversity in the nurse practitioner workforce, as proposed by the NLN (2016). Having a diverse group of faculty and peer mentors, a diverse group of mentees and providing professional knowledge and support to the mentees promotes inclusion in the academic setting and, ideally, in the nurse practitioner workforce in the future. This will help meet the needs of the diverse population that nurse practitioners serve. Full engagement in the programme by the minority mentees was a promising result. This data informed efforts for the second offering of the programme, which started in autumn 2022. For example, an additional goal was added to focus on high-quality relationships before moving into the professional goals. The hope is a stronger relationship will increase participant engagement. In addition, eight hours of faculty and peer mentoring training are planned. Faculty coordinators will continue to evaluate these efforts as the mentorship programme evolves.

References

American Association of Colleges of Nursing (AACN, 2020a). *Holistic Admissions*. https://www.aacnnursing.org/our-initiatives/diversity-equity-inclusion/holistic-admissions

American Association of Colleges of Nursing (AACN, 2020b). *Promising Practices in Holistic Admissions Review: Implementation in Academic Nursing [White paper]*. https://www.aacnnursing.org/Portals/42/News/White-Papers/AACN-White-Paper-Promising-Practices-in-Holistic-Admissions-Review-December-2020.pdf

Baker, V. L., Pifer, M. J., & Flemion, B. (2013). *Process challenges and learning-based interactions in stage 2 of doctoral education: Implications from two applied social science fields*. The Journal of Higher Education, **84**(4), 449–476.

Bice, A. A., Kantor, R., Parker, D., Ellington, K., & Conde-Zuege, R. (2021). *Holistic review of BSN to DNP applicants: A step-by-step approach to implementation*. Journal of Professional Nursing, **37**(5), 971–977. https://doi.org/10.1016/j.profnurs.2021.07.020

Brook, J., Aitken, L., Webb, R., MacLaren, J., & Salmon, D. (2019). Characteristics of successful interventions to reduce turnover and increase retention of early career nurses: A systematic review. *International Journal of Nursing Studies*, **91**, 47–59.

Cook, E. (1942). Letter to a friend, quoted in *The Life of Florence Nightingale* (p. 406). Macmillan.

Doran, G. T. (1981). *There's a S.M.A.R.T. way to write management's goals and objectives*. Management Review, **70**, 35–36.

Hadjioannou, X., Shelton, N. R., Fu, D., & Dhanarattigannon, J. (2007). *The road to a doctoral degree: Co-travelers through a perilous passage*. College Student Journal, **41**(1), 160–177.

Jacobs, S. (2018). *An analysis of the evolution of mentorship in nursing*. International Journal of Mentoring and Coaching in Education, **7**(2), 155–176.

Karimi, H., & Alavi, N. M. (2015). *Florence Nightingale: The mother of nursing*. Nursing and Midwifery Studies, **4**(2), e29475.

Lunsford, L. (2012). *Doctoral advising or mentoring? Effects on student outcomes*. Mentoring & Tutoring: Partnership in Learning, **20**(2), 251–270.

https://doi.org/10.1080/13611267.2012.678974

Lyman, B., Gunn, M. M., & Mendon, C. R. (2020). *New graduate registered nurses' experiences with psychological safety*. Journal of Nursing Management, **28**(4), 831–839. https://doi.org/10.1111/jonm.13006

McCauley, L. A., Broome, M. E., Frazier, L., Hayes, R., Kurth, A., Musil, C. M., Norman, L. D., Rideout, K. H., & Villarruel, A. M. (2020). *Doctor of nursing practice (DNP) degree in the United States: Reflecting, readjusting, and getting back on track*. Nursing Outlook, **68**(4), 494–503. https://doi.org/10.1016/j.outlook.2020.03.008

National League for Nursing (NLN) (2016). *Achieving Diversity and Meaningful Inclusion in Nursing Education: A Living Document from the National League for Nursing*.

https://www.nln.org/docs/default-source/uploadedfiles/professional-development-programs/vision-statement-achieving-diversity.pdf

Rush, K. L., Adamack, M., Gordon, J., Lilly, M., & Janke, R. (2013). *Best practices of formal new graduate nurse transition programs: An integrative review*. International Journal of Nursing Studies, **50**(3), 345–356.

Szalmasagi, J. D. (2018). *Efficacy of a mentoring program on nurse retention and transition into practice*. International Journal of Studies in Nursing, **3**(2). https://doi.org/10.20849/ijsn.v3i2.378

Wen, P., Chen, C., Dong, L., & Shu, X. (2019). The role of mentoring in protégés' subjective well-being. *Journal of Career Development*, **46**(2), 171–183. https://doi.org/10.1177%2F0894845317731864

Wynn, S., Holden, C., Romero, S., & Julian, P. (2021). *The importance of mentoring in nursing academia*. Open Journal of Nursing, **11**, 241–248. https://www.scirp.org/journal/paperinformation?paperid=108652

Chapter 10
Mentoring in Social Work in the UK

Interview with Suzanne Triggs & Carolyn Smith

How has mentoring evolved in the social work field?

Suzanne: There is a pervasive fixing archetype in the profession that can be characterized as '*I don't need help, I help, I fix things for others*'. In social work leadership, management and front-line roles there is still a strong culture of telling, transmitting and '*here are the benefits of my professional experience*'.

The nature and frenetic pace of social work also contributes to the 'quick fix' culture. People are often listening in order to tell people what to do, to populate an assessment and to feed the system. Some social workers recently articulated this to me as 'listening to record' or 'listening through the laptop'. They have specific performance indicators and outcomes that they have to meet. The workforce has been decimated by people leaving the profession, so a lot of the time you have agency staff propping up services and there are a lot of people working in a context with very little organizational or institutional memory.

It is easy to see how this culture has arisen. Most people come into the profession with a strong value base of wanting to make a difference for people, and early in their careers this is tied to telling people what to do, which the process-driven, linear, computer-facing systems reinforce.

Carolyn: Time constraints are a huge problem, so mentoring can be seen as helping to provide a 'quick fix' and not necessarily providing time for reflection and thinking, or looking at the longer term. It does not really allow time to unpick the reasons why we might be doing something. Reflection is often the first thing to go when under pressure, and from a practice standpoint the mentoring role is very much 'solve a problem, move onto the next problem'.

This is a very different approach to mentoring in other professional contexts, where it is explicitly a relationship in which reflection and longer-term thinking is nurtured and encouraged. Should anything be done to help mentoring in social work evolve?

Suzanne: From the point of view of someone who trains others in coaching and mentoring, a lot of the key work involves helping people remember why they came into the job, and stripping things back to look at core skills so that people can step out of the 'fixer' mindset. During training, often people struggle with the mindset shift for the first half day, but by the afternoon the penny has dropped regarding who they are, how they want to show up and who they want to be. The difficulty comes on returning to the office, and how that environment shapes their behaviour. I can help them create allies with one another and step out of the mindset that is a barrier to mentoring and coaching, but the environment unwittingly demands a fixing professional identity of them.

A big factor is screen-based listening where people are having to listen and talk while at a computer screen in order to take electronic efficiency short cuts. Technology not only has many advantages, but also has disadvantages in terms of encouraging people's attention to be fractured and extremely time limited. Just asking people to turn their phones off for the duration of the training can cause lots of anxiety for people, and they need to adjust to being really and truly present. The overaccessibility of technology, particularly in the hybrid-working world, can provide a barrier in terms of people reading each other's social cues effectively, which can lead to a sense of empathy decline. This makes it difficult for mentoring to be more exploratory, attuned and thoughtful.

Carolyn: My experiences of mentoring have been fulfilled at various stages through my career by advanced social work practitioners or team managers. I think I got some mentoring through formal supervision, when there is a chance to ask questions and get guidance that way. Also, there is day-to-day and more informal mentoring, via the role modelling that senior colleagues might show you, when you can have conversations in the office. I think there is a similar picture for mentoring in the profession today. If we look at mentoring in social work as described just now, then we just learn from senior colleagues so there's little room for change.

In order to receive coaching of the sort that Suzanne describes, there has to be a culture shift in the organization and an element of top-down support. In Wakefield, where we have had a number of staff trained in coaching by Suzanne, for me personally that was life-changing as it helped to change my approach to work and particularly my approach to supporting other staff, both formally and informally.

That is a really limited definition of mentoring that seems to be in play in social work. Our direct experience and that of many other contributors to the handbook is that mentoring can be part of a reflective process that can pose questions and go deeper into people's values and goals. Why do you think mentoring has evolved in that way in social work?

Carolyn: There is no real training or discussion about the value of mentoring, so in the end any mentoring is very much dependent on the supervisor and it is very much led by the person supervising. So, even if the supervisee brings an agenda, it becomes very case-focused very quickly and there is usually not enough time to explore things more widely. Supervision very quickly becomes focused on quick fixes and what tasks need to be done by what date, and these rigid statutory timescales soon dictate what is discussed.

As Suzanne's doctoral research is really the only research into coaching for social workers out there, the coaching that is generally available tends to be more corporate coaching that is available to anyone in the council. While some of that coaching is transferable, it is not something that many social workers have experience of and it is not something that is directly relevant to our day-to-day roles. So, it takes a lot more work for anyone to transfer those coaching experiences into a social work and practice context.

Suzanne: There is very little language for coaching and mentoring in social work, there is just no lexicon for it. We are involved in trying to create a language and framework, but it depends very much on funding, and because social workers are such a precious resource it is very hard to carve out the time for training. The crisis-driven and chaotic nature of social work means that someone doing training may say that they have to leave and go to a court hearing in the middle of a training day. Reflective time is valued theoretically but pragmatically, when there are calls like this on social workers' time, then it is very difficult to make it happen.

The Frontline organization that trains new social workers uses coaches and mentors during their training, but as soon as the trainees get out there it stops – so there is no continuity. I am trying to win people over in local authorities to support it more, but what tends to happen is that they ask their practice educators and managers to have the training, and then they say *'all our staff need this'*, but then they realise that this is not possible without large-scale funding and without a change toward a coaching and mentoring culture.

So, change is very incremental, very dependent on funding and very much dependent on word of mouth because there is no national imperative to put coaching and mentoring into social work. Significantly, Carolyn recently got some funding for me to train practice educators across Leeds and Wakefield.

Carolyn: We have teamed up with Leeds and Wakefield's Children's and Adult's Social Services and with the University of Leeds and Leeds Beckett University. The Department for Education (DfE) provided some sustainability funding to set the partnership up and now we are established as an organization we have to maintain the offer. So, we now have a standardized training programme offered via the universities. The DfE are also offering continuous improvement funding which we can bid for each year for very specific pieces of work. That is where I put the bid in last year for training from Dr Triggs in coaching skills and techniques for practice educators. Having experienced a coaching approach directly and having seen the effect on others I am able to promote this, particularly for students who might have been struggling. This aligned with the increasing number of students put on remedial action plans during the COVID-19 pandemic. The feedback from the coaching training so far has been overwhelmingly positive, but again the continuation depends on funding because a lot of the local authorities do not have the funding to provide it. This involves being creative and finding external sources of funding to continue.

Can mentoring in social work evolve into a different kind of relationship that is more driven by the mentee's needs, as it has in other professional contexts?

Carolyn: Something that we are working on in one of our projects is a space for reflective supervision, peer mentoring that really unpicks the 'why' and the context behind things. Currently in social work, mentoring and coaching are very far apart, so there is a lot of scope to align them but currently we are a long way off from doing that.

Suzanne: This goes back to the problem that there is no language for coaching and mentoring in social work, so we are now trying to create one and defining the need for it. There is definite scope for this to evolve but we need clear definitions and a vision of what we want it to look like. So, looking at real examples, like the Médecins Sans Frontières approach, could be a great way to appeal to the social work community in terms of what mentoring could provide. That is a reflective and supportive role rather than the deficit model which is probably how it would be perceived right now – typically *'there's something wrong with you, you need to improve so go and have some mentoring'*, which is a little bit like how coaching is sometimes misinterpreted. There are myths about what mentoring and coaching are, and that is why my training always starts with exploring and unpicking what people think it is.

It would be really useful to the social work community to have some clear examples of what mentoring can do that are relevant and appealing, and particularly to have some examples of what it can do in other organizations that are related to them and that they can respect.

It would be great if the DfE or Directors of Children's and Adult's Social Services could come out and clearly state an ambition for the role of mentoring and coaching in training social work – it could easily be part of a module in university pre-qualification training programmes. In the research I conducted the social workers said exactly this, that there should have been coaching and mentoring in their training and it should be in student training going forward. It is difficult for more experienced practitioners, when you have been in practice a long time and developed a clear professional identity – how do you deconstruct the behaviours and attitudes that the system and environment has been re-enforcing for years? It really does depend on a lot of people being willing and able to deconstruct their mindset and take on another one – not all the time but some of the time.

What could happen to make mentoring really cutting edge in social work?

Carolyn: There are so many different routes into social work and so many different training courses that some consistency would be needed to be able to move it forward.

Suzanne: At the moment, I am on a committee for the 'Coaching for Social Good' Award with the Institute of Coaching at Harvard. I won the award in 2021, and it was the first time they had ever awarded it, which was great for me. But it was also important that this prestigious institution was recognizing that coaching and mentoring existed beyond the corporate leadership and executive world and that it could be of benefit to a wider world rather than just to those who could afford to pay for it. It is clear now that there is a growing movement internationally to apply coaching for social impact. There are voluntary organizations, third sector organizations and people giving their time differently. There are examples of coaching taking place now during the war in Ukraine. It would be really cutting edge to have an alignment with an international organization that promotes coaching and mentoring that says, *'we're going to sponsor this within social work'*.

When I first finished my PhD, my plan was to go to universities and try to get coaching and mentoring students in the same room as social work students, and I started that at Goldsmiths, University of London just before the pandemic. The two sets of students could quickly see that there was an overlap in their professions, how coaching could be used within social work and how the understanding of what social work does could be useful to coaching students.

There could be regular cross-fertilization sessions for social work students with coaching and mentoring students that would encourage a much broader alliance or community of practice going forward. It could certainly help social work students to consider alternatives to 'fixing' if they were in regular groups or modules with coaching and mentoring students, who did not equate their strong desire to help primarily with fixing.

There is definitely scope for some kind of organizational alliance or sponsorship to address how coaching for the social good and mentoring fits with the social work mission to empower, and how the two different sectors can help each other. We need to innovate social work communication with its clients, within the profession, and adapt the social work mindset.

To what extent is mentoring in social work evaluated?

Suzanne: It is not evaluated in general – I develop evaluations of coaching training, but social care organizations rarely give much detailed thought to evaluations of impact. They focus on the need to transform the way social workers communicate and to add to their communication repertoire. Measuring the impact of this is very difficult and would require long-term involvement and more funding to evaluate impact effectively.

As demonstrating impact can be so difficult, I will often do this through gathering powerful stories from social workers. When I train people, I leave a gap in between training days and people have to come back and give examples of how they have used coaching conversations and skills in their practice groups, supervision or team meetings. I pull all of those stories together and I find that retelling them has much more impact than the 'stats'. When I approach other local authorities and say, '*here are some stories about how other social work and social care staff are using it*', the stories are the things that generate curiosity and win people over to want this training intervention for their workforce.

It sounds as though, in some ways, you are acting as a mentor to senior staff in these organizations by asking them to reflect on what their training programmes are for, and giving examples of what training can do.

Suzanne: I agree there may be an element of that. I do not know for sure if the organizational memory of these impact stories persists with the rapid turnover of staff. So, I may deliver something, and it will have an impact, and stories will be told. For example, I met someone recently who remembered the training, and the impact it had had on their practice, that I had delivered over ten years ago. What you really need is regular 'on-the-ground' peer coaching and mentoring experiences, word of mouth recommendations of the approach, learning alliances between different social work and social care organizations, a coaching and mentoring culture as the norm, and all-in institutional, DfE and chief social worker sign-up. You want systematic impact monitoring processes, you want long-term funding, and ultimately you want a wide range of allies so that you are not just relying on interested and committed individuals or just one person in an organization trying to spread the coaching and mentoring message in a vacuum.

Carolyn: There are people in many organizations who will champion coaching following on from our training, but unless you have more organizational support then you are not going to change the culture. It is asking a lot for an organization to change its culture like that, so now we are chipping away because we do not necessarily have the top-down support needed.

Based on Suzanne's training, I have developed a training session for newly qualified social workers to support them in learning and applying coaching skills and techniques. The hope of this is that we can catch staff as they are starting out and give them a different skill set to use.

Are there any key messages that you would like to give to colleagues regarding mentoring and coaching in the social work profession?

Carolyn: For me, coaching and mentoring sit really well with a restorative practice approach, and that it is doable within the role. We know that if people are involved in their own goal-setting the outcomes are much more positive. So, it does not have to involve a huge shift in the work you are doing day to day.

Suzanne: My key message is that we need cultural change, and it is possible, but it needs buy-in. In Norwich, I have been working with a team who are the first ever team of practice coaches. So, they coach and mentor social workers. They have training from me, and they have also become qualified as coaches. That team has now been expanded in Norwich. It is now doubling in size, because social workers and the director have recognized the impact that it has had on social workers and their practice. This model could be used as an example for roll-out elsewhere in the profession.

To reiterate a key message would be that we need coaching and mentoring input right from the start of social work education, we need modules and it needs to be part of ongoing professional development. Recruitment, retention and burnout are at the top of everybody's agenda right now and the impact here could be significant. People come into the job to make a difference, and coaching and mentoring can help people understand that they can make a difference in ways other than fixing people. If they can do that people will stay in the job, but if the workplace is not supportive of this they will walk. Coaching and mentoring can help people stay in the job because they will get value and they will be connected to their values through it.

Is there anything else you would like to say about mentoring that we have not touched on already?

Suzanne: There is clearly a need for it. The majority of my one-to-one clients are social workers. It is time that we service that need organizationally beyond a 'nice to have' training input which is dependent on a funding stream being available. It can radically innovate the way that social workers communicate as part of a relationship-based practice approach.

Carolyn: I know of several examples of how a more supportive approach to mentoring has enabled people to stay in the profession when they are struggling by helping them to see a way through using their values and skills.

Suzanne: Very recently in Tower Hamlets, somebody told me that they had mentored someone who was thinking they could not do the job and could not stay in the job as they were overwhelmed, and there was a case in particular that they were struggling with to do with domestic violence. The coaching and mentoring not only helped them with the case, but they also decided they wanted to become the local domestic violence champion for the local authority. From a point where they were thinking they could not do the job and wanted to leave, a coaching conversation helped them to stay in the job and recognize that they were good at it. So, the coaching and mentoring not only made a difference for that mother and child, but also for the social worker in terms of their longevity and effectiveness in the role.

Finally, I am one of the founders of a new of collective or supportive community of practice called 'Coaching for Social Impact' which is about creating a coaching community for change, inclusion and social justice. We produced a British Association for Counselling and Psychotherapy report in 2022 which sets out different examples of coaching practices that are going on around the UK now. We are keen to grow our numbers and become a movement within the coaching and mentoring profession. My involvement with this community inspired me to develop a new theoretical model for coaching for social impact as it is an extremely undertheorized area. The model addresses how to build personal power and personal responsibility and connects it to social power and social responsibility. It seeks to mobilize individuals to achieve goals and purpose and to positively adapt to setbacks under conditions of uncertainty, adversity and structural disadvantage. The hope behind the model is to try to harness any emergent uplift in social power through coaching and mentoring as leverage for social change and social justice. We welcome anyone who would like to tell us about what they do to coach for the social good or would like mentoring from others about how they can start.

Further reading

British Association for Counselling and Psychotherapy (2022). *Coaching for Social Impact* https://www.bacp.co.uk/media/14826/bacp-coaching-for-social-impact.pdf

Triggs, S. (2020). *Making a difference again: How using coaching enabled children's social workers to enhance their practice and fulfil their vocational aspirations. International Journal of Evidence-based Coaching and Mentoring*, **S14**, 77–87. HYPERLINK "10.24384/rvjp-r583" https://radar.brookes.ac.uk/radar/items/7e945a10-f0f5-4c99-9e09-d80f6eb8c986/1/

Triggs, S. (2021, October). *Power from within: A coaching approach to social work. Coaching Today.* https://www.coachdoctor.org/wp-content/uploads/2022/11/Coaching-Today-Article-Power-from-Within.pdf

Chapter 11
Peer Mentoring as an Overlooked Health and Social Care Method

Gillian Buck

Peer mentoring, delivered by people with shared experiences, has grown rapidly across the globe in recent decades (Munn-Giddings & Borkman, 2017). This (multi)national development is underpinned by 'lived experience' movements pressing for democratic inclusion, and consumerist notions of user involvement as a lever of efficiency and effectiveness (Beresford, 2002). While health and social care professionals might not deliver peer mentoring directly, they may facilitate, support or refer to such activity.

Definitions of peer and mentoring vary broadly (Bozeman & Feeney, 2007; Finnegan et al., 2010). In human services,

> *a peer is generally...a person who has shared experiences in common with the client and uses these to provide support... exchanging practical and emotional help, generally in ways that are outside the realms of a professional relationship.*

> (Schinkel & Whyte, 2012, p. 361)

Peer mentoring is therefore a 'method' to implement the 'theory' of lived experience involvement and the closely related theories of participation and co-production,[4] but it has largely been overlooked in health and social care texts and consequently in professional training. To bridge this gap, this chapter will introduce lived experience involvement in health and social care and examples of peer mentoring, before focusing on criminal justice as a case study to explore how the strengths of peer mentoring can be harnessed and the pitfalls avoided.

Lived experience involvement

Lived experience refers to experience of a social issue or issues. *Experts by experience* use their lived experience to inform social purpose work (Sandhu, 2017). The movement toward experience-informed services originated in disability activism in the 1990s but has been mobilized by a range of marginalized groups, including women, the LGBTQ + community and criminalized individuals, who have called for 'nothing

---

4   For a discussion of the varied conceptions of coproduction, see Mazzei et al. (2020).

about us, without us' (Bakshi, 2021; Buck et al., 2021). Lived experience involvement is now a feature of health and social care in several places around the globe, including Australia, Indonesia (Iryawan et al., 2022), New Zealand (Voronka, 2017), North America and the UK. Involvement is advocated on the basis that lived experiences enable people to contribute to service improvements (Bergerum et al., 2019), resulting in methods that better meet people's needs and reduce divisions between recipients and providers (Buck, 2020).

While health and social sectors increasingly recognize the importance of lived experience, they can fail to fully cultivate the knowledge of experts by experience, viewing them as informants, rather than leaders of change (Sandhu, 2017). Methods developed and delivered *by* people with lived experience are one way to harness this insight, yet many health and social care textbooks overlook peer or user-led approaches completely (e.g., Aveyard & Sharp, 2017; Musson, 2017; Peate, 2017).

Peer mentoring

The terms *mentoring* and *support* are often used interchangeably and peer mentoring can be difficult to sort from adjacent concepts such as training, coaching and even friendship (Bozeman & Feeney, 2007). Tracy and Wallace (2016) define peer *support* as non-clinical assistance from those in similar circumstances, whilst peer *mentoring* involves people in later recovery assisting those in earlier recovery. This definition constructs mentoring as hierarchical, wherein a person with more knowledge 'corrects' another, yet (peer) mentors often strive to be egalitarian; this is not an intervention delivered by an expert 'other', but a peer, theoretically facilitating a less hierarchical, more mutual relationship (Buck, 2020).

Peer mentoring can be especially valuable to stigmatized and marginalized groups and is an established approach in hundreds of mental health settings across England (Wagstaff et al., 2018). These initiatives stemmed from the mental health recovery movement which rejected what was considered an outdated and stigmatizing medical model (Miler et al., 2020). Peers can often connect in ways that traditional outpatient care cannot, and their support can result in fewer psychiatric symptoms and reduced hospitalization (O'Connell et al., 2018).

Peers can also promote physical health and there is a long history of those with lived experience working in disease prevention and intervention (Scannell, 2021). The informal, less hierarchical approach of peer mentoring has supported people to give up smoking, get more active, breastfeed effectively and lose weight (Williams et al., 2018). Peer mentors trained in self-management of the autoimmune disease lupus helped mentees in South Carolina to experience lower disease activity and decreased anxiety and depression (Williams et al., 2018). Importantly, this study also highlighted peer mentoring's potential as a culturally sensitive means of improving health outcomes for minority groups, whose trust in health services may be lower.

In the context of substance use, peer mentoring can increase treatment adherence and abstinence (Bucur et al., 2020) and reduce risks associated with injecting drugs (Tracy & Wallace, 2016). It is theorized that visible 'recovery champions' help people to believe that recovery is possible and desirable (Kidd, 2011). There has been a dramatic rise in peer support in substance use recovery (Tracy & Wallace, 2016) and peer involvement features in national drug and alcohol treatment strategies in at least Australia, Canada and Scotland (Miler et al., 2020).

Peer-led approaches also hold potential for a range of other stigmatized groups. For example, the World Health Organization has emphasized the importance of peer support in HIV prevention (Iryawan et al., 2022). Benefits were found too for adolescent mothers in Zimbabwe experiencing social isolation; peer mentoring improved mental health, social support and skills (Tinago et al., 2021). In the US, peer mentoring was found to increase a sense of agency among parents in child welfare systems, increasing the chances of reunification after child removal (Frame et al., 2006). In the UK, peer mentors offered emotional and practical support to survivors of child sexual exploitation, too often missed or misunderstood by statutory services (Buck et al., 2017). People with intellectual and developmental disabilities (IDDs) experience stigma around the world, limiting their inclusion. Peer mentors were found to mitigate stigma by providing emotional and practical connectedness, particularly in low-income countries where government-led initiatives are minimal (Jansen-van Vuuren & Aldersey, 2020).

Having considered lived experience involvement and peer mentoring across health and social care, I will now focus on criminal justice to explore the strengths and potential pitfalls of peer mentoring as a 'method' of intervention.

Criminal justice case study

Criminalized people deliver peer mentoring around the world, including Finland (Helminen & Mills, 2019), Sweden, the UK and Ireland (Jaffe, 2012; O'Sullivan et al., 2018), and the US (Seppings, 2016). Peer mentoring is an increasing feature in prison, probation, and youth justice settings, with peer mentors making up about 90% of criminal justice mentors in parts of England (Willoughby et al., 2013, p. 7). Peer mentors in criminal justice are community members, often with lived experiences of criminalization, who work to inspire, motivate and support mentees. Practices are diverse, encompassing one-to-one sessions, groupwork and leisure activities but are all based on the theory that behaviour is influenced by close contacts (Buck, 2020).

As inspirational role models, peer mentors offer reassurance that change is manageable and possible (Buck, 2019), instilling *hope* in prison settings (Nixon, 2020); youth justice settings (Creaney, 2020); and post-incarceration (Lopez-Humphreys & Teater, 2020). Peer workers are also claimed to have a credibility that 'professionals' may not, because they have experienced many of the same problems and found ways to navigate them (Prince's Trust, 2012). This provides a sense of security in contexts where people may have experienced authority figures as inconsistent or dangerous (Buck, 2019).

In addition to role modelling, Freire (1997 p. 324) emphasized the importance of mentors centring mentee goals:

> *The fundamental task of the mentor is a liberatory task. It is not to encourage the mentor's goals and aspirations to be reproduced in the mentees...but to give rise to the possibility that the students become the owners of their own history...[to believe in] the total autonomy, freedom, and development of those he or she mentors.*

This definition invites empowerment-based practice, which could counter experiences of feeling powerless, unskilled or untrusted that can be common in prison and probation settings (Pollack, 2004). Buck (2018) traced three 'core conditions' within criminal justice peer mentoring: caring, listening and encouraging small steps. These person-centred features mark a shift from practice that problematizes people, toward healing approaches nurtured by and for criminalized people. This shift is especially important for disproportionately incarcerated groups, including people from ethnic minorities (Anthony et al., 2020). In contrast to confinement and surveillance, peer mentoring can offer relationship-based practice enabling people to unburden suffering and discover new self-direction (Buck, 2018).

Evaluations of peer mentoring have evidenced reductions in reoffending (Sells et al., 2020) and feelings of isolation (Pollack, 2004), along with increased employment outcomes, self-worth (Taylor et al., 2013) and feelings of autonomy (Pollack, 2004). This is important given that leaving crime behind correlates with a sense of feeling able to influence one's own life (Maruna, 2001). There is also evidence that peer mentors work as an effective 'bridge' to other resources, increasing cooperation with courts (Jalain & Grossi, 2020), statutory supervision (Her Majesty's Inspectorate of Probation [HMIP], 2016) and services for substance use, mental health, housing and employment (Reingle Gonzalez et al., 2019; McLeod et al., 2020). Additionally, peer mentoring can benefit mentors, offering employment pathways for people whose histories can pose barriers to employment (Moran et al., 2014).

Besides functional and interpersonal benefits, there are some less noted, but important effects of peer mentoring. For example, peer mentors often highlight flaws within systems and work toward reform by writing, speaking at conferences and striving for structural changes to 'the system' from within (Buck, 2020). Maruna (2017) suggests these efforts are building a social movement, like the US civil rights movement (1954–1968) or addiction/mental health 'recovery movements', wherein grassroots organizations and ex-prisoner activists are reframing understandings of desistance (leaving crime behind), as not just an individual process, but a path with structural obstacles which require social changes.

There have been concerns from professionals that (volunteer) peer mentors may be used to substitute paid professionals (Buck, 2020) but mentors with lived experience are 'valid adjuncts', providing a sense of joint ownership of recovery (Payne, 2017). There are still important roles for social (care) workers who can learn from lived expertise and construct richer interventions. Professionals can facilitate peer support within groupwork and recovery settings, given it aligns with narrative concepts of 'retelling' and 'witnessing' to enhance well-being (Loumpa, 2012). Professionals can also work as allies, creating less stigmatizing services, providing trauma-informed management where required (Buck et al., 2021) and promoting progression routes to avoid peer roles being co-opted (Byrne et al., 2018).

The pitfalls of peer mentoring

Despite the promise of peer mentoring, it is not a panacea. Those developing services should recognize potential problems to increase safety and effectiveness. Spencer (2007, p. 331) highlighted six elements of failed mentoring relationships, including abandonment by a mentor or mentee, a perceived lack of mentee motivation, mismatched expectations, deficiencies in mentor skills, family interference and inadequate agency support. Problems can also arise due to differences in gender or culture, boundaries not agreed in advance or broken confidentiality (McKimm et al., 2007, pp. 13–14). These are important areas for employers to consider when developing training, supervision and development structures.

Mentoring in penal contexts also presents unique problems, given that secure environments which restrict and dehumanize people can constrain healthy working relationships (Gosling & Buck, 2015). Criminalized mentors can experience exclusion in prison and community settings due to criminal histories (Buck et al., 2021) and have high expectations placed upon them for little or no financial reward (Buck, 2018). Punitive environments can also cause mentoring to depart from core principles, extending the coercive reach of the criminal justice system (Hucklesby & Wincup, 2014).

Working as a peer mentor can take a high personal toll and there are risks of secondary trauma and burnout (Perrin et al., 2018). Good-quality training, supervision and peer support are vital, particularly where people are drawing upon their own (potentially trauma-invoking) life experiences (Buck et al., 2021). Cody et al. (2022) argue that any organization facilitating peer support should consider six issues: the 'readiness' of potential peer supporters; opportunities to shadow peer supporters in their role; ongoing training; regular support and supervision, including self-care; ensuring that other forms of support are available to people being supported; and taking the time to reflect on how these initiatives are developing and working. Managers should consider these dynamics to support mentors, strengthen the quality of services and avoid exclusion and exploitation.

Conclusion

Peer mentoring is a method of interpersonal support, which centres lived experience, and is growing in diverse settings (internationally). Experts by experience can help to develop accessible, culturally sensitive services that better meet people's needs and improve people's mental and physical health, relationships and well-being. Despite its prevalence and effectiveness, peer mentoring has been largely omitted from health and social care textbooks to the detriment of professional training and the people using and delivering services. Health and social care workers are well placed to facilitate and encourage peer support to promote recovery, rehabilitation and inclusion across diverse settings (Loumpa, 2012).

Focusing on peer mentoring in criminal justice, this chapter draws out some valuable messages for health and social care. In prison and community contexts, peer mentors can be positive role models who instil hope for the future and a sense of security where trust in professionals is low. Peer mentors often employ core conditions of caring, listening and encouraging small steps. This empowerment-based approach enables (often traumatized) people to unburden suffering, focus on strengths and discover new self-direction. This can result in improved self-worth and decreased isolation. It can also form a 'bridge' to other services. On a practical level, peer mentoring provides valuable work opportunities for people with criminal records who experience social exclusion. More radically, peer mentors (and mentees) can highlight flaws within systems and work toward removing structural obstacles.

Despite clear benefits, peer mentoring is not a universal remedy. Relationships require careful matching and management. Penal contexts which dehumanize people can undermine aims and mentors can have overly high expectations placed upon them. Professional facilitation of lived experience involves delegating decisions and guiding individuals' development as leaders (Buck et al., 2021). Commissioners and facilitators should prioritize mentor training, supervision and development to harness the benefits of peer mentoring while preventing secondary trauma, burnout and exploitation.

References

Anthony, T., Sentance, G., & Bartels, L. (2020). *Transcending colonial legacies: From criminal justice to Indigenous women's healing*. In L. George, A. N. Norris, A. Deckert, & J. Tauri (Eds.) *Neo-Colonial Injustice and the Mass Imprisonment of Indigenous Women* (pp. 103–131). Palgrave Macmillan.

Aveyard, H., & Sharp, P. (2017). *A Beginner's Guide to Evidence-Based Practice in Health and Social Care* (**3rd ed.**). Open International Publishing.

Bakshi, S. (2021). *Peer support as a tool for community care: 'Nothing about us, without us'*. Columbia Social Work Review, **19**(1), 20–43.

Beresford, P. (2002). *User involvement in research and evaluation: Liberation or regulation?* Social Policy and Society, **1**(2), 95–105.

Bergerum, C., Thor, J., Josefsson, K., & Wolmesjö, M. (2019). *How might patient involvement in healthcare quality improvement efforts work: A realist literature review*. Health Expectations, **22**(5), 952–964.

Bozeman, B., & Feeney, M. K. (2007). *Toward a useful theory of mentoring: A conceptual analysis and critique*. Administration and Society, **39**(6), 719–739.

Buck, G. (2018). *The core conditions of peer mentoring*. Criminology & Criminal Justice, **18**(2), 190–206.

Buck, G. (2019). *'It's a tug of war between the person I used to be and the person I want to be': The terror, complexity and limits of leaving crime behind*. Illness, Crisis & Loss, **27**(2), 101–118.

Buck, G. (2020). *Peer Mentoring in Criminal Justice*. Routledge.

Buck, G., Lawrence, A., & Ragonese, E. (2017). *Exploring peer mentoring as a form of innovative practice with young people at risk of child sexual exploitation*. British Journal of Social Work, **47**(6), 1745–1763.

Buck, G., Tomczak, P., & Quinn, K. (2021). *This is how it feels: Activating lived experience in the penal voluntary sector*. British Journal of Criminology, **62**(4), 822–839.

Bucur, H. M., Beckett, D. S., Perry, G., & Davies, T. H. (2020). *Peer recovery provides sustainable avenues for addiction treatment but is not a one-size-fits-all proposition*. Addictive Disorders & Their Treatment, **19**(1), 1–6.

Byrne, L., Stratford, A., & Davidson, L. (2018). *The global need for lived experience leadership*. Psychiatric Rehabilitation Journal, **41**(1), 76–79.

Cody, C., Bovarnick, S., Peace, D., & Warrington, C. (2022). *'Keeping the informal safe': Strategies for developing peer support initiatives for young people who have experienced sexual violence*. Children & Society, **36**(5), 1043–1063.

Creaney, S. (2020). *Children's voices: are we listening? Progressing peer mentoring in the youth justice system*. Child Care in Practice, **26**(1), 22–37.

Finnegan, L., Whitehurst, D., & Denton, S. (2010). *Models of Mentoring for Inclusion and Employment: Thematic Review of Existing Evidence on Mentoring and Peer Mentoring*. Centre for Economic and Social Inclusion.

Frame, L., Conley, A., & Berrick, J. D. (2006). *'The real work is what they do together': Peer support and birth parent change*. Families in Society, **87**(4), 509–520.

Freire, P. (1997). *Mentoring the Mentor: A Critical Dialogue with Paulo Freire*. Peter Lang.

Gosling, H., & Buck, G. (2015). *Mentoring: Crossing boundaries with care?* Criminal Justice Matters, **99**(1), 22–23.

Helminen, M., & Mills, A. (2019). *Exploring autonomy in the Finnish and New Zealand penal voluntary sectors: The relevance of marketisation and criminal justice policy environments in two penal voluntary sector organisations. The Howard Journal of Crime and Justice*, **58**(3), 404–429.

Her Majesty's Inspectorate of Probation (HMIP) (2016). *An Inspection of Through the Gate Resettlement Services for Short-Term Prisoners.* Her Majesty's Inspectorate of Probation.

Hucklesby, A., & Wincup, E. (2014). *Assistance, support and monitoring? The paradoxes of mentoring adults in the criminal justice system. Journal of Social Policy*, **43**(2), 373–390.

Iryawan, A. R., Stoicescu, C., Sjahrial, F., Nio, K., & Dominich, A. (2022). *The impact of peer support on testing, linkage to and engagement in HIV care for people who inject drugs in Indonesia: qualitative perspectives from a community-led study. Harm Reduction Journal*, **19**(1), 1–13.

Jaffe, M. (2012). *Peer Support and Seeking Help in Prison: A Study of the Listener Scheme in Four Prisons in England.* PhD thesis, Keele University.

Jalain, C. I., and Grossi, E. L. (2020). *Take a load off Fanny: Peer mentors in veterans treatment courts. Criminal Justice Policy Review*, **31**(8), 1165–1192.

Jansen-van Vuuren, J., & Aldersey, H. M. (2020). *Stigma, acceptance and belonging for people with IDD across cultures. Current Developmental Disorders Reports*, **7**(3), 163–172.

Kidd, M. (2011). *A first-hand account of service user groups in the United Kingdom: An evaluation of their purpose, effectiveness, and place within the recovery movement. Journal of Groups in Addiction & Recovery*, **6**(1–2), 164–175.

Lopez-Humphreys, M., & Teater, B. (2020). *'It's what's on the inside that counts': A pilot study of the subjective changes among returned citizens participating in a peer-mentor support initiative. Journal of Social Service Research*, **46**(6), 741–755.

Loumpa, V. (2012). *Promoting recovery through peer support: Possibilities for social work practice. Social Work in Health Care*, **51**(1), 53–65.

Maruna, S. (2017). *Desistance as a social movement. Irish Probation Journal*, **14**, 5–16.

Maruna, S. (2001). *Making Good: How Ex-Convicts Reform and Rebuild Their Lives.* American Psychological Association.

Mazzei, M., Teasdale, S., Calò, F., & Roy, M. J. (2020). *Co-production and the third sector: Conceptualising different approaches to service user involvement. Public Management Review*, **22**(9), 1265–1283.

McKimm, J., Jollie, C., & Hatter, M. (2007). *Mentoring theory and practice.* Imperial College School of Medicine.

McLeod, K. E., Korchinski, M., Young, P., Milkovich, T., Hemingway, C., DeGroot, M., Condello, L., Fels, L., Buxton, J. A., Janssen, P. A., Granger-Brown, A., Ramsden, V., Buchanan, M., and Elwood Martin, R. (2020). *Supporting women leaving prison through peer health mentoring: A participatory health research study. CMAJ Open*, **8**(1), E1–E8.

Miler, J. A., Carver, H., Foster, R., & Parkes, T. (2020). *Provision of peer support at the intersection of homelessness and problem substance use services: A systematic 'state of the art' review. BMC Public Health*, **20**(1), 641–641.

Moran, G., Russinova, Z., Yim, J. Y., and Sprague, C. (2014). *Motivations of persons with psychiatric disabilities to work in mental health peer services: A qualitative study using self-determination theory. Journal of Occupational Rehabilitation*, **24**(1), 32–41.

Munn-Giddings, C., & Borkman, T. (2017). *Reciprocity in peer-led mutual aid groups in the community: Implications for social policy and social work practices.* In M. Törrönen, C Munn-Goldings, & L. Tarkiainen (Eds.), *Reciprocal Relationships and Well-Being* (pp. 57–76). Routledge.

Musson, P. (2017). *Making Sense of Theory and Its Application to Social Work Practice.* Critical Publishing.

Nixon, S. (2020). *'Giving back and getting on with my life': Peer mentoring, desistance and recovery of ex-offenders. Probation Journal*, **67**(1), 47–64.

O'Connell, M. J., Sledge, W. H., Staeheli, M., Sells, D., Costa, M., Wieland, M., & Davidson, L. (2018). *Outcomes of a peer mentor intervention for persons with recurrent psychiatric hospitalization. Psychiatric Services*, **69**(7), 760–767.

O'Sullivan, R., Hart, W., & Healy, D. (2020). *Transformative rehabilitation: Exploring prisoners' experiences of the Community Based Health and First Aid programme in Ireland. European Journal on Criminal Policy and Research*, **26**(1), 63–81.

Payne, M. (2017). *Peer support in mental health: A narrative review of its relevance to social work. Egyptian Journal of Social Work*, **4**(1), 19–40.

Peate, I. (2017). *Fundamentals of Care: A Textbook for Health and Social Care Assistants.* Wiley.

Perrin, C., Frost, A., & Ware, J. B. (2018). *The utility of peer-support in enhancing the treatment of incarcerated sexual offenders. Therapeutic Communities: The International Journal of Therapeutic Communities*, **39**(1), 35–49.

Pollack, S. (2004), *Anti-oppressive social work practice with women in prison: Discursive reconstructions and alternative practices. British Journal of Social Work*, **34**(5), 693–707.

Prince's Trust (2012). *Evaluation Summary: Working One to One with Young Offenders*. Prince's Trust.

Reingle Gonzalez, J. M., Rana, R. E., Jetelina, K. K., & Roberts, M. H. (2019). *The value of lived experience with the criminal justice system: A qualitative study of peer re-entry specialists. International Journal of Offender Therapy and Comparative Criminology*, **63**(10), 1861–1875.

Sandhu, B. (2017). *The Value of Lived Experience in Social Change*. The Lived Experience. www.thelivedexperience.org

Scannell, C. (2021). *Voices of hope: Substance use peer support in a system of care. Substance Abuse: Research and Treatment*, **15**.

Schinkel, M., & Whyte, B. (2012). *Routes out of prison using life coaches to assist resettlement. The Howard Journal of Criminal Justice*, **51**(4), 359–371.

Sells, D., Curtis, A., Abdur-Raheem, J., Klimczak, M., Barber, C., Meaden, C., Hasson, J., Fallon, P., & Emigh-Guy, M. (2020). *Peer-mentored community reentry reduces recidivism. Criminal Justice and Behavior*, **47**(4), 437–456.

Seppings, C. (2016). *To Study the Rehabilitative Role of Ex-Prisoners/Offenders as Peer Mentors in Reintegration Models*. Winston Churchill Trust.

Spencer, R. (2007). *'It's not what I expected': A qualitative study of youth mentoring relationship failures. Journal of Adolescent Research*, **22**(4), 331–354.

Taylor, J., Burrowes, N., Disley, E., Liddle, M., Maguire, M., Rubin, J., & Wright, S. (2013). *Intermediate Outcomes of Mentoring Interventions: A Rapid Evidence Assessment*. National Offender Management Service.

Tinago, C. B., Frongillo, E. A., Warren, A. M., Chitiyo, V., Cifarelli, A. K., Fyalkowski, S., & Pauline, V. (2021). *Development and assessment of feasibility of a community-based peer support intervention to mitigate social isolation and stigma of adolescent motherhood in Harare, Zimbabwe. Pilot and Feasibility Studies*, **7**(1), 1–12.

Tracy, K., & Wallace, S. P. (2016). *Benefits of peer support groups in the treatment of addiction. Substance Abuse and Rehabilitation*, **7**, 143–154.

Voronka, J. (2017). *Turning mad knowledge into affective labor: The case of the peer support worker. American Quarterly*, **69**(2): 333–338.

Wagstaff, C., Palmer, M., & Salkeld, R. (2018). *An interpretative qualitative study into the experiences mental health peer mentor of an inner city mentoring and advocacy service. Psychiatry and Mental Disorders*, **1**, 103–108.

Williams, E. M., Hyer, J. M., Viswanathan, R., Faith, T. D., Voronca, D., Gebregzaibher, M., Oates, J. C., & Egede, L. (2018). *Peer-to-peer mentoring for African American women with lupus: A feasibility pilot. Arthritis Care & Research*, **70**(6), 908–917.

Willoughby, M., Parker, A., & Ali, R. (2013). *Mentoring for Offenders: Mapping Services for Adult Offenders in England and Wales*. Sova.

Chapter 12
Where Careers Intersect with Parenthood: How Mentoring Makes a Difference

Nicki Seignot

If Parent Mentoring was a metaphor it would be... a lifeline.
That might be a bit dramatic, but the way I was feeling was
dramatic. It was a massive shift.'

Looking back, I don't know how I would have made
the transition so easily without having had the
mentoring support.

Introduction

The Parent Mentor[5] has a mission; to raise awareness of the significance of the point where careers intersect with parenthood and the impact that this has on individuals and the organizations that employ them. This chapter builds up a case for the role of mentoring in supporting transitions to working parenthood. It elaborates on how mentoring can make a difference, offering benefits to individuals and organizations in a range of public and private sector settings with references to research and programmes developed over the last ten years.

Following parental leave and return to work, employees rarely reference an organization's policy provision for pay and time off; rather the narrative is one of deep personal change, raw emotions, seemingly endless questions, dilemmas, and tensions with the competing priorities of work and family. This is the vortex in which careers have the potential to derail.

What is the cost to an organization of disconnected or lost talent and expertise? The challenges are multifaceted: How does someone navigate a successful return to work and career AND still be the parent they want to be? What are the compromises? What are the non-negotiables? Who decides what is possible? How does someone ask for what they want when they have not even worked that out yet? Where, when, how and with whom should these conversations take place for best effect?

---

5   http://www.theparentmentor.co.uk/

We are clear on the power of internal mentoring as a triple win:

For mentees, one-to-one conversations which span the vital transition moments, questions and needs. Mentees feel 'invested in' at a time when returners (in organizations without mentoring programmes) may be left feeling unseen/forgotten. As one mentee put it: *'It is nice to know that there is someone I can talk to about my struggles and that the company cares.'* Critically mentoring is conducted in an offline space and peer-to-peer where there is a mutuality and shared understanding of the issues concerned with combining work and parenting.

> *You sometimes need to voice your concerns, be heard, and receive encouragement and advice from a believable person – my mentor provided that.*
>
> (Mentee)

For mentors, when upskilled to mentor, there is an opportunity to reflect on their own personal growth and learning through the experience of helping another parent-to-be. Mentors give a level of support they did not have themselves, but through mentoring recognize the difference it would have made to their own transition to working parenthood and the resumption of their career. Mentors tell us that it reconnects them to the organization through the investment in time and space.

> *I found it really healing. It refocused my belief in the business. It's an intimate time – you grow together.*
>
> (Mentor)

And for the organization, mentoring parents is a strategic investment in returning talent. Remember that these individuals were the future once; the high potentials, the graduates, the individual on track for a next promotion or landing that next key project. Its impact can be measured, for example, in levels of engagement, career progression, diversity of talent pipeline and reduced turnover. Mentoring is an opportunity to continue investing in the growth and development of an organization's people. The benefits apply to organizations in a wide range of areas, including the private and public sectors. Furthermore, mentoring contributes to a culture of inclusivity that acknowledges this key stage in life and career. From an return on investment (ROI) perspective, it is a self-sustaining development activity in that successive generations of mentees have the potential to become the next generation of mentors.

> *The organization is getting better and I am reaching out to mentor other young parents. Let's change the culture!*
>
> (Mentee)

A research perspective

Concerned with the retention and progression of women in the workplace, previous research has focused on the nature and influence of coaching and mentoring across maternity transitions (Seignot, 2013; Moffett & Seignot, 2020). Jane Moffett (2017) found coaching addressed key elements of returns to work including raising of profiles, signposting essential conversations, negotiating post-return work options and reflecting on long-term career development. It also offered women space to focus on 'self', evidencing broad and deep outcomes including developing greater self-kindness, cultivating a more positive mindset about themselves in a work context and establishing a work–life balance that works for them.

My own research into maternity mentoring (Seignot, 2013) set out with the aim of answering a specific question: In what ways does mentoring support the transition to working parenthood and reconnection with work and career post maternity? My findings revealed mentoring navigated a complex transition witnessing multiple endings and beginnings: ending work, beginning a maternity leave, beginning a different life with a new unremunerated, but 24/7 job, forging new networks, a life without the structures and rhythm of the working week, loss and separation from ending maternity leave, restarting work and finding the 'work me' again. The research evidenced a shift from career as the primary focus to that of realistic pragmatism associated with setting boundaries on time and working practices. For some of the participants, this shift was manifested in putting 'on hold' their plans for promotion, while for others, the career path was still on track, though interestingly not at any cost. Across the data set, and for both mentees and mentors, decisions for the future and career were qualified by wider considerations characterized by a new relationalism that had not been evident in their pre-maternity descriptions of self and work. Additionally, mentees sought affirmation and gained strength from mentors' confirmation of what was 'normal'.

> *She was reassuring, grounding me again, that it was ok; I wasn't being completely irrational because it was normal. But actually, it wasn't reality. If nothing else you get to drink a cup of coffee hot, and you get to sit and have lunch with adults. I remember the first day back sat at lunch thinking she was absolutely right.*
>
> (Mentee)

As members of the House of Commons All-Party Parliamentary Group for Women and Work, in 2019 Jane Moffett and I undertook an examination of policies and practices through the lens of working parenthood.[6] As professional coaches and advocates for

---

6   Moffett, J., & Seignot, N. (2020). *Policies and practices through the prism of working parenthood: An analysis of factors that help and hinder the engagement and retention of returning talent post parental leave.* The Parent Mentor/Kangaroo Coaching. https://onedrive.live.com/?cid = df0c597ed0ae7f42&id = DF0C597ED0AE7F42 %21165092&authkey = %21AMD7BHK335B11QI

coaching and mentoring we were curious to know the extent to which this specialist form of support was widespread across employers and its impact on work and the continuation of careers. Of our survey respondents, just 10% had received coaching, mentoring or support from workshops and family networks. Of the other 90% who had not had this, 83% wished that they had. What was clear from the research was the impact of coaching and mentoring in the following key areas:

- expediting their sense of being 'back up and running'
- increasing their confidence in asking for what they needed
- having their experiences validated through the connection with another working parent.

Our research showed that there were two key moments post return; at three months and six months respectively. When we correlated these moments with those respondents who had received additional support versus those without support, the impact was evident.

- 60% of returning parents felt 'back' in three months after enjoying coaching and mentoring support, compared to just 39% without support.
- 90% of people who had been mentored or coached reported they felt they were 'up and running' within six months, as opposed to 68% who received no additional support.

It made me feel more confident about coming back and that any challenges I would experience had already been overcome by others.

(Mentee)

Our findings indicated coaching and mentoring do make a difference – opening conversations which go beyond the everyday conversations in work. Additionally, the commentary and feedback from respondents built on previous research findings, suggesting benefits such as a safe space to focus on reconnecting with work self, to air emotions, to work through questions and concerns that perhaps would not be brought direct to a line manager and to address the myriad challenges associated with ending parental leave and returning to work.

It is important to reference the fact that research into coaching and mentoring to date has focused on the maternity context and the impact on women and their careers. While our most recent (2019) research had the ambition to gain insights into experiences of both mothers and fathers returning to work, with a respondent rate of 98% mothers, the reality was that the report did not generate the insights into men's experiences of fatherhood as hoped. We return to the theme and importance of mentoring fathers later in this chapter.

Learning to date

With over ten years' experience behind us working within organizations to establish mentoring programmes for returning parents, we wanted to share some key lessons within our specialist field of mentoring.

1. **The tension between a mentor's eagerness to offer guidance and a contrasting readiness by the mentee to engage.** Mentors bring their unique lived experience; they have been there, navigated their return, tackled the seismic challenges and questions associated with combining career and parenting, and hopefully they have come out the other side acknowledging the journey is never truly completed! Typically, they have a passion to help, to share their story and experiences with the aim of giving someone else the help they did not have but now recognize the absolute value of – '*I wish I'd had this help when I was coming back to work. It would have made such a difference to me.*' In contrast, a parent-to-be may not immediately 'buy' the need for mentoring and consequently can take time to engage and commit. Without careful positioning, mentoring programmes for parents-to-be can be regarded by prospective mentees as a deficit model, the inference being there is a problem to 'fix', a gap, that they need 'help' – none of which are likely to resonate with a prospective mentee. Mentoring, at this point, can feel like an unnecessary time-stealer, fighting for space in a diary that is already at capacity. Someone is offering to fix an issue they do not yet identify with, as opposed to a positive investment in the 'future' them. Positive communication is everything.

2. **Stop, start, deep dive – fluctuations in pace and progress.** These mentoring journeys are defined by visibly steep highs and lows, driven in no small part by the scale of change, the all-consuming new job of becoming a parent and the individual's physical and psychological absence from the work environment. Mentees are appropriately absorbed in their new arena, living the reality of this new 'job', writing and rewriting the emerging script of first-time parenthood. In parallel, occupied by a full-on work schedule, perhaps with a mentee off grid, not seeking their time or help, mentors can sometimes disconnect themselves from the mentoring programme. Understanding the contrasting priorities and distractions of mentor and mentee, and overlaying these with good practice approaches to communication and engagement, will help keep your mentoring programme on track and is an essential element of effective preparation workshops. The top tip is to know when to connect and when to give space, recognizing that there will be points of absolute need and other times where there is zero capacity or need for mentoring.

3. **Prioritizing mentoring – seeing it as a legitimate work activity.** A busy returner can feel submerged by the demands on their time as they bring together the competing priorities of home and getting back up to speed in a busy job. In the vortex of this new life, creating space for mentoring, where they effectively pause, take time to reflect and put the work in on 'self', can feel an indulgence. Mentors need help to recognize this dilemma in a mentee and to be resourced with 'how and when' to encourage their mentee to see this as a legitimate work activity and positive use of time. As one mentor shared: '*It was just another work meeting she didn't have time for. We reached the point where she let her guard down and she was able to share her struggles with me. After then we could turn the corner.*'

Mentoring is an enabler to get back up and running sooner. Employers need talented people, with the skills and experience they bring, to return motivated and ready to engage. In the words of one mentee:

> *Mentoring lets me talk about myself, when there is no more time for myself.*

(Mentee)

4. **The mentor's burden.** As parent mentors we bring what we have learned through experience to a mentoring relationship but this knowledge can sometimes lead to mentors dropping into solution mode; having the answers and trying to fix, to solve *for* rather than *with* the mentee. We see this with questions prefixed by phrases such as *'Have you thought about...?', 'Have you tried...?'* and *'Have you asked...?'* The key here is preparing mentors well, working with their positive desire to help, encouraging them to balance advice with questions, to remain curious and to hold space for a mentee to speak their own truth, self-resource, and work through their own ideas and possibilities. Not every mentoring conversation can achieve resolution to an issue. Sometimes a mentee may leave a discussion still stuck, but with options or ideas to reflect on at their own pace. The conversation can be a catalyst to different thinking. We remind mentors their role is not to solve all their mentee's issues and problems. It is not possible and, quite frankly, it is an exhausting proposition.

5. **Supervision reviews** are an opportunity to signpost and explore dilemmas with well-meaning mentors. It is a skilled mentor that can just listen and be in the moment with their mentee; at the same time noticing what is triggered within themselves as a consequence of what gets brought to mentoring but not necessarily bringing that into the conversation. In one supervision review, one of the dads shared this anecdote: *'I just spent an hour talking with my mentee about hypnobirthing and he's got all the plans sorted. I was absolutely sitting on my hands thinking I can't tell him that this is all going to go out the window on the day. I was desperate to tell him how it was actually going to be!'* The key is the effective set up of a mentor, for them to know their own story and to be able to walk alongside their mentee, nudging, and asking questions from their own experience that prompt thinking and possibilities. Well-timed questions can also help the individual to evaluate what is important to them and what now constitutes success, which may well look different from life before.

6. **Mentoring returners is a business-based activity.** There is a clear objective that mentoring programmes of this nature are about retention and engagement of much needed talent, skills and experience. On this basis, when a mentor connects with a mentee on parental leave, even though they are not the line manager, this is still someone from 'work' getting in touch. Depending on what is happening for the mentee still on leave, they may not even be ready to engage with the thought of work yet. Good practice is for mentors to remain sensitive in this context when brokering the reconnection. Communications do not have to be synchronous (emails can be responded to when ready as opposed to a phone call), but the reality is that a mentor getting in touch signals a change in dynamics and the start of a different phase for the mentee.

7. **Mentoring needs to end as well as it starts.** For some mentoring pairs, there can be a reluctance to bring things to a close. Returns to work are often emotionally charged and both parties will have achieved a level of trust, with some becoming work-based friendships, having engaged in a level of disclosure not typically associated with work-based conversations. With this in mind, it is important to prepare mentors for ending well. We need to go back to the original objective, that is to support a return to work and, when that is done, to facilitate a conversation around moving forward. Ending well is a time to look back, to acknowledge progress and to give thanks for the journey as well as encourage a mentee to plan for how they will resource this next stage of their career and working life.

> *Quite honestly, I didn't know the value of that session until I'd done it. You get a real sense of what you've achieved through the process. It was also a chance to share what I personally took from the mentoring and what I was proud of.*

> (Mentor)

Mentoring new fathers at work

> *Men only have a couple of week's leave and then they're back into it. It's the single biggest upheaval in your life.*

> (Mentee)

Our early mentoring programmes were positioned as 'parent mentoring' in an effort to be as inclusive as possible and encourage new fathers to engage with the process as well as returning mothers. Correspondingly, David Clutterbuck and I wrote *Mentoring New Parents at Work* (Seignot & Clutterbuck, 2017), taking what we believed to be an inclusive approach to encourage internal mentoring programmes as sustainable good practice for support for all parents returning to the workplace. In acknowledging the volume of support and need (particularly in terms of gender diversity) is concerned with women combining a career and parenting, it followed that most of the programmes in those early years were in fact mentoring maternity returns to work.

Today, our experience of working within organizations indicates modern-day fatherhood is in the midst of a shift; a shift in how we talk about fatherhood and how dads see their role in the broader context of family and work. The more businesses we worked with, the more fathers were coming to our sessions as mentors and mentees. These were a new generation of millennial fathers wanting a different experience of family and career. Research by Daddilife (2019) indicates that the current generation of fathers want to be actively present in family life with 87% of millennial dads saying they are mostly or fully involved in day-to-day parenting and 63% requesting some form of flexibility at work since becoming a father. Correspondingly, we saw more dads joining our programmes.

Of course, some of the approaches and frameworks for mentoring mothers can also be applied to new fathers, but working with these fathers in our mentoring programmes illustrated the need to differentiate, and not homogenize under one umbrella of 'parenthood'. From listening to these fathers, it was clear that their journey is demonstrably different to that of a new mother – with its own distinct cadence and lexicon, and extended timeline with a bunch of new themes, challenges and tensions.

There's so much support for new mums – not so for dads. I come home from work and give her a break – but you're not getting any support yourself. Having mentoring meant I was not alone, didn't have to be resentful and it did help our conversations. We were both getting support.

(Mentee)

Working with Han-Son Lee, author and founder of Daddilife,[7] whose mission is to shine a new light on modern-day fatherhood, we have since reshaped what good looks like for mentoring dads. Correspondingly, our mentoring tools and approaches have been tailored to meet the specific challenges of modern-day fatherhood to enable productive conversations and effective support. Our learning so far indicates:

- It takes time and trust for dads to open up beyond the transactional conversations.
- Men's emotional language at work is different to women's and men are not always the best at being truly open. This is why mentoring is key. As men, safe spaces for dads are hard to find, especially when modern-day fatherhood at work is at odds with previous generations of fathers – who are potentially sitting in senior leadership roles within an organization.
- Many fathers are working in business cultures which are defined by outdated expectations of gender and parenting stereotypes. Mentoring has the potential to broker conversations to disrupt this.
- Contemporary fathers are looking for tips, ideas and solutions to help with: conversations with partners; dealing with the 'banter'; and conversations with 'dyed-in-the-wool' line managers in relation to flexible working and taking extended time off/sharing parental leave – and value the reminder that 'it is not just me'.
- Last, mentors bring their (gendered) experience to a mentoring relationship first. Therefore, good practice must be for working mothers to mentor returning mothers and fathers to mentor fathers, in a context and language that is theirs and implicitly understood from the outset.

'You're dealing with the challenges at local level and you don't get that chance to think bigger about how does this interact with our entire lives and careers. It comes at you with such high speed!'

(Mentee)

---

7   https://www.daddilife.com

As more employers seek to enhance shared parental leave and paternity leave, we believe it is essential to normalize parenting across genders. But we need to help employers engage with working fathers differently, validating their role as parents as well as employees. We would argue that employers are interested but do not have the road map. If we encourage dads to talk and collaborate, mentoring has the potential to make a difference. Mentoring is also a positive reinforcement to those who may not have many role models when it comes to senior representation of modern-day dads at work. We often call this the 'boardroom dad' vs the 'modern-day dad' and that is a huge part of why mentoring can be so powerful. It creates the examples and real-time breakthroughs which may not be evident at a more senior level.

Conclusion

We remain passionate about the potential of mentoring to change conversations around working parenthood – for individuals and the organizations that employ them. While we acknowledge mentoring is not a panacea, we argue that its very nature makes it an essential element of diversity and inclusion and talent strategies. It is a long-term investment in people, and in the future of business and public sector organizations. That team member who has just announced they are about to become a new mum, or a new father – what is possible? Let's start the conversation.

References

Daddilife (2019). *The Millennial Dad at Work*. https://www.daddilife.com/wp-content/uploads/2019/05/The-Millenial-Dad-at-Work-Report-2019.pdf

Moffett, J. (2017). *'My Life Has Fundamentally Changed': The Relationship between Maternity Coaching and Mothers' Transitions Back to Work'* [Unpublished MSc dissertation]. Henley Business School.

Moffett, J., & Seignot, N. (2020). *Policies and Practices through the Prism of Working Parenthood: An Analysis of Factors that Help and Hinder the Engagement and Retention of Returning Talent Post Parental Leave*. The Parent Mentor/Kangaroo Coaching. http://www.theparentmentor.co.uk/news

Seignot, N. (2013). *'MumtoMum': A Reflective Study into How Mentoring Supports the Transition to Working Parenthood and Reconnection with Work and Career Post Maternity*. Sheffield Hallam University Business School.

Seignot, N., & Clutterbuck, D. (2017). *Mentoring New Parents at Work: A Practical Guide for Businesses and Organisations*. Routledge. https://www.amazon.com/Mentoring-New-Parents-at-Work/dp/1138188719

Chapter 13
Mentoring for Psychologists: A Support Infrastructure for Diverse Needs

Rachel Scudamore, Dawn Gosden, Angela Carter & Helen Pote

The psychology context

Members of the British Psychological Society (BPS), the UK's professional body for the psychological professions, occupy diverse roles and work contexts. The domains of practice identified by regulated titles (Clinical, Counselling, Educational, Forensic, Health, Occupational and Sport & Exercise Psychologist) and non-regulated domains, such as coaching psychology and cyberpsychology, embrace a broad range of interactions with people in settings varying across schools, homes, workplaces, health centres, prisons, the military and hospitals, and in contexts of public service, private employment, the third sector and independent practice. This is, of course, alongside the academic branch of psychology with its focus on research and education as a complement to practitioner activity.

Across this diversity, there is a common call to the BPS to support mentoring activities as a core contribution to both professional development and to personal well-being. This demand reflects Kram's (1983) early identification of both the career development and the psychosocial benefits that can accrue from mentoring relationships, which have been more recently developed by Merrick (2017) to underpin a step-by-step guide to establishing a purposeful mentoring programme. In the Society's recent extensive consultation project, BPS members placed a clear emphasis on community building and mutual support as central to members' development. This demand from psychologists is evident in the context of clinical psychology in Rao et al.'s (2021) identification of the importance of a caring work culture, with a particular focus on the related activity of supervision. For a practicing psychologist supervision, broadly characterized as the regular discussion of current practice with an experienced colleague, is an essential component of the culture of professionalism. Rao et al.'s (2021) publication, issued by the Society's Division of Clinical Psychology, identifies 'reflective spaces' as important for offering 'intellectual challenge and reflective decision-making' (Rao et al., 2021) and highlights mentoring as contributing to this aim, illustrating both the ubiquity of the demand and the specificity of need in any one context.

This chapter addresses the challenge for the BPS of meeting a universal professional need for mentoring situated in a range of cultures and contexts with varying purposes.

The Society is also keen for mentoring to contribute to its commitment to '*promote and advocate for diversity and inclusion within the discipline and profession of psychology...*' (British Psychological Society [BPS], 2021) as informed by voices such as those from NHS England (2022), from trainees in the profession (Wright, 2020) and from those seeking to enter the profession (Ragaven, 2018). We will first review two mentoring schemes that were already being led by BPS members before the Society took up this challenge. One scheme addresses the inclusion of under-represented groups in geographically spread members in the south-west of England. The other addresses the development of leadership skills in the context of clinical psychology in National Health Service (NHS) services. These pen portraits give an insight into the contribution of mentoring in the psychological professions and demonstrate a common thread of the application of supervision expertise in the mentoring context. We will then outline how the Society, as the learned society and professional body for psychology and psychologists, has worked with experienced members to develop a Mentoring Service that establishes core governance to ensure high-quality and safe practice while providing an infrastructure within which members can run and evaluate distinct mentoring programmes, offering mutual support for their identified needs and audiences.

BPS South West of England Branch career mentoring case study

The BPS South West of England Branch Coaching and Mentoring Programme (hereafter the scheme) was introduced in November 2020 following a compelling case made by its members wanting career support, not just at the beginning, but at various stages in their career journey. The scheme caters for the range of psychology roles and contexts of the branch, taking a non-specialist approach where individuals can feel safe talking about their career aspirations through coaching conversations and providing an opportunity to showcase how involvement in the branch would add value to their BPS membership. Highlighting leading-edge, evidence-based coaching and mentoring, we include coaching as a 'third generation' practice focusing on a collaborative and co-creative approach (Stelter, 2014). Further, with an aim to build a coaching and mentoring community, an innovative supervision process is provided by the scheme leader to support the coach mentors to learn from each other in the safety of the supervision environment (Merrick & Stokes, 2011). Therefore, using a mixture of coaching and/or mentoring approaches, depending on the requirements of the mentee, the scheme provides benefits to mentees and mentors alike.

Building the programme

Research evidence supports the value of coaching cultures in organizations, but, until recently, there has been a lack of evidence about how to embed coaching cultures to benefit all, and not just the talented few (Passmore & Crabbe, 2021). While acknowledging differences between mentoring and coaching, there are also fundamental similarities and synergies that can be useful in career development mentoring. Key skills such as supporting through building trust and commitment, attentive listening and challenge are common to both (Garvey, 2014, pp. 364). As mentoring now increasingly takes place in a coaching world, we draw the evidence base for our scheme from these similarities and differences between coaching and mentoring (Garvey, 2014, pp. 362–363).

With experience of 'third generation' coaching practice (Stelter, 2014) and knowledge of the benefits coaching provides to individuals seeking to make career transitions, the scheme leader put together a series of coaching questions that could be used as part of the mentoring process. The sessions (three, one-hour virtual meetings) were designed for the coach mentors to create a reflective space for the mentees to explore their career aspirations. Questions were drawn from recognized approaches to coaching, for example, GROW (Whitmore, 2002), enabling individuals to develop a deeper knowledge of themselves to better equip them to pursue career search activities. Evaluation of the first pilot scheme revealed mentees initially lacked self-confidence and self-efficacy in terms of their belief in their abilities to achieve career goals. The coaching questions were a valuable tool to support reflection and build confidence.

Additionally, the scheme leader's experience of design and implementation of a previous 'coaching for all' strategy, which included coach supervision, led to a confidence that this scheme did not need to rely solely on experienced coach mentors. Individuals with a passion for coaching and mentoring, but with little experience, could be equally effective coach mentors provided that sufficient high-quality training and supervision is provided.

The scheme leader provides regular group supervision for the coach mentors, giving opportunity to discuss problems and concerns, to obtain feedback and to gain knowledge and skills through networking with the supervisor and their peers. Additionally, ad hoc one-to-one coach supervision sessions are offered, providing further support for the coach mentors and valuable opportunities for quality assurance. Access to these supervision sessions proves valuable when things go wrong, or when an ethical problem arises where the coach mentor requires support and guidance that cannot wait until the next group coach supervision meeting.

Evaluation and recommendations for development

The scheme was reviewed using the Totado Model of evaluation (Birdi, 2010), examining effectiveness at an organizational level by surveying the views of the BPS branch committee, and at team and individual levels by surveying mentors and mentees. Since its conception, three cohorts of mentees have taken part in the scheme and each cohort is thoroughly evaluated before commencing the next intake to ensure lessons learned are taken forward.

The latest evaluation survey in May 2022 revealed, at the organizational level, the value of the scheme being: money well spent; a source to improve members' career well-being; improvement of mentees' knowledge of career opportunities; and improvement of opportunities across the region. At team level, mentors saw the benefits of the scheme for themselves (e.g., in performance and development) as well as for the mentees. Mentors reported satisfaction with the materials and training as summed up in the following comment:

> *It has boosted my confidence and I really enjoyed being able to support and offer value to the mentees, the feedback they gave was fantastic and I really enjoyed being a small part of their journey. I was able to be true to myself whilst using the guidance questions and notes to offer structure and a framework for the sessions.*

(Mentor)

At the individual level, mentees saw the benefits of the scheme supporting their career planning and decision-making. Mentees reported gaining value from the scheme that changed how they felt about their career prospects and possibilities. For example:

> *I now have a much clearer understanding of the differences between roles in the psychological profession which has helped me to become clearer with where I am headed.*

> (Mentee)

Overall, the evaluation provides evidence at all levels of the effectiveness and impact of the scheme. Differences were noted between mentors and mentees in terms of preference for the number of sessions provided; mentees stating they would have preferred more sessions, but mentors reporting that three sessions were sufficient for the mentees to identify and make progress with their career goals. Successfully recruiting two past mentees to train to become mentors, and their positive feedback after their experiences in Cohort 3, demonstrated that those with no experience can be trained and quickly become effective within mentoring schemes. Based on this evaluation, Cohort 4 will move forward with an unchanged design, offering mentees three coaching and mentoring sessions over a three-month period.

Sharing our work to inspire others

As the scheme acts as a pilot to the wider BPS Mentoring Service and in pursuit of spreading the word to other branches about the benefits of mentoring, a working relationship has been forged with the North West Branch chair with the aim of sharing successes and lessons learned and to encourage the branch to set up a mentoring scheme. This objective was achieved through a BPS webinar event on 16 June 2022, open to all members of the BPS: *Coaching Community and Career Development – A North West and South West Branches Event*, receiving positive feedback from the attending delegates.

Clinical Psychologists as Leaders (CPL) mentoring scheme

The BPS Division of Clinical Psychology (DCP) launched the Clinical Psychologists as Leaders (CPL) mentoring scheme in 2018, building on the success of two separate schemes for junior and senior psychologists.

Leadership skills are a central part of the Care Quality Commission (CQC) agenda, and the evolving landscape of the National Health Service (NHS) suggests that psychologists need strong leadership skills to manage change processes. These contextual priorities, along with evidence connecting better leadership to better patient care (West et al., 2015), place leadership competencies as core competencies for the profession.

The scheme intends to promote a culture of mentoring and to develop the capacity within the profession to provide leadership support for itself, particularly addressing barriers to leadership that are to do with exclusion, such as race, ethnicity and gender. The aim is to engage all DCP Clinical Psychologist members to move beyond direct clinical applications of their doctoral-level training and to make greater use of applied psychology expertise in organizational strategy, behaviour change and people management, research and media communication. NHS commissioners and senior managers were clear that psychologists can have greater impact on the mental health and well-being of the four nations by playing a key leadership role in strategy, service development and delivery.

A combined development and mentoring programme

The Division set up a steering group to oversee its mentoring developments in 2016 and gained funding from the BPS to support the next-phase CPL scheme in 2018. As is increasingly common in psychological settings, the plans included input from the Experts by Experience group – people who have lived experience of mental illness and the use of psychological services – to ensure that leadership development efforts can be connected to enhanced services delivered to clients.

The new CPL programme had a dual purpose of developing a mentoring infrastructure across the career span, and developing a complementary leadership and mentoring resource.

The DCP has been active in leadership development for many years, including publishing the Clinical Psychology Leadership Development Framework (Skinner et al., 2010) that maps clinical, professional and strategic skills across the career span, from trainee through practicing and consultant psychologist to clinical director roles. This CPL mentoring scheme was also informed by the NHS Healthcare Leadership Model (NHS Leadership Academy, 2013) which sets out domains, including 'engaging the team' and 'holding to account', which characterize the expected impact of leaders. Both these models underpinned the CPL mentoring scheme's initial self-assessment questions for mentees, and the evaluative post-mentoring surveys and interviews.

Leadership resources were designed for busy NHS clinicians and included simple tips on how to approach senior managers for experience, seek opportunities outside psychology, locally and nationally, and ideas to set up new initiatives. In addition, there were self-directed learning materials for short just-in-time learning, and a programme of face-to-face (until March 2020) and virtual development seminars on topics such as 'using your voice' in advocating for the role of psychology. Guidance for mentees and mentors on conducting a constructive and effective relationship was provided, setting out the expectations of each party for safe practice, and encouraging participants to take account of the challenges of facing exclusion and the well-being of the psychological workforce.

Participation

Recruitment to the scheme was through a presence at formal BPS events, articles in newsletters and emails, plus social media activity, conversations in the DCP chat room and reaching out to doctoral training alumni networks.

In November 2020, the scheme reported that 149 mentees and 54 mentors were engaged in the programme, with at least 39 self-reported pairings ongoing, from an initial expression of interest from 306 members of the Division. Of the mentees, 20% had been qualified for less than five years, and a further 30% between six and eleven years, with the remaining having more than twelve years' experience as a practicing psychologist. The cohort were majority female (79%), reflecting the profession as a whole, and were working in a range of specialities with varying client groups. Many already held service development and staff supervision roles that required leadership skills.

The scheme's self-matching model allowed mentees to select from a list of mentors, each of whom had been asked to provide a short vignette to outline their clinical and leadership experience, location and ability to support those from under-represented groups. Mentors were generally selected from outside the mentee's immediate managerial and supervisory structures.

All pairings were intended to run for six monthly sessions of an hour, plus a review. At an initial meeting, the pair evaluated their potential to work together and formally agreed to proceed and collaboratively set goals, or to decline the match. Both mentor and mentee completed pre-mentoring and post-mentoring evaluation forms and standardized ratings of their leadership skills, detailing also their goals for engaging in mentoring.

Regular and focused communication with participants, and with potential participants, was key to the scheme's momentum, including a monthly bulletin highlighting relevant developmental opportunities and offering ideas for mentoring session discussions, a quarterly call for new joiners, updates to the wider Division members to maintain the profile of the programme, communications with the thirty UK DClinPsy education programmes, and contributions to the BPS online blog, *The Psychologist* *magazine* and the Division's own *Clinical Psychology Forum* newsletter.

Experience, impact and developments

Mentees who completed the six sessions reported that their leadership skills improved significantly after mentoring (score comparison pre- and post-mentoring $p = 0.022$, $n = 23$) and many of the twenty-three reflected that mentoring helped them achieve their goals. Qualitative feedback provided specific examples of how mentoring improved mentees' ability to work with others and to take responsibility within their job role. As hoped for by Rao et al. (2021), participants reported the value of the experience in creating a reflective space for considering challenges and alternative perspectives.

Mentors reported finding value in the experience as one that developed their own understanding of their leadership skills, including identifying effective elements of leadership in a range of contexts. While they felt valued and useful to mentees, they also noted that they would welcome further support in understanding differences between coaching and mentoring, and insight into different models of mentoring that they might employ during sessions.

Senior psychologists have been requesting a similar programme for peer mentoring between colleagues facing common challenges in advancing the contribution of clinical psychology at an organizational level in NHS Trusts. An additional demand for mentoring by those still in training underlines how this approach to career development is well suited across the career span of the profession.

In the words of the steering group's Expert by Experience, Robert:

> *From a service user's perspective...the overall purpose of the CPL project, and of each psychologist's career, is to aid and improve the ability to understand better clients' mental health conditions, and therefore increase an ability to treat them more effectively.*

> *...though we tread the higher corridors of the profession, we are only as good as our ability to listen, to understand, and to help to heal, and everything flows from that – our positions of leadership, our academic papers, the teaching and mentoring, formal or informal, which we may do. It is not that we should aim to travel upwards, but to travel deeper, and our guide in all these things is that frail, uncertain, timorous voice of the client, a frail voice, yes, but one which should provide the lead in all we do, and which alone gives us real authority and leadership.*

The DCP is looking to enable new initiatives, making use of a new BPS Mentoring Service infrastructure, in line with our increased emphasis on looking after the psychological workforce, particularly in the light of the COVID-19 pandemic, to ensure sustainable services that are best able to provide effective help to others.

Acknowledgements: Professor Helen Pote (Project Principal Investigator and Finance Lead) would like to thank the steering group and particularly Dr Jenny Taylor (Project Lead), who managed the scheme, and Melissa Stock (Research Assistant), who supported the administration and evaluation of the scheme.

BPS Mentoring Service: The role of the professional body in empowering members

For Finkelstein and Poteet (2007), it is important to align the design of a mentoring scheme with its purposes and organizational culture, and Allen et al. (2009) advise establishing scheme-specific objectives and guarding against adopting a one-size-fits-all model. As illustrated across these two case studies, for BPS members there is no singular purpose or culture and it would be inappropriate, therefore, for the Society to launch a single mentoring scheme and fail to embrace the specificity of our two case studies here. As an organization, the Society has a long history of supporting flexibility across the professions and to enable context-specific variations would be essential to its role. Megginson et al. (2006) identify separate roles for organizations and for scheme leaders in contributing to mentoring success, and for the BPS it was important both to attend to the organization's responsibilities, including funding, evaluation, quality assurance, safeguarding, data control and risk management, and to ensure scheme leaders are supported in attending to their responsibilities within their member-focused schemes.

The Society established a Mentoring Service Steering Group (MSSG), reporting to the Trustees through its strategic Member Board, to address this challenge. The Steering Group comprised members with experience of running mentoring schemes, including the case studies here, so that the Society could be guided by knowledgeable voices. The group also includes the BPS Careers Manager to ensure that an understanding of the individual schemes contributes fully to the development of the Society's mentoring offer and its position within wider strategic objectives.

A core proposal for the BPS Mentoring Service was to provide an evidence-based framework to steer scheme leaders in considering the relevant factors in their particular scheme designs, to set expectations of the roles involved, to provide evaluation materials and to offer an infrastructure of technology and community to support their efforts. The MSSG has completed its work on the design of governance and preparation of guidance and has steered the selection and implementation of a technical platform on which Society schemes now run.

Potential scheme leaders applying to be a part of the BPS Mentoring Service are guided in setting up the detailed specifications of how their scheme is to run, underpinned by adaptable templates and core policies to ensure safe and impactful practice. They are also required to commit time to run their scheme, to support their mentors, and to engage in monitoring and evaluation activity. This process engages new scheme leaders in a conversation with experienced colleagues and begins their involvement in a community of practice around mentoring.

For approved schemes, the Service offers an online environment that has been built to host mentor and mentee profiles, to enable self-matching by participants or administrator-led matching according to the preference of each scheme leader, to offer a structure for setting goals and reviewing progress, to facilitate regular communication between the scheme leader and participants and between mentor and mentee to keep the relationships on track, and to simplify evaluation methods with customizable survey tools. All of this operates on a scheme-level basis so that each scheme leader has control over their own scheme but cannot view anybody else's scheme, while BPS admin can take an overview of all schemes and support the establishment of new schemes as demand grows. On an ongoing basis, the Member Board will oversee the portfolio of schemes and their evaluation, and BPS careers staff will lead on community building between Society scheme leaders with regular forums and input from specialist contributors.

As such, the BPS is running a decentralized model, as described by Koczka (2017), granting autonomy in scheme design, with associated responsibilities, to scheme leaders, and providing infrastructural support, alongside the expectation of minimum service levels and ongoing evaluation to contribute into Society-wide development.

An emerging theme from psychologists' mentoring schemes is the adaptation of the cultural and practice norm of supervision to support mentors in their roles. This will be important in ensuring sustainability for schemes by foregrounding the value to mentors as well as mentees, as described by Holland (2018). Although the Mentoring Service is in its nascent phase, it is clear that a supervisory approach is relevant to supporting scheme leaders in their roles too. A further contribution of the professional body is to develop and support a scheme leader community and to ensure that lessons learned are shared broadly across schemes for application in individual schemes where appropriate, or to change the BPS Mentoring Service infrastructure where they are evidently of value across the profession's approach to mentoring. Our ongoing Service evaluation, underpinned by members who are at the forefront of developing a psychologists' take on mentoring, will be key to capturing good practice and enabling the flourishing of a range of focused mentoring schemes.

References

Allen, T. D., Finkelstein, L. M., & Poteet, M. L. (2009). *Designing Workplace Mentoring Programmes: An Evidence-Based Approach.* Wiley-Blackwell.

Birdi, K. (2010). The Taxonomy of Training and Development Outcomes (TOTADO): A New Model of Training Evaluation [Conference presentation]. BPS Division of Occupational Psychology Conference, Brighton, UK.

British Psychological Society (2021). *Strategic Framework 2021–2022.* British Psychological Society. https://www.bps.org.uk/news/strategic-framework-2021-2022

British Psychological Society (2022). *Coaching Community and Career Development: A North West and South West Branches Event,* Online Webinar, 16th June, 2022.

Finkelstein, L. M., & Poteet, M. L. (2007). *Best practices for workplace formal mentoring programs.* In T. D. Allen, & L. T. Eby (Eds.), *The Blackwell Handbook of Mentoring: A Multiple Perspectives Approach* (pp. 345–367). Blackwell Publishing.

Garvey, B. (2014). *Mentoring in a coaching world.* In E. Cox, T. Bachkirova, and D. Clutterbuck (Eds.), *The Complete Handbook of Coaching* (**2nd ed.**, pp. 361–374). SAGE.

Holland, E. (2018). *Mentoring communities of practice: What's in it for the mentor? International Journal of Mentoring and Coaching in Education,* **7**(2), 110–126.

Koczka, T. (2017). *The role of the mentoring programme co-ordinator.* In D. A. Clutterbuck, F. Kochan, L. G. Lunsford, N. Dominguez, & J. Haddock-Millar (Eds.), *The SAGE Handbook of Mentoring.* SAGE.

Kram, K. E. (1983). *Phases of the mentor relationship. Academy of Management Journal,* **26**(4), 608–625.

Megginson, D., Clutterbuck, D., Garvey, B., Stokes, P., & Garrett-Harris, R. (2006), *Mentoring in Action: A Practical Guide* (**2nd ed.**). Kogan Page.

Merrick, L. (2017). *Design of effective mentoring programmes.* In D.A. Clutterbuck, F. Kochan, L.G. Lunsford, N. Dominguez, & J. Haddock-Millar (Eds.) *The SAGE Handbook of Mentoring.* SAGE.

Merrick, L., & Stokes, P. (2011). *Supervision in mentoring rogrammes.* In T. Bachkirova, P. Jackson, & D. Clutterbuck (Eds.), *Coaching and Mentoring Supervision: Theory and Practice* (pp. 207–215). Open University Press, McGraw Hill Education.

NHS England (2022). *NHS Workforce Race Equality Standard.* NHS England. https://www.england.nhs.uk/about/equality/equality-hub/workforce-equality-data-standards/equality-standard/

NHS Leadership Academy (2013). *NHS Leadership Model.* NHS England. https://www.leadershipacademy.nhs.uk/healthcare-leadership-model/

Passmore, J., & Crabbe, K. (2021). *Developing a coaching culture in your organisation.* In J. Passmore (Ed.), *The Coaches' Handbook: The Complete Practitioner Guide for Professional Coaches* (pp. 24–35). Routledge.

Ragaven, R. N. (2018). *Experiences of Black, Asian and Minority Ethnic Clinical Psychology Doctorate Applicants within the UK.* [ClinPsy.D thesis, University of Hertfordshire].

Rao, A. S., Kemp, N., Bhutani, G., Morris, R., Summers, E., Brown, K., Clarke, J., & Neal, A. (2021). *Building a Caring Work Culture: What Good Looks Like.* Division of Clinical Psychology, British Psychological Society.

Skinner, P., Toogood, R., Cate, T., Jones, G., Prescott, T., Coak, A., Lamers, C., Reed, E., McCusker, C., Robertson, A., & Rooney, N. (2010). *Clinical Psychology Leadership Development Framework.* Division of Clinical Psychology, British Psychological Society.

Stelter, R. (2014). *A Guide to Third Generation Coaching Narrative: Collaborative Theory and Practice.* Springer.

West, M., Armit, K., Loewenthal, L., Eckert, R., West, T., & Lee, A. (2015). *Leadership and Leadership Development in Health care: The Evidence Base.* Faculty of Medical Leadership and Management, Center for Creative Leadership, The King's Fund. https://www.kingsfund.org.uk/sites/default/files/field/field_publication_file/leadership-leadership-development-health-care-feb-2015.pdf

Whitmore, J. (2002). *Coaching for Performance: GROWing People, Performance and Purpose* (**3rd ed.**). Nicholas Brealey.

Wright, R. (2020). *Navigating Blackness in educational psychology: Reflections of a trainee educational psychologist. Educational Psychology Research and Practice,* **6**(1), 1–9.

Part 2:
Mentoring Approaches to Leadership Development and Legacy

Part 2:

Chapter 14
Mentoring Leaders for Courage, Compassion and Change

Stephen Murgatroyd

The four futures for leadership

This is a volatile, uncertain, complex and ambiguous (VUCA) world in which trust in organizations, professionals and sources of information are being questioned (Edelman, 2021) and leadership is challenged to create future-focused narratives which inspire, enable, engage and encourage their colleagues to work together for a different future. For leaders, this work is challenging and demanding and requires a real sense of both what it is to be themselves and what it is to be part of a team (Tillich, 1952; van Loon & Buster, 2019). They have to be both leaders and followers and be their authentic selves in both aspects of their intertwined selves.

They also have to work from the future back to the present, keeping the future constantly in mind when leading teams and initiatives focused on present- and near-term concerns. Indeed, as one leader said in a recent mentoring session, '*I have to be a learner and stay futures focused if I want to position this organization for its emerging and different future.*'

Many leaders cannot do this, which is why many speak of a crisis in leadership (Lipman-Blumen, 2006; Kellerman, 2012; Tourish, 2020). In part, this is because self-interest ('what's in it for me?') has become more prevalent (Davis, 2009). But it is also because leadership has increasingly been focused on the current and future financial performance of organizations, revenue potential and cost control, rather than the achievement of the organization's purpose and the development of meaningful work that has a real impact in terms of achieving the organization's larger mission.

Also, leaders are often so engaged with 'the present time' that they do not really see possible and probable futures. They are paying attention to what is clear to see – current challenges, operational issues, people issues, money – rather than what should matter most, what the organization and its people need to become if they are to be a positive influence on the future world and the sectors in which they operate. Getting past the 'small stuff' and focusing and aligning all on the direction being taken is the task of leadership.

Benjamin Bratton (2017) has explored the nature of these challenges using two dimensions, derived from reading Deleuze and Guattari (1977) and others: (a) *sensing* (what we pay attention to) and (b) *connectedness* (the work of becoming and following).

- **Dimension one – Sensing:** What we pay attention to

  This is what we refer to as the 'sensing' dimension. It refers to the issues, developments and activities we pay most attention to: what do we attend to, whom do we attend to and why? Some pay attention to a great many of the features that will shape our future (changing technologies, demographics, patterns of work, global developments) and see patterns and connections between them. Others live their lives paying little or no attention to what is happening around them, but focusing on the specific operational challenges.

- **Organizing question:** What is noticed and counted by whom and why?

- **Dimension two – Connectedness**

  Some live their lives as if they were 'masters of their universe' and see the world through the lens of 'self' and 'me'. Others see the world through the lens of connections between people, lands and social action. In psychology, we refer to this dimension in terms of the relationship domain which refers to whether one is motivated by self-interests (a sense of a separate atomistic self (Kerridge, 2020), personal accountability and responsibility) or by a focus on the interconnectedness to others, both living and non-living (ecology, altruism and transcendence). Linked to connectedness are issues of ethics and moral distress, matters which will be returned to below.

  Organizing question: What kind of person is being imagined and what is the work of becoming?

When we put these two key dimensions together,[8] we can begin to imagine a number of different leadership positions taken by individuals. This helps us understand the work of mentors, since not all leaders are open and available as mentees to the work they need to do to both become and to follow. Further, the same leader may move between the four positions captured in Figure 14.1, depending on the issues, internal and external dynamics, and the emerging challenges they feel the organization is facing.

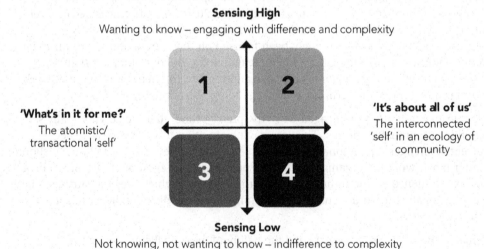

Figure 14.1: Four different leadership positions.

8   I am most grateful to my colleague, Dr J. C. Couture, for his insights and suggestions related to this analysis.

Some leaders, especially those occupying position 3 in the four positions in Figure 14.1 (about me/not wanting to know), are less likely to seek mentoring than others. For example, those in position 2 (about us/wanting to know more and to be connected) are more likely to recognize the need for mentoring and support.

Mentoring for courage and compassion

Most of the leadership challenges in caring and health-related organizations relate to people: how to facilitate their growth and development as individuals and as team members; how to connect the work that one team does with that of others; how to challenge and push teams to reimagine performance, productivity and success; and how to help teams and the individuals within them imagine a different future.

Behind these 'people' issues are issues of money, policy and ethics. In particular, those who work in health and the caring professions often face what is known as moral distress: situations in which the person knows exactly what should be done and what is needed, but feels constrained or unable to act because of money, policy, risk-aversion or some other factor. Such moral distress has real consequences: diminished sense of team cohesion; avoidance of certain situations or patients in need of care; medical mistakes and errors; burnout; decreased job satisfaction; and faster exit of staff from situations in which moral distress occurs frequently, such as in intensive care units (ICUs) or end-of-life care (Ulrich et al., 2007; Zuzelo, 2007).

Some of the mentoring relates to management and governance practices: how to build a strategy based on futures literacy and thinking; how to reimagine the work of governance; how to rethink and re-engineer business processes; and how to demonstrate value, outcomes and impact. A task for mentors is to prepare leaders to do what is right for their organization and to prepare them to face the consequences (Ismail et al., 2014). Courage is the hallmark of effective leadership, especially in a VUCA world and a complex health and care system.

The real work of the mentor: Five key challenges

Mentors are not there to coach or change specific behaviours, this this may occur as a consequence of their work. Others do this work – teachers of leadership, competency and skills coaches and performance coaches. There are effective models for performance coaching (McLean, 2012; Mukherjee, 2014), and sufficient and substantial 'best practice' and 'next practice' guides that leaders can access.

The real work of the mentor is to help the leader become their authentic self and build their courage as leaders. As Warren Bennis (2009), the great authority on leadership, wrote: *'becoming a leader is synonymous with becoming yourself – it is precisely that simple and it is also that difficult'*. It is also about developing courage and reach – stretching and becoming more than you thought possible, something Peter Drucker (2004) captured:

> *Leadership is the lifting of a man's vision to higher sights, the raising of a man's performance to a higher standard, the building of a man's personality beyond its normal limitations.*

In order to 'become yourself' as a leader, it is important to recognize that 'becoming' is a process, not a goal. Along the way, if things slow down or are not going according to plan, keep in mind that this might be impacting the depth of thinking and conversation being used and the degree of engagement. Key to this work, in addition to building resilience and a sense of mastery (Aris & Murgatroyd, 2017), and ensuring physical health and well-being, is to accept a degree of vulnerability. Leaders who are invulnerable in their own minds are usually more likely to fail than those who understand that their vulnerability is a source of strength (Fahkry, 2018). Indeed, vulnerability is the birthplace of innovation, creativity and change (Brown, 2010; 2018), and the starting place for effective mentoring. It is what usually triggers 'the call' for support and mentoring.

The mentor works with the person who finds themselves with leadership responsibilities and helps them in five specific ways:

1. **Finding their authentic self and voice**

   Rather than following some sort of leadership prescription, of which there are a great many, the key is to become the genuine and authentic self and to live that truth through relationships, interactions and actions. This is what Max de Pree identified as the art of leadership (De Pree, 1989) – the art of finding generosity of spirit, compassion and meaning in each day's work, the art of not being caught up by the minutiae of the organization, but rather attending to what matters most to the people within the organization and those who use its products or services. In care organizations, this is about looking out and recognizing moments of truth in which empathy, warmth and genuineness were displayed toward a client or patient while delivering appropriate services.

2. **The importance of creating belief**

   A key component of the work of the leader is to develop the capacity of people within the organization to believe and commit to its meaning and purpose. In care-focused organizations, the work is about more than adopting statements, business plans and evaluation methods – it is about living beliefs in action daily. Effective leaders find and focus the attention of followers on aspects of their daily reality which reinforce beliefs and support a future focus for the work of the organization (Bateson, 1972; Merleau-Ponty, 2012). They demonstrate what might be called an 'empirical sensitivity' (Nyak et al., 2020) and use evidence and data storytelling to connect the work done every day to the bigger purpose. Mentors work with leaders to help them identify moments of truth and support them in developing and articulating a narrative that helps all in the organization and those connected to it 'make sense' of its work, its strategic direction and its people.

3. **The power of recognition and noticing**

   Leaders need to develop the skills of recognizing: (a) potential risks and challenges; (b) opportunities to leverage a moment of truth or development to strengthen and build the organization and its narrative; (c) people who do remarkable work without seeking praise; (d) people who are underperforming or who do not share the belief system of the organization; and (e) interactions either among staff or between staff and patients which speak to the powerful opportunity for successful transaction. Noting and then processing these opportunities and recognizing them as narratives and stories can strengthen the organization's resolve, reinforce strategic moves and engage colleagues in building and bettering the organization. As Nyak et al. (2020) suggest, this work is about sensing, seizing and transforming the work of the organization through these noticed moments. Mentors work with leaders to strengthen their ability to notice, recognize, seize and build narratives.

A key part of this work is to help reveal the rules of the organization (Mills & Murgatroyd, 1990) – the explicit and tacit assumptions which shape and drive organizational behaviour and are the core of its culture. Given Peter Drucker's observation that 'culture eats strategy for breakfast', the leader's understanding of the culture and its rules is key to their ability to lead. Mentors help them unravel these rules.

4. The power of adaptive action

An Edmonton-based organization working on a range of projects focused on health, well-being, community capacity-building and safety – REACH Edmonton – has developed a reputation for effective partnership and alliance building, and for responding rapidly to emerging developments. Those outside the organization talk of 'working at the speed of REACH'. But the key to their success and the hallmark of agile and nimble organization is focused and effective leadership driven by a set of beliefs in the positive futures of groups who others have seen as 'problematic'. Championing new, collaborative and creative responses and working quickly, even with small budgets, REACH can respond in meaningful and purposeful ways and make a difference. It has taken a decade of work to achieve this nimbleness and agility and its small team have spent considerable time exploring not just the shared leadership model (Persaud, 2018) with which it works, but also the nuances of working together on a diverse range of projects. REACH uses a mentor to discuss with four to six colleagues each month how the organization is working for them, what their positives are and what concerns them. These conversations become the basis of a mentoring dialogue with leaders. The aim is to challenge leaders to adapt to both the shifting internal conversations and the developing external realities.

What is key here is the building the sense of 'agency' which staff across the organization feel: empowerment coupled with accountability without the negatives of 'datafication' (Ruckenstein & Schull, 2016), and focusing on recognizing performance with meaning and purpose.

5. The importance of compassion, courage and commitment

Sometimes leaders must do tough things: request the resignation of a senior colleague, refuse to comply with a request from a funding organization, challenge an emerging policy, change the way in which certain aspects of the work within the organization is done, or reorganize and refocus the entire organization given changed conditions and circumstances. This work is always demanding, no matter how 'seasoned' and experienced the leader is.

But such work is essential for an adaptive and nimble organization. How it is executed matters: done badly, leader actions can set an organization back and disrupt its culture, which can take years to heal.

What leaders seek from mentors is an opportunity to explore the nuances of the work they need to do and to have their courage both tested and reinforced. They are also seeking support to strengthen their commitment to act: 'Am I doing the right thing?' is not a simple question. Mentors cannot give leaders courage or compassion, but they can help them find these components of their leadership and strengthen them. They can also help prepare them for both the intended and unintended consequences (Nichols et al., 2020).

In terms of the Bratton model introduced in the first section of this chapter, the task of the mentor is to help the individual they are working with understand their current position in the model and identify a position that, for them and their organization, makes most sense for them. The work just described helps with this journey to becoming.

What mentors cannot do

Mentoring, like leadership, is an art based on experience, insights and empathy. The intention is that the more experienced mentor helps a developing leader mature (Eby & Robertson, 2020). Sometimes, the mentor and the leader are equally experienced, so the role of mentor is more like that of confessor, conscience keeper and challenger. The role evolves as the relationship between mentor and mentee develops.

As a mentor who has run large organizations, including those shaped by public policy and the powerful forces of new public management (Zanetti & Adams, 2000; Peters, 2001; Çolak, 2019), as well as small private enterprises and consulted for organizations worldwide across a range of industry sectors, it is clear that some mentors do not understand the boundaries within which they work.

There are seven aspects of mentoring that give rise to concerns, especially in organizations focused on health and care services. These are the seven 'do nots' and 'dos' of mentoring:

1. **Focusing on what the leader could, should, must or can do and not attending to the issues, concerns and challenges followers face** (Yip & Raelin, 2012). The mentor's role is to encourage reflection, looking at the 'becoming leader' opportunities of a given situation and exploring the followership challenges the situation will give rise to. Mentors do not side with the leader, but keep the 'big picture' in mind at all times.

2. **Offering specific solutions to challenges, threats or changes as opposed to encouraging the leader to develop options and strategies for action which they fully own.** Even if the mentor has been in similar situations a hundred times, they are not in the specific situation in the organization at this time. The key definition of empathy which Carl Rogers (1975) used was that the mentor or counsellor should '*perceive the internal frame of reference of another with accuracy and with the emotional components and meanings which pertain thereto as if one were the person, but without ever losing the "as if" condition*'. This is not to say that mentoring is a passive endeavour, but it is to say that mentoring is not about giving instructions and directions.

3. **Mentoring is about learning for all engaged in the work.** The work is a two-way street. The most powerful and effective mentoring occurs when there is a strong sense that both the mentor and the mentee are actively engaged in inspired conversations that are intended to advance the work of the organization through insight, learning, connections and collaboration (Labin, 2017). Mentoring fails when the mentor appears to 'know it all'.

4. **The mentor dominates the relationship.** Mentors exist as supports to leaders, not as substitutes. They are also there to help the leader reflect on where they are in their development as a leader and team member and what is next for them on their journey aimed at developing their authentic self and their voice. When mentors dominate the relationship, the mentee quickly realizes that the agenda is not theirs and that the benefits of this relationship are likely to be marginal. Having the right chemistry in the relationship is key (Jackson et al., 2003).

5. **The mentor avoids the hard conversations.** Sometimes, the mentor needs to challenge the leader they are working with. They need to confront either obvious issues or concerns they are avoiding, or they need to draw attention to 'the elephant in the room' (or the herd of elephants if the concerns are complex). Mentoring requires directness from time to time if the leader is to grow and develop their authentic and courageous self. On more than one occasion a mentor has asked *'are you still the right person for this work at this time?'* or *'can you accept that this challenge is beyond your own capabilities?'* or *'you appear to be underestimating the degree and potential impact of resistance within the organization!'* But the mentor uses these moments to build capabilities, understanding and a sense of purpose – they are not 'confrontations' for the sake of confronting. They are purposeful interventions aimed at strengthening the leadership of the mentee.

6. **The mentor is too quick to dismiss anxieties, concerns, fear or stress.** When the mentee signals that their emotional state is beginning to be both of concern to them and getting in the way of their ability to offer authentic leadership and followership, then the mentor should take this signal very seriously. While mentoring is not therapy and a mentor cannot address all aspects of life (Glazman, 2020), they need to be able to recognize signals that suggest that the leader is not coping and needs additional support from a counsellor or therapist. Leaders need their own mental health to be strong so that they notice, show compassion and engage in shared leadership.

7. **The mentor seeks to enforce the 'rules'.** The rules may be imposed by government, governance or external body. The rules may be created by a professional body or by a regulatory organization. The rules may be buried in the 'way we do things here' rule book. But they are there, whether the rules are explicit or tacit (Mills & Murgatroyd, 1990). The rules are not what the mentoring work should focus on. The focus should be on what is needed to ensure that the organization develops and functions effectively, efficiently and in the best interest of stakeholders. Often this means that the rules need to be broken, changed, challenged or amended. The task of the mentor is not to 'police' the rules, but to use the opportunity of needing to break them to explore consequences (intended and unintended), risk and opportunity. The task is to encourage the leader to reflect on the moment of truth and answer the question: *'what are you*

trying to do here and what does it mean for all in the organization?'. The best mentors are those who were successful and did not play by the rules as most people understood them. They understood that 'forgiveness is easier to get than permission' and that courageous leaders 'never let a good crisis go to waste'.

When the basic tenets of effective mentoring – listen, encourage, empower, engage and connect to develop courage, compassion and an ability to change in agile ways – are displaced by the behaviours just listed, then the mentoring relationship is likely to fail, as a study by Straus et al. (2013) of mentoring in health care clearly shows. Failure can set back the leader's journey to authenticity and courage.

In a recent mentoring relationship, an individual was able to use our work together to leave her 'safe', pensioned job and become a successful artist and maker, now selling her work all over the world. More importantly, she has rediscovered her passion, her sense of energy and excitement, and finds life much more intensely rewarding and satisfying. The mentoring enabled her to 'let go' of the feeling that she needed to be 'always secure' and to find passion and energy through being creative and always unsure.

Conclusion: What really matters in the work of mentors

Reflecting on thirty years of mentoring others, including leaders of manufacturing, financial services, forestry, health, eldercare and social organizations, three key observations seem to capture the essence of this work.

First, the most significant work is helping leaders overcome their assumptions about what leadership is and to guide and encourage their discovery of their authentic self as the basis for leadership. Leadership is an art, a beautiful risk and a journey. A key component of this work is supporting the leader's work in becoming an excellent team member who can share the work of leadership with others.

Second, and challenging, is the work of maintaining a futures focus. One practical problem leaders face is the demands of the now – urgent issues, reports to read and file, accountability requirements, people issues and the rest of the 'busy' work. While the busy work needs to be done, the work of the leader is to think strategically, act through shared leadership to engender focus and alignment across the organization, value people and do so with compassion, and to serve the purpose and meaning of the organization (Denhardt & Denhardt, 2000). Mentors need to help their mentees stay focused on the 'big' work of leadership and encourage them 'not to sweat the small stuff' (Carlson, 1997). Thinking back from the future and being ready for a number of different possible and probable futures is at the heart of this work.

Finally, the most important work is to encourage and develop the leader's courageous spirit. Change leadership, teamwork for an emerging future, and making bold and creative moves aimed at improving performance all require degrees of courage and commitment. In public services this can sometimes involve endless meetings, presentations and legal issues which often give rise to doubt, uncertainty and a sense of risk. In the private sector the challenge is maintaining a sense of order and maintaining revenues while redesigning the organization and its business processes. All can be challenging. Commitment to the strategy, courage in seeing through and determination are all essential components of the work of leaders. Mentors can support leaders by attending to the need for moments of real courage.

The rewards of mentoring are continuous learning for all involved in the journey and the experience of sharing moments of real learning as the leader becomes more of their authentic, courageous and compassionate self.

References

Aris, S., & Murgatroyd, S. (2017). *Beyond Resilience – From Mastery to Mystery: A Workbook for Personal Mastery and Transformational Change*. Lulu Press.

Bateson, G. (1972). *Steps to an Ecology of Mind*. University of Chicago Press.

Bennis, W. (2009). *On Becoming a Leader*. Basic Books.

Bratton, B. (Ed.) (2019). *The New Normal*. Strelka Institute.

Brown, B. (2010). *The Gifts of Imperfection: Let Go of Who Think You are Supposed to Be and Embrace Who You Are*. Hazelden.

Brown, B. (2018). *Dare to Lead: Brave Work, Tough Conversations, Whole Hearts*. Random House Canada.

Carlson, R. (1997). *Don't Sweat the Small Stuff…and It's All Small Stuff: Simple Ways to Keep the Little Things from Taking Over Your Life*. Hachette Books.

Çolak, C. D. (2019). *Why the new public management is obsolete: An analysis in the context of the post-new public management trends*. Croatian and Comparative Public Administration, **19**(4), 517–536.

Davis, G. (2009). *The rise and fall of finance and the end of the society of organizations*. Academy of Management Perspectives, **23**(3), 27–44.

Deleuze, G., & Guattari, F. (1977). *Anti-Oedipus: Capitalism and Schizophrenia*. Penguin Group (USA) in translation from the French.

Denhardt, R. B. & Denhardt, J. V. (2000). *The new public service: Serving rather than steering*. Public Administration Review, **60**(6), 549–559.

De Pree, M. (1989). *Leadership is an Art*. Doubleday.

Drucker, P. F., with Maciariello, J. A. (2004). *The Daily Drucker: 366 Days of Insight and Motivation for Getting the Right Things Done*. Harper Collins.

Eby, L. T. & Robertson, M. M. (2020). *The Psychology of Workplace Mentoring Relationships*. Annual Review of Organizational Psychology and Organizational Behaviour, **Volume 7**(1), 75–100.

Edelman (2021). *Edelman Trust Barometer*. Edelman Ireland. https://www.edelman.com/sites/g/files/aatuss191/files/2021-01/2021%20Edelman%20Trust%20Barometer_Final.pdf

Fahkry, T. (2018, February 5). *How to embrace vulnerability as your greatest strength*. Mission. org. https://medium.com/the-mission/how-to-embrace-vulnerability-as-your-greatest-strength-d2ac2b80ba52#:~:text=Vulnerability%20is%20not%20a%20sign,no%20control%20over%20the%20outcome.&text=Your%20association%20with%20vulnerability%20requires,strengthen%20your%20emotional%20well%2Dbeing

Glazman, M. (2020, October 18). *5 things to stop expecting from a mentor*. Chief Learning Officer. https://www.chieflearningofficer.com/2020/10/18/5-things-to-stop-expecting-from-a-mentor/

Ismail, S., Malone, M. S., & Van Geest, Y. (2014). *Exponential Organizations – Why New Organizations are Ten Times Better, Faster, and Cheaper than Yours (and What to Do About It)*. Diversion Books.

Jackson, V. A., Palepu, A., Szalacha, L., Caswell, C., Carr, P. L., & Inui, T. (2003). *'Having the right chemistry': A qualitative study of mentoring in academic medicine*. Academic Medicine, **78**(3), 328–334.

Kellerman, B. (2012). *The End of Leadership*. HarperCollins Business.

Kerridge, R. (2020, January 18). *The Self Delusion by Tom Oliver review: how we are connected and why that matters*. The Guardian. https://www.theguardian.com/books/2020/jan/18/the-self-delusion-tom-oliver-review

Labin, J. (2017). *Mentoring programs that work*. Association for Talent Development.

Lipman-Blumen, J. (2006). *The Allure of Toxic Leadership: Why We Follow Destructive Bosses and Corrupt Politicians – and How We Can Survive Them*. Oxford University Press.

McLean, P. (2012) *The Completely Revised Handbook of Coaching: A Developmental Approach*. Jossey-Bass.

Merleau-Ponty, M. (2012). *Phenomenology of Perception*. Routledge.

Mills, A. R., and Murgatroyd, S. (1990). *Organizational Rules – A Framework for Understanding Organizational Action*. The Open University Press.

Mukherjee, S. (2014). *Corporate Coaching: The Essential Guide*. SAGE.

Nichols, C., Hayden, S. C., & Trendler, C. (2020, April 2). *4 behaviours that help leaders manage a crisis*. Harvard Business Review. https://hbr.org/2020/04/4-behaviors-that-help-leaders-manage-a-crisis

Nyak., A., Chia, R., and Canales, J. I. (2020). *Noncognitive microfoundations: Understanding dynamic capabilities as idiosyncratically refined sensitivities and predispositions*. Academy of Management Review, **45**(2), pages 280–303.

Persaud, D. (2018). *Shared leadership in healthcare organizations*. In A. Örtenblad, C. A. Löfström, & R. Sheaff (Eds.), *Management Innovations for Healthcare Organizations: Adopt, Abandon or Adapt?* Routledge.

Peters, B. G. (2001). *The Future of Governing*. University Press of Kansas.

Rogers, C. R. (1975). *Empathic: An unappreciated way of being*. Counselling Psychologist, **5**(2), 2–10. http://www.elementsuk.com/libraryofarticles/empathic.pdf

Ruckenstein, M., & Schull, N. (2016). *The datafication of health*. Annual Review of Anthropology, **46**(1), pages 1–18.

Straus, S. E., Johnson, M. O., Marquez, C., & Feldman, M. D. (2013). *Characteristics of successful and failed mentoring relationships: A qualitative study across two academic health centers*. Academic Medicine, **88**(1), 82–89.

Tillich, P. (1952). *The Courage to Be*. Yale University Press.

Tourish, D. (2020). *Introduction to the special issue: Why the coronavirus crisis is also a crisis of leadership*. Leadership, **16**(3), 1–12.

Ulrich, C., O'Donnell, P., Taylor, C., Farrar, A., Danis, M., & Grady, C. (2007). *Ethical climate, ethics stress, and the job satisfaction of nurses and social workers in the United States*. Social Science and Medicine, **65**(8), 1708–1719.

van Loon, R., & Buster, A. (2019). *The future of leadership: The courage to be both a leader and follower*. Journal of Leadership Studies, **13**(1), 1–2.

Yip. J., & Raelin, J. A. (2012). *Threshold concepts and modalities for teaching leadership practice*. Management Learning, **43**(3), 333–354.

Zanetti, L. A., & Adams, G. B. (2000). *In service of the Leviathan: Democracy, ethics and the potential for administrative evil in the new public management*. Administrative Theory & Praxis, **22**(3), 534–555.

Zuzelo P. R. (2007). *Exploring the moral distress of registered nurses*. Nursing Ethics, **14**(3), 344–359.

Chapter 15
A Systems-Psychodynamic Approach to Mentoring and How It Can Help Individuals and Organizations to Develop Leadership Capacity

Robyn Vesey

> *If distrust of the organization predominates, the capacity of staff to face the realities and complexities of patient need, to make the difficult decisions required and to act humanely inevitably suffers.*

> (Ballatt & Campling, 2011, p. 137)

To effectively perform and deliver, health and social care organizations need people with mature decision-making capacities. This is sometimes called leadership or management but applies to every role, and therefore processes to nurture and develop these capacities are a crucial part of people development. This chapter offers an overview of the systems-psychodynamic perspective to mentoring, including an understanding of the nature of health and social care organizations, and how the wider context impacts upon individuals within their work roles. Individual effectiveness is understood in relation to the anxieties and other emotions elicited by the work, which have a particular nature in health, social care and public service organizations.

In addition, the new organizational forms, the process of change, and the sudden changes brought about by the COVID-19 pandemic and workplace technology are understood as a source of uncertainty and anxiety. These add to the need for, but detract from the possible providers of, containment – the psychological condition that enables reality-based evaluation and decision-making in the face of stress or anxiety (Bion, 1961). It is argued that mentoring is an intervention that can address the need for containment and develop individuals' leadership capacities in complex and challenging organizational environments. Mentoring can therefore impact the organization itself through enhanced individual effectiveness, especially when carried out with a systemic awareness, a capacity for containment and a generative sense of development.

Individuals in their work context

In this section, examples based on real cases are provided, but disguised to preserve confidentiality.

Abby is a consultant clinical psychologist in a perinatal mental health service in a small city, serving a largely rural community. Her organization, a mental health trust, has recently merged with a neighbouring trust, and she sees the disruption and turmoil in her colleagues, who have become distant and detached. Her role involves overseeing the psychologists who work embedded within the perinatal multidisciplinary teams, and constant questions hang over the demands of the teams in terms of therapy referrals, care coordination and risk management. Some of the team's psychologists seem able to manage the requests and demands, whereas others seem either to overwork and become resentful, or to seek rescue leaving them dependent on Abby's help.

Abby has also been appointed as a clinical lead for mental health in the maternity provider collaborative network across the region, which involves chairing multiorganizational meetings and working on care pathways across different services for pregnant women. The network includes maternity units and community services, non-statutory sector children's services, child and family health services, and adult mental health services. Abby is keen to improve the cooperation between organizations and sees this as central to the quality of the service, but it can be difficult to agree on priorities, agendas and, crucially, funding decisions. She finds this work rewarding but it takes much more time than the half-day allocated in her week.

Abby finds it frustrating that she so often feels out of control of her diary, unable to complete the tasks she wants to as well as she would like. She worries that others see her as either absent or inconsistent as a leader. Her new trust is bringing in performance targets for psychologists in her team, and she is negotiating with the nurse service manager about how these should be implemented. She cares passionately about the quality of the service, in touch with the motivations that brought her into her NHS career, but has increasingly become concerned, and somewhat disillusioned, by the impact of change and of staff turnover.

Abby is a lesbian woman who has recently married her long-term partner and is exploring the possibility of having children of her own. She sometimes finds that not yet having children of her own is a challenge in working in this service, as if she is considered inexperienced in relation to those who are mothers. Realising that she was struggling with some aspects of her new leadership role, she contacted a senior psychology colleague in a different part of her organization and set up mentoring with them.

David is a team leader in a charity which offers support to people experiencing homelessness, in a city in the UK. The charity is primarily funded by the local authority, although it has some fundraising activities. It offers a range of services, including case worker follow-ups for people in new homes, one-to-one counselling, groups for developing skills of independent living, and running information campaigns on social media. The charity has just had to close a residential hostel and this has been experienced as a huge loss, with only five of the hostel staff being able to apply for jobs in other parts of the organization. David feels strongly connected to the place, proud of the fact that this charity is local and that it has maintained the contract in the face of strong competition from national providers, but he often feels unsettled by the commissioners' demands which play out in changes such as the closure of the hostel.

David takes time to nurture relationships with his team and feels that his staff depend on and look to him for help when needed, but he has noticed a higher staff turnover than before the COVID-19 pandemic, and more problems with staff sickness. While most staff have long since returned to offering face-to-face sessions with clients, the team meetings still occur primarily on video conferencing, and he is rarely in a room with his whole team. He feels a loss of team cohesion, a sense of disconnection and a sense that he cannot keep an overview of what everyone is doing. As it is such a small charity he reports directly to the charity's deputy director and he is under pressure to provide more up-to-date data in relation to the key performance indicators (the outcomes against which the service is evaluated, set by commissioners). David sometimes accompanies his boss to commissioner meetings and understands how important the data is but is aware his team struggle to complete the reporting forms, which they feel are unnecessarily difficult, unimportant and a waste of their time.

David sometimes feels burdened and exhausted by the responsibilities and a sense of powerlessness in his role, and at the worst moments, a sense of pointlessness and disillusionment, as if there is nothing that he can do that will really make a difference and a lot of the effort is for no real benefit. He sometimes finds himself looking forward to early retirement but worries that the team need him and wonders who would replace him. After a conversation with his boss, the deputy director, David set up a mentoring relationship with an external mentor, recently retired from a position running a children's home that was part of a charity.

In these examples we can see how organizational context around an individual leader or manager has important influences on the individual's experience of taking up their role. David is involved in coordinating and sustaining the work of his team and responding to the needs of commissioners and funders for information as they monitor key performance indicators. David must offer encouragement in the face of his team's confusion, stress and resistance to submitting data and must contend with his own sense of powerlessness about what his organization is able to offer the homeless people they work with. Abby has a multifaceted role and stands on different boundaries: the boundary between her psychology team and multidisciplinary colleagues within her trust, and the boundary between her trust and the wider network of partners in the provider collaborative network. One requirement of her role is that she must secure resources and influence decisions in what is a turbulent and stretched organizational environment. Working with mentors using a systems-psychodynamic approach, Abby and David were able to consider in depth how they were being impacted by their work context, and how they might want to experience themselves differently in their leadership roles. Their mentors were able to offer their own experiences and knowledge of both the systems they work in, and the nature of leadership amid organizational conditions.

In the following section, we will take an overview of key features of the systems-psychodynamic approach. The emotional impact of the work and wider context will then be examined in more depth, and finally, organizational change and possibilities for containment will be outlined. The individual examples in this section will be revisited to show how the systems-psychodynamic approach can be used in mentoring to help individuals and organizations develop their leadership capacity.

Overview of the systems-psychodynamic approach

The systems-psychodynamic approach (Neumann, 1999; Gould et al., 2006) originates from the Tavistock Clinic in London, with some of the key texts emanating from this and now related organizations: the Tavistock Clinic (Obholzer & Roberts, 2019), Tavistock Consultancy Service, (Huffington et al., 2004; Armstrong, 2005) and the Tavistock Institute (Sher & Lawlor, 2021). This approach combines theories from psychoanalysis and open systems theory and has a 'genealogy', including the work of Kurt Lewin, Wilfred Bion, Sigmund Freud and Melanie Klein, with subsequent theorists and organizational practitioners developing and linking with these earlier ideas (Miller, 1997, p. 188). The approach explores organizational phenomena from a number of perspectives, connecting psychoanalysis, group relations and open systems theory with concepts such as 'social defences' (Jaques, 1955; Menzies-Lyth, 1960, Armstrong & Rustin, 2015) and 'organization in the mind' (Hutton et al., 1997; Armstrong, 2005). These concepts bridge the individual with the collective; the external and explicit with the internal and unspoken; the rational or conscious with the irrational or unconscious.

Fundamental to this approach is an understanding that individuals in organizations are acting in relation to, and being acted on by, others. The others might be people within their organization with whom they work in teams or groups, as outlined by group dynamics (Bion, 1961). The 'others' might also be particular aspects of the organization itself (for example, 'HR' or 'the management'), real or imagined leadership figures, and even the wider 'public' at large. David Armstrong (2005) describes how the organization as a whole, or what he calls the organizational field, has a dynamic life of its own, which acts on and impacts the experience of individuals, as well as being acted upon (or co-created) by individuals in groups. Therefore, the emotional experience of the individual at work is not only individual (Hirschhorn, 1997; Roberts, 2019), but also contains an aspect of the emotional experience of the organization as a whole and this is related to the organization's task, structure, culture and context (Armstrong, 2005; Hoggett, 2006; Stokes, 2019).

The emotional impact of the work and the wider context for those working in health and social care

Systems psychodynamics pays particular attention to the emotional impact of the work that is being done in any organization (Menzies-Lyth, 1960; Hughes & Pengelly, 1997; Obholzer & Roberts, 2019; Cardona, 2020). Health and social care work is work with people, involving the relationships and emotions when helping others in difficulty. Individuals are drawn to this work for the purpose and meaning, for the satisfaction of helping and caring for others, and for deeper, perhaps unconscious, reasons to do with their own personal histories and psychology (Ballatt & Campling, 2011; Cardona,

2020). There are particular emotions around difficult situations, such as experiencing homelessness or having a traumatic experience of birth, and there are also emotions and relational tensions that inevitably emerge around the experience of helping and being helped: compassion, sadness, frustration, pity, repulsion, guilt (Menzies-Lyth, 1960; Armstrong & Rustin, 2015). One way of understanding what can happen in groups and organizations is to use the psychoanalytic term 'projection' that Bion (1961) describes as central to group dynamics. In this understanding not only might someone at work experience their own feelings – of frustration, sadness or fear – but they might also be receiving projections of others' feelings, absorbing as it were, the feelings of colleagues, as well as service users and carers. Francesca Cardona developed the metaphor of 'team as sponge' to describe the impact of emotions from the work on the whole team; for example, becoming cut off from feelings and each other when facing huge anxiety about risk, or becoming untrusting of outsiders when facing hostility from the people they are trying to help (Cardona, 2020).

Researchers and writers have developed these ideas to include the impact of the wider context, understanding how social expectations and narratives impact upon people working in both health and social care (Hoggett, 2006). The health service not only has to deal with the reality but also the social expectations and anxieties to do with illness, death and dying (Obholzer, 2019). Children's social services have to contend with social anxieties about the protection of children at risk of abuse (Cooper & Lousada, 2005). Organizations themselves are often put through changes which are designed to decrease the likelihood of any harm; for example, through regulations, requirements and structures that are put in place to manage risk and potential failures. As well as maximizing the success of these initiatives, leaders in health care organizations might also need to resist both the sense of blame and the fantastical thinking that all harm can be prevented (Ballatt & Campling, 2011). Stokes (1994, p. 313) identifies the way the pressures and expectations from wider social anxieties evoke a '*struggle at an organizational level, between ... manic or omnipotent states of mind and ambitions and more realistic and sober views of reality and what is possible*'.

Mentoring conversations using a systems-psychodynamic approach offer space to consider the emotional impact of the work dynamics and the wider context, and in this way, individuals can make sense of some of the more difficult experiences, including of failure or shame. Mentors facilitate this process by asking questions, by appropriate sharing of their own experiences in leadership roles and by offering their understanding of the way the organizational system operates.

For example, the mentor working with Abby to think about her experience of effectiveness at work helped her to make sense of her many and contradictory feelings in her work and organizational context. The psychologists she supervised seemed to be either resentful or dependent, and with her mentor she explored the parallels with a parenting role and the need to respond to infant demands without either depriving or indulging. They considered how she might offer consistent and clear messages about her availability and her confidence in her colleagues' abilities. For Abby there was also a personal impact of the work: the ambivalence the mothers in the services felt toward their babies connected with her own ambivalence about having children. She was able to talk about this in the mentoring and identify that her workplace may be distorting her expectations of motherhood.

David was able to explore with his mentor the experience of losing colleagues when the hostel closed, which had brought up mixed feelings toward the commissioners of his service. He identified that on the one hand he wants to deliver the performance and data required, and on the other he feels frustrated and resentful that commissioning decisions have closed the hostel they were previously able to offer. David was also able to discuss what is reasonable and possible for his service to provide in the context of significant cuts in social care spending, as well as the impact of economic changes during and since the pandemic. Such mentoring conversations enable exploration of what might have been internalized from the system as a sense of personal failure or inadequacy for not delivering what is needed. Adopting a systems-psychodynamic perspective helped David and Abby to consider the dynamics they were caught up in with their teams in the context of the wider pressures and priorities in their organizations.

Organizational change and the place of containment

Organizational change is widely understood as evoking emotions, and the systems-psychodynamic approach offers an understanding of how such emotions can impact the individuals and the collective capacity to work effectively during times of change and transition. Service restructures, changes in service provision and then the sudden crisis responses to the onset of the COVID-19 pandemic are different kinds of change that have been introduced in health and social care organizations in recent years. Significant emotions arising at times of change include anxiety in relation to uncertainty and grief, which can be expressed destructively in some circumstances (Krantz, 2006; Stokes, 2019). The loss of colleagues or changes in the nature of work are emotive issues for staff, and alongside these there are changes to organizational structures, at both concrete and psychological levels. Reliably available others, clear boundaries around remit and responsibility are aspects of organizational structure that contribute to a containing experience, and of course these become uncertain at times of change (James & Clark, 2002).

Managers and leaders have a particular place in organizations to offer containment to enable staff to carry out their work. This is offered not only by individual managers and leaders, but also by structures and processes in the organization, and the predictability they can provide is especially important (Cooper & Dartington, 2004). Alongside the potential disillusionment that can be experienced at times of organizational change, individuals can be vulnerable to reinforcing destructive or uncompassionate relational dynamics (Ballatt & Campling, 2011), especially when trusting relationships with others, including those in senior roles, are no longer available (Lohmer & Lazar, 2006). A challenge for organizations during times of change, is to maintain a relationship with its members that allows for productive work through adequate containment. In a mentoring intervention there is the chance for individuals to receive support from outside of supervision processes that may be necessarily focused on a high volume of client content. This can be particularly beneficial to individuals going through organizational change, where containment might be limited by the reconfiguring of structures and relationships.

For David his mentoring helped him to work through his feelings of despondency that followed the closure of part of his service. David was also able to speak about his ambivalent feelings about leaving, on the one hand wanting to move away from the feelings of burden and disillusionment, and on the other hand feeling tied to the organization. Having the benefit of a retired mentor who had recently undergone a similar transition helped David not only to imagine the option of leaving in a healthy way, but also to reconnect with the reasons he enjoyed and valued his work role and he decided to stay. For Abby, the recent merger in her trust, as well as the new coming together of the provider collaborative network meant new relationships forming across old boundaries and differences. Discussing the lack of progress and lack of trust with her mentor she came to see how this could be understood given the impact of change and the nature of past relationships, with previous mistrust or division emerging into the present as the new network forms. Abby could therefore identify where and how she could intervene to address particular issues, and which areas were best left for others to address and for her to seek influence in more subtle ways. Her mentor helped her to prioritize her time and activity across the provider collaborative network, with insights on the structural changes and history of key figures.

Conclusion: How systems-psychodynamic mentoring can help individuals and organizations to develop leadership capacity

In this chapter outlining a systems-psychodynamic approach to mentoring, it has been argued that mentoring can develop leadership capacities through attention to the individual's experience of themselves and their effectiveness at work in relation to the people they influence, lead and manage. A systemic awareness identifying the many wider factors that influence an individual's experience at work can counter negative feelings, such as failure and guilt, that are a feature of organizational dynamics in health and social care work. In the same way as coaching, a mentoring relationship can offer a space for exploratory conversations to help with improved performance and personal awareness through conversation, a supportive relationship and a developmental focus on the work role. However, in mentoring individuals can also seek advice around their leadership challenges and learn from the experiences shared by their mentor. Mentors can offer their understanding of systems and organizations, and in this way help mentees to make strategies to more effectively navigate their role in the organization (Lancer et al., 2016). Mentors also role model, for example, ways of taking up authority, and so communicate important aspects of organizational culture and values (EMCC Global definition, 2024).

From this perspective, the benefits for the organization are three-fold. First, in terms of sustaining, retaining and developing members of staff in their complex and challenging work roles through an awareness of the impact of the wider system, and in some cases preparing individuals to take on roles of greater seniority. Second, in promoting a dynamic of containment and kindness through the experience of a containing, supportive and understanding relationship which can act as a counter to the more destructive organizational dynamics that surround work and the impact of change. Finally, in setting up an exchange between a more senior, more experienced member of staff, and a less senior, less experienced member of staff, mentoring invites a generous approach to succession, and indicates the value and status of senior members. Recognition, and the chance to offer something when ending a career, can be a powerful and effective position for individuals to take as they manage stepping down from senior posts. In this sense, mentoring can be of benefit to mentor and mentee, and enable a good chance of a successful succession, with key experience and knowledge passed on and internalized as well as individual contributions and capacities recognized and celebrated – so facilitating healthy, rather than destructive, endings.

Questions for reflection

Think about your current or past experiences in work roles in health and social care:

1. What do you notice about the impact of the wider context on your experience:
   - the work of the organization and the emotional experience of this work?
   - the commitment to naming the realities and the challenges that were faced at work – or not?
   - the use and impact of reflective space in which the experience at work could be thought about?
2. What might mentoring offer you as either a mentor or a mentee?
   - What might mentoring offer your organization?

Exercises

1. The systems-psychodynamic approach to mentoring pays attention to the internal experience of individuals and how this is linked to the external realities of the workplace. Talk with colleagues about the difference that the COVID-19 pandemic and/or remote working has made to your working practices and to your experience of work. Notice, without judgement, what has changed and how this feels.
2. Consider two perspectives on workplace effectiveness: individual and systemic. Whenever you have a conversation about effectiveness, make a record of how many times individual factors are named and how many times wider workplace systemic factors are named. Where is the emphasis in your conversations? What difference does this make to the 'solutions' that are suggested or taken on as ways to improve effectiveness?

Practical summary

1. The organizational context that an individual is working in can have a significant impact on their experience and their effectiveness in their work. This is via four key mechanisms:
   - the challenges of the work itself and the emotional experience of this;
   - the ways in which challenges are responded to both individually and in groups, and how far these create healthy decision-making cultures or untrusting, more difficult ones;

- the uncertainties of organizational change, including restructures, changes in leadership and in the nature of the work; and
- the capacity of the organization to offer containment in terms of the leadership and management, organizational role clarity and the culture or nature of working relationships.

2. Mentoring can offer a containing space in which an individual can reflect on their experience and pay attention to the impact of the organizational context. To do this, it is important that the mentoring is relationally safe, predictable and that there is an approach that conceptualizes the wider organizational context and dynamics in order to pay attention to their impact upon the mentee.

3. Mentoring can have an impact at an organizational level in addition to, and through, the impact on individuals:

- increasing individual effectiveness, satisfaction in complex and challenging roles and therefore increasing staff retention through effective and supportive leadership, with a systemic awareness of the sources of stress and difficulty;
- promoting a work culture where generative exchange and reciprocal appreciation is offered between people; and
- improving the chances of successful succession, both by developing members of the organization and equipping them to take up more senior positions, and by valuing and recognizing more experienced members of staff and inviting them into a generative exchange.

References

Armstrong, D. (2005). *Organization in the Mind: Psychoanalysis, Group Relations and Organizational Consultancy*. Karnac Books.

Armstrong, D., & Rustin, M. (2015). *Social Defences against Anxiety: Explorations in a Paradigm*. Karnac Books.

Ballatt, J., & Campling, P. (2011). *Intelligent Kindness: Reforming the Culture of Healthcare*. Royal College of Psychiatry Publications.

Bion, W. R., (1961). *Experiences in Groups: And Other Papers*. Tavistock Publications.

Cardona, F. (2020). *Work Matters: Consulting to Leaders and Organizations in the Tavistock Tradition*. Routledge.

Cooper, A., & Dartington, T. (2004). *The vanishing organization: Organizational containment in a networked world*. In C. Huffington, D. Armstrong, W. Halton, L. Hoyle, & J. Pooley (Eds.), *Working Below the Surface: The Emotional Life of Contemporary Organisations* (pp. 127–150). Karnac Books.

Cooper, A., & Lousada, J. (2005). *Borderline Welfare: Feeling and Fear of Feeling in Modern Welfare*. Karnac Books.

EMCC Global (2024). *Mentoring*. https://www.emccglobal.org/leadership-development/leadership-development-mentoring/

Gould, L., Stapley, L. F., & Stein, M. (2006). *The Systems Psychodynamics of Organizations: Integrating the Group Relations Approach, Psychoanalytic, and Open System Perspectives*. Routledge.

Hirschhorn, L. (1997). *Reworking Authority: Leading and Following in the Post-Modern Organization*. MIT Press.

Hoggett, P. (2006). *Conflict, ambivalence, and the contested purpose of public organizations*. Human Relations, **59**(2), 175–194.

Huffington, C., Armstrong, D., Halton, W., Hoyle, L., & Pooley, J. (Eds.). (2004). *Working below the surface: The emotional life of contemporary organisations*. Tavistock Publications.

Hughes, L., & Pengelly, P. (1997). *Staff Supervision in a Turbulent Environment: Managing Process and Task in Front-line Services*. Jessica Kingsley.

Hutton, J., Bazalgette, J., & Reed, B. (1997). *Organisation-in-the-mind*. In J. E. Neumann, K. Kellner, & A. Dawson-Shepherd (Eds.), *Developing Organisational Consultancy* (pp. 113–126). Routledge.

Jaques, E. (1955). *Social systems as a defence against persecutory and depressive anxiety*. In M. Klein, P. Hermann, & R. E. Money-Kyrle (Eds.), *New Directions in Psychoanalysis* (pp. 478–498). Karnac Books.

James, K., & Clark, G. (2002). *Service organisations: Issues in transition and anxiety containment. Journal of Managerial Psychology*, **17**(5) 394–408.

Krantz, J. (2006). *Dilemmas of organizational change: A systems psychodynamic perspective*. In L. Gould, L. F. Stapley, & M. Stein (Eds.), *The Systems Psychodynamics of Organisations: Integrating the Group Relations Approach, Psychoanalytic, and Open System Perspectives* (pp. 133–156). Routledge.

Lancer, N., Clutterbuck, D., & Megginson, D. (2016). *Techniques for Coaching and Mentoring* (**2nd ed.**). Routledge.

Lohmer, M., & Lazar, R. A. (2006). *The consultant between the lines of fire: The dynamics of trust, mistrust and containment in organisations. Organisational and Social Dynamics*, **6**(1), 42–62.

Menzies-Lyth, I. (1960). *A case-study in the functioning of social systems as a defence against anxiety. Human Relations*, **13**, 95–121.

Miller, E. J. (1997). *Effecting organisational change in large complex systems: A collaborative consultancy approach*. In J. E. Neumann, K. Kellner, & A. Dawson-Shepherd, (Eds.) *Developing Organisational Consultancy* (pp. 187–212). Routledge.

Neumann, J. E. (1999). *Systems psychodynamics in the service of political organizational change*. In R. French, & R. Vince (Eds.), *Group Relations, Management, and Organization* (pp. 54–69). Oxford University Press.

Obholzer, A. (2019). *Managing social anxieties in public sector organisations*. In A. Obholzer, & V. Z. Roberts(Eds.), *The Unconscious at Work: A Tavistock Approach to Making Sense of Organizational Life* (**2nd ed.**, pp. 174–183). Routledge.

Obholzer, A., and Roberts, V. Z. (Eds.). (2019). *The Unconscious at Work: A Tavistock Approach to Making Sense of Organisational Life* (**2nd ed.**). Routledge.

Roberts, V. Z. (2019). *The self-assigned impossible task*. In A. Obholzer, & V. Z. Roberts (Eds.), *The Unconscious at Work: A Tavistock Approach to Making Sense of Organisational Life* (**2nd ed.**, pp. 127–135). Routledge.

Sher, M., & Lawlor, D. (2021). *An Introduction to Systems Psychodynamics: Consultancy Research and Training*. Routledge.

Stokes, J. (1994). *What is unconscious in organizations?* In R. Casemore (Ed.), *What Makes Consultancy Work: Understanding the Dynamics* (pp. 312–319). South Bank University Press.

Stokes, J. (2019). *Institutional chaos and personal stress*. In A. Obholzer, & V. Z. Roberts (Eds.), *The Unconscious at Work: A Tavistock Approach to Making Sense of Organisational Life* (**2nd ed.**, pp. 136–143). Routledge.

Chapter 16
Chief Executives' Perspectives on Mentoring in Mental Health Services

Interview with Paddy Cooney & Paul Jenkins

We are very keen to hear from you about your experiences of mentoring and the mentoring scheme that you set up for NHS staff. What would you most like to share with us for this chapter about your perspectives on and experiences in the field of mentoring that you feel are significant and groundbreaking for CEOs and why?

Paddy: The mentoring scheme was trying to address how you respond in any organization to staff developmental needs, at middle-management level. You go out on a ward and spot some people who have real talent. You know they are having a dilemma: do they remain in clinical work or become a manager? This is a different question in coaching. By the time people go into coaching, there is generally a clarity about where they want to go. Whereas in mentoring, it is more of an exploration about: What is it I really want to do?; What are some of the issues, difficulties I am up against?; Where do I really want to go?; and, Where can I discuss these issues confidentially, with no feedback to the organization? This is an important differentiation about the group that it is being aimed at. A CEO can't put everyone on a King's Fund 'Top Manager' programme, but you can spot talent and suggest putting them in contact with someone who can help them with where they want to go. They may come back to the CEO to feed back and discuss their needs following the mentoring programme. The mentoring has got to be in the context of a plan, with, for example, the CEO, the Director of Operations, or the Director of Nursing – whoever recommends mentoring. An agreement is then made that when the mentoring ends, they will take this up, discuss their learning, and look at what their thinking is and the further developments they may need. It may not lead to promotion, and this needs to be made clear.

Paul: I have used mentoring both as a recipient and as a provider in three contexts:

1. In thinking about development, where people go next.
2. In advising people around transition – when one has entered a new role or new level. Any stepping up is tough. The higher you go in an organization, the tougher it becomes, and the less latitude people give you to learn and make silly mistakes.
3. Where people are managing difficult situations and issues in the organization. The value of mentoring, when done either from within the organization or outside, is the separation from the line management and the immediately

difficult situation and circumstances. You are looking for advice input and support from someone who can relate to the situation from a more objective and detached perspective. They can help you explore and unpack the issues.

As a CEO, I have encouraged people to take mentoring from outside our organization. We are a small organization. Where this is the case and where it has a particularly distinctive culture, then I feel mentoring from outside the organization is essential. They are more likely to benefit from insights and expertise from someone outside that culture who has the distance.

As mentor and mentee, what have you found of most benefit from the mentoring you have been involved in, both as a mentor and as a mentee?

Paddy: One of the issues is making the individual think about it. Clear ground rules are essential in effective mentoring – the mentee needs to be clear that the agenda is their responsibility. A mentee could come to a session without an agenda, having not thought about it, and somehow you as the mentor are responsible for their agenda. The reality is that it's got to be the mentee's agenda. In the initial stages of the relationship, it's getting that through to mentees. I don't expect them to come with a whole coherent set of questions for the agenda, but to set the framework: What do they want to talk about today?; What do they want to focus on and discuss today?; What are the issues: is it something you have recently faced or want to discuss? We would elaborate, if there were issues missing and anything else required. But this is one of the early principles of effective mentoring. In coaching, there is more of a shared responsibility at times, about what that agenda is.

Paul: The value of mentoring conversations has come from people being able to talk about a mixture of current issues that are difficult in the here and now, together with looking at developmental and growth needs. The balance of this in a session can vary. The conversation in the here and now, then leads to observations and further conversations about strengths, weaknesses and areas for growth and development. As Paddy says, it's the mentee's responsibility to set the agenda, to take ownership and value out of the mentoring session. Much depends on honesty and trust in the mentoring relationship. Trust in the relationship then encourages honesty and dictates what you say and don't say in a mentoring relationship.

Can you say something about your experiences of being mentored yourself? Would you say this is in line with what you have experienced yourself?

Paul: Yes, very much so. I have benefitted from mentoring in the past. I benefited enormously from the mentoring in a previous post. With the help of some independent insight, this then allowed me to talk about, face and deal with some very tricky issues. In the particular context of being a CEO, it can be an immensely lonely job; there are not always many people you can fully open up to. Therefore, mentoring has to be grounded in a relationship with someone you trust, [someone you can] be open with and [someone] who you can display your weakness/vulnerability to.

Paddy: For me, with the mentoring I have done over recent years, it seems to be [about] substituting for the lack of contact and connections outside [the mentees'] organizations and with their peer group, and the restrictions and problems they have. That leaves them in quite isolated positions. Networking is important for learning and in its absence how do you learn? So, mentoring seems to be serving a very different function in this context. There is a real pleasure in when mentees use the discussion to really think about their situations and return to later sessions with solutions that have worked for them. It not only validates the mentoring process but benefits the organization through an individual believing they have agency in their day-to-day work.

Bringing in your experiences which have informed your perspective of mentoring, what would be the three key messages you would want to highlight in this chapter, from a CEO's perspective of both receiving and offering mentoring?

Paul: It's about having help outside the constraints, either of the organization, or at least the line management environment you operate in. Whenever you are with someone you manage, for the most part, there is invariably some other business in the room. You have got to deal with issues of performance and the business you are managing. However much you try to separate it off, and focus on the individual and their development needs, you still get caught up in day-to-day issues. Whereas the great thing about the mentor–mentee relationship is that it is separate from this. It is focused on you. You may still talk about the issues, but the mentor hasn't got to decide the outcome. What you can deal with in that relationship is how you are feeling about it and how you are thinking about it, and bring in alternative perspectives. So many problems seem so much bigger when you think you are the only person in the world ever dealing with them. Whereas when you talk to people, in the context of their own experience, [you] can say, '*I have been there, I have been somewhere worse than that*', then a mentee's problems shrink and can seem more manageable.

Paddy: You make a very important point here, Paul. Generally, when I have seen someone as a mentee, it's because someone has recognized something in them that's worth investing in. They don't get to see a mentor because it's part of the capability procedures. If those worries are there, it's internal and a management responsibility. If I am mentoring someone, it's because someone is wanting to put something into your development. It's quite a good starting point.

We [would] always set up six sessions, every six weeks/two months, with a reasonable interval, so issues were still alive and not forgotten about, but not over frequent. This would be for a fixed period agreed with the mentor. I could be mentoring someone, who says, '*I don't know what to do about this*' and you think, '*but we had sorted this out years ago*'. You suggest, '*have you thought about this?*' Some is mundane, about how you manage your day, and some are big issues which are organizational issues/struggles, that you are not going to find the answer to. One of the issues for me is about organizational memory. Some of the content of mentor's sessions and what they come up with, we are constantly relearning. We have dealt with it in the past. The sense mentees can have is that they are the only ones dealing with it. As a mentor, you know that there have been countless others who have also dealt with it since at least ten years ago, and have thought through some of those issues.

For a mentor to be really effective it's important for a them to have that organizational memory.

Can we expand further on your mentoring scheme? What are the key messages for mentoring leaders that are relevant here?

Paddy: It's often not the big stuff you are sweating but managing the little stuff that makes a job more doable. In another world, on management courses you might have learned this, but sometimes putting it into practice can be a different matter. It's therefore the small stuff as well as the big stuff.

Paul: You have reminded me of another point about this. I arranged some mentoring for a very talented person from a minority background who could lack confidence due to their experience of how their race had been responded to at previous stages of their career. Mentoring can be particularly good at helping people overcome confidence issues. Again, because it is detached from the realities of the day-to-day situation. Sometimes you can do that within communities of interest; giving an aspiring female manager a female mentor or an inspiring Black member of staff – someone who has already crossed those thresholds and has progressed up the career ladder. Or you can do it across those thresholds.

Paddy: Can I add something about this which is important in terms of the set up? If Paul contacts me and asks me to mentor a mentee, it can be quite a difficult situation for the mentee, because their boss has approached a mentor he knows to allocate to them. Have they got any agency in the process? What we did when we set up the community interest company, 121support.org.uk, [was that] we worked out an introduction in the first session, to say that if this isn't working for you and it's about our relationship, not whether we like one another personally, you must say so and we will find someone else. You have to give space for a mentee to say no. As Paul was saying, in some cases, I could do with a Black mentor, although that is thought about beforehand. Three of the people I was mentoring were Black managers but they were happy to continue mentoring. They are not looking for all the answers in one person, and often they are dealing with the issues of being a Black, Asian or ethnic minority manager in a predominantly white structure with their peer group or experts with the lived experience. Some are saying, '*I want to concentrate on me and, my management role*'. At the end of the second session, I used to say, '*this is your chance to say, "do you want to change, move or go with this?"'* It never happened. By that time, you had built up a good relationship, but the person you are mentoring always had to be left with the option of being able to say this isn't quite working, without it being seen as rejecting or upsetting both ways.

That relates to setting up the mentoring scheme. Can you tell us more about this?

Paddy: Myself and other colleagues, wanted to put our experiences back into services, and weren't looking for money or payment. We had a number of CEOs come to us to ask us for mentoring support for themselves and employees. We decided to formalize it by setting up a community interest company. We then wrote to CEOs to let them know what we were offering. In the end, we did charge £500 for all six sessions. This paid for purely for fares, travel, the website, etc., but we as individuals weren't paid. We wanted to put something back, understanding, and being a resource to, many of the CEOs we had worked with – to develop a resource which made life easier for them. That worked. We had retired. It ran for six or seven years, until we were celebrating our seventieth birthdays, [which was] when we questioned what we were doing. Predominantly, six or seven Trusts used our services all the time. They were getting good feedback from the staff we mentored so there was scope. It should be said that when approached, we offered mentoring to individuals in the third sector at a significantly discounted rate, so that small organizations were not excluded.

We then had a number of individuals who were still working who wanted to do this, but didn't want to be paid. So, the reward was for them was that we brought them together in a big meeting and paid for this, twice a year. That's important to people to create that sort of mentoring and networking space.

Paul: One of the key things about mentoring is generosity. The idea of being paid for it would in some ways be wrong, because it speaks to people's willingness to give back and help the next generation coming through, to help them make the right choices, to help them manage difficult situations. The value of generosity played into it. Schemes like I was on, and you set up, Paddy, you need space. When you are more experienced you know a number of people who could do this, who are well placed to mentor given their experience and the time in their careers. Mentoring is predominantly informal and does rely on generosity, but nonetheless some formal organization of that is crucial: it gives an infrastructure, creates a range of contacts and perhaps generates some equality of opportunity. Organized schemes are a resource that staff can tap in to and bridge that gap.

Paddy: A structural thing: how do you get knowledge about what's going on around you. Trusts have grown much larger through mergers. So, in the past one might have asked colleagues in next door Trusts to mentor some staff, but as the Trusts become larger, and most people want to go outside their own organization for mentoring, there is a sense in which you have restricted your pool of mentors. As the organizations have become larger and larger, you have reduced your peer group. Your peer group is ever further away.

What happened with the mentoring scheme you set up, Paddy?

Paddy: We formally closed it down because a lot of people we had mentoring were outside London. The numbers of mentees dwindled and it became more difficult. Four of us were doing a lot ourselves. So, we approached a couple of organizations. We talked to the Mental Health Network to see if they wanted to take it over and develop it. Although we charged minimally, we ended up making a profit. We offered to give them all that as well and move it over. For different reasons, such as time to set it up, none of them could do it. So, we decided to close it down and gave the money to a third-sector organization.

The learning is we set it up between the four of us. For mentoring schemes to work organizationally and continue, they need embedding in the organizational structure. Where a mentoring scheme is dependent on individuals, it's not owned by the system.

What do you feel has made mentoring effective from each of your perspectives?

Paul: A mix of things: the ability to be open and honest; the fact that it is outside 'normal business',; and generosity – the fact that people are willing to give their time to someone else, to listen willingly and to share their own experience. It's two ways. When you are a mentor, while it is detached, you are putting your own experience, shortcomings and mistakes on the table to help someone else. Effective mentoring is not judgemental. You can help people come to their own conclusion and view of what they have done/are thinking of doing is the right choice. It isn't an appraisal or to do with a performance management process. It is about helping people, from a spirit of helpfulness and generosity, decide about what they do next in their jobs, either dealing with immediate issues or planning their next moves, or other issues.

Paddy: When you talk about generosity, I think of *The Gift Relationship* by Richard Titmuss (2018). You do end up with a good relationship. From a mentee's perspective, this is someone with a huge range of experience and they are here for me, willing to give me an hour, to talk about anything I want to talk about. From my perspective as mentor, I became quite invested. I wanted the sessions to go well and for them to be happier in their job, not necessarily more successful, but more comfortable. [I wanted them] to be able to walk out and feel it was a worthwhile session; someone who understands what they are going through, who isn't going to judge them, who may have some solutions, or even say, '*I don't know what you can do about it. That's a real problem and the organization is in danger because of that problem, or you are. You need to tell your manager. There is nothing we can do through mentoring.*' This can be affirming, as it is recognized as an issue for the organization, not the mentee's failure.

What might have hindered mentoring from your perspective?

Paul: When the personal chemistry doesn't work properly. I can think of a few examples of when the mentor and mentee are not prepared to share enough of themselves. You have to have that openness and honesty on both sides. There's a critical mass [needed] for the mentoring to take off. If that's not there it will not work.

What Paddy said about recognizing it for what is it. If you think you are going to a mentoring session and it's a coaching session, you have a different expectation of it. You need to be clear what mentoring is and isn't, what makes it work and what doesn't. When you go to a coaching session, it's more formal, an expectation you will get something, whereas mentoring is less formal/a conversation. You get something from that human interaction and sharing experience, not because someone has gone through some management or coaching theory. People do muddle mentoring and coaching from both directions. They cannot expect from/out of mentoring what comes from coaching.

Paddy: If the mentee doesn't take responsibility for setting the agenda: this the key. I had one difficult situation I was involved in. We got on and she felt supported. The organization was under scrutiny. Her position was difficult. I felt the mentoring was having to compensate for the organization's dysfunction. It can't do that. I could not make her situation better in the organization. The organization and managers were going to have to do that. Coming together in mentoring is not the answer to organizational dysfunction. Sort the dysfunction out first, then you have the ability to do something with mentoring. I never felt she got much out of it, though I did feel I was personally able to support her in some difficult circumstances. It became something else.

What are the key headlines and standout messages for you?

Paul: One message is, that in my view, mentoring is not for life. It has a value as a time-limited exercise. That time isn't necessarily six sessions a year, but it doesn't work to try and perpetuate it too long. It becomes something else then. The mentee needs to take the learning and move on. However it is defined, whether it is defined prospectively or retrospectively, it is doing a certain amount of work and reaching a mutual conclusion that the time is ripe to stop. It should always have a stop.

I think what you are saying is to be aware of the time limit.

Paddy: Mentoring needs to be within the structure of the organization. I have seen too many times [instances] where a person has arranged mentoring and that's it. Whereas when it finishes the manager or CEO needs to take responsibility for that individual coming back to discuss [the mentoring] and ask questions like: Where does that leave you?; What does it make you feel about the organization?; and, What's the next step for you? It has to be located back within the organization, whether it's the supervision system or appraisal system, it needs to be part of the structure. The end and beginning of mentoring need to be recognized and responsibility taken back in the organization.

One of the 'standouts' is that mentoring is not used enough. It doesn't need to be national but I do think three or four Trusts could come together and identify two people who would do mentoring. That would give us eight between four organizations that could mentor eight people, or move around. [We should] think of it as a resource but I don't think we do it often enough. I really enjoyed mentoring when I was in post. You realised how far you had come and the learning along the way. You don't recognize how you move on. You don't recognize how the world has changed since I was a social worker in a Community Mental Health Team in Nottingham in 1982–1983, but a lot has changed. You need to look at where we came from. We have made progress. We have got some things right and some things wrong. That's the frustration I can feel when we focus on what's not working well. You need to look at where we came from. That doesn't make what has happening now right, but we are in a much better place than we were. As a mentor, this is one of the things that came home for me. We have moved on. We haven't got it right. As a mentor, that's the feedback I get. It allows me to reflect and realise how much we did that was effective, but also how much has been lost, and about the things we got wrong. For the mentor, it's an enjoyable process, a validation of past experiences.

Reference

Titmuss R. (2018). *The Gift Relationship: From Human Blood to Social Policy*. The New Press.

Chapter 17
Legacy Mentoring

Trevor Waldock

Summary

Mentoring was shaped by the strapline, *'teach him everything you know'*, from the Greek myth of Odysseus. The reality is that mentoring owes more to understanding the role and development of eldership for the twenty-first century. This chapter explores both how we can step up the game of mentoring to legacy mentoring and how we use it to develop this and the next generation of change-makers in the world.

One of the misconceptions of the modern Western mind is that myths are somehow just make-believe stories with little or no power to impact our lives. Actually, myths are central to how the right hemisphere of our brains captures the deeper and wider truths of the world we live in and how it works. They provide us with a more insightful view of reality than much of what passes as modern views of 'truth' (McGilchrist, 2021). One of the better known ancient Greek myths has given the leadership world the word *mentor*, which is seen as a key conversation in the leader's toolkit. Often, when I was training mentors, whether it was for business, social or non-profit leadership, I would start by telling the myth that explains the origin of the word. I would begin the story by saying, *'when Odysseus went off to the Trojan wars, he left behind his young son Telemachus. Before he departed, he called on his old friend Mentor and gave him oversight over his son with those well-known words, "teach him everything you know" – and that is where the name MENTOR comes from.'* Yet this version of the myth is somewhat incomplete and short-changes us of the potential that mentoring offers the world.

Looking more closely at the forgotten details of the myth of Odysseus and Mentor, we discover that it goes more like this... Father Odysseus went off to war and asked his old friend Mentor to teach his son everything he knew (so far so good). However, there are two extra important dimensions that have been lost from this popular version of the myth. First, while Mentor was his name, his role wasn't simply that of a mentor, as we often understand it; he was, more accurately, an elder. Second, Mentor didn't do the real mentoring for Telemachus, the goddess Athena did.

Mentor's contribution

Much of the discussion about mentoring, as a dimension of the leadership conversation, has lost sight of the real opportunity for a deeper, more transformational, conversation. The key insight, that has frequently been overlooked, is that Mentor was not primarily a mentor (as we currently use the word) – he was an elder. *Mentor* was his name, but *elder* was his role. Mentor was Odysseus's elder. Naturally, Odysseus, who had experienced the value of Mentor's eldership, wanted his son to also gain all the wisdom he could from this older man. The role of elder has been woven into the fabric of traditional culture since time immemorial. Nelson Mandela, a global icon of an elder, had his own personal elders integrated into his life from his birth to his death. He recognized his utter indebtedness to the wisdom, perspective, challenge, neutrality, courage and insight of these elders across his lifespan, in shaping who he became. Mandela's view of the vital importance of elders in developing him as a leader and then an elder himself, was perfectly summed up by Reuel Khoza (2006), when he wisely noted that, *'leadership is formed in the cradle of elders'*. The man Mentor was such a cradle, an elder, to Odysseus and so it was no surprise that he wanted his son to have the same excellent cradle of development and support, to aid Telemachus in his journey into adulthood.

By viewing the mentoring role through the lens of eldership, we can offer so much more to the development of mentors (Waldock, 2021). By taking this perspective, we lessen the risk of reducing mentoring to simply imparting skills development, having encouraging conversations, sponsoring career aspirations, helping people navigate their way through organizational politics and facilitating a personal development 101. To be clear, mentoring can legitimately include all of these things if you are an elder, because elders are mentors (in the common usage of that word), but not all mentors are elders.

Those who have embodied the qualities of eldership help others in deeper ways. They are able to look at the wider context (including historical), the whole picture, the deeper and wider purpose and meaning of what is happening (both at work and beyond), the deeper motivations of our actions and the legacy we are creating. They help their clients wrestle with their own ego and get beyond it. They assist in the recovery of the essential leadership qualities of humility, kindness, courage, generosity and speaking truth to power. Such people I call *legacy mentors*.

Legacy mentors help a leader to have the existential developmental conversations that no one around them seems to be having, that include such questions as: *Who are you becoming? Why are you here? Who does your life or your organization exist for? What legacy will you leave behind?* (The kind of seminal questions raised by another famous myth, that of King Arthur and his knight Parsival).

Kirsten Powers, CNN analyst and *New York Times* best-seller, talking in an interview about her latest book *Saving Grace* (Powers, 2021), shares a pivotal point in her mid-fifties where she says, *'One of my life turning points was asking myself, who do I want to be? … I am supposed to be, at this point in my life, becoming an elder.'*

There are thousands of experienced leaders asking themselves exactly the same questions: *What now? Is this all there is? I'm meant to retire, but I feel there is another chapter in me. How can I make a real contribution to the world?* Who will help all of those in the world, like Kirsten Powers, who are entering the second half of their life and are asking themselves, on the early morning commuter train, or in the coffee queue between back-to-back meetings, questions like; *Who am I beyond this job? What is the true end in mind of my life? What is the legacy that will outlive me?* Whether you are an experienced or emerging leader, all of us need the opportunity to explore these profound and challenging, life-shaping questions. Connecting with our deeper sense of purpose is foundational to all meaningful contribution at work and in wider life.

Athena's contribution

Our children may have little appreciation for the music, books, podcasts, advice, etc. that we have found most helpful. Odysseus found Mentor an invaluable elder in his own life, but his son plainly didn't! The second revelation in the ancient Greek myth is that Mentor wasn't much help to Telemachus. Odysseus's fatherly idea didn't go to plan. By all accounts the young Telemachus was left pretty much unchanged by his mentoring experience with Mentor! It is at this point that we are introduced to the goddess Athena. She comes to meet the young Telemachus, disguised as Mentor, but she brings an entirely different quality of conversation, that really did change things for this young man. The goddess was the embodiment of a holistic humanity, a more complete integrity. She was the goddess of both warfare *and* wisdom, of courage *and* creativity, of justice *and* inspiration, the strategic *and* the empathic. It was her integrated humanity that facilitated the real transformation in the life of Telemachus. Interestingly, if we look at the impact of elders on Mandela's life, he developed from the macho young man into the same integrated blend of qualities that Athena modelled. Mentor was ineffective without the soul-work of Athena. Legacy mentors are an integration of Mentor and Athena, they can work with leaders in discerning the right battles to give energy to, defining their strategy, and building their courage, they can help process the leader's ambitions, focus their desires for justice and navigate their career path – the 'doing' part of leadership. They also help leaders to integrate within themselves their heart-centred aptitudes for exploring creativity, honouring intuition, developing generosity, cultivating empathy and compassion, investing in inspiration, distilling wisdom (Ket de Vries, 2022) and prioritizing kindness – the qualities of 'being' and of soul. Doing and being. Mentor and Athena.

Recovering the fullness of the myth of Mentor, and embracing and integrating our 'Athena' within the public face of our 'Mentor', is essential if we are to develop a generation of mentors into legacy mentors, who in turn transform current and emerging leaders to become legacy mentors themselves.

When Rachel asked me to mentor her through a career change, she was initially very focused on getting the right skills, honing her CV, mapping out a career plan and networking with the right stakeholders to help her further her personal brand in the marketplace. Once we had outlined all these immediate 'wants', I did two things. First, I said, *'why don't we just pause for a minute of silence. Use the time as you want. Meditate. Pray. Reflect. But let's practice the core leadership skill of making silent space.'* I made this suggestion in the broadest terms, knowing how some people get snagged up on associating deep mindfulness with religion, or 'soft' leadership. As she began reflecting on how she now felt after that minute, she said she felt a little calmer (I had noticed how there had been an underlying anxiety behind all her immediate wants, which had prompted me to seek a quieter rhythm in the conversation that followed.) I then asked her another question, *'At the start of the conversation we outlined all that you want from this mentoring and from life right now. Can I ask you what life is wanting from you right now?'* She was clearly disrupted by this question. I encouraged her to sit with it and see what emerges. I was reframing the conversation at a deeper and higher level of meaning and purpose. She began to talk about an experience she had had months previously that had made no rational sense to her, and how she dared not talk to anyone about it for fear they would think her a little whacky. As she told me about the experience, we began to listen without judgement to what it might have been saying to her, regardless of whether it was imagined or from some deeper, intuitive space within her. My conversation with Rachel had now shifted to a totally different place from where it started, and yet was still very much an exploration of where her life was going. Her immediate needs and wants were now being shaped by a deeper narrative of purpose, meaning, vocation and life's deeper call to her. Over the following months we deepened these conversations, as she discovered more about the source of her life's motivation, her sense of why she was here on this planet at this time. She looked more at her contribution to life, rather than her performance at work. She investigated practices that would keep her rooted and grounded in living from that place of source within herself, rather than being driven by other people's agendas of success. She came to a place in the mentoring relationship where although she had developed a plan of action, she was more focused on who she was becoming, rather than what was the right thing to be doing.

How we become legacy mentors

Making the journey toward getting over ourselves

The first half of life is very much about building the ego identity structures. We are wrapped up with questions such as: *How do I make my mark? Who do I know? What gives me self-worth? Where do I belong? What can I achieve? What positions do I hold?* And then there is the second half of life, which can be summed up by the word *aspiration*. The Greek root of this word means, to *stretch beyond your ego*; to get over, or beyond, ourselves. Beyond this all-important ego-self, that we constructed in the first half of life, lies the true self. The true self is more conscious of its interdependent role in the world, is concerned with meaning, loving and leaving a legacy. Legacy mentors can facilitate the crossing over from 'doing' to 'being'.

To mentor leaders well, the legacy mentor first needs to do the hard work of getting over themselves. It is the legacy mentor's personal experience of this journey that equips them to help others to navigate it too. We cannot mentor anyone beyond, or deeper, than where we have journeyed ourselves. How can I help a leader get beyond their own ego, if I haven't begun to get beyond my own? I won't have experienced that painful journey. I won't be familiar with the territory that needs to be navigated by those I mentor.

Working on my heart and character requires the same discipline as a daily trip to the gym, because the ego would almost do anything rather than surrender its hard-fought identity. Who am I if I am not successful, famous, respected, wealthy and well known? The 'doing' aspect of the self feels it is better to keep on investing in and defending the identity that it *thinks* is the real self, rather than to risk discovering that much of it is an illusion. It is that very awareness of those moments in our day, where we feel ourselves tightening up, responding defensively, getting protective, acting more tribally, building a moat around what we possess, or holding on, rather than letting go, that provides us with the clues as to how to get beyond our defended ego.

Becoming bigger people and asking bigger questions

An egocentric life limits our vision of who we are, who we can become and how we see the world. Once the ego work begins, we are able to see that there is so much more potential within us than we ever imagined. We all have greater capacity for cognitive development, for emotional development, for talent and skill development, for empathy development, for relationship development and for consciousness development. We also have a greater capacity to discover our role and contribution to the wider world, which we uncover as we begin the move from a self-centred focus to a more global and universal-centred view of the world. The opportunity to explore our potential is available to us every single day, across every single moment of our lives, through every choice we make about our thoughts and our actions. Each step creates another brush stroke on the canvas of who we are becoming.

The legacy mentor, who is becoming a more expansive person, is not afraid to ask bigger questions of themselves and others. I have a few people who continue to mentor me. One of them asked me recently, *'Do you actually need to earn money?'* This came at a time when I was wrestling with what felt like a tension between leaving a legacy and still earning some money. I was taken aback, surprised by their question. It certainly felt challenging and I felt a tightening around my ego as it rose up, wanting to respond, *'Of course I do, you don't understand my situation.'* It was an invitation for me to stretch my understanding of myself, beyond the expected comfortable norms of work, of retirement and my relationship to money, as well as confront my insecurities. Her question was coming from a larger view of life, its meaning and my innate potential. Another mentor challenged the leader in me recently by saying, *'You aren't the boss anymore.'* He wasn't referring to my transition around my job, he was calling me to think about how the universe works and the fact that I'm not in control. To be honest, the leader's instinct to be in control is actually an illusion. None of us are really in control of much at all and he was inviting me to trust who I was, within the universe, in a way that I needed to hear. My mentors weren't trying to tell me what I should think, or do, or what to believe, but they were both asking bigger questions of me, to give me an opportunity to become a bigger person. They could both do that, because they themselves, as legacy mentors, had faced and explored these tough questions for themselves.

Moving away from collusion

The 'non-directive' approach in coaching and mentoring teaches us just that – that we should only be following the client's agenda and not influencing the direction the conversation takes. They and they alone set the agenda. In a conversation I had with a very well-known thought leader in the field of mentoring, he challenged this particular stance because, he said, it doesn't address the temptation to slip into *collusion*. As we know, collusion is an unspoken agreement to not talk about something. Sometimes, it's consciously avoided, like the proverbial 'elephant in the room' and at other times it is unconsciously avoided. He was challenging the mentoring shibboleths as to why coaches and mentors were remaining quiet on the big issues of our time. Why weren't mentors asking challenging questions to CEOs about their lack of ambition and action with issues such as their organizations response to the climate crisis, or the threatening of democracy, or the inequality against women?

Another area where collusion may happen is in relation to the economy. The word economy has become limited in many people's minds to for-profit organizations. Actually, the word 'economy' comes from the Greek word *oikos*, which means 'house'. The economy was built on the metaphor of a house with many rooms. 'Rooms' bartered with one another for the benefit of everyone, the whole house, the oikos, the economy. In an individualistic society, we often forget that our room, and indeed our personal benefit, comes from our interdependence with the other rooms. Life is an interdependent reality. Some CEOs focus on *their* business (*their* room) and how to make it the best and outdo other rooms. We have department heads who focus on their corner of their room. The oikos/economy, is the whole house and is the context that each 'room', or organization, or department, sits within. When we allow a conversation to just focus on our clients' individual concerns, or their particular patch, or myopic perspectives (even if that happens to be a whole organization), then we collude with those CEOs or leaders. We do this by not *lifting up* the conversation to the higher, 'house' level, and not *drawing out* the depth of the whole person within the whole 'house'. The climate crisis, for example, is a global issue that is recognized as one of the top current existential threats to organizations, and organizations are simultaneously impacting on the sustainability of the planet. However much a leader might want to avoid it, it is actually an unavoidable conversation within the context of the whole picture.

A legacy mentor courageously holds the bigger picture by embracing and introducing into the conversation such questions as:

- What are we not talking about here?
- What are the long-term consequences of your current choices, in a few generations from now?
- What is your relationship to money and wealth creation?
- What legacy do you want to leave behind?

These questions will inspire new insights as we take legacy mentoring conversations into a more expansive place. At the very least, this means that we need to invest more deeply in ourselves as legacy mentors, so that we take a more holistic approach with our questions. In this way we ensure that we are not just developing partial areas of a person's life, but the whole. Can we ask the deeper questions about the centrality of kindness (Timpson, 2021), along with love and empathy, which are the issues of *being*? These go alongside the issues of doing, such as explorations around strategy, leadership and direction. Together Mentor and Athena had a complete view of leadership development through legacy mentoring.

It is sobering to reflect that if a westerner had mentored Nelson Mandela on his approach to ending apartheid, he would probably have been as ineffective as Mentor was with Telemachus. Why? Because the world view that was needed to end apartheid, Ubuntu, is not a western mindset, it is African. Ubuntu is a highly interdependent mindset that is woven into the fabric of community development. It is a philosophy deeply rooted in human identity – '*I am because we are.*' My experience of working in India and Africa taught me that business leaders have a different relationship to community, meaning and spirituality at work, than their western counterparts. My friends who work in the Middle East tell me the same. Extending our points of view by understanding different views of the world, is an essential component of legacy mentoring, if we are to learn to ask the deeper questions.

The confidence to invest in the next generation

One of the dimensions of my working week is offering pro-bono mentoring to the youth ambassadors of *One Young World*,[9] the global youth organization. I recently extended this by making an open invitation to experienced mentors and coaches to join me on a team to expand our support offering. The people I approached to join my team were all very experienced professionals, with impressive coaching and mentoring CVs, covering many decades. So, it was surprising to hear a significant number saying, *'I'm not sure I'd be much good at this ... I don't think I have much to offer these young people.'*

I've observed a surprising lack of confidence from experienced mentors to step into the legacy-mentoring space with young people. This potential impostor syndrome can continue in us all across a lifetime; sometimes it is obvious and sometimes it is well disguised. The legacy mentor takes the opportunity to listen to their own fears and then turn it around within themselves and receive it as an important piece of insight about humanity, not just themselves. We are all fearful that we are 'not enough' and young people are also fearful that they are 'not enough'. Young people may be working extra hard to extinguish their fear through activity and achievement. Older people fear their lack of usefulness after a certain point in their working life. None of us, young or old, are experts in making this life journey. We are all making our maiden voyage. We are not just fearful that work will expose our shortcomings, but that life itself, with all its unforeseen challenges, may reveal us as inadequate. The issue of confidence doesn't just apply to people stepping up to become legacy mentors, but to everyone alive. Our anxiety about mentoring certain groups of people is actually a window into the human condition. We can say to ourselves and to those we mentor, *'I'm stepping up to offer you all that I have, with humility and confidence. I don't have the answers but I'm willing to walk alongside of you. Together we will face life with an open heart, with courage and fragility, because that is what it means to be human.'*

Our lack of confidence is not simply a barrier to get over, but an invitation to a more real, more genuinely helpful, mentoring relationship.

Legacy mentoring is just another name for eldership. The world desperately needs us to aspire towards being elders in our mentoring and to seed the next generation of elders through our mentoring conversations. Whatever age you find yourself working with, being a legacy mentor is truly a high calling and great honour, and a way of ensuring something of real value that can outlive us. It calls us to deepen the conversation within ourselves, in order that we can deepen the conversation with those we support. Rather than simply facilitating tactical, career, strategic or organizational–political manoeuvring, legacy mentoring offers the chance to be involved in the transformation of who someone is becoming; making an investment in how they can learn to lead, love and leave a legacy in the totality of their life.

---

9   www.oneyoungworld.com.

References

Kets de Vries, M. F. R. (2022). *Leading Wisely: Becoming a Reflective Leader in Turbulent Times*. Wiley.

Khoza, R. J. (2006). *Let Africa Lead: African Transformational Leaders for 21st Century Business*. Vezubuntu.

McGilchrist, I. (2021). *The Matter with Things: Our Brains, Our Delusions, and the Unmaking of the World*. Perspectiva.

Powers, K. (2021). *Saving Grace: Speak Your Truth, Stay Centered, and Learn to Coexist with People Who Drive You Nuts*. Convergent Books.

Timpson, J. (2021, October 17). *Kindness always comes first for successful leaders. The Sunday Times*.

Waldock, T. (2021). *Becoming Mandela: Be Your Legacy*. Trevor Waldock.

Chapter 18
Changing Minds through Futures-Focused Mentoring

Stephen Murgatroyd

Mentors help leaders and followers become authentic change leaders, able to imagine the future and help team members design and redesign their organization and business processes to enable that future. Mentors help build courage and the capacity of leaders to share leadership and become followers as well as leaders. They mentor for authenticity, courage and transformative leadership coupled with compassion.

Mentoring for courage is not a new aspiration (Hobgood, 1999) and the practice of mentoring is essentially a Socratic process of engaged and inspired conversation aimed at exploring ideas, beliefs and values that underdetermine action and shape strategy (Mills & Murgatroyd, 1990). Sometimes, the work focuses on the particular challenges and issues of the moment, but often the mentor pushes the leader to consider the bigger picture – strategic intentions, impacts of competing forces on the 'direction of travel' the organization is embarked upon and the ways in which different teams and tribes within the organization are responding (Murgatroyd, 1984, 1988; Mills & Murgatroyd, 1990). Always, the mentor is working to reveal to the leader the leader's own authentic self, which is the source of their courage and is the basis for their work as a leader – it is how they develop personal mastery (Murgatroyd & Simpson, 2011).

Futures literacy and the work of mentoring

Some see mentoring as always about a conversation – a unique form of 'talk-therapy' for the practice of leadership, without the work becoming therapy of a different kind – self-exploration and psychotherapy. It is in part psychological work, but also about exploring the practices of leadership, based on the significant practical experience of the mentor.

It is also about using analytic frameworks and tools to design a different future for the organization and to understand the dynamics of leadership and change management. These tools help leaders better articulate just how their futures-focused understanding of their organization can be communicated, and also enables an interrogation of the future landscape of the organization – what it will look like, who might be doing what and what it will take to change, adapt and reconfigure it to make that future possible.

In this chapter, I outline the five tools used most often in the mentoring and foresight work undertaken within organizations since the mid-1980s. These organizations include schools and school systems, universities and colleges, large international banks, large retail organizations, airlines, health care systems, manufacturing organizations, global IT companies, forestry and ecosystem service organizations, local care providers and non-profit organizations. Each claim their situation is unique, and they are in part correct. But the generic tools are easily tweaked. Each claim that the challenges and dynamics they face are very specific and they are in part right, but they are also locked into their own company and industry sector and are not looking across boundaries and niches and seeing the bigger picture. When they are helped to do so, they realize that the network of potential supports and solutions found in a completely different industry in a completely different part of the world is just what they need to deal with an immediate or near-term challenge.

The tools come from work in foresight literacy and from the world of design. These two disciplines are strongly connected. Design focuses on complex problems and uses tools to develop both innovative ideas and practical, workable solutions to the challenges faced (Martin & Hanington, 2019). Futures literacy is focused on what might be called 'the cone of anticipation' (Voros, 2003; 2017; 2019), shown in Figure 18.1.

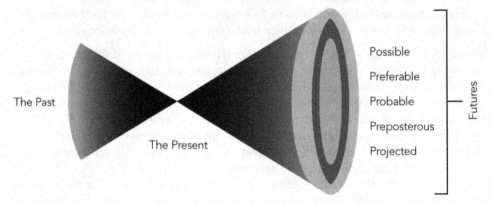

Figure 18.1: The cone of anticipation.

Those who work in futures literacy make extensive use of design tools when they do so. In particular, scenario development (Bishop et al., 2007) and causal layer analysis (Bishop & Dzidic, 2014) coupled with 'A Thing from the Future' (Situation Lab, 2015) are commonly deployed in workshops and consulting activities aimed at building a picture of possible, probable and projected futures. This work is different from a lot of what passes as strategic planning, which is essentially taking the present and projecting it forward. Futurists begin with the assumption that the future is not and does not have to be a straight line from the past and that we need to imagine different futures, given all that is happening in the world (Larsen et al., 2020).

When leaders are excited about an emerging technology, for example, futures-focused mentors encourage them to look at the Gartner hype cycle (Dedehayir & Steinert, 2016). Produced annually by a technology-focused consulting organization, the hype cycle places current and emerging technologies appropriate for the organization in a specific place on a curve ranging from 'peak of inflated expectations' through a 'trough of disillusionment' through the 'slope of enlightenment' to the 'plateau of productivity'. The mentor may also encourage them to imagine the deployment over time, which is where the Three-Horizon tool (Curry & Hodgson, 2008) can be helpful.

The tools to be described here each aim to develop the futures literacy and strategic thinking skills of leaders through focused tools where mentors engage in guided conversations about their use and their application to the work of the organization. The basic idea is simple: given that the future depends on actions we take today and that there are many possible futures, effective leaders develop a deep understanding of their preferred future and work back from that future to the present.

Five tools to focus the mentoring conversations

In a review of mentoring practices related to developing capabilities, Crisp and Cruz (2009) suggest that there are essentially three kinds of mentoring:

1. mentoring that is focused on the growth and development of the individual (Hernandez et al., 2017);

2. mentoring that is focused on supporting the mentee in dealing with the current and near-term challenges they face – psychological, practical and connecting them with others; and

3. mentoring that is both personal and reciprocal – creating a 'blanket' of support for the work the mentee has to do, both now and in the future (Ragins & Verbos, 2007).

This chapter suggests a fourth kind of mentoring: building the capacity of the mentee to think back from the future and act now to enable a preferred future.

The tools to be described here are devices to shift the conversation and engage in a bigger exploration of where they are headed in terms of their work as a leader and in terms of the work of the organization they are a part of. They can be used in any order and at any time, but their use does tend to create an intense and focused dialogue about the nature of leadership, the future focus for their work and the challenges of organizational change and development.

Tool 1: The Futures Consciousness Scale

The Futures Consciousness Scale was developed by colleagues at the University of Turku in Finland (Ahvenharju et al., 2018; Lalot et al., 2020). It explores the tendencies, biases and mindsets of leaders as they think about their future and that of their organization. It also suggests the ways in which leaders will react to aspects of the future as they become apparent. It consists of questions on these dimensions:

- **Time perspective** – Understanding the past, present and future and how actions today have consequences in the future. Valuing long-term thinking.

- **Agency beliefs** – Trust in one's ability to influence future events. Understanding of what can be influenced and how.

- **Openness to alternatives** – Critical evaluation of alternatives and questioning of established truths. Seeing future possibilities broadly and innovatively.

- **Systems perspectives** – Seeing the interconnectedness within and between human and natural systems. Understanding the complex consequences of the decisions we make.

- **Concerns for others** – Understanding the interdependences between all humanity. Motivation to improve the lives of others, beyond self. Commitment to act according to own morals.

In all there are twenty questions which take two to five minutes to complete. The system used to collect responses then generates an individual spider map of the results, which can be quickly shared between the mentor and leader. Such maps look can look like Figure 18.2, the results of a particular leader in a health care organization:

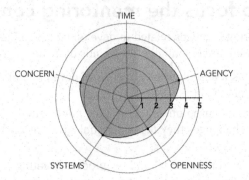

Figure 18.2: Spider map for a leader in a health care organization.

As can be seen, they are not that open to change and development and have a weak understanding of systems dynamics and how systems work. My own map looks like this (Figure 18.3):

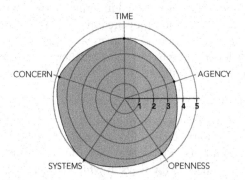

Figure 18.3: Spider map for the author.

Sharing these maps and exploring their implications for their readiness for a different or quickly changing future, and/or exploring their sense of agency or their sense of 'entrapment' in a culture of rules, accountability targets and complex dynamics provides a powerful starting point for conversations about their preparedness for the 'big' work of leadership – driving performance with passion, leading change as a result of thinking back from the future and building shared leadership.

In practice, these kinds of tools trigger powerful conversations about what leadership in the context of their own organization actually means and what a path for their own development may look like.

Tool 2: Scenarios: Seeing as far as you can see

Futures thinking is often associated with the development of scenarios – frameworks for different futures. The idea is simple – understand the patterns and trends shaping the future and distil these into some key dimensions that will give shape to the future. For example, one dimension in looking at a post-COVID-19 world would be the speed of economic recovery (from fast to slow) and the other the nature of trust in government, business and related organizations (from high to low). The resultant analysis might suggest these scenarios for the future (Table 18.1):

Table 18.1: Future economic recovery and trust scenarios.

Economic recovery/Rebound

	Division/Enclaves/Tension	Vibrant and connected communities	
Social trust low	■ Economy rebuilds but remains volatile and fragile ■ People and organizations adopt new behaviours – virtual interactions, small groups, home-based work ■ Family and local interests 'trump' provincial and national interests ■ Digital divide exacerbated by the persistence of online activity (especially school, college and university) ■ Not all can find meaningful work	■ Virus is well controlled and many accept vaccination ■ People crave human interaction and find ways of balancing interaction and safety ■ Companies, many with fewer employees, deploy technology smartly to secure profit ■ Trust in government returns and private sector strengthens its influence ■ Inequality remains but is 'quietened' by the growth in employment	**Social trust high**
	Growing tense divisiveness	'We're in this together'	
	■ Prolonged recession with a fear of second and third waves of COVID-19 – no sign of a vaccine ■ Significant, prolonged unemployment with youth unemployment at an all-time high ■ Trust in government, employers and each other shaken and fragile ■ Tribalism and bitterness between peoples ■ Increase in crime and malicious behaviour ■ Mistrust of information from public bodies – rumours beat facts	■ Prolonged impact of COVID-19 brings communities together – a spirit of 'we can overcome' ■ Bail outs for key industries and continued support for workers through guaranteed basic income ■ Significant tax incentives for upskilling and reskilling – learning key to the future ■ New and quickly emerging public–private partnerships respond to social need ■ Non-profit mergers and collaboration a hallmark of this scenario ■ High expectations around transparency and social good	

Economic recession/Depression

These scenarios, which came from mentoring work within an organization, are not intended to present a choice. The question being asked is not 'Which one of these four scenarios do you think will happen?' It is 'How ready are you and this organization for *all four* of these possible futures?' This is then followed by the question 'What is the work you and your team need to do to build the future you prefer while being ready for the other three?'

In a recent mentoring session, one leader suggested that they had spent so much time defining their 'preferred' future that she had neglected to explore the implications and challenges of the 'probable' future or the least desirable future. She suggested that this made agile and nimble responses to emerging events difficult, since they had anticipated things moving in a different direction.

In the mentoring relationships, developing a scenario map takes time. The big picture sketches of the four scenarios are hard work, but it is the exploration of their implications for leadership, organizational design, change and transformation which is where the mentoring work is. It requires the leader being mentored to have both a systems perspective and openness to new ways of thinking about old ways of working. Not all do.

Tool 3: Three Horizons: 'Shift happens!'

Scenarios are hard work and take time. Not all mentoring situations permit their use and development. An alternative is the Three Horizons planning tool. Developed by McKinsey in the early 2000s, the tool involves looking at three versions of the future, each labelled a horizon:

- **Horizon 1 is 'business as usual'**, or *'the world in crisis'* **(H1)** – It is characterized by 'sustaining innovation' that keeps 'business as usual' going. For example, what happened in the pandemic to enable certain activities to persist and thrive?

- **Horizon 2 represents** *'world in transition'* **(H2)** – The entrepreneurial and culturally creative space of already technologically, economically and culturally feasible innovations that can disrupt and transform H1 to varying degrees and can have either regenerative, neutral or degenerative socioecological effects. For example, the growing deployment of artificial intelligence (AI) as a basis for diagnostic work in the treatment of eye disease and cancer and the use of robotics in surgery – do these suggest a different future?

- **Horizon 3 is how we envision a** *'viable world'* **(H3)** – We may not be able to define this future in every detail — as the future is always uncertain — yet we can suggest what fundamental transformations lie ahead, and we can pay attention to social, ecological, economic, cultural and technological experiments around us that may be pockets of this future in the present. For example, is the use of telehealth and virtual counselling during the pandemic a harbinger of future care?

Putting these together gives us three very different patterns for the future (Figure 18.4):

Three horizons framework applied to the transition towards a regenerative culture

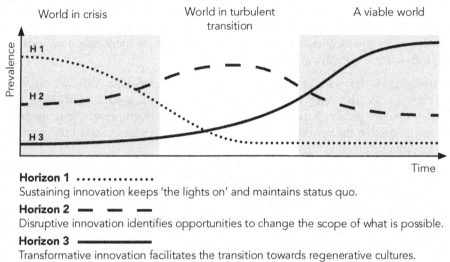

Horizon 1 ··············
Sustaining innovation keeps 'the lights on' and maintains status quo.
Horizon 2 ▬ ▬ ▬
Disruptive innovation identifies opportunities to change the scope of what is possible.
Horizon 3 ▬▬▬▬▬▬
Transformative innovation facilitates the transition towards regenerative cultures.

Figure 18.4: The Three Horizons framework applied to the transition toward a regenerative culture.

This too is hard work. It requires facilitating a conversation about what in the present time is worth persisting with (what do we improve or need to redesign?) and what needs to end so as to better prepare for a different future (what do we need to stop?) – a critical reflective understanding of the precarity of the present moment (Horizon 1). It requires us to examine what emerging opportunities, trends and patterns will emerge from the present (Horizon 2) and what truly disruptive events and innovations are occurring which will fundamentally change what we do, how we do it and where we do it (Horizon 3). As one commentator on this approach has noted:

> *Three Horizons thinking allows us to acknowledge what is valuable in each of the three horizons' distinct perspectives and ways of relating to the future. It helps us to see the opportunities and future potential of the present moment. It can help us to ask deeper questions as we engage in conversations informed by 'future consciousness' that turn rigid mindsets into valuable perspectives.*

(Wahl, 2017)

It also requires, as do most of the tools described here, the development of systems thinking on the part of emerging leaders as well as their ability to develop a strong sense of their own agency about the future. As Sharpe et al. (2016) observe, the work here is making explicit both what matters about the future of the organization and where the real power of leadership lies. These are sometimes both exciting and painful conversations, especially if the future involves major change and transformation and the leader being mentored recognizes that 'this work is not for me!'

Tool 4: A Thing from the Future

Some of the leaders with whom the author has worked need to think in concrete, tangible terms. The Situation Lab's (2017) 'A Thing from the Future' helps for these kinds of leaders. It is described thoroughly by Stuart Candy (2018) and the 'prompt' cards (if needed) can be downloaded[10] and produced to stimulate the mentoring conversation, though they are not always needed.

The basic idea is that a series of 'prompts' are used to stimulate a conversation about a specific topic or 'the thing' (e.g., well-being through work, the future of eldercare, excellent psychological services for all, the future of psychiatric assessment, medical diagnosis) and that the conversation aims to help refine an idea of what the future should be. The prompts are:

- **Grow** – ten, twenty or thirty years from now we will see... [in relation to 'the thing']
- **Collapse** – what, in the future will no longer be done, possible or acceptable – what has fallen apart?
- **Discipline** – what, in the future, will be carefully managed, controlled and analysed?
- **Transformation** – what in the future will be so transformed and different that we will hardly recognize it?
- **Mood** – the mood now is … but ten, twenty or thirty years from now the mood will be more one of…

A recent mentee explored what the 'thing from the future' would like if schools in Ontario became regenerative learning spaces (Denichaud, 2020), while another used it to examine what would happen if mentoring was done entirely through digital means, including AI-enabled mentor chatbots (French, 2020). Their work was shared as part of the UNESCO 2050 Futures of Education expedition.

What happens when this tool is used is that the leader begins to find new ways to articulate strategic direction and the cognitive–emotional components of the changes that this strategic direction will require.

Tool 5: Looking at myself and my organization in the future

Stories can entertain, delight, engage and inspire. In leadership writing and work, stories are everywhere. They range from the heroic ('you probably couldn't do this!''), through the cautionary ('never do this!'), to the motivational ('you should try to do this!') and the expository ('I did this and this is what I learned!'). As Harris and Barnes (2006) observe, engaging leaders in focused storytelling can help reveal a lot about them. They suggest a focus on themes, such as:

- mistakes and failures
- unexpected opportunities
- risk and reward
- choices and consequences
- lessons learned
- obstacles and challenges
- someone who inspired me…

---

10   The cards can be downloaded from http://situationlab.org/futurething-print-and-play-edition/.

These are all reflective and involve learning from the past. In the authors' work, the stories are set in the future and are triggered by starting lines, such as:

- *'Five years after we began our change journey, I found that...'*
- *'When we discovered that our budget was reduced by 15% but we were expected to increase our performance, we had no choice but to...'*
- *'The six big things we had to do to get to where we are now in 2030 were amazing ... First...'*
- *'We had no choice but to change. At first ... but then...'*

In all these kinds of storytelling, the mentor asks leaders to craft their stories in terms of:

1. a *story of now* that communicates the urgent challenge we are asking others to join us in acting on.

2. a *story of us* that speaks to the shared values, experiences or aspirations of our organization.

3. a *story of self* that describes our own challenge and the choice that led us to this outcome of taking leadership on the issue in question.

– based on the work of Chris Riedy (2020) at the University of Technology in Sydney, Australia. The value of these stories, as Riedy observes, are that they help the leader:

- make sense of, and learn from, the complex past and present;
- provide a window into other worlds and lives that can reveal hidden perspectives and build the case for change;
- *'imagine what might happen in the future, and so prepare for it – a feat no other species can lay claim to'* (Cron, 2012, p. 1);
- warn against future dangers;
- inspire and persuade people to adopt new practices;
- provide meaning, agency and direction;
- make future possibilities tangible and recruit people into realizing those possibilities; and
- build and maintain the institutional fabric to deliver a sustainable future.

From experience, leaders begin by being reluctant and hesitant but soon warm to the task. We often ask them to develop a PechaKucha presentation – twenty slides of images with no or just a few words which tell a powerful story with they can speak to from the heart as well as from experience. They are given just twenty seconds per slide, but the result is powerful. PechaKucha[11] is an established process used by organizations around the world to capture stories about the present and the future. Normally, some fifty thousand people would present their PechaKucha at one or more of eleven hundred events around the world. The power of these storyboards is the power of images – another skill set which futures-focused leaders need to master.

---

11   For more information, see https://www.pechakucha.com/about.

The value of futures-focused tools for the work of mentoring

The work of mentoring is not always about the present moment and the challenges faced by a leader. Indeed, too much of a preoccupation with the 'now' can inhibit the growth and development of the leader. Such mentoring is more like problem-solving and option-finding than about the development of authentic, courageous and transforming leaders. The tools outlined here are devices aimed at shifting focus from the 'now' to the 'what if?' and the 'then what?' and 'so what?'

One focus for my own work is learning from failure – not just my own or that of the mentee, but of many others who have gone on to be successful. As a late colleague wryly observed, *'failure is inevitable – learning from failure is an option!'* When we explore what has happened either within the organization or at other organizations with major futures-focused change efforts, we soon see that a great many of these efforts fail (Zigarmi & Hoekstra, 2008). The key learning comes from those who fail but persist, so as to get to the next place on their change journey. Decreasing the fear of failure while strengthening the resolve to engage in change is a key part of the mentoring work for authentic, courageous leadership (Schon, 1983).

So few leaders engage in serious, systematic examinations of the future – they are 'busy' with the work and demands of the present. Mentoring is an opportunity to get them to look up from their spreadsheets and reports and explore the emerging futures of the sector in which they work and the challenges these will give rise to in their own organization. Only when they can really see the futures clearly, can they act with purpose and strategic intention. Mentoring can be a vehicle to make a real difference to their growth and development.

References

Ahvenharju, S., Minkkinen, M., & Lalot, F. (2018). *The five dimensions of futures consciousness. Futures*, **104**, 1–13.

Bishop, B. J., and Dzidic, P. L. (2014). *Dealing with wicked problems: Conducting a causal layered analysis of complex social psychological issues. American Journal of Community Psychology*, **53**(1–2), 13–24.

Bishop, P., Hines, A., & Collins, T. (2007). *The current state of scenario development: An overview of techniques. Foresight*, **9**(1), 5–25.

Candy, S. (2018). Gaming futures literacy: A thing from the future. In R. Miller [ed.] Transforming the Future: Anticipation in the 21st Century. Routledge and UNESCO, pp. 233–246.

Crisp, G., & Cruz, L. (2009). *Mentoring college students – A critical review of the literature between 1990 and 2007. Research in Higher Education*, **50**(6), 525–545.

Cron, L. (2012). *Wired for Story*. Ten Speed Press.

Curry, A., & Hodgson, A. (2008). *Seeing in multiple horizons: Connecting futures to strategy. Journal of Futures Studies*, **13**(1), 1–10. https://jfsdigital.org/wp-content/uploads/2014/01/131-A01.pdf

Dedehayir, O., & Steinert, M. (2016). *The hype cycle model – A review and future directions. Technological Forecasting and Social Change*, **108**, 28–41.

Denichaud, D. (2020). *Learning to become 2050: Ontario schools as regenerative learning spaces. Education Futures Partnership*. https://education-futures-partnership.education/wp-content/uploads/2020/11/Learning-to-Become-DENICHAUD.pdf

French, R. (2020). *Why the future of mentorship needs to extend to the digital world. Education Futures Partnership*. https://education-futures-partnership.education/wp-content/uploads/2021/02/Feb-2021-French-Final-Paper.pdf

Harris, J., & Barnes, K. (2006). *Leadership storytelling. Industrial and Commercial Training*, **36**(7), 350–353.

Hernandez, P. R., Estrada, M., Woodcock, A., & Schultz. P. W. (2017). *Mentor qualities that matter: The importance of perceived (not demographic) similarity. Journal of Experimental Education*, **85**(3), 450–468.

Hobgood, M. E. (1999). *Mentoring moral courage: Resources in liberation ethics, community service, and the social commitment of the academy. Horizons*, **26**(1), 85–104.

Lalot, F., Ahvenharju, S., Minkkinen, M., & Wensing, E. (2020). *Aware of the future? The development and validation of the Futures Consciousness Scale. European Journal of Psychological Assessment*, **36**(5), 874–888.

Larsen, N., Mortensen, J. K., & Miller, R. (2020., February 11) *What is 'futures literacy' and why is it important? Copenhagen Institute for Future Studies*. https://medium.com/copenhagen-institute-for-futures-studies/what-is-futures-literacy-and-why-is-it-important-a27f24b983d8

Martin, B., & Hanington, B. (2019) *Universal Methods of Design: 125 Ways to Research Complex Problems, Develop Innovative Ideas, and Design Effective Solutions*. Rockport.

Mills, A. R., & Murgatroyd, S. (1990). *Organizational Rules: A Framework for Understanding Organizational Action*. The Open University Press.

Murgatroyd, S. (1984). *Relationships, change and the school. School Organization*, **4**(2), 171–179.

Murgatroyd, S. (1988). *Consulting as counselling – The theory and practice of structural consulting*. In H. L. Gray, (Ed.), *Management Consultancy in Schools*. Cassell Educational Publishing.

Murgatroyd, S., & Simpson, D. G. (2011). *Renaissance Leadership: Rethinking and Leading the Future*. Lulu Press.

Ragins, B. R., & Verbos, A. K. (2007). *Positive relationships in action: Relational mentoring and mentoring schemas in the workplace*. In J. Dutton, & B. R. Ragins, (Eds.), *Exploring Positive Relationships at Work: Building a Theoretical and Research Foundation* (pp. 91–116). Lawrence Erlbaum & Associates.

Riedy, C. (2020). *Storying the future: Storytelling practice in transformative systems*. In P. Molthan-Hill, H. Luna, T. Wall, H. Puntha, & D. Baden (Eds.), *Storytelling for Sustainability in Higher Education: An Educator's Handbook* (pp. 71–87). Routledge.

Schon, D. A. (1983). *The Reflective Practitioner: How Professionals Think in Action*. Basic Books.

Sharpe, B., Hodgson, A., Leicester, G., Lyon, A., & Fazey, I. (2016). *Three Horizons: A pathways practice for transformation. Ecology and Society*, **21**(2), 46–61. https://www.ecologyandsociety.org/vol21/iss2/art47/

Situation Lab (2017). *A Thing from the Future*. Situation Lab. http://situationlab.org/project/the-thing-from-the-future/

Voros J. (2003). *A generic foresight process framework. Foresight*, **5**(3), 10–21.

Voros, J. (2017, February 24). *The futures cone, use and history. The Voroscope*. https://thevoroscope.com/2017/02/24/the-futures-cone-use-and-history/

Voros, J. (2019). *Big history and anticipation: Using big history as a framework for global foresight*. In R. Poli (Ed.) *Handbook of Anticipation: Theoretical and Applied Aspects of the Use of Future in Decision Making*. Springer International.

Wahl, D. C. (2017, June 7). *The Three Horizons of innovation and culture change. Regenerate the Future*. https://medium.com/activate-the-future/the-three-horizons-of-innovation-and-culture-change-d9681b0e0b0f

Zigarmi, P., & Hoekstra, J. (2008). *Leadership Strategies for Making Change Stick*. The Ken Blanchard Companies. https://eoe.leadershipacademy.nhs.uk/wp-content/uploads/sites/6/2019/04/1317116579_MWdw_leadership_strategies_for_making_change_stick.pdf

Part 3:
Generative Conversations in Mentoring – Power Dynamics, Equality, Diversity, Inclusivity

Chapter 19
Fully Human: Working Creatively with Race and Identity in Public Services through Mentoring

Leslie B. Brissett

The European Mentoring and Coaching Council (EMCC) uses the following definition for mentoring:

> *Mentoring is a learning relationship, involving the sharing of skills, knowledge, and expertise between a mentor and mentee through developmental conversations, experience sharing, and role modelling. The relationship may cover a wide variety of contexts and is an inclusive two-way partnership for mutual learning that values differences.*

> *The inherent nature of the relationship between mentor and mentee is rooted in the appreciation and ability to work creatively with difference. In our current context, particularly in UK, the differences of race and identity are offering a chance to engage with what it means to be fully human and how to honour the humanity in 'the other'.*

Since the death of a black man, George Floyd, in the US in May 2020, race has become a central issue for public services. Occurring at the same time as this death, were the beginnings of the government social distancing responses due to the COVID-19 pandemic. At the confluence of these two moments in time emerged a phrase that has been indelibly etched in our minds, 'Black Lives Matter'. In the context of this text exploring mentoring and coaching, we have to ask ourselves, *do* Black Lives Matter, *to whom and why?* But before that, I invite us to engage with the question, 'What *is* a black life, and *who* lives it?' Within the boundary of a mentoring relationship, where both mentor and mentee may be exploring the lived experience of role taking, arguably in that endeavour, they are both living inside a black life, whether it belongs to the mentor, the mentee or someone from the mentee's work system.

Public services is a term used to capture a range of ideas and activities that when put together form a domain of activity, funded through taxation and delivered through a network of agencies, some owned by the state, some by the voluntary/ third sector and others by private wealth. What makes a public service 'public' is the fact that the beneficiaries of the service are on the one hand individuals and on the other a collective, known as the public. In the context of mentoring and coaching relationships, public services are a barometer for the way that a society takes care of and makes provision for all of its members/citizens. And when considering matters of equity and inequality, the legacy that colonial practices have left.

The lens I wish to use in this chapter is that of *group relations*. Developed at the Tavistock Institute of Human Relations in 1957, the group relations conference was a methodology formed out of a body of theory and practice later termed systems psychodynamics (Miller & Rice, 1967). As we enter this chapter, it is worth thinking and feeling your way into your own role in your mentoring context and how these concepts can illuminate how you make sense of your organization, your role and the context in which both exist.

The chapter begins by setting out how group relations can be helpful in thinking about roles at work and the nature of work itself. It then goes on to describe some of the identity dynamics that take place in our working lives, and the historical roots of contemporary structural and organizational inequities and biases that hinder career progression and development. Thinking about role can be a helpful tool in mentoring and coaching relationships seeking to identify and address such inequities. It ends with a look at issues of creativity and imagination as tools to access the fullness of what it means to be human in a world that seeks to (perhaps unconsciously but certainly systematically) constrain and limit the capacity of human flourishing, regardless of the bodies they inhabit. This is important for mentoring because roles in systems carry with them a set of assumptions about the authority that is invested in certain types of bodies in certain roles. As such, the mentoring relationship gains strength and impact by exploring how those assumptions affect the role holder and the system that they belong to.

Why is group relations a helpful lens to study matters of public services?

Group relations thinking is rooted in a deep understanding of the idea of connectedness between individual human beings (Bion, 1962). As a chain of connection, it can be seen that interconnectedness forms groups, and the interdependence of groups of human beings and their environment clusters to manifest as our cultures.

Systems theory is relevant here to understand how individuals and groups function in an organization – another way to describe an organization is a set of systems within a larger framework of systems. For example, the liver is a system of cells functioning within a larger system called the body. But if you remove a liver, you kill both the liver and the body of which it was a part. Drawing on the early work of biological systems, it is postulated that an organization is a set of coordinated behaviours, practices and conversations that guide its members toward a shared end or primary task. The primary task is the set of actions that must be achieved for the system to survive (Sher & Lawlor, 2022). The concept of boundary is vitally important here, because the boundary determines what is 'inside' and what is 'outside'. The task of the management of an organization is to regulate the import of raw materials across the boundary into the organization. Once inside the organization, a process can be undertaken that turns that raw material into a new product or service that can then cross the boundary out of the organization. This journey across the boundary is both observable and experienced by participants in the activities of the organization (Fraher, 2004). For such a transformation to take place, the people in the organization have to activate their creativity and skill, and work collaboratively to make it happen.

Coaching and mentoring play a vital role in supporting actors in the system to achieve the primary task by mobilizing available resources. How one holds on to the complexity of role and task and identity is a profound challenge, especially in the face of the underlying assumptions that shape expectations and relationships between actors in the system (Gertler & Hayden, 2015).

Our experiences of roles at work are embedded in a particular time and place. For example, traffic wardens once existed to keep the roads clear of cars that would park and cause annoyance, or block the flow of traffic. Speeding fines were intended to discourage people from driving at speeds that could lead to accidents and cause injury to motorists or pedestrians. Medical receptionists had the task of assisting doctors to ensure that their patients could be seen as soon as possible. These public service roles were classified by an understanding of their primary task as the framework of the action that would be taken by the role holder. It could be argued that times have changed and now the emphasis of these roles has changed. So, traffic wardens and speeding fines still use the language of safety and efficiency, but their actual purpose is to generate increased revenue for their employers, some being incentivized to 'catch people/increase issue rates' Le Grand (2010) and other scholars have studied the impact of regime change and the use of policy triggers to change public and system behaviours – not all intended consequences were achieved. Likewise, medical receptionists are now experienced by many members of the public as existing to keep people out of the surgery and safeguard doctors from potentially burdensome patient loads. The UK *Daily Mail* newspaper ran an article in October 2023 that outlined the role of receptionists as 'care navigators' who not only gatekeep services but can have a critical role in ensuring access to care (Foster, 2023).

The above paragraph demonstrates what we might call a drift from the primary task of a particular public service or role. As drifts in task and role occur, there is a corresponding emotional experience that is encountered within and outside the boundary of the role and service. The primary task is a source of survival for the role holder, and drifts cause anxiety. The various pictures of the roles we hold are accompanied by images in the mind (along with thoughts, feelings, sensations) about the organization (Armstrong, 2005). Feeling about these role shifts also gives rise to emotional experiences that need to be managed. Mentoring can create a space to reflect on the impact of these primary task or role changes and shifts in a system. Emergent emotional experiences can be explored to provide space for the further reconceptualization and new action on the part of the role holder or those shaping the context of the system as a whole. It is at this juncture that role consultation as a tool for the mentor can be helpful for role holders that they are mentoring. It offers a systematic way of thinking about role as purposeful action to achieve the purposes of the systems we serve (Armstrong, 2005).

Individuals in roles are part of an organizational system with interconnections and interdependence. Role consultation, using the group relations, offers a framework to consider wider systemic factors, such as professional and organizational culture and accompanying assumptions. For the purpose of this chapter, the focus is particularly on race and identity and how they can be addressed creatively in mentoring.

Race and identity: What does it mean to be human?

Many of our professions have at their roots untested assumptions, about matters of what we now term race. Before we look more closely at race and what it might mean for us in the coming digital age, I would like to share one example from the field of anthropology. Anthropology is a discipline that is undergoing a resurgence of interest and, particularly in organizational consultancy, many people are drawing on anthropological and ethnographic systems of thought. Young (2000) argues that all systems of knowledge are rooted in a colonial, Western hegemonic set of narratives, designed to privilege the European over the colonized. A quote that aptly illustrates this is taken from eminent palaeontologist and evolutionary biologist, E. D. Cope's 1890 text 'Two perils of the Indo-European'.

> *The highest race of man cannot afford to lose or even to compromise the advantages it has acquired by hundreds of centuries of toil and hardship, by mingling its blood with the lowest. It would be a shameful sacrifice, fraught with evil to the entire human species.*

(Young, 2000, p. 117)

Similar sentiments can be found in the origin stories of the all the professions and institutions in the European West from medicine, education and psychology to policing. It was a short forty years after E. D. Cope that Freud (1929) wrote *Civilisation and its Discontents*, where he extended psychoanalytic thought to the level of the group and society. Processes of dehumanization have been the hallmark of the Western civilization, and it is perhaps this discontent that Freud tried to bring to attention with his approach of psychoanalysis applied to the level of the group.

As we enter a digital age in the mediation and delivery of public services, we will face increasing changes to the way that roles are described and therefore how they are taken up. Our attitudes and behaviours to the roles and role holders will likewise face a pressure and need to change. As the technology becomes more dispersed and artificial intelligence (AI) and more sophisticated algorithms enter the realm of public services, our relationships to the Internet, telemedicine and data-analytic forms of diagnostics and treatments will radically alter. This alteration in the technical matrix of the public services will force us to pause and contemplate the following questions to consider our assumptions about race and identity, to address the process of dehumanization and to unpack the experience of being fully human:

■ What does it mean to be human?
■ How do we support staff to be fully human?

- How do we treat patients and clients in their full humanity?
- What needs to change in order to treat the full human?

These questions can be helpfully explored in the framework of a mentoring relationship, where both sides of the dyad can look at what these questions evoke and how the understanding of the role one takes up in the realm of public services can be affected. Particularly, when considering the hidden, untested assumptions and processes of dehumanization affect both black and white (melanin-rich and melanin-deficient) role holders. Group relations is a body of practice that can be particularly empowering in the mentoring relationship by holding a systemic lens to the identity dynamics in our working lives and the historical roots of contemporary structural and organizational inequities and biases that can hinder career progression and development. The next section further elaborates on this by exploring ways of seeing and being beyond the five-sense reality to work creatively with race and identity in mentoring.

Ways of seeing and being

To treat the full human, mentors and mentees can learn to embrace 'not knowing' in deeper and sustained ways. For example, while reading this chapter, you are invited to suspend the usual critical, deconstructive voice when reading and locate the way of listening that one uses when reading a poem or listening to children telling a story. Another way to enter the not knowing is to engage with the type of listening that emerges when one is watching a sunset. In that kind of space, which can be thought of as 'radical openness', we are able to suspend our usual judgements and render ourselves open to what may be emerging as the apparent 'what is-ness' of the external reality (Wells, 1998). As such, we may discover something new and original regarding being fully human as a mentor, coach or mentee.

Opening to the emergent reveals a world view that is broader and more encompassing than our five-sense reality. This is a journey into our social conditioning and the possibility of the unravelling of our social conditioning through enquiry. We have all been programmed by 'science' and its reductive method (van Manen, 2014), which has reduced the human subject to a collection of parts and conditions that can be systematically isolated and treated. The cutting and reductive mind has removed our capacity to see the whole or the full complexity of the world that we live in. And even more striking, it has disempowered us from being able to recognize that we are active participants in this world that we co-produce. As a result, we have lost the capacity to see and apprehend our full humanity, which is most strikingly visible for us in the way that systems dehumanize and eradicate the humanity of 'others' to pursue profit, power and privilege.

It may seem like a diversion, but understanding our histories is vital for the mentoring relationship. Western thought has formalized the training of professions from the renaissance in Europe since around 1500. That education has taken the form of science and rationality as the basis for progress and the best method for understanding the world that we inhabit. If one cannot see, taste, touch, smell or hear it, it has been declared to be unreal. Focusing on the five senses, which can be described as the materialist paradigm – promulgates a view of the world that says that 'all that is real is solid, and what is not solid is not real'. This view has privileged the senses of sight and hearing on the one hand, while ensuring that our experiences are rooted in the senses of taste and touch. As such, food and the importance of externally verifiable phenomena provide a context of a stable shared reality and the establishment of our cultures. The growth of the northern European empires, in what was termed the industrial revolutions, was rooted in the acquisition, control and distribution of spices and food products from the east and south of the global order in the Age of Discovery from the fifteenth to seventeenth centuries. On return from their travels, European merchants sought to replicate what they encountered in Africa, China and India. The resultant globalized industries and their offshoots are predicated on extracting materials from the earth, principally, in the form of tea, coffee, sugar, chocolate and oil.

Mentors and coaches and their clients are invited to hold a critically reflective stance that seeks to understand what is at the root of the systems of belief and assumptions that underpin what we term 'knowledge'. This can involve questioning our connection to the earth and its produce – a common focus in Indigenous cultures. So, as a full human, what does it mean to be an earthling: made from and dependent on soil?

Let us take a brief look at the five senses and how they impact or limit our sense of being human. Sight as a reality and a metaphor. The faculties that make sense of what is seen and heard are function to mysterious internal, invisible processes that can profoundly alter our shared sense of reality. Matters of sight and hearing have been declared to be 'in the eye of the beholder' and so, in an aesthetic sense, have been rendered labile and unstable. Conversely, the causes of many diagnoses of mental 'ill health' by the medical and legal professions (or those responsible for the underlying thinking of those professions) are rooted in the idea that sanity exists when reality is shared by self and other.

So, in our work as mentors we are bound by the social conditions that move us toward the development of processes of thinking and being that seek verification and approval by external sources. This focus on esteem, verification and approval to form 'legitimate authority' is the hallmark of our industrialized contexts. These processes of acquisition, control and distribution, and their impacts, are the essential descriptors of colonization. Colonization is a profoundly homogenizing power and can provide a backcloth to mentoring those from different cultures or those who hold different world views.

How is the sense of smell related to mentoring? The colonial project has sought to cut off the relationship with the olfactory senses and regulate it in relation to social stratification and value. This has shaped the location of certain industries and who works in or with them. In London, on very early trains or late-night buses, the large numbers of cleaners and refuse workers who take care of the toilets, sewers and kitchens or our public works departments can still be seen. However, thankfully they are no longer referred to (in public) as 'the great unwashed'. In your role as a mentor or mentee, how do you engage with smell and smelling and how it subtly impacts your role or your industry? Is attention paid to the room and your body, and do the impacts of these smells get discussed or reflected upon during your work as a collaborating pair?

The impact of the colonizing force is that it creates a matrix in which we are trapped in our physical manifestations as the key determinants of our humanity. The nature of the body and the way that it is constructed in language, its size, shape, way of movement and of PRIME importance, its colour, are background onto which meaning is projected and power and authority attributed.

The matters of sentience – our capacity for feeling and relating – are invisible and indeterminate about our five senses or our capacity to 'Be' where being is described as our ontology. Yet, phenomenologically, by experience, that what makes life meaningful is our felt sense, or what is described in the systems-psychodynamic context as our sentient selves. Work with race and identity in mentoring requires exploration of our sentient parts and an opening to the emergent to unravel a world view that is broader and more encompassing than our five-sense reality. Such a way of seeing, noticing and being can open up the possibility of the unravelling of our social conditioning through enquiry to consider how these dynamics impact individuals at the workplace.

Liberation and emancipation through group understanding

Imagination and creativity

As outlined earlier, the materialist paradigm has constructed the human as the physical, verifiable manifestation of the body. However, the domain of the invisible, accessed by the sentient system, is what creates meaning and the experience of being alive (Lawrence, 2006). The entry way to the other senses, those of inner sight, inner hearing and other sensory systems, has been considered to be imaginal and therefore unreal in daily living. However, in the digital era, a re-emergence of the demands for new thought and new action are the products of these very inner states and senses. The area where the inner senses are validated and deemed meaningful is when we are considering the role of those senses in matters of creativity, design and innovation.

It is this creative space that opens the possibility for understanding what it is to be human and to capture and utilize all the senses could be said to be Fully Human – a new paradigm in which we actively and consciously consider our historical and multidimensional selves, not just the materialist paradigm of five-sense reality. And importantly, these senses and their activation cannot be externally verified or authenticated by an objective expert. The nature of intersubjectivity and mutual recognition and shared experience is crucial.

The UK public sector has been a site of considerable innovation and change for over a century. Perhaps, it is time for us to move to a new level of discussion and exploration that questions the underlying nature of the systems that seem to be perpetuating these inequalities?

Mentoring and coaching can have a profound impact here, if both partners in the relationship are prepared to explore the fundamental assumptions about our embodied experiences new resources open up for the mentee. A mentoring relationship could usefully explore the feelings about: What does it mean to be in a male or female body? What does it mean to inhabit a body rich in melanin or deficient in melanin? What are the assumptions that we make about the religions and beliefs that shape our cultures and how we behave at work?

So many of these untested assumptions about our social systems are unthinkable and so remain in the realm of the unconscious, unable to be explored. For example, the foundational idea of God sits at the heart of much of our social fabric, whether it is when there are going to be bank holidays, our taxation systems and the distribution and eligibility criteria for benefits and services, or who the legal and policing systems serve. The capacity of a mentor to hold themselves psychologically and not become overwhelmed or try to save their mentee is a key skill. Being able to accompany or 'be with' such depth of exploration with a mentee can assist them in identifying the web of cultural myths and unquestioned assumptions that shape the forces of demand and expectations in roles in society and organizations. This awareness opens vistas for mentors to support their mentees in being fully human. Mentees can discover that they have let go of their agency and capacity to act due to internalized ideas about what is possible for them based on the whether they are male or female, black or white, etc. – while recognizing that these binaries are no longer sufficient heuristics for embodied selves.

Awakening to integrated spirituality at work

Spiritual traditions have often been conflated with religious traditions. What this chapter is suggesting is that there is a creative possibility available to us by exploring the unseen realities. Wilfred Bion (1962) developed the ideas of psychoanalyst Melanie Klein to suggest that there is an 'ineffable O' that could be engaged by psychoanalytic exploration, in particular working in and with groups. Essentially, there are things that are beyond our ability to put into language but that fundamentally shape our ability to take roles in life. An openness to explore these matters can enrich the mentoring relationship.

Such a recentring of the other senses may mirror a decentring of the colonized privilege of the sense of sight and sound. The reidentification of the body as the site of a new ways of being and knowing could not only yield results for mentors and mentees in their relationship, but also a wider benefit for role holders in organizations, and above all the customers of public services.

Conclusion

We have described the processes of colonization and seen the way that the land and minds of the people have been trapped in the materialist paradigm and that this has shaped how roles are identified and acted out in public service systems. We then looked at the concepts of the Tavistock Institute of Human Relations and how they have made possible, through several insights from systems theory and psychoanalytic thinking, the creation of group relations and the systems-psychodynamic field. The nature of the unconscious influence of systems on organization and role taking have been elucidated and yet we have discovered how the endemic nature of inequity and inequality is designed into these systems in such a way that conscious actions on the part of an individual are insufficient to unlock them. Finally, we explored how the ideas of creativity and imagination offer a way of seeing and being that open possibilities and options in the face of enduring systemic and structural oppression, such that people in roles can find new agency and potency to act in small ways to further their careers and deliver better service to the public. Mentoring is a powerful tool to unleash creativity and agency in the mentee, so that they can have the courage to bring all of what makes them human to their work. The approach suggested here is a subtle one – not a checklist – almost like osmosis, change is possible through conversation and accompaniment (Shaw, 2002).

It is worth ending with a section of text taken from the epilogue of *'Awakenings'* a book on Parkinson's disease and parkinsonism. In describing a patient who could not walk alone but could walk when accompanied, Oliver Sacks says:

> *Her own comments on this are of very great interest:* 'when you walk with me', *she said,* 'I feel in myself your own power of walking. I partake of the power and freedom you have. I share your walking powers, your perceptions, your feelings, your existence. Without even knowing it, you make me a great gift.' ... *One must be touched before one can move. This patient, whether speaking of others or music, is speaking of just this, the mysterious 'touch', the contact, of two existences. She is describing, in a word, the sense of communion.*

(Oliver Sacks, 1991, p. 282)

The relationship between the mentor and mentee walking side by side, exploring role and mentee context, is the power of transformation and can be long lasting. When the mentor has done their inner work, the results are a shared capacity, authority, power and freedom.

References

Armstrong, D. (2005). *Organisation in the Mind: Psychoanalysis, Group Relations, and Organizational Consultancy.* R. French (Ed.). Karnac Books.

Bion, W. R. (1962). *Learning from Experience* (**1984 edition**). Karnac Books.

Foster, K. (2023, October 26). *Receptionists refer patients for treatment in bid to cut cancer waiting times. Daily Mail.*

Fraher, A. L. (2004). *Systems psychodynamics: The formative years (1895–1967). Organisational and Social Dynamics,* **4**(2), 191–211.

Freud, S. (1929). *Civilization and Its Discontents* (**2014 edition**). Penguin Classics.

Gertler, B., & Hayden, C. (2015). *Uneasy on the boundary: reflections on the culture and effectiveness of group relations conference work in the USA, 1965–2012.* In E. Aram, R. Baxter, & A. Nutkevitch (Eds.), *Group Relations Work: Exploring the Impact and Relevance within and beyond its Network* (pp. 139–159). Karnac Books.

Lawrence, W. G. (2006). *Dreaming to access the infinite: Thoughts and thinking that led to the discovery of the social dreaming matrix. International Journal of Psychotherapy,* **10**(1), 13–21.

Le Grand, J. (2010). *Creating Incentives to Improve Public Services.* The London School of Economics and Political Science. https://www.lse.ac.uk/Research/research-impact-case-studies/creating-incentives-to-improve-public-services

Miller, E. J., & Rice, A. K. (1967). *Task and sentient systems and their boundary controls.* In: E. J. Miller, & A. K. Rice (Eds.), *Systems of Organization: The Control of Task and Sentient Boundaries.* Tavistock Publications, 1967; Routledge, 2001.

Sacks, O. (1991). *Awakenings.* Pan Books.

Shaw, P. (2002). *Changing Conversations in Organisations: A Complexity Approach to Change.* Routledge.

Sher, M. & Lawlor, D. (2022). *An Introduction to Systems Psychodynamics: Consultancy Research and Training.* Routledge.

van Manen, M. (2014). *Phenomenology of Practice: Meaning-Giving Methods in Phenomenological Research and Writing*. Left Coast Press.

Wells Jr, L. (1998). *Consultants as nautical navigators: A metaphor for group-takers. The Journal of Applied Behavioral Science*, **34**(**4**), 379–391.

Young, R. J. C. (2000). *Colonial Desire: Hybridity in Theory, Culture and Race*. Routledge.

Chapter 20
Designing Group Conversations for High-Quality Insights: Application to Mentoring

Amina Aitsi-Selmi & Cathy Presland

Introduction

Good decision-making to handle complexity and achieve societal transformation requires a level of individual self-awareness, insight and emotional development. In other words, to operate successfully in today's increasingly complex environment and solve its big challenges, individuals including leaders and practitioners need to develop an inner capacity (Inner Development Goals [IDG], 2022). Developing this *inner capacity* for flexible and innovative thinking, and understanding the limits of individual awareness, can then support societal transformation by cascading the beneficial effects of possibility thinking, effective decision-making and complex problem-solving (Fredrickson, 1998; Hunter et al., 2013).

Coaching and mentoring directly support individuals in developing their inner capacity, and group approaches can help to foster interpersonal dynamics that allow for insight and healthy exploration of 'psychological friction', within and between individuals. The challenge then becomes less about whether inner capacity development is worthwhile and more about how to design, and consistently reproduce, effective approaches. This chapter qualitatively reviews the RSA Coaching Network's (RSA, 2022) process of designing one such approach to generative group conversations in the virtual medium, using theory-informed reflections and pragmatic tools. It aims to offer support for practitioners in health, social care and beyond, and to contribute to the emerging body of work on optimizing group dynamics and the use of technology.

The RSA coaching conversations: Supporting social impact in uncertain times

Those who work in service-driven fields including health and social care, or transformational professions such as psychology, mentoring, coaching, and spiritual guidance tend to hold timeless values such as justice, sustainability and compassion. The RSA is one organization that has been at the forefront of significant social impact for over 260 years, supporting the ecosystem of service– or social impact– driven individuals and communities (RSA, 2022).

In March 2020, when the pandemic was declared, the steering group of the RSA's Coaching Network had just initiated a series of online conversations entitled *21st Century Challenges* through a serendipitous intuition that the world was headed toward more digital working.

Valuing access and community, the virtual format made meetings available to Fellows and non-Fellows across the world and was hoped to create a generative space for ideas to emerge, enriching the dialogue and strengthening bonds between individuals in the RSA's orbit.

The dual objectives for these events were to: 1) facilitate specific insights for participants to shift thinking and see new solutions; and 2) experience a process for generating insights which had applicability beyond the individual events.

Method, theoretical lens and definitions

Coaching and mentoring are concerned with catalysing and sustaining human development within particular contexts. They are more pragmatic than technical in their knowledge generation and for this reason we use a qualitative approach designed to share the authors' experience and pose questions rather than derive scientific facts. Our intention is to offer practical tools and points of reflection for practitioner and professional groups who want to use an online space for coaching and mentoring.

An Integral view

To position individual insights within a social context, we chose a simple but comprehensive analytical tool derived from Integral Theory called the AQAL model (all quadrants, all levels, all lines, all states, all types) (Wilber et al., 2008). Integral Theory is a transdisciplinary framework based on the subject–object theory of Robert Kegan and the integral theory of Ken Wilber (Esbjörn-Hargens, 2009).

Integral Theory proposes that the myriad ways individuals may perceive reality can be assigned to one of four quadrants characterized along a pair of axes – a continuum between poles of internal and external realities, as well as individual or collective realities (Reams, 2005). These are: individual subjective experience (upper left (UL) quadrant); the interpersonal domain of relationships and collective meaning-making (lower left (LL) quadrant); objective measurable phenomena, including behaviours and biology (upper right (UR) quadrant); and socio-economic systems and societal structures (lower right (LR) quadrant).

The qualitative analysis in this chapter draws on the underlying principle that reality can be perceived through multiple world views and that world views can evolve. The RSA Coaching Conversation space engaged with world views in all four quadrants without privileging any.

Coaching conversations

Coaching and mentoring differ from other types of conversation because of the unique lens through which coaches/mentors see their clients, i.e., as agents of their own transformation and solution-finding through insight. The International Coaching Federation (ICF) defines coaching as: *'partnering with clients in a thought-provoking and creative process that inspires them to maximize their personal and professional potential'* (ICF, 2022).

Although operating within a coaching context, we take the European Mentoring and Coaching Council (EMCC) view that *'Coaching and Mentoring share many of the same characteristics, lying along a structured conversational continuum rather than being discrete modalities with no overlap and that, common to both, is a structured, purposeful and transformational process, helping clients to see and test alternative ways for improvement of competence, decision making and enhancement of quality of life'* (EMCC, 2022).

It is worth a side note that the RSA events were not explicitly mentoring the group *as a team*, but a collection of individuals, and the relationships between facilitators and participants, as well as within breakout groups surfaced rich material for conversation.

Generative space

We use the term *generative* to describe the process by which an individual's experience is constantly created and recreated as their awareness shifts (Fleming, 2020), which facilitates the safety to let go of frames of reference and perceptions, challenge received ideas or beliefs, and allow new ones to form. This is distinct from a discursive space for the exchange of existing ideas, which is usually for the purpose of information gathering or consensus forming.

The objective of the RSA Coaching Conversation was to create the conditions to make insights/new ideas more likely to arise and facilitate the transformation of frames of reference. When humans are willing and able to engage in creative or playful cognitive and actual experimentation, they expand both their possibility thinking and their thought–action repertoire (Fredrickson, 1998; 2004). Thus, the generative space can both help create ideas and motivate the actions that arise from them.

Positive affect was used to allow disorientation to be experienced in a safe space, accepting the range of views without reacting to doubts and confusions. This enhances the capacity to continually reshape experience and ideas, and the effect can be enduring beyond a single event (Fredrickson, 1998; Kelley et al., 2019, 2020).

Method: Retrospective reflection on the RSA generative space

The COVID-19 pandemic amplified the inherent uncertainty of modern work and created new challenges in the domains of leadership, social impact and human connection. During a period of twenty-four months, the RSA Coaching Network facilitated sixteen online group meetings that coincided with the onset of the COVID-19 pandemic in 2020, engaging a global community of around 300 impact-driven individuals engaged in social impact work. A list of all the series' topics (at the time of writing) can be found online (RSA, 2020a; 2020b; 2021)

For the purposes of this chapter, we qualitatively reviewed the series content, post-meeting reflections which were shared with the network, and materials used (including context-setting questions and breakout room questions). We also reviewed the available feedback from attendees, which was usually collected at the end of each meeting. Our measures of success during the meetings were: 1) the expression of sparks of insight or 'aha' moments; and 2) expressions of relational and internal satisfaction from participants.

Results and discussion: Five principles for creating virtual generative spaces

Reviewing the series through the combined reflections of the authors, five practices were identified that we believe supported the success of the series.

As a result of the series, the Coaching Network has continued to grow since the pandemic and is considered one of the most active at the RSA at the time of writing, taking account of the frequency meetings, attendance, participation, and feedback. Close to half the participants in the series were not previously associated with the RSA and we believe that the readiness to operate online, the topicality of the themes selected for the series and the design of the Coaching Conversations as a generative space is precisely what enabled this success.

1) Setting context without agenda

One of the things we do as human beings is to make sense of experience and events, and create shared meaning to guide our individual and personal activities. In a generative space, with a focus on *individual* insights, shared meaning can be a distraction. The aim of the facilitation, therefore, was to intentionally direct the conversation away from debating ideas or reaching agreement, diverting or cutting off extensive intellectual enquiry, and resisting any need to resolve ambiguity prematurely, and toward the personal exploration of a theme with no particular destination in mind.

This was done by setting a broad *context* and *principles of engagement*. At the start of the meetings, we reminded participants of: 1) the purpose of the RSA and RSA Coaching Network; and 2) the context of the meeting. Other principles included: 1) listening attentively, 2) speaking intentionally; and 3) caring for the shared space (Baldwin & Linnea, 2010).

From an Integral perspective, collective meaning-making (the LL quadrant) was not an objective or a necessity – convergence and divergence were invited throughout. We allowed space for individuals to concentrate on their own experience (UL quadrant), to explore ideas around systems and social impact (LR quadrant), or to reflect on actions (UR quadrant).

For example, the event *The Individual in Society*, did not intend to reach a definition of 'society' but to allow individual exploration of the ever-present experience of being with others, to raise awareness of that, and to give space to reflect on its implications.

Toolbox 1: Examples of contexts and dos/don'ts.

At the start of the meeting have you explained the following:

- It is an exploratory space in which individuals can uncover and examine their own insights.
- We do not aim to teach or provide information.
- We are not aiming for shared agreement or consensus on ideas.
- It is not a coaching space – participants should not expect to give or receive coaching, feedback or problem-solving input (this is a key pitfall in any group of service professionals)

---

2) Creating safety and openness

Groups tend to go through a process of settling into the collective space – navigating doubts, anxiety or tension – before moving into a generative space (think of Tuckman's 'forming and storming, norming and performing' (Tuckman, 1965)). This settling process does not occur by accident and was attended to throughout.

Creating a sense of psychological safety facilitates insight and sharing (Rozovsky, 2015) and, from an Integral perspective, allows individuals to move freely between quadrants (or subjective experience) and encounter resonance and dissonance without judgement.

We created this safety by: 1) modelling vulnerability – sharing difficult thoughts and feelings as they arose; 2) inviting others to share, sometimes scanning for signs of willingness to speak or open body language such as a nod or smile.

In the breakout rooms, participants were encouraged to share as much or as little as they felt comfortable with and were reminded that it was a *listening* space. The listener was requested to allow pauses and to resist interrupting or validating, and the speaker was encouraged to flow with their thoughts rather than make sense of them.

We found that the optimal breakout room size was three. Pairs elicited more intimacy but were heavily affected by affinity between individuals. The depth of intimacy and trust achieved between individuals in small groups is very high – *'events always provide a safe exploratory space and provide me with fresh insights or clarity'* (participant feedback, 2021).

Toolbox 2: Creating safety and openness

- Model vulnerability to set the tone in the group, create psychological safety with guidance on expectations and positive affect.
- Give clarity about objectives and context and set up the breakout rooms.
- Use the plenary to health check the experience.

---

3) Allowing for disintegration (and reintegration)

At the heart of our approach is the view that human experience is, by nature, subjective, and fostering *insight* is how individuals transform their perspectives and expand their capacity to be with complex and large-scale challenges, thus developing their inner capacity (as defined above).

This letting-go or disintegration of existing beliefs and world views can be disorienting (Mezirow, 1997), and can be emotionally and cognitively challenging. However, it is necessary to loosen habitual thinking and assumptions, our so-called 'generative entanglements' (Clark, 2019), which come about when personal experience, mental predictions, or sociocultural contexts are 'entangled' with objective reality. The more one can disassociate the objective from the subjective, the more likely they are to see ideas beyond current limits.

Disorientation/disintegration can occur within the individual, and also between individuals operating from different world views (e.g., from different disciplines, values systems or AQAL reality domains). The facilitators treated this not as a negative experience but as part of the insight-generating process.

The tools and processes employed were: 1) listening without comment, judgement, or validation; and 2) structured questions to move around the topic and open new perspectives, sometimes according to the preference of the facilitator, but always with a focus on generating insights rather than answering intellectual questions.

These tools allow individuals to explore for themselves without any need for direction or challenge, for example, in an event on *Power Dynamics*, one individual saw that a long-held view was based on a potentially false assumption, and they had the space and structure to explore, dissolve and re-form this for themselves during and after the event.

Toolbox 3: Conflict dos and don'ts

- Treat conflict or disagreement as a source of insight and hold it with presence and non-reactivity, while offering positive support and acknowledgement for different perspectives.
- Use coaching and disorienting questions to challenge assumptions and explore how our ideas arise and can therefore be dissolved, for example, 'how do you know … ?'; 'what if … ?'
- Use the AQAL model to identify the different reality domains that participants are operating from and understanding the source of conflict (without needing to name them).

---

4) Inviting diverse voices

Diversity goes beyond measurable differences and includes subjective perspectives and meaning-making. In the RSA Conversations, we wanted to encourage diverse perspectives, not to change the *content* of the conversation, but to reinforce the subjective nature of the knowledge base, and the dominance of certain lenses.

We called on people at the start of the meeting who seemed to signal an openness or confidence and, as the meeting progressed and the group settled, invited those who had not spoken (while also respecting that some prefer to remain silent). The room was scanned for those who might represent a 'minority voice', or who had expressed one, including those we identified as outside the dominant group of white, British participants. The approach had a ripple effect of bringing in more of those voices.

For example, a facilitator checked in with a black participant from South Africa as to whether they would like to share something during a conversation on power. The participant shared that as a black person they cannot risk making their white colleagues feel unsafe as they end up paying a social and professional penalty due to structural lines in which the black person tends to be blamed. This share had a strong impact on the group and generated a lot of questions as well as insight. It enriched the conversation along diverse dimensions. While not everyone understood or agreed with the experience, the participant said that they felt very accepted and seen in this predominantly white group.

Toolbox 4: Engaging a range of voices

- Scanning the room.
- Toggling facilitator roles, with one person checking the experience of participants while another leads the exploration.
- Calling on people who looked engaged through their facial expression and posture, using the 'raise hand' function.
- Calling on people who appeared to be from a non-dominant group (by name or appearance).
- Inviting dissent by asking for 'comments, questions or objections'.

---

5) Owning and letting go of experience

Operating at the experiential level (naming one's thoughts, emotions and experience as a phenomenon rather than a fixed state or set of meanings) was used to modulate group and individual tension by enabling participants to be more aware of their impulses and to resist acting on them automatically or reactively. Encouraging participants to speak an opinion as a transitory thought rather than a fixed truth softened the dialogue and exchanges between members. For example, a recent event on *Integrity* focused on the feeling of integrity rather than the behavioural rulebook. This facilitated a stronger sense of awareness and inner development for individuals, which can make it more likely for individuals to speak or act from a sense of curiosity rather than strongly held opinions – thus strengthening solution-seeking and collaboration in the workplace.

Two tools facilitated this: 1) peer listening guidelines described in the earlier section on 'Creating safety and openness', i.e., sharing personal experience, without judgement, comment or (dis)agreement, which can run counter to the norms of professional gatherings; and 2) carefully constructed questions for breakout discussions. The questions aimed to stimulate a 'disorienting dilemma' (Kitchenham, 2008), revealing the transitory nature of ideas and experience, reducing attachment, and opening a space for new insights and transformation of frames of reference.

Toolbox 5: Inviting a sharing of experience not ideas

- Open the meeting with a grounding/centring mindful pause focused on breathing.
- Give examples of coaching questions or question stems that focus on experience not ideas. How do you know you are having experience X (angry, frustrated, etc.)? What did you notice when you heard X?
- Slow down the pace and making use of pauses throughout the conversation.

Discussion: Using generative spaces to facilitate small but significant insights

The RSA Coaching Conversations aimed to expand individual inner capacity through the mechanism of insight, by creating a safe space where the dissolution of existing perceptions and their reshaping, with the help of disorienting questions, could take place. We believe this approach can be easily reproduced by mentors (online and offline) to complement other aspects of their role which may be more content- or action-oriented.

Generativity was enhanced by allowing space for different world views to interact without privileging any particular one (for example, insights around systems and strategies, which are often the preserve of workplaces, were held in the same space as emotional content, which is often relegated to mindful or therapeutic spaces).

Uncomfortable experience or tension was treated as fertile soil for insight and perceiving a situation or challenge through a different reality quadrant in the AQAL model was a generative opportunity that could lead to new relationships, ideas and depth of relationality (the experience of intimacy). This required openness and skill from the facilitators, and cooperation between co-facilitators in designing the sessions, to go beyond individual preferences. For example, some were more interested in mindfulness approaches (UL), and others were more interested in behavioural ones like improvisation (UR). All were interested in systems (LR) and large-scale social impact and change.

From feedback, we believe that this approach to designing a generative space enriched the experience for the participants, and created a sense of coherence (as distinct from shared meaning) and intimacy at the individual/group level. This is easily transferable to a range of coaching and mentoring situations.

Conclusion

Individuals often engage in mentoring and coaching with practical growth goals. What the RSA Coaching Conversations series did was to create a generative space where big ideas about systems and our individual experience of them could be expressed and transformed for practical purposes but without a focus on practical discussion. We designed a checklist to support the creation of (virtual) generative spaces which all co-facilitators contributed to and has become a living document.

We propose that mentoring and coaching for service-driven leaders and professionals in health and social care can integrate this approach to develop generative spaces, and consciously bring individual interior and the systemic exterior realities together. Through care, trust and acceptance, generative spaces allow the disintegration/reintegration of world views to lead to transformational insight which can ripple through the fabric of society. Accepting that this is a qualitative and reflective piece, rather than experimentally validated, further research could examine the experience of participants over the long term.

Generative groups tend not to seize on initial solutions but create space to view challenges from different, often evolving, perspectives. As old views disintegrate and new ones form, the individuals and groups become increasingly at home in the fluid process of how awareness and perspective interact to generate insight, transforming our understanding of, and agency in, the world we inhabit.

References

Baldwin, C., & Linnea, A. (2010). *The Circle Way: A Leader in Every Ehair*. Berrett-Koehler Publishers.

Clark, A. (2019). *Consciousness as generative entanglement*. Journal of Philosophy, **116 (12)**, 645–662.

Esbjörn-Hargens, S. (2009). *An Overview of Integral Theory: An All-Inclusive Framework for the 21st Century*. Integral Institute, Resource Paper No. 1.

European Mentoring and Coaching Council (EMCC) (2022). *Definition of Mentoring*. https://www.emccglobal.org/leadership-development/leadership-development-mentoring/

Fleming, S. M. (2020). *Awareness as inference in a higher-order state space*. Neuroscience of Consciousness, **6(1)**.

Fredrickson, B. L. (1998). *What good are positive emotions? Review of General Psychology*, **2(3)**.

Fredrickson, B. L. (2004). *The broaden-and-build theory of positive emotions*. Philosophical Transactions of the Royal Society B: Biological Sciences, **359(1449)**, 1367–1377.

Hunter, J., & Chaskalson, M. (2013). *Making the mindful leader: Cultivating skills for facing adaptive challenges*. In H. Skipton Leonard, R. Lewis, A. M. Freedman, & J. Passmore. (Ed.) *The Wiley Blackwell Handbook of the Psychology of Leadership, Change, & Organizational Development* (pp. 195–220). Wiley Blackwell.

Inner Development Goals (IDG) (2022). *Inner Development Goals*. https://www.innerdevelopmentgoals.org/

International Coaching Federation (ICF) (2022). *Frequently Asked Questions.* https://coachingfederation.org/faqs

Kelley, T. M., Hollows, J., & Savard, D. M. (2019). *Teaching health versus treating illness: The efficacy of intensive three principles correctional counseling for improving the mental health/resilience of people in an English prison. Journal of Offender Rehabilitation,* **58**(**8**), 1–17.

Kelley, T. M., Pettit Jr, W. F., Sedgeman, J. A., & Pransky, J. B. (2020). *Psychiatry's pursuit of euthymia: Another wild goose chase or an opportunity for principle-based facilitation? International Journal of Psychiatry in Clinical Practice,* **25**(**4**), 1–3.

Kitchenham, A. (2008). *The evolution of John Mezirow's transformative learning theory. Journal of Transformative Education,* **6**(**2**), 104–123.

Mezirow, J. (1997). *Transformative learning: Theory to practice. New Directions for Adult & Continuing Education,* **1997**(**74**), 5–12.

Reams, J. (2005). *What's integral about leadership? A reflection on leadership and Integral Theory. Integral Review,* **1**, 118–132.

The Royal Society for the Encouragement of Arts, Manufactures and Commerce (RSA) (2020a). *RSA Coaching Conversations on 21st Century Challenges.* Eventbrite. https://www.eventbrite.co.uk/e/rsa-coaching-conversations-on-21st-century-challenges-tickets-101328977700

The Royal Society for the Encouragement of Arts, Manufactures and Commerce (RSA) (2020b). *Deep-Dive Conversations on 21st Century Challenges: Think, Connect, Explore.* Eventbrite. https://www.eventbrite.co.uk/e/deep-dive-conversations-on-21st-century-challenges-think-connect-explore-tickets-266746103777

The Royal Society for the Encouragement of Arts, Manufactures and Commerce (RSA) (2021). *RSA Coaching Conversations 2021.* Eventbrite.

https://www.eventbrite.co.uk/e/rsa-coaching-conversations-2021-tickets-139652465283

The Royal Society for the Encouragement of Arts, Manufactures and Commerce (RSA) (2022). *Coaching Networks.* https://www.thersa.org/fellowship/networks/coaching-network

Rozovsky, J. (2015). *re:Work: The five keys to a successful Google team.* Re:Work. https://www.michigan.gov/-/media/Project/Websites/mdhhs/Folder4/Folder10/Folder3/Folder110/Folder2/Folder210/Folder1/Folder310/Google-and-Psychological-Safety.pdf?rev = 7786b2b9ade041e78828f839eccc8b75

Tuckman, B. W. (1965). *Developmental sequence in small groups. Psychological Bulletin.* **63**(**6**), 384–399.

Wilber, K., Patten, T., Leonard, A., & Morelli, M. (2008). *Integral Life Practice: A 21st-Century Blueprint for Physical Health, Emotional Balance, Mental Clarity, and Spiritual Awakening.* Random House/Integral Books.

Chapter 21
Reciprocal Mentoring: Introducing the Concept of Generative Conversations

Rita Symons

In this chapter, we explore the shift from mentoring being about imparting wisdom, to a true partnership, based on the premise that all change happens one conversation at a time. We explore social constructivism and the fact that reality is created through human connection and dialogue. And if we believe that, how then can we use mentoring as a tool to have more meaningful conversations that allow collective growth? We explore how to have truly generative conversations, introducing this concept as an enhancement to existing mentoring practice.

In order to do this, we need to explore the role of power dynamics in society and in organizations. What do we need to pay attention to? Recent years have brought a welcome focus on social justice. My suggestion is that mentoring programmes, if conceptualized in the right way, have a part to play in challenging traditional power structures and in creating a shift in the tectonic plates of global society. They can be a powerful tool for change.

> *Connect deeply with others. Our humanity is the one thing*
> *we all have in common.*
>
> (Melinda Gates)

The history of mentoring

Mentoring has been around for a long time and is thought to come from Homer's *Odyssey* where Odysseus charged his good friend Mentor with the care of his son Telemachus while he fought for many years in the Trojan Wars. This genesis framed how mentoring has been considered for many generations, with the sense that an older, shrewder mentor shares their wisdom with a mentee. This has been perpetuated by famous mentoring pairs, such as Sigmund Freud mentoring Carl Jung in the field of psychology and in business, where mentoring has been used as a tool to induct new employees. All too often, in the past, this turned into a narrow, didactic education into 'this is how we do things around here'.

There are many examples of mentoring in health and care, and where it is done well it can be impactful. However, it still predominantly works on assumptions which reinforce hierarchical power and assumes more experienced staff have increased knowledge, thus reinforcing the inequality in the relationship. One of the most heartbreaking moments in my career was when I was a director of a health and social care trust. I attended a preceptorship meeting, where a wonderful, committed newly qualified nurse told her story of starting work in a community hospital and daring to offer a suggestion in terms of more up-to-date practice. I saw her at week three and she said she would not be offering any more ideas.

So, the question we need to ask is – in the rapidly changing, VUCA environment we live in, does this model based on hierarchy still serve us?[12]

What's power got to do with it?

We know from power dynamic theory that power is at play in all human interaction and we also know, in terms of the way modern society is constructed, that power is asymmetric. We sit today in a world shaped by our shared human history that has created the inequality we see, and culture is contextual and ever changing.

Power is a word that is used in so many contexts; so, what does it mean and why is it so important? Stewart Black and Bright (2019) define power as *'an interpersonal relationship in which one individual (or group) has the ability to cause another individual (or group) to take an action that would not be taken otherwise'.*

In establishing mentoring as an intervention, indeed in any transformational intervention, there is a need to apply deep curiosity to the prevalent power dynamics in your setting and reflect on whether specific action is needed to redress the balance of power.

The way power is exercised in an organization underpins a large part of the organizational norms that form culture. There are good tools to assist in an exploration of organizational culture. One such model is that developed by Johnson and Scholes in the 1990s (Figure 21.1) which is still current and in regular use.

They reminded us that there are often hidden dynamics in organizations and a good way to reflect on culture is to consider both the structural and human dynamics. Their model invites us to look at control systems, power structures and organizational structure, but it also considers stories and symbols. Often the narrative and myths in an organization shape the behaviour. This also links to what they term 'rituals and routines'. This is related to the norms in any organization. The invitation is to reflect on the current culture, but we can also use this structure to look for the desired state and identify what needs to change.

---

12   VUCA is an acronym that stands for Volatility, Uncertainty, Complexity and Ambiguity.

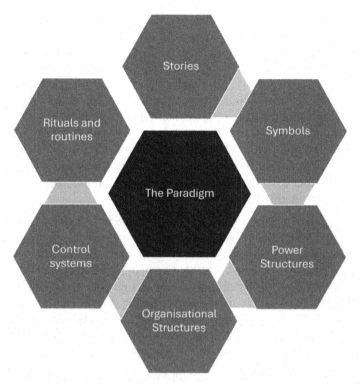

Figure 21.1: Cultural web (Johnson & Scholes, 2015).

Reflection on Practice:
Thinking about your own organization:

- Who has the formal power?
- Where does the informal power sit?
- What stories are told about the organization?
- What strategies might you employ to navigate and make positive changes?

New models of mentoring

Jack Welch (2001) who was the retired CEO of General Electrics in the US shared his experiment with reverse mentoring in one of his books on leadership. He had noticed that with the rapid development of technology-based working practices, some of the more long-standing members of his organization were struggling to adapt and, therefore, he set up a scheme which matched senior managers with young new starters. The purpose was for the young graduates to effectively teach older colleagues how to operate in the new environment. The programme was purportedly successful, and by being conceptualized as *reverse* suggested a shift or reversal of power. It would have been interesting to explore whether there was any real or permanent shift or whether the skills of the younger employees were simply commodified.

Reverse mentoring was used in a number of areas, including in inclusion. It became popular in the last decade and programmes were established in both the private and public sector, with mixed success. Anecdotally, I know of schemes that were established without appropriate thought and that subsequently did real harm. Unearthing racial trauma with too little understanding and no attention to the systemic inequity in the health and care system is beyond foolhardy and arguably immoral. The adage about the path to ruin being paved with good intentions comes to mind. And any positive action comes with the risk of the majority population feeling others are being favoured. The politicization of othering is not a subject for this book, but it is important for practitioners to be cognisant of the resultant polarity in society, fuelled by politicians and social media, and the impact this might have on any mentoring initiatives.

In parallel to the development of reverse mentoring, we have seen models which start to present greater mutuality, such as co-mentoring, peer mentoring or reciprocal mentoring. In my work on reciprocal mentoring, we have tried to reframe the relationship as a partnership which is about two people connecting at a human level, bringing their unique and resourceful selves to a shared endeavour. These interactions are characterized by the assumption of positive intent, deep-rooted respect and the psychological safety to allow vulnerability and mistakes. In reciprocal mentoring, there is clear intent and purpose and while individuals undoubtedly benefit, it is largely a systemic intervention designed to create a desired organizational change.

There is no doubt that thinking about mentoring models will continue to develop, but at its heart it remains about human connection.

Understanding generative conversations in mentoring?

Osborne and Hinson (2015) describe generative conversations in the following way:

> *Generative conversations are conversations that generate new value or meaning.*

This is consistent with the theory of social constructivism in which we propose reality is a construct of sensemaking though interaction and dialogue. The derivation of the word dialogue from Greek suggests meaning though words. Weick (1995) states, '*People make sense of things by seeing a world on which they already imposed what they believe. In other words, people discover their own inventions. This is why sensemaking can be understood as invention and interpretations understood as discovery.*'

In terms of paradigms, this leans to an interpretative rather than positivist view. In other words, there is no single version of the truth and our relationships and emotional capital are our greatest gifts because they are the tools through which we create meaning in our lives. And yet, how little time do we spend thinking about the quality of our conversations?

My experience in Reciprocal Mentoring for Inclusion in the NHS has led me to observe that where a framework of generative conversation and sensemaking is used in a mentoring partnership, this unleashes a creativity and shared solutions emerge, in terms of what needs to change. In this programme, the power differential was actively considered and addressed to enable this outcome.

How to create the environment for great conversations in mentoring?

Adding value and meaning through something as basically human as conversation feels like a no-brainer. So, why do we not do more of it? The simple answer is because our biological and organizational design does not always make this easy.

In order to realise the power of generative conversation, certain conditions need to be in place. They include:

- psychological safety;
- the opportunity to be heard;
- a willingness to examine self; and
- commitment.

Psychological safety

Amy Edmondson (2019), in her work on psychological safety, identifies psychological safety as:

> *A belief that one will not be punished or humiliated for speaking up with ideas, questions, concerns or mistakes.*

In terms of our basic risk-averseness as humans, she identifies four things that none of us want to appear. They are ignorant, incompetent, intrusive and negative. So, what do we do? We stay quiet, not offering ideas or suggestions, not questioning and not showing any vulnerability or sharing the fact we might not know. How many times in meetings has someone said, can I ask a stupid question? And we all sigh with relief because the rest of us didn't know the answer?

If psychological safety exists, we feel we can bring our authentic selves into the room and we can summon the courage to speak up. This creates a sense of community and belonging, but it also makes business as well as moral sense. Matthew Syed (2019), in his book *Rebel Ideas*, cites examples of disastrous consequences where there has been no thought diversity, leading to groupthink or where team members have not felt able to speak up and challenge the leader. Edmondson too talks of the concept of 'avoidable failure'.

This speaks to how we want to be as leaders. In the complex world we live in, we cannot know everything and the best leaders are those that admit this and actively seek out different views. A strong leader is one who is prepared to be told she has got it wrong.

The opportunity to be heard

Another prerequisite is the ability for everyone to be heard and for equality of contribution. For those of you who mentor or coach, you will understand what a powerful gift it can be for someone to feel truly heard.

I am a big fan of Nancy Kline's Thinking Environment (Kline, 2002) here and the *concept of rounds*. This works well in mentoring in a group setting where you would decide on an order, maybe by drawing names on a clock face, and people speak in turn. There is no pressure as individuals can pass. The ease which is created when individuals know they will get their turn and not be drowned out by the loudest voices in the room creates a fabulous canvas for generative conversation. We, therefore, need to consider how we structure our meetings and conversations. We also need to bring openness, presence and deep listening. If we are honest with ourselves, how often in our workplace do we truly listen? Deep listening requires empathy and attention which is key to effective mentoring.

Stone (2009) introduced the concept of Continuous Partial Attention where we juggle and do not allow ourselves to focus on any one thing. This has been exponentially amplified since then by social media and online working, where we are expected to be constantly available, keeping us in a hyperstimulated state. You cannot do your best thinking in amygdala hijack, and yet that is where so many of us spend large proportions of our life.

Listening is often just about being present and resisting the desire to come in with your story, but generative conversation may also be helped by open, incisive questioning. It is worth spending time considering how you can use the right questions to elicit new insights.

We need to consider listening between the lines. Susan Scott (2002) in her book *Fierce Conversations* states, '*When we listen beyond words for intent, for the scaffolding on which a story hangs, clarity and character emerge.*'

Willingness to examine self

I do work in the area of inclusion and when I work with groups and start by demonstrating we all have biases and assumptions and that is normal, there is often a palpable sense of relief.

We are not socialized to talk openly about our biases and the things we hold to be true about others. It is essential, however, that we develop acceptance of and curiosity about our assumptions and biases if we are to truly move into creating new knowledge and realities.

Our assumptions shape how we respond to others, as we find it hard to resist going into a conversation without preconceived ideas. And then of course, confirmation bias means we selectively listen for facts that reinforce our world view. Noticing what assumptions we are holding is essential if we are to listen without judgement.

Self-awareness is critical and this is a life's work, through genuine reflective practice. We need to practice self-compassion as increasing self-awareness can be an uncomfortable process. Leaning into the discomfort to allow growth is, in my view, a price worth paying and something encouraged by all health, social care and therapeutic professions.

I am constantly surprised, however, by how many people I come across in these professions who are unable or unwilling to open Pandora's Box. I have also come across some deeply committed individuals, leaders who are prepared to forensically examine the impact of their privilege and commit to learning and change. The challenge for us all is creating the environment where people can be in the space taken up with growth, not resistance.

Commitment

We all have finite energy and in order to give our attention, we need to feel some sense of ownership for a goal or vision. In work teams, this is normally about delivering organizational strategy or delivering better outcomes for citizens. If we have no connection to purpose then we will find it hard to motivate ourselves to invest the considerable energy required to engage. Not getting down in the weeds and getting off the dance floor and onto the balcony is a useful skill. Some meetings and topics are more challenging than others, but if we constantly remind people of the dream – of what the team is trying to achieve – it is easier to maintain forward momentum and encourage people to engage in the work.

Reflection on Practice:
Thinking about you and your organization:

■ How well do you understand your own biases and assumptions?
■ Do you feel there is psychological safety?
■ Does everyone have the opportunity to speak?
■ What might you want to change to stimulate fresh thinking?

Going beyond our need to be right in mentoring

We are conditioned from our earliest experiences in education that there is a right and a wrong answer and we should always strive to be right and get good exam results. This becomes inextricably linked with our thoughts about success. This is ingrained in our psyche and creates environments at work and at home which create a polarity where there are differing views. We each hold on to our need to be right. Rosenburg (2012) introduces the concept of non-violent communication and offers practical suggestions for how we can reframe our need to defend our positions. He identifies a number of practices we need to work on if we are to avoid conflict and move to cooperation and co-production.

They are the need to be clear about our own needs, identifying the needs of others, however they are expressed, and checking understanding of those needs, ensuring they have been heard. There is also a need to create the right setting with both empathy and an environment of positive framing and language. All too often in our dialogue, we fall back on a deficit approach. We need to actively notice and counter this.

This approach appears simple but can be effective in bringing trust, respect and, ultimately, improved thinking. The key is to bring clean communication and to constantly check that there is no dissonance between intent and how a message is actually being received. In mentoring relationships this is critical to success.

Practical Tips: Establishing Reciprocal Mentoring

In thinking about planning for success in establishing a mentoring scheme, we need to go back to the issue of power. If you are trying to create equality, with people from different places in the hierarchy, think very carefully about the signals. You will not create the environment for generative conversations if a junior member of staff is summoned to the CEO's office by his or her PA. Neutral venues and direct contact, even if you are the CEO; these send important signals in terms of how people perceive a mentoring programme.

It is also important to ensure the internal communications are right. Do people know why you are setting up mentoring? Organizations should be explicit about intent and spend time thinking about crafting the messaging. How does it link to a higher purpose and what is in it for them? It is important in this that any negative history is acknowledged and a focus placed on why this is different.

A robust process is essential in terms of support for all participants to understand the basic elements and what forms good contracting. Evidence shows that mentoring works best where there is an element of choice in terms of mentoring pairs and there needs to be clarity in terms of what individuals do if it isn't working.

And for mentoring to be reciprocal, it is not about one individual helping another with their goals, it is about an interdependent learning contract where both partners consider how they want to use the mentoring as a vehicle for growth.

Closing thoughts: Intergenerational conversations

A slight play on words as we consider generative and generational, two quite similar words. A theme that underpinned early mentoring was age, with an implicit assumption that wisdom came with age. But what is the evidence that is true? When we look around us, we could draw the conclusion that the Baby Boomers and Generation X have made a bit of a mess of things. And yet, we find it quite hard to accept this and continue to be stuck in a narrative that reinforces an unsustainable focus on growth and perpetuates inequality.

And can we honestly say the two post-war generations behave better than the young? You only have to consider Greta Thunberg as an example of this. The vitriol directed at her by powerful, rich, older men has been shameful. And why? Arguably, because she dares to speak the truth. She dares to challenge. Because she doesn't fit the Northern Hemisphere view of what young girls should be concerned about. In their eyes, she should be focused on makeup, dieting and her selfie filters.

The young are the future and they are the ones who are going to have to find creative solutions to the precarious situation we find ourselves in, so I would encourage you to listen to your children and consider how the focus of mentoring needs to be targeted at young people.

References

Edmondson, A. C. (2019). *The Fearless Organisation: Creating Psychological Safety in the Workplace for Learning, Innovation, and Growth.* Wiley.

Johnson, G., & Scholes, K. (2015). *Cultural web.* In J. Atkinson, E. Loftus, & J. Jarvis (Eds.), *The Art of Change Making* (pp. 134–137). Leadership Centre.

Kline, N. (2002). *Time to Think: Listening to Ignite the Human Mind*, Graewood Business Services.

Osborne, D., & Hinson, J. (2015). *Generative Conversations: – Results Through Connection and Meaning.* ChangeFusion. https://change-fusion.com/wp-content/uploads/2015/12/GenerativeConversations.pdf

Rosenburg, M. (2012). *Living Nonviolent Communication: Practice Tools to Connect and Communicate Skillfully in Every Situation.* Sounds True.

Scott, S. (2002). *Fierce Conversations: Achieving Success at Work & in Life, One Conversation at a Time.* Piarkus.

Stewart Black, J., & Bright D. S. (2019). *Organisational Behavior.* Openstax.

Stone, L. (2009). *Beyond simple multi-tasking: Continuous partial attention?* https://lindastone.net/2009/11/30/beyond-simple-multi-tasking-continuous-partial-attention/

Syed, M. (2019). *Rebel Ideas: The Power of Diverse Thinking.* John Murray.

Weick E. K. (1995). *Sensemaking in Organisations.* SAGE.

Welch, J. (2001). *Jack: Straight from the Gut.* Warner Books.

Chapter 22
The Mentoring Relationship: Layers of Meaning and How to Work with Them

Lydia Hartland-Rowe

Introduction

This chapter looks at what might be going on 'under the surface' in the mentor/ mentee relationship, and how to work creatively with these complexities. Based on applied psychoanalytic and 'systems-psychodynamics' frameworks, the chapter identifies developmental, unconscious and systemic influences that are an unavoidable part of all relationships. It includes examples of what this looks like in practice, and suggestions about how to work with these influences, for both mentor and mentee.

Vignette

Grace and Michaela meet for mentoring sessions as part of a professional development programme. Grace is working on a portfolio that will help her be approved as a specialist practitioner in her field. Michaela has been identified as a mentor because she has been through the process, now required for all practitioners as part of an organization-wide restructure, which itself is part of an improvement mandate. They come from different fields of expertise, but the overarching scheme of accreditation is shared. They work in different teams; Grace is a long-standing senior member of her team, whereas Michaela is at a more junior level and is younger than Grace. Michaela is also one of very few staff members who are people of colour in her organization.

In the first two meetings Grace said how busy she was in her team, and how she wasn't sure she would have time for the portfolio – she was not hostile but seemed to make light of its purpose, framing it as 'jumping through the hoops'. She did little work in the interim, which made it harder to find a focus beyond this mood of busyness and a slight belittling of the task. This has felt difficult for Michaela to respond to. She had submitted her own portfolio when it was still optional, had enjoyed the experience of reviewing her knowledge and experience, and had appreciated working with her mentor, an older woman in her team who was a familiar senior colleague, and who as another woman of colour in the organization had been a helpful role model. Using this experience as a model, Michaela has expressed interest in Grace's career, and made suggestions about how she might use this narrative to create the portfolio, but her efforts seem to fall flat. ➔

Michaela approached the next meeting determined to find a way to help Grace to find interest and energy for the project. The more Michaela tried to be encouraging and helpful in this meeting the more gently rejecting Grace seemed to become. Michaela herself began to feel frustrated, found herself getting quite impatient, and afterwards felt completely inadequate as a mentor, unsure if she was up to the role. Grace cancelled their next meeting giving overwork as a reason, and Michaela felt slightly relieved. She got back in touch with Grace to reschedule, but later than she meant to, and it began to be difficult to get back on track.

Even this short vignette shows how much can be going on in a mentoring relationship, and how much feeling can be evoked in both mentor and mentee. Being aware of the different influences likely to be at work in the relationship can help both partners to identify what might be getting in the way of the mentoring experience working as well as it can.

Developmental influences

As adults, we go on developing, and we draw on earlier experiences of development. Like a set of Russian dolls, our smaller 'learning selves' are always present within us, and can either resource us well, or at times make it more difficult to learn and grow. These key ideas about development can be helpful in approaching the mentor/ mentee relationship.

From infancy, relationships are central to the way that we grow and develop

The study of early experience shows the importance of the relationships that we have with primary carers right from the very beginning, from first experiences of learning to find the breast and feed with the help of an adult gaze and supportive holding (Miller, 2002). Our first experiences of walking, talking and playing 'peepo' are framed by relationships with minds bigger than our own. As we move out into the wider world, from our first day at school, learning to learn with others, and through all the different developmental milestones that we then approach, relationships that support growth and learning are key.

But they are not without their challenges. Being dependent on someone else in order to learn can feel exposing, leave us feeling vulnerable, and, as adults, even ashamed of needing to have help while at the same time wanting to be supported. Being aware of the mentoring relationship as a dependency relationship can help to recognize the possibility that either party could have unexpected feelings about working together, either about being more vulnerable through being dependent, or about being the person on whom someone else depends.

Early relational experiences can have an impact in later life

The way that we approach relationships, and particularly ones where we are dependent, or might feel more vulnerable, is influenced by the way in which these very early experiences unfolded. This doesn't mean that if someone had a very easy and straightforward experience of these early developmental stages they won't ever face challenges in dependency relationships later in life. It also doesn't mean that if someone had difficult early relational experiences they will always struggle in relationships where they are vulnerable to someone else. There are multifactorial influences on us as we grow and develop, and different points at which meeting the right environmental influences can really help us to move forward, even if earlier experiences have been less straightforward. But it does mean that it is worth being aware of what can be evoked in a mentoring relationship 'now' that may have its origins in a different relationship 'then', which can help to make sense of feelings that don't seem to fit with who we are as our adult selves.

We enter into all relationships with our personal and cultural history

Who we are, how we have grown, and the social and historical contexts in which we have grown, all influence how we see and experience each other – and how we interpret what we see. Relationships where power is a feature, as in all dependency relationships, add a complicated dimension for both partners – so, what does it mean to depend on someone who may represent the kind of authority figure that is aligned to the possible misuse of power that has led to experiences of racism? And what does it feel like to take on such a role while being mindful of how one might be experienced? The question of *'who am I to you'* and *'who are you to me'* may need to be openly talked about and revisited in the course of a mentoring relationship, whether or not there appear to be significant differences present within the pair.

Unconscious influences

The developmental influences on relationships are unlikely to be unconscious, because they are so often rooted in very early experiences of dependency and learning. An applied psychoanalytic framework suggests that there are unconscious processes that go on between people all the time, in all kinds of contexts (Bower, 1995). Noticing and recognizing where these processes might be influencing a relationship can be helpful in making sense of experiences that otherwise don't seem to fit with what we expect to happen, or what we expect it to feel like.

Psychoanalysis is a broad field, with different approaches and an evolving body of theory and practice. The perspectives of 'applied' writers, such as Isca Salzberger-Wittenberg (1970), Biddy Youell (2006) and Marion Bower (2005), is helpful here, building on work rooted in a psychoanalytic tradition that started with Freud and Klein. Here are a few core ideas that are helpful in thinking about what influences the mentor/mentee relationship from 'under the surface'.

The 'internal world'

A core idea in psychoanalytic thinking is that as well as our conscious thoughts, wishes and feelings, we all have aspects of who we are and how we feel that we keep ourselves from knowing. This might be because they don't fit with who we feel ourselves to be, or don't fit with our social environment, or would cause us too much distress and anxiety if they were present consciously. A lot of what is unconscious is helpfully so, keeping us able to relate healthily to ourselves, and to each other. But it doesn't go away, and instead is part of our 'internal world', a parallel to the conscious version we have of the world and ourselves in it. The 'internal world' is partly based on what has happened to us and what kinds of experiences we have had, particularly early in life. But it is also influenced by how, as an individual, we understand and process our experiences – and different individuals process the same kinds of experiences very differently. To some extent our 'external world' can be a shared one, in that different individuals can be exposed to the same experiences in the environment, for better or worse. But everyone's 'internal world' is unique. This may be very important to remember as someone who has received mentoring and is now providing it – your own experience of the relationship you had with your mentor, and how you interpreted it and processed it, is particular to you. Each pair needs to find their own way of working together, without expectations that what feels productive and fruitful in one mentoring relationship will feel the same in another.

Transference

One feature of the 'internal world' is that it holds versions of what relationships are like, based on previous experiences of relationships, and on how we made sense of those experiences. When we encounter a relationship that has some shared features of a relationship as it is represented in the 'internal world', particularly early relationships, we tend to 'transfer' the qualities that we see *inside* onto the relationship that we are actually part of *outside*. Sometimes this can be helpful – if we are someone whose experience and whose way of processing dependency relationships and of being vulnerable in learning has been positive, then we are more likely to see new people on whom we might need to depend in a more positive way. If we are someone whose 'internal world' has instead led to an interpretation of such figures as unreliable or even unkind, or someone whose experiences have actually included being left unheld or even mistreated, then the way new figures are approached may well be less straightforward. Our 'transference' to new relationships is coloured by what internal versions we have of other, older relationships. Just to make it more complicated, this all happens at an unconscious level, so we won't always know if we are distorting the reality of the person in front of us because we are encountering them through an internal lens coloured by who we expect to see. In a mentoring relationship, where there is some dependency and perhaps also some beliefs about who has power and authority, it is very possible that the 'transferences' between mentor and mentee may start out distorted until enough knowledge and trust of the actual relationship has been developed. Awareness that this might be part of the process can help to slow down judgement or potentially unhelpful responses.

Projection and projective identification

Some of what goes on inside each of us at an unconscious level also communicates itself, subtly and often through non-verbal signs and signals, to those with whom we are interacting. Two key processes that are at work here are *projection* and *projective identification*. In the clinical psychoanalytic literature in which these terms were developed, they refer to the processes at work between a psychoanalytic therapist and their patient, where they are a central focus of interest in understanding the 'internal world' of the patient (Salzburger-Wittenberg, 1970). But they are also at work in all kinds of other relationships. It can be useful to be aware that they might be influencing what the relationship feels like, especially when things feel unaccountably difficult.

In this context, the definitions can be greatly simplified. 'Projection' is simply the way in which we disown aspects of ourselves that we don't want to know about, or feelings we don't want to have, by ridding ourselves of them and locating them in those around us through subtle, non-verbal means of unconscious communication. Babies and teenagers are particularly good at projecting their feelings – the upset and unsettled feeling we can all have on hearing a tiny infant crying, or the fear and frustration we can feel when an adolescent seems totally unaware of risks they may be taking. Infants need to project their experiences because their other ways of communicating are limited. Adolescents often need to project unwelcome feelings so that they can get on with the difficult job of growing away from childhood and into adulthood. But we all project, every time we attribute qualities to someone else that might be ones we would helpfully recognize in ourselves. Sometimes, these are qualities we don't want to have because they are felt to be negative – 'she's so competitive', 'they're so lazy'. But sometimes they can also be qualities that we are not able to recognize that are more positive but don't fit with our conscious version of who we are – 'I wish I was as focused as her', 'I will never be able to manage the kind of job she does'. In a mentoring relationship, it can be helpful to be aware of what might be projected 'onto' the mentor by the mentee (for example, being the one who knows, being someone judgemental) and vice versa (for example, being the one who is vulnerable, or competitive).

'Projective identification', in this context, is simply what happens when we are the recipient of someone else's projections – and what we do with them. So, if what is projected is someone else's anxiety, and we then find that we get so anxious ourselves that we can't function as well as we usually do in similar circumstances, we have 'identified' too much with the anxiety rather than recognizing it as something we can't entirely identify with because it is not in keeping with our own sense of who we are.

Countertransference

Countertransference in the clinical psychoanalytic literature is also a big subject, but in the context of the mentoring relationship, it is possible to simplify it as the way that it feels when you are on the 'receiving end' of someone else's projections, including who you might be connected to in their 'internal world' (i.e., the 'transference'). So, if what is being projected is someone else's extremely critical self-view, something they don't want to know about consciously, we might find ourselves feeling unaccountably critical of them in a way that doesn't quite sit with who we usually are. The projection has got inside us, we have identified with it – and the risk is that we then find ourselves acting on it. The clue that tells us when there might be an unhelpful projection is the extent to which the way we feel does or doesn't fit with what we would expect of ourselves in a similar circumstance. So, it might be very important to know how you usually feel going into a new relationship with someone you are meant to support or to be supported by – the level of anxiety, or enthusiasm, or concern that you would expect. That makes it more possible to be aware of what might be happening within the relationship, and what belongs to whom.

These processes are part of ordinary human contact all the time – we can't help 'projecting' aspects of ourselves that we don't want to know. But sometimes they get in the way of a relationship working well, which is the main reason to have an interest in them.

Systems psychodynamics

As well as the unconscious processes that are always at work within each of us, and between us as individuals, there is also a body of work that emphasizes the importance of recognizing what is at work unconsciously within the wider system in which individual relationships are located. 'Systems psychodynamics', an approach to organizational life that brings together both the impact of systemic structures and processes, and the dynamics between people within the system, adds a very important perspective to the understanding of what might be going on 'under the surface' in the mentoring relationship. It connects the impact of the wider social currency, the particular dynamics at work within the organizational structure framing the relationship, and the intimate network of unconscious communications happening within the pair. It is a helpful way of ensuring that the impact of the structural characteristics of the organization or system in which relationships sit is also recognized as a significant influence on the relationship. If the organization as a whole is struggling to ensure that there is sufficient time to support professional development activity, for example, then it might well be that this quality of organizational life will emerge in the mentoring relationship as well. It may be helpful to consider it as a systemic rather than a purely individual phenomenon as it may help in finding a way forward. Issues that look like individual problems connected to a person or a pair might more helpfully be thought about in the context of what they represent for and of the wider system – this can take the pressure off, and reduce the potential to lay blame rather than find meaning when things aren't going well.

Systems psychodynamics also emphasizes the importance in any work taking place in an organizational context of 'boundary, authority, role and task'. In other words, it is important to have clarity about the definition and boundary around the mentoring pair (i.e., Is it a separate contract for a particular development activity? Is it part of an ongoing line management relationship? Does it have a time frame?), under whose authority the work is taking place (i.e., Is there organizational support for the time needed, and an expectation that the work will take place?), what each role means (i.e., What are the responsibilities for mentee and mentor?), and what the shared task is (i.e., Is it the process of working together or is it the outcome?). These things might look easy to define as a way of looking at the mentoring relationship in the context of a specific organizational system – but the psychodynamics of what then takes place between the individuals, and between the mentoring pair and the teams and organization around them is very likely to make this more complex. Being ready to question what might be getting in the way at a systemic level, and what the wider difficulties encountered at an individual level might represent about the system, can be a helpful way of getting unstuck.

The systems-psychodynamics framework also helps to ensure that the wider social structures, histories and organizational experiences of the use and misuse of power are recognized as important influences throughout the organizational system, including within a mentoring relationship.

Helpful questions

So, how are these ideas helpful in practice? Obviously, the mentoring relationship has as its core focus the development and enrichment of the mentee, alongside the mentor's development of their own capacity to promote development in others. The main aim isn't to analyse, but to work with the interests, preoccupations and issues affecting the specific developmental aims of the mentee. When all goes well, there may be no need to explore what is going on at a deeper level in the relationship – but when there appear to be stumbling blocks that are hard to get round using other ways of approaching things, questions that promote a deeper exploration are worth considering.

A systems-psychodynamics perspective

Some of these questions might be:

- Are we aware of who 'holds authority' for this mentoring work organizationally, i.e., is it supported by management/a professional body/a peer group?
- Are we clear on the boundaries of the mentoring relationship, what it is and isn't?
- What do each of our roles require of us and provide us with?
- What is our shared task? What we are trying to do?
- Are there things going on in this relationship that may echo what is going on elsewhere in the organizational structure in which the mentoring takes place?
- Are there things going on in the organization that may be having a significant impact on our work together?

Looking at the vignette, there are aspects of the situation where a systems-psychodynamics 'lens' might be helpful in getting unstuck. The fact that the mentoring is part of a process that is mandated is likely to be significant as a systemic pressure – and the experience for Michaela of feeling that she is not doing a good enough job might be an expression of something present at an organizational level. For Michaela, as one of very few women of colour within the organization taking up a mentoring role in relation to an older, more senior white woman, the situation may mean that the mentoring relationship is holding both a developmental aspiration for the organization, but also an uncomfortable reminder of the extent to which groups have been minoritized in the organization's history. Finding ways to notice these influences as possible barriers to working well together could help to move the relationship forward. It might also be helpful for the pair to think about the questions of boundary, authority, task and role to get back on track.

Developmental and unconscious influences

When things get so stuck, it can be helpful to stop and reflect on possible unconscious dynamics that might be holding an influence. This doesn't necessarily need to happen within the pair for this to make a difference. Even just reflecting as individuals can open up space and help to get things moving.

Helpful questions for reflection might include:

- How do I feel about a relationship where there is an element of dependency?
- How do I think my mentor/mentee 'partner' might feel about dependency?
- What kind of person might we each represent to the other – including where our perceived identities might bring preconceptions about who we are and how we might treat each other?
- Are there feelings I have here that feel unfamiliar to how I usually feel in similar contexts?
- Am I responding in this context in ways that surprise me?

Again, in the vignette there are some examples of where these questions might arise. For example, what might it mean for Grace to be in a role where she is in some way dependent on someone else in a new way? What does it mean to Michaela to have someone relating to her in this more dependent way – and what is the meaning for her of the difference between her own mentor and herself as Grace's mentor? Is there anything in particular for Grace that touches her about being in a potentially exposing position in relation to someone younger than her, and someone in a more junior position? Grace consciously frames this development opportunity as something she is essentially too busy and senior for, and something she is only doing because she has to, but it is possible that there might also be a more anxious Grace in her 'internal world', who feels uncertain about success, or is even humiliated by having to undergo an accreditation process when she already feels well established. Just having these possibilities in mind can help to make a difference to the way that a mentor like Michaela might approach her mentee, even if they are never discussed or explored.

It also seems likely that some of what Grace might feel about the experience is being 'projected' into Michaela – and that she finds herself identifying with it in a way that leaves her with very uncomfortable feelings. Although Grace is consistently cheerful she also doesn't do any work on her portfolio, and gradually Michaela gets more frustrated. That makes some sense for Michaela in her own right, but she feels afterwards that she acted out of character when she was impatient with Grace – so one helpful question might be whether or not some of what Grace is feeling is actually anger and frustration, which is being projected into Michaela? The feelings afterwards of not being good enough, and of uncharacteristically not following up quickly when Grace cancels, might also be points when it could be helpful to ask 'what belongs where?'

Health warning!

It's really important to remember that these ideas are for reflection and to start an *internal* conversation about what might be going on. They are not something to be applied 'to' a mentee by a mentor, but an additional bit of equipment for both partners to use in navigating what can at times be a complex relationship. These dynamics might never be talked about – or they might, if it felt like it might be helpful to think together about what the mentoring relationship feels like to each partner. But even just considering the possibility that there are processes going on that are not conscious, and that have meaning, can sometimes really help to regain focus on the actual, adult relationship in the 'here and now'.

References

Bower, M. (1995). *Early applications: children and institutions*. In M. Bower, & J. Trowell (Eds.), *The Emotional Needs of Young Children and Their Families: Using Psychoanalytic Ideas in the Community* (pp. 22–33). Routledge.

Bower, M. (2005). *Psychoanalytic Theory for Social Work Practice: Thinking under Fire*. Routledge.

Miller, L. (2002). *Babyhood: Becoming a person in the family*. In D. Hindle, & M. V. Smith (Eds.), *Personality Development: A Psychoanalytic Perspective* (pp. 33–48). Taylor & Francis.

Salzberger-Wittenberg, I. (1970). *Psychoanalytic Insight and Relationships: A Kleinian Approach*. Routledge & Kegan Paul.

Youell, B. (2006). *The Learning Relationship: Psychoanalytic Thinking in Education*. (Tavistock Clinic Series). Routledge.

References

Chapter 23
Mentoring in a Rainbow Nation

Colleen Qvist

Background to our Rainbow Nation

On 27 April 1994, my husband and I planned to pop out quickly to vote in the South African General Election before coming home for breakfast. Many hours later we were still standing in the line and we realised that there would be no breakfast (South Africa History Online [SAHO], 2013). This was the first democratic election where all South Africans over eighteen years of age, irrespective of race, were allowed to vote. Previously, only White people were allowed to vote.

It was also on this day that Archbishop Desmond Tutu referred to South Africans as a Rainbow Nation (Buqa, 2015).

I think it was then that many South Africans set about unlearning what had been ingrained in us and relearning a new way. I think our focus at that time was on being the 'same'. Looking back, I think we should have focused on being 'equal but different'. When I think of Archbishop Tutu's Rainbow Nation, we were focusing on being one rainbow and not on the individual colours that collectively make up a rainbow. It is easy to think of diversity, especially in a South African context, as only referring to race. Diversity is so much more than only race and includes the mainstream categories of age, gender, gender identity, ability and sexual preference. It is tempting to scan a selection of photographs and think that when your eyes see 'same' that there is no diversity. Diversity is not always visible. As a mentor I have realised that people have different answers to:

- Does your milk come from a bottle or directly from a cow? Or don't you drink milk?
- Did you grow up in a child-led household?
- Do you know your father?
- Do you have to walk to fetch water, or do you switch on a tap?

For years, South Africans have embraced that we are all the same – the concept of the single rainbow. It is only relatively recently that we have felt safe enough to stop tiptoeing around race. It is now that more people are comfortable enough to be curious about other people's lived experiences and to share ours. We have started to explore each part of the rainbow and to celebrate that red isn't blue and there are many shades of red. We now know that what makes our Rainbow Nation immeasurably rich in diversity extends beyond colour and race. It helps me to think of the OSHO quote when I muddle equality and similarity.

Everybody is equal in the eyes of existence. But remember,
equality does not mean similarity. Everybody is
uniquely unique.

(OSHO, 1987)

My formative years

I was educated in a White-only school in South Africa where we spoke English and prayed at assembly. It was an era when sexual preference was not spoken about – there were two genders, and socio-economic status was ignored. We also believed that all people were Christian and spoke English. Diversity was there, although hidden. There were no Black, Indian, Coloured or Asian children in my school (Statista, n.d.). We existed in a 'sea of sameness'.

I grew up in a Christian, English-speaking home where my parents celebrated uniqueness and my brother and I were taught to accept all people (and animals) as having unique value. I have spent more than 87% of my working life in post-apartheid South Africa. Our Rainbow Nation.

It has been somewhat of a shock for me to be exposed to other people's belief systems about race. I had naively believed that everyone thought the same way as me. An example of this was when I employed the company's first Black salesperson in the 1990s and sent her to a hospital to be trained by one of our medical specialists. The new sales rep phoned me in a state of upset to say that the doctor would not let her into the theatre because she was Black, and I had not shared that with him. It was a time of anger, hurt and epiphanies.

I have spent much of my life reflecting on my lived experiences from my perspective and the perspective of others. What we see often depends on where we are standing. Imaging standing looking at a giant number six. If your mentee was standing opposite you, they would see a nine not a six. It is important that you move to your mentee's side of the story or picture to see what they are seeing (Figure 23.1).

Figure 23.1: Perspective.

I have seen people look for connection with others by mentally ticking off the list of the things they have in common (for example career, mom, parent) and be surprised when they did not click with the person despite the similarities.

My daughter said the other day that Humans aren't just White or Black or parent, or whichever label we choose to use. They are the perceptions you have of those labels.

My experience as a mentor

I spent twenty-two years working in medical devices in sales, product and management and now I am credentialed as a COMENSA Master Coach and COMENSA Master Mentor who has worked with clients for the last ten years in their personal and work lives. My clients come from a variety of industries including retail, manufacturing, commerce, finance and health care. I mentor salespeople in the medical devices and pharmaceutical industries, and executives looking for how to maintain balance and equilibrium, and how to juggle parenting and career. I have also mentored as a mom to a 25-year-old daughter, to unemployed youth moving into retail, and to coaches and mentors in my recent voluntary capacity as Gauteng Chair and National Vice President of Coaches and Mentors of South Africa (COMENSA).

I am writing this chapter from the position of being aware of my privilege as a White woman in South Africa and I am sharing what I have learned as a mentor in a Rainbow Nation. I have empathy for those who have had less or different privilege, but I do not disappear into the 'Oh shame' of sympathy. Different is not wrong. Different is not less or more. Instead, I ask how can I use my 'different' to empower others and how their 'different' can empower me? How can we use our differences as a strength?

Below, I share specific pointers that have helped me to become a more effective mentor.

Screen dump, stereotypes and blind spots

Mentoring can involve sharing our knowledge, wisdom and experience of what worked for us. It can be tempting to screen dump our lived experience onto our mentee as if it is a one-size-fits-all template. What worked for you cannot be a direct template for your mentee. It takes time to understand your mentee and to work out which part of your experience can be shared and how that experience can be adapted to produce results in the mentee's situation.

My belief is that to be totally effective as mentors we need to utilize both coaching and mentoring skills (European Mentoring and Coaching Council [EMCC], 2022). It is useful to look at the COMENSA Behavioural Standards for Coaching (COMENSA, 2022). I ask my mentee to share their story in our first session. I ask questions and I listen. I realise that I may hold stereotypes of my mentee and could offer suggestions that uphold that stereotype. By asking questions and listening I connect with the real mentee and not the stereotype I hold of them.

Activity

Write down your thoughts about your mentee who is:

- a 22-year-old man
- a pregnant 15-year-old
- heavily tattooed
- a graduate
- in a wheelchair
- wearing a LGBTIQ support t-shirt
- grey-haired and stooped over

Have you noticed any biases come up?

Another phrase to look out for in your thinking and conversation, as a mentor, should you use it, is 'you just' as it implies that something is easy. You might tell your mentee that they should 'just' approach a stranger at an event and start talking. Yes, it may be easy for you now, but was it always easy? During the COVID-19 pandemic, people spoke about us all being 'in the same boat'. This was later corrected to 'being in the same storm in different boats'. Your mentee may have a similar goal but they may have very different opportunities and resources.

Contracting and recontracting

In my sessions, I contract around us speaking out if either of us uses terminology that the other finds uncomfortable or offensive. At a workshop I was facilitating, I watched two women from the same racial classification argue over whether they were Black or African They finally compromised by agreeing to use both terms.

Other English words that may result in discussion – ladies, girls, guys, senior, boys, old, feminist. The list is endless.

I contract to not assume, to be naturally curious and to seek to understand. We cannot be expected to know everyone's beliefs, traditions, rituals and cultures. It is wiser and more respectful to ask about and to share one's own lived version (Matambo, 2021). As mentors we need to develop the courage to challenge and to use deep, probing coaching questions in our mentoring. As an example, if my mentee shared that they were not happy about going home for Christmas, I would ask questions such as: Where is home? What usually happens during Christmas? What does your unhappiness feel like?

U theory has the concept of removing our jacket. If we think of our opinions as jackets, we can remove our jacket to try on someone else's jacket. I contract in my sessions for us to follow 'I have a jacket versus I am my jacket' (U.Lab, 2015a).

When I feel that we have wandered off the path of what we have agreed to, I make a point of recontracting by raising what we have agreed to, asking whether it is still valid or does it need tweaking, and then lovingly bringing us back onto the path. Upheld boundaries are comforting for both mentor and mentee, and models for the mentee the behaviour of upholding boundaries.

Systems and structure and beliefs and behaviours

In U theory there is the Iceberg model (U.Lab, 2015b) that shows the visible situations in the world portrayed at the top of the iceberg. These are the bits that stick out. We can see poverty and environmental crises, and discrimination. We can see corruption. We can also see all the positive parts.

We cannot see what lies underneath the surface. In this model, immediately below there is a layer of systems and structures and beneath that another layer of behaviours and beliefs. Do be mindful that you cannot see these layers in your mentee. You need time to unpack and understand them. Your mentee may not know what is in their own layers. By being mindful of the invisible layers, you can avoid falling into the trap of thinking you know what is in the layers because you have worked with previous mentees who tick the same boxes. Black unemployed youth do not all have the same backstory. Older, stooped-over people are not immediately bad at technology. Young people are not automatically good at tech.

I have always worked in a culture of individualism versus collectivism. The Western way is to recognize the person who stands out and to celebrate individual achievements while encouraging competition and winning at all costs. The culture is such that you speak out, disagree, debate, motivate and are seen.

The African way is one of community, of Ubuntu, I am because you are. The power is in the collective and in the community (Battle, 2009).

It helps to know which system and culture your mentee identifies with because their approach to getting ahead, setting goals, and dreaming of the future will be very impacted by this.

Narrative

What is the story in your mentee's head? I worked with a young woman who told me that she would never be able to go in a plane. I asked her why and she said that it was because she lived in a squatter camp (Your Dictionary, 2022) and had no electricity. The words that are spoken into our lives have power. As it turns out, the young woman was employed by a bank and the bank sent her from Johannesburg to Cape Town in a plane for training. Many people are defined by where they come from as opposed to where they are going.

Makhalima (2022) speaks about the psychology of geography and space and how growing up in a four-roomed house affects the size of the imagination because it acts as a psychic constraint and permeates everything that you do. Prison cells are squares, instead of L-shaped or U-shaped, as it removes the perceived sense of freedom. Makhalima also mentions that people who grow up in too much open space may have issues with impulse control and being overwhelmed by choice. How does the psychology of space affect your mentee?

Role models and representation are also so important. A kwaito artist shared with me that so many of our youth see the success of the drug dealer, the pimp and the person stealing cars and in the absence of other successful role models that they seek to emulate these people (Qvist, 2016).

When a young girl doesn't see people like her as scientists, it is written into her DNA that people like her do not become scientists. In South Africa currently, many university/college graduates are the very first graduate in their families. They may feel pressured by their family and community to perform.

Community and families hold a lot of power in some cultures and very little in others. Many people are also driven by what other people will think and they tend to make life decisions based on this. I have seen mentees working in corporate organizations being summoned home by family/mom/gogo or gran and they have had to go to the detriment of their career and the confusion of their colleagues. Defining culture, heritage and identity in South Africa is complex (SAHO, 2019). This complexity needs to be considered for you to mentor successfully.

In South Africa, in some cultures, being seen to be humble and not arrogant is highly valued. Unfortunately, many think that being humble means not having a voice. I have seen people try to take up as little space as possible and to fade into the background. There has been many a facilitator or manager who has been very confused that everyone had agreed to a project with no questions being asked but they have then not delivered on that project. The expectation of being humble or voiceless leads to people agreeing and going away and not doing anything, instead of seeking to understand by asking questions. Your mentee may therefore not feel they have the right to decide on the frequency of your sessions or to reach out to you when they need a mentoring session.

As mentors, we also need to understand behaviours like keeping eye contact, raising our voice and disagreeing are welcomed and expected behaviours, especially in the Western work culture, but can be seen as very disrespectful in other cultures. Do you see the person who does not hold eye contact and who whispers as shifty, guilty or respectful?

Language can also cause many problems in a South African mentoring setting as we often mentor people in a language which is not their home language. South Africa has eleven official languages and respects many others (SAHO, 2019). As a mentor, it is important to make a point of giving feedback of what it is that you are hearing and understanding. This gives your mentee an opportunity to correct any misunderstandings. In a group setting, especially in South Africa, you will often hear more than one language in a single conversation. This works very well if you can understand the other language but causes problems if you cannot follow. It is tempting to feel that you are being kept out of the conversation on purpose and to feel isolated. It is easier to communicate in our home language. People need to be lovingly reminded to swop to a common language or for someone to translate. Often, I have followed the conversation in a group by asking the person sitting next to me to translate.

Change

No man ever steps into the same river twice, for it is not the same river, and he's not the same man.

(Heraclitus in Marks, 2019)

It has become apparent during the COVID-19 pandemic how fast and radically the world can change. The world was changing anyway, but the pandemic was a catalyst for change. The question I then ask myself regularly, is whether I have kept up with the topics that I mentor on, or am I trying to share information from years ago that is no longer relevant? I am also aware that our fast-paced lives, fed by social media, have meant that people today like instant gratification. I remind myself that this is not wrong and that if we only had the skills from 1820, we would not survive in the 2020s.

Two examples from my experience with change are with young people. I was surprised when youth in retail expressed a need to frequently rotate through different departments. I felt that I would need to spend forever in a bakery to learn how to make everything, but they explained that they could always go back. Rotation introduced excitement and warded off boredom for them, but rotation would have introduced another layer of fear in me because of the reduced amount of time to become an expert.

Another situation saw a medical representative advise me that they had reached the pinnacle of their career after a year in their discipline, and it was time for a change. I could have felt offended if I thought they were thinking that I was slow to have spent seventeen years somewhere when they were ready to move after only one year. The adage 'different is not wrong' is key: people need to find what works for them. As an aside, do check that your mentee is not running away and avoiding something, but instead they are running towards something. When we run away, patterns repeat.

Crime, trauma and healing

South Africa is a country with well-documented high crime levels. It is also a country with people who have multilayered and complex trauma (Navsaria, 2021). We have different ways of addressing or avoiding the trauma and different rituals for healing and grief. As a mentor, it is better to respectfully ask. I am reminded of a client who expressed that she felt guilty because she was grieving her brother before he had died from a terminal illness. It was important that I understood her background and beliefs and did not mentor from my perspective of grief.

Disconnecting

Your mentees will bring parts of themselves that you may battle to understand or process. Individuals in the caring professions tend to be prone to burnout. Do introduce a process to replenish and maintain your energy and to mindfully disconnect from their story. You cannot serve hundreds if you do not learn to process and detach. There are numerous options here to ground you and you will need to find a method that suits you such as regular supervision, meditation, journaling, prayer, angel work and breathing.

Your lived experience is not a one-size-fits-all template. Be open and curious to diverse cultures, beliefs, behaviours, rituals and systems, and contract and recontract to respectfully explore different approaches and different narratives. It is when we embrace the differences and see that different is not wrong that belonging changes from only being a word to an actual lived experience.

When you see diversity as a strength and acknowledge, embrace and celebrate our differences, you will discover that mentoring in a Rainbow Nation can be extremely rewarding.

References

Battle, M. (2009). *Ubuntu: I in You and You in Me*. Seabury Books.

Buqa, W. (2015). *Storying Ubuntu as a rainbow nation*, *Verbum et Ecclesia*, **36**(2), Art. #1434. http://dx.doi.org/10.4102/ve.v36i2.1434

Coaches and Mentors of South Africa (COMENSA) (2022). *Annexure A: Behavioural Standards for Coaching Framework*. https://www.comensa.org.za/wp-content/uploads/2022/05/Behavioural-Standards-Framework-for-Coaching.pdf

European Mentoring and Coaching Council (EMCC)(2022). *Thought Leadership and Development: Mentoring*. https://www.emccglobal.org/leadership-development/leadership-development-mentoring/

Makhalima, M. (2022, April 11). *You are where you live... Well sort of*. The Museletter. https://themuseletter.wordpress.com/2022/04/11/you-are-where-you-live-well-sort-of/

Marks J. E. (2019). *No man ever steps in the same river twice*. The Startup. https://medium.com/swlh/no-man-ever-steps-in-the-same-river-twice-867ec5afc857#:~:text=Heraclitus%2C%20a%20Greek%20philosopher%20born,he%27s%20not%20the%20same%20man.%E2%80%9D&text=For%20two%20and%20a%20half,Sceptical%2C%20Seeking%2C%20Secular

Matambo, C. (2021). *The Perceptions of South African Executive Coaches on the Role of Cultural Intelligence in Cross-Cultural Executive Coaching* [Research project, unpublished]. University of the Witwatersrand.

Navsaria, P. H., Nicol, A. J., Parry, C. D. H. , Matzopolous, R., Maqungo, S., & Gaudin, R. (2021). *The effect of lockdown on intentional and non-intentional injury during the COVID-19 pandemic in Cape Town, South Africa: A preliminary report*. South African Medical Journal, **111**(2), 110-113.

OSHO (1987). *In existence there is no inferiority*: In *The New Dawn*. Osho Media International. https://www.facebook.com/osho.international/posts/everybody-is-equally-unique/10156724008962069/

Qvist, C. (2016, January 31). *Creating Positive Role Models for Youth*. LinkedIn. https://www.linkedin.com/pulse/creating-positive-role-models-youth-colleen-qvist

South Africa History Online (SAHO) (2013, April 25). *South Africa's First Democratic Elections*. https://www.sahistory.org.za/dated-event/south-africas-first-democratic-elections

South Africa History Online (SAHO) (2019, August 27). *Defining Culture, Heritage and Identity*. https://www.sahistory.org.za/article/defining-culture-heritage-and-identity

Statista (n.d). *Total Population of South Africa in 2022, by Ethnic Groups*. Statista. Retrieved May 2022, from https://www.statista.com/statistics/1116076/total-population-of-south-africa-by-population-group/

U.Lab (2015a). *Transforming Business, Society, and Self (Co-Sensing)* (**Source Book**). Massachusetts Institute of Technology; Presencing Institute. https://courses.edx.org/c4x/MITx/15.S23x/asset/U.Lab_SourceBook_v2.pdf

U.Lab (2015b). *Transforming Business, Society, and Self (The iceberg model)* (**Source Book Version 3A**). Massachusetts Institute of Technology; Presencing Institute. https://courses.edx.org/asset-v1:MITx+15.671x+3T2015+type@asset+block/U.Lab_SourceBook_v3a.pdf

Your Dictionary (2022). *Squatter-camp definition*. https://www.yourdictionary.com/squatter-camp

Chapter 24
Integrating Compassion and Mindfulness in the Mentoring Relationship

A. Maya Kaye

Compassion is the radicalism of our time.

(Dalai Lama)

Mindful compassion: Could it be an antidote to adverse mentoring outcomes?

Although life has always been riddled with uncertainties, it is becoming increasingly clear that we live in exceptionally challenging times. With the last two years of the global pandemic, war and economic insecurity, distress has been present in every corner of the Earth. It is safe to say that many of us have experienced loss, grief and trauma to varying degrees. In addition to societal pressure for high achievement, post-pandemic educational and occupational restructuring, stress and burnout may take centre stage during mentoring sessions (Hookmani et al., 2021).

As an interpersonal phenomenon that aims to nurture well-being through formal and informal encounters (Hookmani et al., 2021), mentoring can be a buffer for those experiencing psychosocial difficulties and professional burnout (Eby et al., 2008). Meaningful mentoring is a trustworthy relationship focused on guiding, inspiring, revealing and amplifying mentees' strengths. When done correctly, it is a significant responsibility that can positively impact both mentors and mentees and overall organizational cultures and communities (Hookmani et al., 2021).

Nonetheless, these unprecedented times, coupled with a lack of 'good enough' self-awareness and caring-compassion motivation (Gilbert, 2009a), can exacerbate adverse mentoring relationship outcomes and ethical implications (Hu et al., 2021). In fact, besides the negative impacts of compassion fatigue and burnout, several ethical tensions have been raised in developmental relations with mentees, such as power differential, boundary violations, competitive motivations and self-enhancement values (Moberg & Velasquez, 2004; Straus et al., 2013; Johnson, 2016).

With that in mind, readers are invited to visualize how to approach the complexities and challenges of the mentoring relationship in ways that allow for openness and responsiveness while promoting growth and preventing unethical behaviours. How could mindful compassion be an antidote to adverse mentoring outcomes in highly competitive environments?

Integrating compassion and mindfulness in the mentoring relationship could assist mentors and mentees in increasing self-awareness, compassion levels and emotional regulation skills (Gilbert, 2010; Solomon & Barden, 2016; Weber, 2017). Through mindful compassion, mentors recognize environmental and relational challenges affecting the mentoring relationship and take the necessary steps to be helpful to themselves and their mentees. In turn, mentees will see their mentors as someone they can trust, share perspectives with, ask questions of without fear of judgement and rely on knowledge and insight that formal education may not have provided.

Drawing on Johnson's framework for conceptualizing competence to mentor and Gilbert's CFT approach, we explore how compassion and mindfulness could:

- facilitate engagement with environmental and relational challenges that may interfere with the mentoring process;
- foster strong mentoring working alliances; and
- promote ethical and prosocial behaviours in and beyond mentorship.

The chapter starts with a brief overview of compassion as a motivational system. Next, we present a CFM conceptual model and demonstrate how it could guide mentors in developing compassion-focused competencies that lead to a compassionate self-identity and way of life that drive the mentoring relationship.

Compassion-motivation: 'To be helpful, not harmful'

Although the study of compassion has deep roots in spiritual communities, it has only been in the last thirty years that the cultivation of compassion and its psychosocial and neurophysiological benefits have received attention in Western research and practice. Understanding the origins of care and compassion may provide mentors with insight into a broad spectrum of biopsychosocial processes that tend to influence the mentoring process (e.g., self-interest, competitiveness, cooperation, sexuality, prosocial behaviours, ethical boundaries, institutional biases) (Johnson, 2016; Gilbert, 2020).

Throughout the literature, compassion has been conceptualized in various ways, from a spiritual virtue to a relational and multidimensional process (Gilbert, 2020). This chapter focuses on understanding compassion from the evolutionary approach proposed by Gilbert and Simos (2022). In his extensive research and the development of CFT, Gilbert defines care and compassion by combining ancient wisdom, motives and algorithmic ideas. Based on the Mahayana Buddhist tradition and evolutionary psychology, care and compassion are basic motives rooted in the evolved caregiving systems of mammals. In other words, the transformation of basic caring behaviours into compassion happened because of human beings' insight, conscious intentionality and objective sense of self. Thus, Gilbert defines compassion as a *'sensitivity to suffering in self and others with a commitment to try to alleviate and prevent it'* (Gilbert, 1989; Dalai Lama, 1995; Gilbert & Simos, 2022).

Compassion-focused mentoring (CFM) conceptual model

From micro to macro levels of work, compassionate intention could be extended to a wide range of human endeavours, including the mentoring process. Building on Gilbert's CFT approach, CFM delves deeper into caring behaviours that: *1) address individuals' unique needs*; and *2) promote their development and flourishing.*

As shown in Figure 24.1, the CFM conceptual model draws on Johnson's framework for conceptualizing mentor competence (Johnson, 2003; 2016) and Gilbert's CFT approach (Gilbert, 2009a; Gilbert & Simos, 2022). From the bottom up, compassion-motivation and mindfulness are in a state of interconnected balance, giving rise to a self-identity guided by the mindful intention: *'to be helpful, not harmful'* in all areas, while cognizant that human minds may be easily influenced to act in harmful manners (Gilbert et al., 2019). Such self-identity could inform and extend well-known mentoring-specific abilities and competencies depicted in the upper part of Figure 24.1. For a detailed review of mentors' abilities and competencies in the mentoring relationship, please see Johnson (2003; 2016).

In this conceptual model, in addition to discussing challenges within the mentorship process, a critical point in unfolding compassion-motivation, encouragement and empowerment is that mentors and mentees make space for cultivating a compassionate identity within their minds that encourages transformation through kindness, acceptance and non-judgement. Mindful compassion training could assist mentors in developing and strengthening their compassionate self-identity through mindfulness and insight into their own motivations (e.g., compassion vs competitive motives), emotions and behaviours (Gilbert, 2009a, 2009b; Defoor et al., 2020; Gilbert & Simos, 2022).

While compassion and mindfulness have been addressed as independent processes in Western research (Weber, 2017), in the CFM conceptual model, they are understood as interdependent. Understanding the interconnection of mindfulness and compassion is central to developing and modelling a compassionate self-identity in the mentoring relationship. In other words, mindfulness without compassion may become an unregulated activity that merely tends to the concept of well-being. And compassion without mindfulness may lead to emotional exhaustion and burnout (Brensilver, 2017).

Furthermore, while compassion-motivation is sensitivity to, alleviation of, and prevention of general distress (Gilbert & Simos, 2022), mindfulness is awareness and acceptance of any experience that may arise – good, bad or neutral (Nhat Hanh, 2011). For example, mentors and mentees may be aware of feeling burnt out – a form of distress – and make space for such experience in a non-judgemental way; however, they may choose to 'just power through' if competitive instead of compassion motivation is the dominant motive. Oppositely, mentors and mentees may conduct their lives based on compassion-motivation – *'to be helpful, not harmful'* – but underdeveloped awareness may hinder their ability to perceive distress in self and others (e.g., toxic positivity; dismissive behaviours).

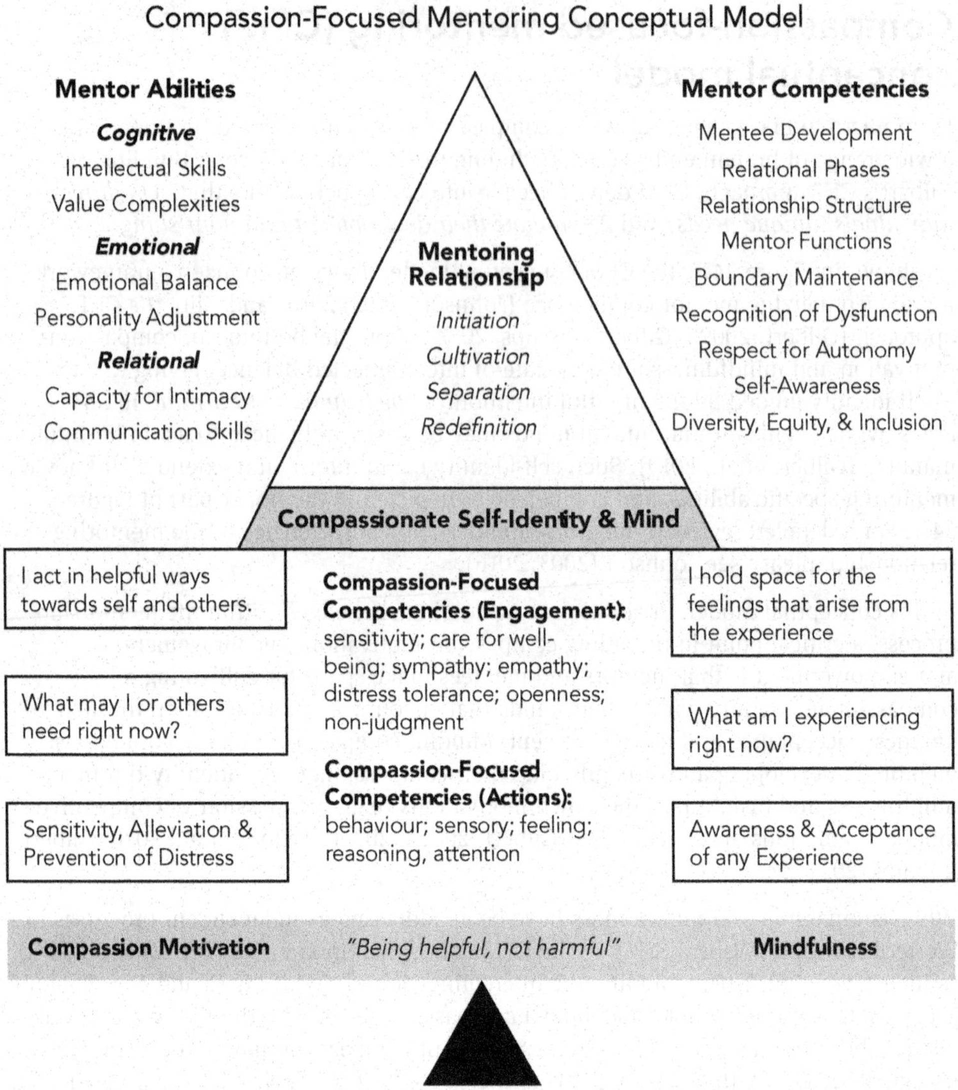

Compassion-Focused Mentoring Conceptual Model

Mentor Abilities

Cognitive
Intellectual Skills
Value Complexities

Emotional
Emotional Balance
Personality Adjustment

Relational
Capacity for Intimacy
Communication Skills

Mentoring Relationship

Initiation
Cultivation
Separation
Redefinition

Mentor Competencies

Mentee Development
Relational Phases
Relationship Structure
Mentor Functions
Boundary Maintenance
Recognition of Dysfunction
Respect for Autonomy
Self-Awareness
Diversity, Equity, & Inclusion

Compassionate Self-Identity & Mind

I act in helpful ways towards self and others.

Compassion-Focused Competencies (Engagement): sensitivity; care for well-being; sympathy; empathy; distress tolerance; openness; non-judgment

I hold space for the feelings that arise from the experience

What may I or others need right now?

Compassion-Focused Competencies (Actions): behaviour; sensory; feeling; reasoning, attention

What am I experiencing right now?

Sensitivity, Alleviation & Prevention of Distress

Awareness & Acceptance of any Experience

Compassion Motivation   *"Being helpful, not harmful"*   **Mindfulness**

Figure 24.1: Compassion-focused mentoring (CFM) conceptual model (building on Johnson (2003) and Gilbert & Simos (2022)).

Therefore, the balance between compassion-motivation and mindfulness facilitates the development of compassion-focused competencies for engagement and action in mentoring. This interconnected and complex learning process gives rise to a compassionate self-identity and mind (Gilbert & Simos, 2022) that becomes the foundation in which mentors develop and strengthen mentoring-specific competencies and abilities (Johnson, 2003; 2016). When compassionate self-identity informs mentoring abilities and competencies, mentors and mentees may form a solid working alliance and better cope with potential challenges to the mentoring process. Consequently, in addition to education and career development, the mentoring relationship could become a vehicle of sustainable psychosocial support. Next, we continue to unpack the CFM conceptual model and what a compassionate self-identity could be like in the mentoring relationship and beyond.

Going beyond empathy: Compassion as self-identity

A brief literature review provides promising evidence of incorporating compassion and mindfulness into mentoring programs (see Foukal et al., 2016; Trube, 2017; Esposito et al., 2018; Deefor et al., 2020; Freedenberg et al., 2020; Hookmani et al., 2021). Nonetheless, there is a dearth of information on how compassion and mindfulness could inform the mentoring relationship, fostering solid working alliances, prosocial behaviours, goal agreement and reflective learning.

Such exploration requires an open discussion about the interchangeable use of empathy and compassion in mentoring. Furthermore, it is not uncommon for compassion to be confused with kindness, sympathy and love. As those represent different psychological functions in individuals, Gilbert (2009a) emphasizes the importance of differentiating them through the understanding of motives, emotions and competencies. For example, while compassion is a motive, human empathy is a competency that leads to understanding of how self and others feel. As a competency, empathy could be used for any purpose (e.g., ethical, unethical, neutral) (Gilbert & Simos, 2022).

Therefore, within the mentoring relationship, it is critical to understand how empathy is used, as well as the motivation behind it. For example, mentoring in competitive workplace cultures, including higher education, for-profit and not-for-profit settings, may prove daunting. Often, mentoring relationships are becoming more about managing and performance metrics and less about approachable and compassionate support while achieving professional and educational development. Thus, some mentors may be empathic but lack compassion-motivation to help their mentees in non-hazardous, meaningful ways, while others have compassion-motivation but lack empathy skills (Gilbert & Simos, 2022).

Applied compassion-focused competencies for engagement and action in mentoring

Adapted from Johnson (2016, p. 125) and seen through the lens of the CFM conceptual model, the case vignette below illustrates how empathy without compassion and mindfulness may lead to intentional or unintentional harm in the mentoring relationship. Dr Blurred Lines is part of a well-organized mentorship program in his university. He is a dissertation chair and advisor and is facing an ethical complaint by a female doctoral student.

Case vignette: Boundary maintenance, mentor functions and relationship structure

A female doctoral student in her last year filed an ethical complaint with the university ethics commission, alleging that her dissertation chair and advisor, Dr Blurred Lines, abandoned her, leaving her extremely distraught.

Dr Blurred Lines' department has a well-organized mentorship programme that uses a multimethod approach to evaluating faculty mentoring effectiveness.

Dr Blurred Lines is an experienced and successful researcher and faculty member. The mentor is achievement-driven and believes he must succeed with all his mentees.

Due to regular socializing and the development of a personal relationship that many at the university saw as 'intense', it appears that the mentor and mentee established an uncommon level of attachment.

Given the pressures and the prestige of his research university, Dr Blurred Lines was preoccupied with his reputation and believed that if one of his mentees failed, it would show that he had failed as a mentor and was a failure.

During his student training, she experienced various personal crises and emotional problems that alarmed Dr Blurred Lines. The mentor would conduct what amounted to 'psychotherapy sessions' as frequently as three to four times per week. He pushed her to call him after hours and often invited her to gatherings with his family. Although the relationship was never sexualized, the student's level of dependence and enmeshment with her mentor was so intense that she was upset when he attempted to cease the mentorship after she graduated.

As Gilbert's definition of compassion asks us *'to be helpful, not harmful'* to self and others (Gilbert & Simos, 2022), mentors aspire to develop a mindful and compassionate identity that drives the entire mentoring process. With that in mind, we invite the reader to reflect on how compassion-focused competencies for engagement and action in mentoring (see Case vignette box) could have informed Dr Blurred Lines' mentor functions, relationship structure and boundary maintenance.

In higher education, mentors naturally fulfil numerous roles with most mentees (e.g., instructor, evaluator, supervisor, advocate). Furthermore, from the perspective of mentees, the most well-regarded mentors are those who give a wide range of support and guidance functions. Although mutuality is an essential component of solid mentorship working alliances, it can also increase the possibility of boundary crossings. However, having numerous responsibilities with a mentee does not have to result in unethical behaviours (Johnson, 2016).

In Dr Blurred Lines' case, in using the CFM conceptual model, he could have exercised compassion-focused competencies such as *attention* by tuning into self and the mentoring relationship and checking his motives, needs, boundary violation cues and harmful behaviours (Johnson, 2016; Gilbert & Simos, 2022). Whether Dr Blurred Lines' motivations were self-serving (e.g., need to be needed, voyeuristic curiosity), competing (e.g., need to succeed, fear of failure) or caring-compassion (e.g., helping the mentee stay afloat emotionally and achieve graduation goals), his poor mindfulness of boundaries induced excessive dependency and intense emotional enmeshment in a student, resulting in a worsening of her condition (Johnson, 2016; Gilbert & Simos, 2022).

Moreover, while Dr Blurred Lines might have acknowledged and understood his student's challenges (*sympathy, empathy*), he could have benefited from reflecting and consulting with a trusted colleague about his inner motivations and mentoring concerns (Johnson, 2016). Perhaps, undeveloped mindful compassion prompted the mentor to pay *attention* to what was unhelpful, leading to reactive and unskilled *reasoning, feeling,* and *behaving*. Training and development of compassion-focused competencies could have guided his decisions concerning professional mentoring and personal counselling boundaries (Gilbert & Simos, 2022).

Compassion-focused competencies for engagement and compassionate listening

Whether mentoring is focused on psychosocial support or career and education development, compassionate listening can help mentees create an emotional resonance that soothes the nervous system, leading to optimal learning states and emotional regulation (Gilbert, 2009a, 2009b; Siegel, 2014; Jinpa, 2016). It involves compassion-focused competencies for engagement in mentoring, such as *sensitivity, care for well-being, sympathy, empathy, distress tolerance, openness* and *non-judgement*. Besides actively listening, Thich Nhat Hanh, a pioneer in bringing mindfulness to the West, clarified that compassionate listening serves the purpose of assisting another person in emptying their heart (*care for well-being*). In other words, even if the mentor disagrees with the mentee's point of view, they can still listen attentively and compassionately (Nhat Hanh, 2011).

The compassionate listening process involves:

- being fully present and bearing witness to the mentee's felt experience (*sensitivity, sympathy, empathy, distress tolerance*);
- the genuine desire to learn more about the mentee through non-judgemental, open-ended questions (*care for well-being*); and
- meaning-making of how life experiences are part of the human condition and how they may affect the mentee (*care for well-being, openness, non-judgement*) (Gilbert, 2009a, 2009b; Caldwell, 2017).

In Dr Blurred Lines' case, slowing down the process and bearing witness to the mentee's felt experience could have helped him engage with her emotional difficulties while maintaining his mentor functions, emotional balance and boundaries. Instead of reacting by offering unrestrained emotional, psychological and social support, compassionate listening could have assisted the mentor and the mentee in turning toward the difficulties interfering with the mentoring process and outcomes (e.g., student's personal crisis and emotional problems, successfully graduating).

Compassion-focused competencies for action in mentoring

As seen in Figure 24.1, training in compassion-focused competencies for action in mentoring, such as shifting attention to what's helpful to self and others, could have assisted Dr Blurred Lines and his mentee in exploring different resources while attending to mentoring relationship structure, functions and boundary maintenance. For example, given that Dr Blurred Lines was a dissertation chair and advisor, he could have referred the mentee to the university's counselling department and academic success coaches while briefly making emotional check-ins before each mentoring session *(behaviour)*. When developing compassionate mindfulness, Dr Blurred Lines could have benefited from consulting with a caring colleague about his concerns and developing mindful awareness of the motivation behind his mentoring work *(attention)*. Mindfulness training through body, mind and emotional awareness exercises *(sensory)*, as well as the identification and challenging of limiting beliefs *(reasoning)*, could have helped Dr Blurred Lines navigate environmental and relational challenges interfering with the mentoring process (Gilbert & Simos, 2022).

Final comments

Your mind may be blooming with ideas, and you probably wonder where to start. This chapter explored integrating compassion and mindfulness in the mentoring relationship by developing a compassionate self-identity that informs mentoring competencies. I suggest you start by sitting with this content for a moment and observing what comes up for you. How does it resonate with your mind and body? Where are you in your compassionate self-identity journey? And how can it be translated into your mentoring journey?

References

Brensilver, M. (2017). *Mind the Hype: Reflections on a Critique of Mindfulness Research.* Mindful Schools. https://www.mindfulschools.org/foundational-concepts/response-mind-hype-article/

Caldwell, M. (2017, January 30). *How to Listen with Compassion in the Classroom.* Greater Good Magazine. https://greatergood.berkeley.edu/article/item/how_to_listen_with_compassion_in_the_classroom

Dalai Lama (1995). *The power of compassion.* Harper Collins.

DeFoor, M. T., Moses, M. M., Flowers, W. J., & Sams, R. W. (2020). *Medical student reflections: Chaplain shadowing as a model for compassionate care training. Medical Teacher,* **43**(1),1–7. https://www.tandfonline.com/doi/full/10.1080/0142159X.2020.1817880

Eby, L. T., Allen, T. D., Evans, S. C., Ng, T., & Dubois, D. (2008). *Does mentoring matter? A multidisciplinary meta-analysis comparing mentored and non-mentored individuals. Journal of Vocational Behavior,* **72**(2), 254–267. https://www.sciencedirect.com/science/article/abs/pii/S0001879107000401?via%3Dihub

Esposito, M. J., Roychoudhury, S., & Fornari, A. (2018). *A professionalism and mentoring curriculum for pathology residents in training. Academic Pathology,* **5**, p.237428951880506. https://www.sciencedirect.com/science/article/pii/S2374289521003225?via%3Dihub

Foukal, M. D., Lawrence, E. C., & Jennings, P. A. (2016). *Mindfulness and mentoring satisfaction of college women mentoring youth: Implications for training. Mindfulness,* **7**(6), 1327–1338. https://link.springer.com/article/10.1007/s12671-016-0574-0

Freedenberg, V. A., Jiang, J., Cheatham, C. A., Sibinga, E. M., Powell, C. A., Martin, G. R., Steinhorn, D. M., & Kemper, K. J. (2020). *Mindful mentors: Is a longitudinal mind–body skills training pilot program feasible for pediatric cardiology staff? Global Advances in Integrative Medicine and Health*, **9**, p.216495612095927. https://journals.sagepub.com/doi/10.1177/2164956120959272

Gilbert, P. (1989). *Human Nature and Suffering*. Laurence Erlbaum Associates.

Gilbert, P. (2009a). *A Compassionate Mind: A New Approach to Life's Challenges*. Constable.

Gilbert, P. (2009b). *Introducing compassion-focused therapy. Advances in Psychiatric Treatment*, **15**(3), 199–208. https://www.cambridge.org/core/journals/advances-in-psychiatric-treatment/article/introducing-compassionfocused-therapy/ECBC8B7B87E90ABB58C4530CDEE04088

Gilbert, P. (2010). *Compassion Focused Therapy*. Routledge.Gilbert, P. (2020). *Compassion: From its evolution to a psychotherapy. Frontiers in Psychology*, **11**. https://www.frontiersin.org/articles/10.3389/fpsyg.2020.586161/full

Gilbert, P., & Simos, G. (Eds.) (2022). *Compassion Focused Therapy: Clinical Practice and Applications*. Routledge.

Gilbert, P., Basran, J., MacArthur, M., & Kirby, J. N. (2019). *Differences in the semantics of prosocial words: An exploration of compassion and kindness. Mindfulness*, **10**(11), 2259–2271. https://link.springer.com/article/10.1007/s12671-019-01191-x

Hookmani, A. A., Lalani, N., Sultan, N., Zubairi, A., Hussain, A., Hasan, B. S., & Rasheed, M. A. (2021). *Development of an on-job mentorship programme to improve nursing experience for enhanced patient experience of compassionate care. BMC Nursing*, **20**(1), 175. https://bmcnurs.biomedcentral.com/articles/10.1186/s12912-021-00682-4

Hu, Z., Li, J., & Kwan, H. K. (2021). *The effects of negative mentoring experiences on mentor creativity: The roles of mentor ego depletion and traditionality. Human Resource Management*. https://onlinelibrary.wiley.com/doi/10.1002/hrm.22076

Jinpa, T. (2016). *A Fearless Heart: How the Courage to Be Compassionate Can Transform Our Lives*. Avery Publishing Group.

Johnson, W. B. (2003). *A framework for conceptualizing competence to mentor. Ethics & Behavior*, **13**(2), 127–151. https://www.tandfonline.com/doi/abs/10.1207/S15327019EB1302_02

Johnson, W. B. (2016). *On Being a Mentor: A Guide for Higher Education Faculty* (**2nd ed.**). Routledge.

Moberg, D. J., & Velasquez, M. (2004). *The ethics of mentoring. Business Ethics Quarterly*, **14**(1), 95–122. https://www.cambridge.org/core/journals/business-ethics-quarterly/article/abs/ethics-of-mentoring/544EF8C0726F4C5F5108D386D03E59F2

Nhat Hanh, T. (2011). *The Art of Mindful Living*. Plumvillage.org. https://plumvillage.org/mindfulness-practice/

Siegel, D. J. (2014). *Brainstorm: The Power and Purpose of the Teenage Brain*. TarcherPerigee.

Solomon, C., & Barden, S. M. (2016). *Self-compassion: A mentorship framework for counselor educator mothers. Counselor Education and Supervision*, **55**(2), 137–149. https://onlinelibrary.wiley.com/doi/10.1002/ceas.12038

Straus, S. E., Johnson, M. O., Marquez, C., & Feldman, M. D. (2013). *Characteristics of successful and failed mentoring relationships. Academic Medicine*, **88**(1), 82–89. https://journals.lww.com/academicmedicine/fulltext/2013/01000/characteristics_of_successful_and_failed_mentoring.27.aspx

Trube, B. (2017). *Mindfulness practices in mentoring and teaching. Childhood Education*, **93**(2), 159–167. https://www.tandfonline.com/doi/full/10.1080/00094056.2017.1300495

Weber, J. (2017). *Mindfulness is not enough: Why equanimity holds the key to compassion. Mindfulness & Compassion*, **2**(2), 149–158. https://www.sciencedirect.com/science/article/abs/pii/S2445407917300277?via%3Dihub

Section 3:
Practical Applications – Development and Diversity of Mentoring Services

Chapter 25
Beyond the Buzz: Getting Strategic with Mentoring

Ann Rolfe

> *Tactics without strategy is the noise before defeat.*
>
> (Sun Tzu)

The client looked at me aghast.

She had just looked at the fifteen questions (Figure 25.1) that I routinely provided to organizations wanting to plan a mentoring programme.

'I'm not sure we can answer even the first three!' she said.

I reassured her that it was not unusual, it's precisely why I developed the questions, to help planning groups develop their programme.

1. What is mentoring?
2. What is your aim
3. What's the return on investment?
4. Who will mentor and be mentored?
5. What are their roles and responsibilities?
6. How will you recruit participants?
7. How will you match pairs?
8. How often will they meet?
9. How will you develop their mentoring skills
10. What activities will you have in the program?
11. How will you support and sustain mentoring?
12. Who will manage the program?
13. How will you get the mentoring message across?
14. How will you measure results?
15. How long will it take to prepare and implement your program

Figure 25.1: Plan your programme: Fifteen questions you need answered.

Yet, as helpful as these questions are, all but one is merely tactical, and as Sun Tzu, master strategist, observed so long ago, tactics are not enough to succeed.

To get strategic we first need to ask a bigger question: Why do you want a mentoring programme? In exploring the question of why, it turns out mentoring itself is usually a tactic not a strategy. We must change this.

What is the difference between strategy and tactics?

Strategy and tactics are part of a hierarchy of purpose and plans that enable an organization to operate (Figure 25.2). At the very top level is the vision of the organization. Informed by its values, organizational vision describes its aspirational goals and guiding principles. Next, the mission defines the organization's purpose. Together vision and mission express the reasons the organization exists and what it hopes to achieve. To do so, it will need strategies in key areas from the products or services it delivers, the markets it targets, operational support, finances and its people. Each key area has its own strategic goals, objectives, plans and measures, but none operates in isolation, and this is what is easily overlooked when it comes to mentoring. Every area depends on the others. Strategies must complement and support one another. Tactics are the detailed action plans that are implemented to fulfil the strategic plan.

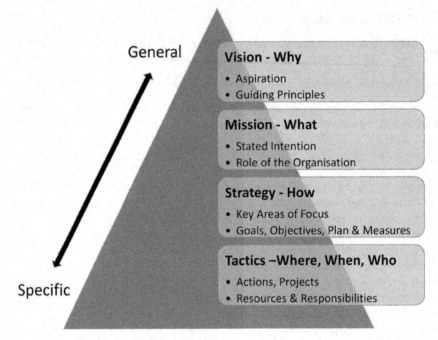

Figure 25.2: A pyramid of strategy.

Sometimes, the area responsible for human resources operates in a silo, and its managers are not part of the overall organizational strategic planning process. A strategy is handed down to them by the top team, placing mentoring on the agenda without the web of support from other linked strategies. Frequently, the budget allocated for mentoring does not reflect either the importance or the scope of what is involved. Often there are unrealistic expectations about what can be achieved by mentoring because the top team have succumbed to the buzz.

The buzz

The buzz began more than thirty years ago in conferences, journals and eventually management programmes. Mentoring became the in-thing, the latest fashion, a must-have asset for everyone. A magic bullet, a panacea for any ailment, mentoring was seen as a low-cost answer to many problems and was seized upon with enthusiasm. Many mentoring programmes reported good results, but few organizations invested in rigorous evaluation and objective before-and-after measures of strategic outcomes.

There is still an abundance of buzz about mentoring. Fortunately, now there is less hype and more research and practical expertise. Often quoted statistics on mentoring suggest: 84% of Fortune 500 companies, and 100% of Fortune 50 companies have mentoring programmes (MentorcliQ, n.d.). Coaching and mentoring ranks fourth on the list of learning and development strategies (Taylor, 2022) and the COVID-19 pandemic led to 30% more mentoring in organizations (LHH & HR Research Institute, 2021). Companies with mentoring programs were 18% more profitable than the average during the pandemic (Cantalupo, 2022) and 50% of professionals surveyed agreed that mentoring was critical (LHH & HR Research Institute, 2021). However, only one of these statistics is an objective measure of organizational performance.

Mentoring is more popular than ever, but popularity does not mean it is effective. It is not enough to have a mentoring programme because everyone else does. It is not enough that there is a warm fuzzy glow in saying to recruits, 'you'll have a mentor', and it is not enough to introduce a mentee to a mentor and leave them to it. For mentoring to be effective we must get beyond the buzz and become strategic.

What does it take for mentoring to be strategic? At the very least, it requires:

- clearly articulated aims and objectives directly linked to the strategic strengths and weaknesses in the organization;
- analysis of the factors that impact on organizational strengths and weaknesses so that other initiatives can be implemented that will support and complement mentoring to achieve specified objectives; and
- a solid, documented business case showing the resources necessary for the initiative, the projected return on investment and how achievement of objectives will be measured.

Why do we want mentoring?

The way to answer the question: Why do we want mentoring? is to start with the strategic plan of the organization and dig into the SWOT analysis (Strengths, Weaknesses, Opportunities and Threats) that drove the plan. Find issues that mentoring could change.

There has got to be a sound reason for the organization to invest in mentoring. We must be clear about the difference we want mentoring to make, not simply to the individuals involved, but to the organization. We need to understand how mentoring will contribute to growth, stability and, yes, profitability for the organization. How will mentoring assist the organization to fulfil its own strategic goals? Unless we know why we want it and what we hope it will do for the organization, mentoring is like a ship without a destination, a rudder or a navigator. We don't know where we are going, we just drift with the tide.

Without linking the mentoring to the organization's strategic goals, it is unlikely we'll be able to make a business case and get the budget required to make it work. It will also be challenging to get the support necessary from decision-makers and those concerned with bottom-line affecting costs unless the strategic value of mentoring is clear. Managers will be difficult to convince to accommodate people who need time off-the-job to mentor or be mentored, unless there are compelling reasons communicated at every level of the organization. Mentoring must be part of some larger goal; strategic reasons such as those shown in Figure 25.3, are imperative.

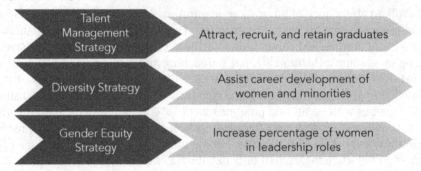

Figure 25.3: Examples of strategic reasons for mentoring.

Frequently, mentoring is associated with increased success in recruitment, retention and engagement. Often, it is aimed at increasing women or minorities in leadership. Sometimes, it strives to increase diversity and equity. Whatever is hoped for from mentoring, it should be stated in the aims and objectives of the programme, supported by other actions and have quantifiable measures of outcomes.

Mentoring (alone) is not the answer!

All too often mentoring is seen as a simple answer to a complex problem. For example, mentoring had long been hailed as an answer to the glacial progress of women and minorities to senior levels in organizations. However, providing psychosocial support to mentees may have welcome benefits – helping them develop confidence and skills – but it does not address the multiple causes of the problem. Structural issues such as stereotypes, unconscious bias, harassment, unfriendly policies, recruitment and promotion practices have far more impact on women's advancement. On top of this, this type of mentoring programme implies that the deficit lies with individuals themselves for their lack of progress.

We can build career development, training and education into our mentoring, we may even include sponsorship (proactive, powerful people who advocate for their protégé) in the mentor's role, but if we want strategic value from mentoring, we must identify the other factors that impact on the situation that we hope to change. The factors that mentoring will *not* change. The list in Figure 25.4 is drawn from a mentoring needs analysis conducted in a government agency, using Kurt Lewin's force-field analysis with potential participants in a programme to increase women in leadership roles.[13]

13   Developed by Kurt Lewin, force-field analysis, facilitates people brainstorming to identify driving forces – factors that support, encourage or propel people toward the desired situation and restraining forces, and factors, pressures and issues that restrict progress or prevent the desired situation. Once identified, you can work to reduce restraining forces and boost driving forces.

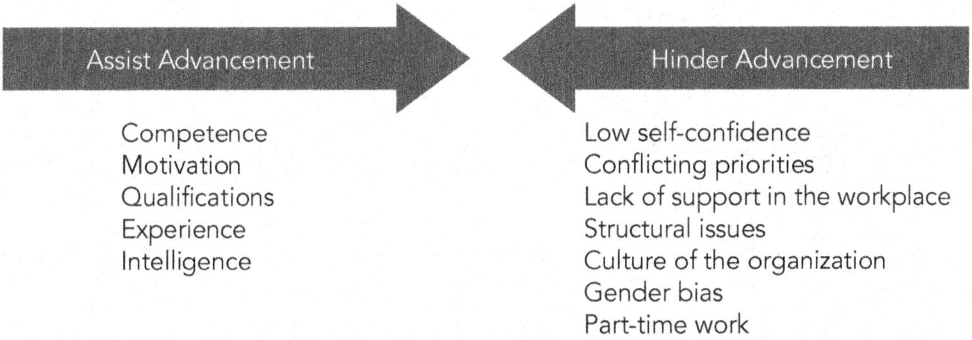

Figure 25.4: The top factors impacting on women's advancement identified in a mentoring needs analysis.

Can mentoring shift self-confidence? Yes, it can! Can it help people sort out their priorities? Yes! Can it help build a network of support? Yes! If you stipulate and make explicit that these are the objectives of mentoring, they are realistic outcomes. But will mentoring change the culture? Not anytime soon. Will it change the structure, or gender bias? Again, not in the short term, and not if mentoring is the only tactic used.

Another example is recruitment. Your mentoring might aim to increase success in hiring talent in a competitive market. Offering mentors might influence a candidate, but you would need to offer worthwhile pay, conditions and development as well. You would have to look at whether recruitment practices were attracting the right applicants, processes were efficient and timely, and what other organizations did better. Another factor is the status of your industry and the reputation of the organization. Unless mentoring is complemented by other strategies in these areas it won't succeed.

If engagement is an organizational goal, mentoring employees may help, but research (Beck & Harter, 2015) tells us the biggest single factor is the relationship with the immediate supervisor. Investment in developing managers' skills (to help them become less boss more coach) may give a better result than mentoring team members (Harter, 2020). You will also need to look at holding managers accountable, organizational culture, communicating mission or purpose, clear expectations and feedback.

Since early 2020, many workers have experienced trauma and stress due to the COVID-19 pandemic. Building coping skills, overcoming isolation, transitioning to working from home/returning to the office and managing dispersed teams could be areas that organizations want to address through mentoring. This would require a well-researched approach and sensitive implementation. We would need to be careful not to assume mentoring will help. I believe it would, but we're dealing with mental health issues, and I would want mental health professionals involved, and data not opinion, as the basis for any mentoring intervention.

Becoming realistic about what mentoring can and cannot change allows you to design a mentoring programme as part of a larger strategy collaboration, embedded in the areas of focus identified as key to achieving the organizational mission.

If we advocate for mentoring, we must find allies who will implement other actions to dismantle barriers and remove obstacles to achieving goals. This will only happen if mentoring has strategic aims to meet organizational needs and add demonstrable value.

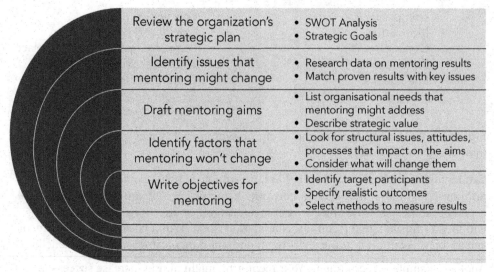

Review the organization's strategic plan	• SWOT Analysis • Strategic Goals
Identify issues that mentoring might change	• Research data on mentoring results • Match proven results with key issues
Draft mentoring aims	• List organisational needs that mentoring might address • Describe strategic value
Identify factors that mentoring won't change	• Look for structural issues, attitudes, processes that impact on the aims • Consider what will change them
Write objectives for mentoring	• Identify target participants • Specify realistic outcomes • Select methods to measure results

Figure 25.5: How to get strategic with mentoring.

Identify target participants

When you have completed the groundwork of reviewing the organization's strategic plan, and identifying the issues mentoring might change and those it won't, you can begin to write objectives for the mentoring programme. These will identify your target participants, specify realistic outcomes and the methods by which you will measure results.

Again, the need for analysis of relevant information will shape your selection of the right participants to target as mentors and mentees.

For example, if the aim is to retain the graduates the organization invested so much in recruiting, you will want information about attrition rates and timing. It can take three years to recoup the cost of hiring, so look at when graduates are lost. One organization that analysed attrition, found they lost a large portion of candidates before they even commenced work! Graduates were recruited in the final year of their studies. So, they began a carefully managed pre-employment onboarding. They provided welcome events, communication and networking, and introduced mentors in the months prior to the graduates taking up employment. This successfully reduced the dropout rate. However, there would be other critical points on the three-year timeline. At one year, two years and three years, an increasingly large investment in the graduate's development has taken place. The employee's experience now makes them a more attractive candidate for other employers and loss is even more expensive. So, a focus on these anniversaries was required.

Graduates need more than one type of mentor or a choice of different mentors at different stages. For example, a senior executive mentor, pre-employment, would encourage them to join and help them see the bigger picture of a future with the organization. A buddy-mentor, perhaps a graduate who had just completed one or two years with the organization, when they start could 'show them the ropes' and handle the simple questions a newbie needs answered but may be afraid to ask their manager. At the same time, a mid-level manager might mentor for career development and their immediate supervisor would mentor and coach the graduate in their learning and development.

Similarly, mentoring aimed at increasing diversity might target new, entry-level employees offering psychosocial support; those that had been employed a year or two for career development; others at higher levels in the organization for transition to leadership roles; or mid-level managers for senior management development. It is a question of making an informed decision on where mentoring can make the most difference. An informed decision is one based on data. A strategic approach means gathering data about the problem you are trying to solve, not guessing.

Once potential mentees have been identified, you can look at the right mentors to match them with. Consider the level of the mentor compared to the mentee – too great or too little disparity can be a problem; gender – a woman may prefer a woman mentor, but there are fewer available at a more senior level, and she needs male as well as female perspective; someone with a disability may benefit from another mentoring them, as well as non-disabled mentors, likewise nationality or culture, but it is very easy to make culturally inappropriate mistakes so you need to consult participants rather than assume.

Specify outcomes

Mentoring can build on an organization's strengths, and address its weaknesses, if we define what they are and write aims and objectives to reflect exactly what we want to achieve. Aims can be broad and general statements of why we want mentoring, but objectives must nail down the who, what, where and how.

For example, if, as part of a gender-equity strategy, an organization in a male-dominated industry aimed to increase its percentage of women in leadership. A needs analysis might identify the strategic value (benefits) of avoiding predicted skills shortages, becoming an employer of choice, and lowered future recruitment costs due to greater talent retention and internal promotions instead of external hires to fill senior roles.

The organization could plan a suite of projects, including (but not limited to):

- recruitment processes aimed at drawing more high-potential female applicants;
- selection practices that eliminate any bias;
- top-down communications about inclusive culture;
- training on merit-based and inclusive management;
- family-friendly work policies; and
- a mentoring programme or programmes.

The collective, stated aim of these projects might be:

'Within five years, create a pipeline of female leaders,
by attracting, retaining, developing, and supporting
high-potential women.'

This is an aim that is clear, specific and can be measured. You can identify quantifiable before and after measures such as the current ratio of female/male employees at various levels of the organization, the percentage of female candidates that apply now and the current retention rate overall, and for female employees. You can track women's progress prior to the programme, during and after, noting promotions and performance. You can compare the number of people in the leadership talent pool now and each year.

Objectives might include:

- increase ratio of female to male grade three–four employees from X to Y within three years;
- increase retention of female employees from X to Y within three years; and
- increase the percentage of women in the leadership talent pool from X to Y within three years.

Participant objectives

Participants – both mentees and mentors – should be volunteers in a mentoring programme. That means they will have their own reasons and motivation for participating. It is very helpful to explore these with individuals at the beginning of mentoring. Doing so can add valuable insights to programme designers and offers other elements for evaluation.

From an individual perspective, mentees often seek mentoring with vague, rather than clear goals. Individuals can benefit from getting strategic, too. Mentors can be trained to lead mentoring conversations that resemble a simplified strategic planning process (Figure 25.6). This model, that I've used successfully over the years, gives mentors a structured approach to their conversations, which can help them feel comfortable and focused. Leading the conversation this way empowers the mentee, helps them develop clear goals and ensures they take responsibility for planning and action.

Figure 25.6: Framework for a mentoring conversation (Rolfe, 2022).

Measure results

You need to design the evaluation process from the beginning, as part of the programme design. You will want to evaluate the programme itself, the mentoring relationships and the results.

Evaluation involves collection of data and the use of that data to answer questions and make judgements about the programme. Therefore, planning evaluation begins with the identification of the questions that need to be answered, and the criteria against which judgements will be made.

During the programme design phase, you need to identify:

- Attributes of success – in the context of your mentoring programme, what does a successful outcome look like?
- Information needed – what performance measures will you require?
- Data sources – what information can you collect?
- Outcomes – how will you measure success?
- Extraneous factors – what else may have influenced the outcomes?
- How and to whom will you report?

Figure 25.7: What to evaluate.

Taking a strategic perspective, we will focus here on the stated aim of the mentoring programme and outcomes.

Basically, you have two avenues to assess outcomes:

1. Qualitative – ask the participants their opinions.
2. Quantitative – numerical and statistical data.

Figure 25.8 shows quantifiable and qualitative outcomes that you could measure pre-programme and annually thereafter.

Sources from which the data can be elicited include the participants who may be surveyed or interviewed and data that you accessed prior to the programme and record during and after it. The former is qualitative data, though you can produce numerical output through rating scales.

Methods for collecting qualitative data include:

- informal contact by the programme coordinator;
- participant survey questionnaires;
- group review processes;
- individual interviews; and
- participant narratives or extracts from journals volunteered.

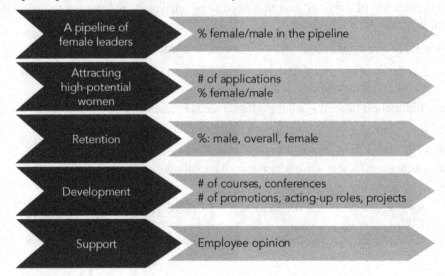

Figure 25.8: Measurable outcomes.

The simplest way to evaluate a mentoring programme is to ask participants what they thought. Open-ended questions also yield valuable qualitative data. For example:

Ask mentors and mentees:

- What do you believe the programme has achieved for the organization?
- What do you believe the programme has provided for individuals?

Ask mentees:

- Did you achieve what you hoped for?
- Were there other outcomes for you?

Ask mentors:

- What were the outcomes, benefits and challenges?

While opinions provide qualitative data, some responses can be quantified, as shown in Table 25.1.

	1	2	3	4
To what extent do you agree that this programme is contributing to…	Strongly disagree	Disagree	Agree	Strongly agree

Table 25.1: Sample question in qualitative survey.

Unfortunately, too few organizations go beyond the buzz of qualitative feedback. Perhaps that's because objective, quantitative evaluation takes time, money and expertise, though some aspects can be measured numerically quite easily and quickly. For example:

- How many participants started/completed the programme?
- Number of mentoring relationships maintained for the life of the programme.
- Number of women participating in training programmes and development opportunities.
- Percentage of female new starters retained after 1, 2, 3, 4, and 5 years.
- Number of target group applying for higher positions.
- Benchmark comparisons with other organizations.

Keep in mind that outside factors may influence outcomes. Mentoring programmes do not take place in a vacuum. Organizations have dynamic environments and outside circumstances may influence outcomes. A balanced evaluation takes these factors into account. For example, an organizational restructure may affect the number of applications received. A highly competitive employment market may inhibit recruitment. Only a small pool may be available from which to draw mentors, and this has implications for the ability to make appropriate matches and whether relationships last.

Sorting out what bottom-line organizational results can be attributed to mentoring is difficult. A statement quoted earlier, *'companies with mentoring programmes were 18% more profitable than the average during the pandemic'* creates a great buzz, but was there a causal relationship? Chances are the fact that they had mentoring programmes was indicative of the culture, diversity and management style of the organization. Teasing out the many variables is a job for statisticians. Going beyond the buzz means being realistic about what mentoring can and cannot achieve and finding rigorous ways to measure that.

Are we heading in the right direction?

People responsible for planning mentoring programmes are getting better at articulating the benefits they hope for from mentoring, and most organizations now demand a business case for any new initiative. These are steps in the right direction. Adding the layers of needs analysis, realistic objectives and proper evaluation described above will continue the path of moving beyond the buzz and getting strategic with mentoring.

References

Beck, R., & Harter, J. (2015, April 21). *Managers account for 70% of variance in employee engagement. Gallup Business Journal.* https://news.gallup.com/businessjournal/182792/managers-account-variance-employee-engagement.aspx

Cantalupo, G. (2022, May 19) *Does mentoring still matter for Fortune 500 companies? Forbes Communication Council.*https://www.forbes.com/sites/forbescommunicationscouncil/2022/05/19/does-mentoring-still-matter-for-fortune-500-companies/?sh = 602bb5335d8c

Harter, J. (2020, February 4) *4 factors driving record-high employee engagement in US. Gallup Workplace.* https://www.gallup.com/workplace/284180/factors-driving-record-high-employee-engagement.aspx

LHH & HR Research Institute (2021, August 20). *The State of Coaching & Mentoring in 2021.* https://www.lhh.com/us/en/insights/the-state-of-coaching-and-mentoring-in-2021/

MentorcliQ *(n.d.). 40+ Definitive Mentoring Stats for 2022.* https://www.mentorcliq.com/blog/mentoring-stats

Rolfe, A. (2022). *Advanced Mentoring Skills: Taking Your Conversations to the Next Level.* Mentoring Works.

Smith, F. (2016, July 5). *Anonymous recruitment aims to stamp out bias, but can it prevent discrimination? The Guardian* https://www.theguardian.com/sustainable-business/2016/jul/05/blind-recruitment-aims-to-stamp-out-bias-but-can-it-prevent-discrimination

Taylor, D. H. (2022, February 8). *L&D Global Sentiment Survey 2022: The Long Shadow of COVID-19.* DHT. https://donaldhtaylor.co.uk/insight/gss2022-results-01-general/

Chapter 26
Mentoring When It Doesn't Officially Exist!: Members of Parliament Staff Wellness Working Group

Steph McTighe, Estelle Warhurst & Tom Fairweather

Introduction

This chapter will explore how any individual can make a positive difference to those with whom they work, if they so choose. *'Life is a matter of choices and every choice you make makes you.'*[14]

Mentoring provides tremendous opportunities and benefits to each of the parties involved in the working relationship: the mentor, the mentee and the employer. Therefore, it should be attractive in any employment scenario. Yet, in some instances, it is not available. The MPs' Staff Wellness Working Group (WWG) for the UK Houses of Parliament explore mentoring relationships in the absence of formal structures. We detail the mentoring journey that led to the WWG's formation and our own use of the informal relationships and arrangements they have employed for the betterment of Parliament. We will guide anyone who leads a team, of whatever size, toward exploring what opportunities they can offer. As the WWG will testify, anyone who wishes to be a mentor can be, regardless of a lack of formal frameworks or structures in the workplace. All that is required is the right type of attitude.

About the Working Wellness Group (WWG)

The WWG is a cross-party group of staff working for Members of Parliament across the UK, in both constituency and Westminster offices. The Executive Committee of the group, comprising three individual office managers, has more than thirty-two years of combined parliamentary experience with senior MPs.

We aim to secure greater focus on the health and welfare of MPs' staff, recognizing the uniqueness of our roles and the stresses we experience. We work with MPs' staff and officials of the House of Commons to put in place support mechanisms, training

---

14   Quote by John C. Maxwell, author on leadership including the books, *Failing Forward* and *How Successful People Think*.

provision, best practice and support for staff. Since our inception, we have provided informal mentoring to our colleagues, particularly in the areas of self-care, well-being and good mental health practices.

Importantly, the WWG was borne out of the efforts of a handful of individuals who, in finding one another, found they had something more fundamental in common: the way they led their teams. As three individual office managers (all for MPs of different political persuasions) we found mentoring in common, without naming it as such. Prior to becoming office managers, we had experienced leaders that had not brought out the best in us. In our individual offices, we used our own negative experiences to run things differently and aimed for better.

Through a passion to extend our approach more widely by combining forces as like-minded individuals and improving the working environment beyond our own small offices, the WWG was forged.

The absence of formal mentoring in Parliament

You would be forgiven for thinking that a workplace with the prestige and grandeur of Parliament would include world-leading employment processes and procedures since it invokes images of grand buildings and suited staff going about the business of keeping the country running.

Surprisingly, this couldn't be further from the truth. In fact, working environments for MPs' staff have long been devoid of many of the common HR functions we come to expect in workplaces, let alone any of the more progressive and 'advanced' schemes, like the facilitation of mentoring relationships.

There are several reasons for this employment oddity but in short, achieving progress and improvement in some aspects of Parliament is hamstrung by the reliance (sometimes over-reliance) on procedure. In a building famed for its continued use of archaic rules and traditions, it is immensely difficult to secure change to things which have evolved over decades upon decades. From an employment perspective, Parliament is an umbrella term encompassing the 650 elected Members of Parliament and at the time of writing, circa 780 peers in the House of Lords, as well as the many staff and clerks who ensure the operation of Parliament as our legislature.

The offices of Members of Parliament are individual, private entities which operate independently of one another, and of the Houses of Parliament. Rather than MPs' staff being regarded as one 'employment ecosystem', think instead of 650 individual small businesses, each entirely separate from one another aside from some back-end administration of payroll. These offices, or silos, come and go as MPs do. There is little corporate memory beside that which is held internally by the Houses of Parliament, and so change often lags behind other sectors.

Each of these individual offices, responsible for supporting every function of an MP's role, is relatively small, usually around four to five staff in size, with staff usually divided between parliamentary work (for example, speech writing and research) and constituency work, known as 'casework' (discussed in the Case Study). These teams also suffer from significant workloads, and it would be easy to say that there is no capacity to take on proactive relationships such as mentoring within such a small unit.

While the House of Commons provides training on various issues it does not offer any formal routes for MPs' staff to access mentors, or to develop their own mentoring skills. In some instances, offices may be working on opposite sides of a partisan coin, so trust can be hard to come by outside of one's own individual silo – and, as we have learned first-hand, trust in the mentoring relationship is key.

However, in spite of all of these barriers, the WWG have managed to mentor colleagues working for Members of Parliament. So, what has been done? How has it been done? And crucially, has it worked?

Case Study 1

This day in the life is typical of caseworkers in MP's offices throughout the UK.

I filter the MP's inbox of more than a hundred emails. I start to work my way through them: an invitation to an event in Westminster for a charity, a campaign email about protecting our oceans, an office bill to pay, all interspersed with pleas for help from desperate constituents.

One email was sent at 2.03 a.m. It is a constant stream of horrendous circumstances and events. It is clear the person is desperate. I think about what avenues of help we might be able to provide.

I am interrupted by a call from a constituent who calls almost every day. He is banned from contacting all other services. I continually try to bring the call to a close, but I hear him as he doesn't have anyone else to talk to.

Now I go through my own inbox. By mid-morning, the MP is starting their first meeting in Westminster. The requests and additional tasks start coming in: changes to the diary, briefs to be found or written, meetings to be arranged, speeches from the Chamber to be 'clipped', subtitled and shared on social media platforms.

I start to tackle a constituent's case, reading through the documents including a GP's letter, a hospital report, court documents and supporting letters from other professionals involved. The phone rings when I am halfway through reading the first letter! An existing constituent looking for an update on their case, but the first contact was two days ago. I have not been able to action her case yet and she repeats her story and begins to cry. I listen, empathize and acknowledge how hard this must be for her and assure her that while I can't promise to fix it, I will do all I can to help. Instantly the phone rings again. I try to gather my strength to bear the emotional burden but this time it's about whether the MP can attend a drop-in event. I not only feel relief but also frustration of how unimportant such a call is compared to what I have just heard.

Back to the case I had started reading. It involves serious mental health problems. There is no pre-warning to the abuse suffered by this person. It is hard to read. I have learnt from working here what it means to have a lump in your throat as you try to hold back the tears.

The phone rings again. This time it is an indignant pensioner furious that the council is not cutting the grass often. It's hard to readjust, but I remind myself that they don't know the other issues I'm dealing with and no one calls their MP lightly.

It's in the context of this small constituency office, overwhelmed by constituents' problems, that the office managers decided to mentor caseworkers, without naming it as such. Worried about staff suffering emotionally, burning out, or going off sick with stress or worse, they knew of the high staff turnover rates and they knew how emotionally draining the job felt having done it themselves for some time. More importantly, they knew how it felt to experience those feelings in isolation. One had had a previous career and had resigned following serious burnout. Others had experienced bullying managers who had undermined them to the extent they believed that they had to resign. They felt strongly that if they had had a mentor, not just to help them be the best at the job but to manage its pace and stresses, if they had had someone they could have been vulnerable in front of, they may not have left a career they loved or believed they had no future. It was feeling let down by others that provoked these managers into being passionate about mentoring.

Out of concern for the well-being of others, these office managers decided to take a different approach. One called everyone into the meeting room for a conversation on the nature of the job, wanting all-round clarity on the obstacles ahead, the inevitable emotional triggers and weight that would come with the endless correspondence and cries for help. They wanted the team to know that it was okay not to be okay and that this would be a support network. They decided to share openly, for the first time and somewhat to their own surprise, the experience of their own burnout, their subsequent depression, their failure to pace themselves, and their failure in leaving a career they loved and had worked so passionately for. They concluded that they wanted to avoid a deterioration in the mental health and well-being of this team by creating a different culture. Furthermore, if colleagues wished to progress, they would be assisted in any way, shape or form and anyone interested in a particular topic was encouraged to find out how it could fit with the day-to-day work and run it as a project, with support. Another decided to be open about the mistake they had made and share up front that it was not 'fatal', and that if a mistake was made, it was safe to come and discuss it. Another put in place daily catchups to discuss any frustrations, whether work-related or personal, enabling staff to bring their authentic selves to work.

In being openly vulnerable about their own journeys, a safe space was created and a connection was ignited between these small teams. It has been said that *'successful mentoring is based upon trust and confidentiality'* (Centre for Higher Education Practice, n.d.). While it may have felt like a leap in the dark to expose past failings, these office managers were comfortable that they never wanted anyone else to experience the feelings of isolation and lack of confidence that they had, simply from the lack of opportunity to have open conversations with those more senior and experienced. Not least because, to become successful, people have to make mistakes.[15]

They all wanted to be approachable and lead teams in the way that they would have appreciated being led, based on a strong value of honesty. Being vulnerable was the first step in creating an environment of psychological safety, although they may not have proclaimed to have had the wisdom at that time to label it as such. Instinctively however, they knew they had not felt safe to be themselves previously. As Maya Angelou said, *'I've learned that people will forget what you said, people will forget what you did, but people will never forget how you made them feel.'* This quote is applicable to the impact of the mentoring relationship and experience.

---

15   See Elizabeth Day's podcast *How to Fail* premised on the idea that 'learning how to fail is actually learning how to succeed better'.

Outcome of mentoring

So, what happened? The teams bonded more and more tightly. They got to know each other's ways of working and built up tremendous working relationships built on foundations of safety and trust. The staff were all trusted to manage their own time and workloads around their home/caring lives. They were actively encouraged to bring their whole selves to work and share ideas.

The result was three high-functioning and motivated teams that produced work over and above the day job, including wordy reports for all-party parliamentary groups or others like the Independent Parliamentary Standards Authority (IPSA). The staff took up different projects in their areas of choice, with one member interviewing and then writing a report on drug policy. Another created support signposting leaflets, using their previously acquired design talents, following a spate of local suicides. And others felt able to give back to the local communities by undertaking regular voluntary work to benefit others. Their mental health benefited because they felt empowered to help in ways that they could. Their productivity and creativity were harnessed and increased. The office managers bought in services, such as vicarious trauma training and formal supervision, in recognition that there was a need for professional input too. Staff were encouraged to share their learnings and areas of expertise with one another, which helped with cross-fertilization of skills.

There was an increased team spirit and, crucially, no presenteeism or absenteeism in two years (until a cancer diagnosis which tragically led to the death of one team member). It was said at her funeral, that, in her own words *'we are more than a team, we are a family'*. When one member of the team later moved on, she wrote this in her resignation letter: *'I am so grateful for the mentorship and friendship you have given me since joining the team. I have a lot to thank all of you for, as the experience, support, friendships and learning opportunities have just been so invaluable and will certainly be hard to come by anywhere else in life. This team will always have a special place in my heart.'* Another decided later that she wanted to return to university to study for a Master's degree and called the office manager to ask her thoughts on the proposed decision. It was the perfect fit for her, and she is flourishing in her new role, alongside her advanced studies. And yet another team has been together for seventeen years, proving the deep bond that is formed by supporting each other at work.

This is what mentoring and its impact can look like: increased productivity, personal development, self-growth, support, confidence, and bigger and better things for those who are nurtured. Mentoring in these cases meant people were treated as having something to offer, rather than disregarded for their lack of seniority. It was key that a two-way street had been created. Some of the mentoring undoubtedly instilled confidence to forge ahead in the workplace and branch out with conviction. Of course, they also had positive attitudes themselves. As one of the managers said, *'No-one has all the information or knowledge, we can all learn, develop and grow, no matter how old we are, how long we have been doing a particular job or whether others look to us for guidance. Mentoring means never resting on your laurels or believing that you are the only person that knows how to undertake a project.'*

As this shows, even in a small team, mentoring is possible. What all three of us had in common was that we were all taking a similar approach. However, while we were doing so, we did not know one another. It was only later that we met and formed the WWG from first-hand knowledge of how things could go well for teams and from wishing to spread the support to others.

The need for mentoring

In thinking about the need for mentoring – either for yourself or others, ask yourself these questions:

- What am I (not the organization) doing for me/staff in terms of well-being or career progression?
- When did we last communicate about progress?
- Where do I/they see themselves in two, five or ten years?

In considering these questions, you might have some wisdom or knowledge you could share that may benefit a colleague. You might be reminded of a time you made a mistake but didn't tell anyone because you felt ashamed. Imagine what this would do for others if you were to share this? Consider how open you are about what you share. Are you approachable? Would they say the same?

In addition, ask yourself these further questions:

- What do I think mentoring means?
- What do I need to do to start mentoring?

Atypical solutions to atypical problems: The formation of the WWG

In the context of mentoring, Winston Churchill said, 'We make a living by what we get, but we make a life by what we give.' So, does what we do work? Feedback from a survey of parliamentary staff suggests so, 'the success of staff initiatives is apparent – like the WWG' (Halliday, 2022). The WWG focuses on support for colleagues, good management and encourages other managers to create a culture of openness. The WWG's motto is collaboration because we are acutely aware of the bigger picture, for example, how several touchpoints in the working lives of staff can be impactful.[16] For that reason, the WWG has striven to break down silos across the House of Commons and work together with the many relevant departments that interact with staff in recognition that well-being cannot be achieved from only one source. The whole culture is relevant and important.

The WWG was created to fill a gap and within that space, informal mentoring can be found. There is an entire web of work woven into this but simplified, it looks like providing staff with solid training and resources to fully understand the job role as well as fostering a culture of honesty, equality, recognizing that everyone has value to

---

16   This includes relationships with, for example, IPSA, the House of Commons library, and the Learning and Organisational Development Team, to name a few.

add and creating a safe environment for people to feel able to be who they are. Being available to answer questions, support people and nurture them to find their own strengths is crucial too.

Informal mentoring obviously isn't the norm but it does not mean that there is no room for it. On the contrary, the scope for creativity and innovation from the lack of structures has been, arguably, one of the best things about it and what has made the WWG so successful. The evidence speaks for itself. The WWG has plugged a gap at the heart of Parliament in being a staff group and a voice run for the benefit of staff. It understands and can relate to those it serves. Human beings will always benefit from empathy, human interaction and connection, which at its heart is how the mentoring relationship could be described. The impact of the COVID-19 pandemic has compounded and proven this, creating a need for networks and open lines of communication.

> *'Mentoring is not only needed when you are under pressure but also for those "normal" times. It is vital having a trusted individual whom I can ask for help, sound ideas out on and look to in times of need. Having someone who may have experienced professional difficulties in a similar way to me can be incredibly reassuring.'*

(A junior member of staff in an MP's office)

Conclusion

Mentoring shouldn't be seen as a labour or negative sum game. It can be a key tenet of potential value and a pillar upon which the future growth of your organization can rest. Depending on how an organization is run, it can be very successful or not.

If mentoring is about allowing the best of people to shine through, then it must also be about how leaders behave. One author, when asked about what makes a great leader, said:

> *'Great leaders recognize, amplify and celebrate the inner brilliance of others ... they build teams with divergent ideas, backgrounds and viewpoints. They listen to them, value them, they show them and they empower them. Some of the best leaders ... possess a significant predilection for coaching, mentoring and diplomacy ... they are also compassionate, collaborative and humble.'*

(Liddle, 2021)

The message is this. While you may not be in overall charge of your organization, if you manage only one other person, think about what opportunities there are for you both to grow. Reverse mentoring means those more senior can also learn skills or knowledge from those more junior (Jordan & Sorell, 2019). As with any working relationship, both parties should be getting something. While ultimately the WWG recognizes it does not have overarching power over the running of Parliament, what we have proven is that, within our own networks and reach, we have created successful cogs in the larger wheel. If others replicate this approach, the ripple effect could eventually be positively impactful for the institution as a whole. It is arguable that it could even alter the organizational culture as it is about evolution, rather than revolution. In any event, for the individuals involved, it is undoubtedly going to be a positive experience.

References

Centre for Higher Education Practice (n.d.). *What is Mentoring?* University of Southampton. https://www.southampton.ac.uk/chep/mentoring/what-is-mentoring.page

Halliday, J. (2022, May 23) *Half of UK MP's staff have clinical levels of psychological distress, study finds. The Guardian.* https://www.theguardian.com/politics/2022/may/23/half-uk-mps-staff-clinical-levels-psychological-distress-study

Jordan, J., & Sorell, M. (2019, October 3). *Why reverse mentoring works and how to do it right. Harvard Business Review.* https://hbr.org/2019/10/why-reverse-mentoring-works-and-how-to-do-it-right

Liddle, D. (2021). *Transformational Culture: Develop a People-Centred Organisation for Improved Performance.* Kogan Page.

Chapter 27
NIHR: National Institute for Health and Care Research Mentoring Programme

Sarah Howarth, Julie Haddock-Millar & Chandana Sanyal

Introducing NIHR

The purpose of the National Institute for Health and Care Research (NIHR) is to develop a highly skilled academic research workforce capable of advancing the best research, which improves health and benefits for society and the economy in England and beyond. We have a central role in England's health and care research landscape. We work alongside other organizations that have an overarching aim to strengthen health research in the United Kingdom (UK). Each UK nation has its own government department that oversees health and care research:

- The Department of Health and Social Care funds health and care research in England through the NIHR. It also supports applied health research for the direct and primary benefit of people in low- and middle-income countries, using UK aid from the UK government.

- Health and Care Research Wales is a national, multifaceted, virtual organization funded and overseen by the Welsh Government's Research and Development Division. It provides an infrastructure to support and increase capacity in research and development (R&D), runs a range of responsive funding schemes and manages the National Health Service (NHS) R&D funding allocation for Wales.

- The Chief Scientist Office (CSO), part of the Scottish Government's Health and Social Care Directorate, supports and promotes high-quality research aimed at improving the quality and cost effectiveness of services offered by NHS Scotland and securing lasting improvements to the health of the people of Scotland.

- The Health and Social Care Public Health Agency (HSC PHA) is the major regional organization for health protection in Northern Ireland. The agency has a mandate to protect public health, improve public health and social well-being, and reduce inequalities in health and social well-being.

The NIHR Academy was established in October 2018 following a strategic review of training across the NIHR to review the past and look proactively at future training needs. It set out a vision underpinned by a series of recommendations which led to the reshaping of the training programmes offered. The NIHR Academy recognizes and rewards:

- collaborative, multiprofessional approaches to research;
- the embracing of innovation and new opportunities and technologies;
- active involvement and engagement of patients, carers and the public;
- respect for the diversity of methodological and theoretical practices; and
- personal and professional development and support of colleagues.

The NIHR Academy comprises of 'Members' and 'Associates'. Members include those on an NIHR academic path and those who play a recognized role supporting academic development. They form a key part of the national health research system that is the NIHR. NIHR Academy Members range from Masters Studentships through to Professorships and Senior Investigators. Membership includes individuals based in both domestic and global health research settings. Some also work closely with industry, developing a cadre of research leaders with combined academic, NHS and industry insight and experiences. Members are able to access a portfolio of NIHR Academy development and support activities. They are also able to access NIHR research training and career development programmes to help ensure that their research meets the current and future needs of patients and the public, as well as developing and sustaining training routes for research skills to support the development of future leaders across all professions and disciplines.

In addition to the awards themselves, the NIHR also provides a range of leadership and mentoring programmes to complement its training programmes, regular networking opportunities, bespoke workshops and events, and personal advice and guidance on funding opportunities. Associate Members are those who are part of the NIHR research training ecosystem. They are either on a research trajectory or plan, or have an NIHR role in supporting research training.

Research has shown that postdoctoral researchers may face structural and cultural challenges in relation to their career trajectory and insecurity about ongoing funding or employment (Akerlind, 2005). Clarity regarding career routes is an ongoing challenge for postdoctoral researchers (Van der Weijden et al., 2016). Research productivity pressures can be a barrier to accessing career development opportunities and pursuing career opportunities (Omary et al., 2019). However, a number of research studies demonstrate the positive contribution and influence mentoring can have on postdoctoral career progression (Ranieri et al., 2015; Ranieri et al., 2016). Mentors are able to facilitate opportunities for interdisciplinary research and offer new perspectives on research career development and future employment (Hafsteinsdóttir et al., 2017; Hafsteinsdóttir et al., 2020).

Introducing the NIHR mentoring programme

The NIHR provides postdoctoral Academy Members with career development support through its mentoring programme. The programme supports postdoctoral researchers from a broad range of professional and disciplinary contexts across our diverse health and social care communities to mentor others and to seek a mentor.

The programme has been developed and guided by a Steering Group whose membership is representative of Academy Members. The refreshed programme builds on the previous NIHR Academy Mentoring Programme that was delivered by the Academy of Medical Sciences. The previous programme was only available to postdoctoral Academy Members from a clinical background, meaning a large proportion of Academy Members were not eligible for the scheme. Following a review in 2020 of the NIHR Academy Mentoring Programme, it was decided to bring the management of the programme in-house and it was expanded to support all Academy Members, regardless of professional background. The refreshed programme was launched in February 2021.

Each year, NIHR provides an opportunity for seventy-five matched mentoring pairs, prioritizing those from backgrounds or disciplines that may not have previously had access to mentoring. The programme aims to support the academic and career development of NIHR postdoctoral communities by:

- extending the NIHR mentoring programme to postdoctoral award holders from disciplines and professional backgrounds which may not have a strong mentoring tradition, or may not have had access to programmes such as this in the past;
- promoting interdisciplinarity working; mentees are able to seek a mentor from a cognate or complementary discipline or professional background, where appropriate;
- supporting mentoring relationships between individuals from different organizations and institutions; and
- promoting equality, inclusion and diversity through engagement with, and learning from, under-represented groups.

The NIHR define mentoring as: '*a non-directive developmental relationship; mentors support mentees to learn and grow. The relationship is often two-way: the mentor also develops. Mentors often draw on shared knowledge, skills, competencies and behaviours; they call on the skills of questioning, listening, clarifying and reframing. Mentors tend to have the organizational and contextual experience relevant to the mentee's organizational and career-related system, and typically mentoring relationships tend to be longer-term than coaching.*'

Mentors and mentees are supported throughout their participation in the programme through regular professional development events and resources. The programme adopts a continuous improvement approach and participants are asked to provide feedback through the formal evaluation process, at six months and twelve months.

The programme takes a cohort-based approach and intake to the cohorts takes place three times per year in April, June and November, with expressions of interest to join the cohorts open for six weeks before the intake date. The programme averages twenty-five matched pairs per cohort. The first year of the programme proved so successful that the target number of matched pairs was increased from seventy-five to ninety and even taking into account the increase in matched pairs we still experienced a significant oversubscription of 50%.

Mentoring programme framework

NIHR adopted the European Mentoring and Coaching Council (EMCC) Global International Standards for Mentoring and Coaching Programmes (ISMCP) as an overarching framework for the design, implementation and evaluation of the programme. The ISMCP is an independent accreditation awarded to organizations designing, delivering and evaluating mentoring and/or coaching programmes either 'in-house' or externally. It is an integral and essential step on the path to establishing the professional credibility and status of good mentoring programme management, ensuring programmes are:

- thoughtfully designed;
- systematically managed; and
- significantly contributing to the development of participants, strategic drivers of the organization and wider stakeholder objectives.

The six Core Standards enable organizations to achieve a baseline standard of programme management that ensures quality and rigour:

1. Clarity of purpose
   - The strategic drivers and objectives of the programme are clearly defined.
   - The intended outcomes and benefits of the programme are understood by all the stakeholder audiences.
   - Participants are encouraged and supported in developing their own purpose for participating in the programme within the overarching context of the programme.
2. Stakeholder training and briefing
   - Stakeholders understand the concept of mentoring and/or coaching and their respective roles.
   - Participants are aware of the knowledge, skills and behaviours they need to apply in their roles as mentors and mentees and they have the opportunity to identify skills gaps.
   - Learning support is available throughout the participants' involvement in the programme.
   - Training and briefing take into account the context and purpose of the programme, balancing the need for core skills and knowledge against the need for flexibility in the manner and timing of delivery.

3. Process for selection and matching
   - Stakeholders understand the selection and matching methodology and criteria.
   - The matching process ensures the match fits the programme and provides sufficient learning opportunities for participants, as relevant to the programme.
   - Both mentors and mentees have an influence on whether they participate and their matched relationship.
   - There is a process for recognizing and unwinding matches that do not work and for rematching the participants, if they wish.

4. Processes for measurement and review
   - There are robust measurement and review processes to evaluate the mentoring relationships, the programme and the organizational/strategic outcomes.
   - The measurement and review processes enable timely adjustments to be made to the programme.
   - A meaningful cost–benefit and impact analysis is in place, appropriate to the organizational and sector context.
   - The measurement and review processes support the mentoring relationships through support mechanisms, including supervision.

5. Maintains high standard of ethics
   - Roles and responsibilities of all stakeholders are clearly defined and communicated to all key stakeholders.
   - The programme adheres to clear guidelines on the behaviour and responsibilities of all stakeholders.
   - There is a process for recognizing and managing conflicts of interest between stakeholders, for example, between mentors or mentees and the organization.

6. Administration and support
   - Participants receive sufficient support, continuing professional development and/or supervision throughout the programme.
   - Participants are supported beyond the programme where appropriate.
   - The programme is managed professionally and in accordance with the programme methodology and processes.
   - The programme methodology and processes are transparent and available to all key stakeholders.

Key design features of the mentoring programme

The mentoring programme uses expressions of interest for both mentees and mentors to apply to the programme. Expressions of interest open six weeks before the cohort launch dates and this information cascades to prospective applicants via the NIHR Infrastructure. All potential mentees and mentors are invited to submit an expression of interest within the application window. This application can be for the upcoming cohort or a later cohort depending on their preferences. Mentees are NIHR Academy Members who hold an NIHR postdoctoral award and/or hold a postdoctoral position and are based in NIHR Infrastructure or in an NIHR School.

Mentors are NIHR Academy Members or Associate Members who are NIHR research leaders. They may be an NIHR research professor or senior investigator, or an NIHR-based postdoctoral researcher with significant postdoctoral experiences (typically, at least five years). Alternatively, they may be an NIHR Academy Member or Associate Member contributing to the NIHR's work at a senior leadership level, for example, an awarding panel member, or a senior leader in NIHR including its centres, infrastructure and schools.

The matching process is broken down into three stages (Figure 27.1), at stage one the team review the matching criteria points that were selected in the expression of interest form. The matching criteria consist of eleven points that all applicants are asked to indicate which are most important to them:

1. balancing professional and academic work
2. career progression
3. career transition
4. research funding
5. developing a global/international research profile
6. networking/building relationships
7. work–life balance
8. diversity and inclusion
9. leadership development
10. research practice
11. managing research teams.

The team then move onto reviewing the free text responses for any additional preferences and supporting information; for example, if a mentee would like to be matched with a mentor in a specific field or with specific experiences. Finally, the team conduct a review at stage three of mentee and mentor preferences to ensure they match up and do not have any conflicts of interest before the match is confirmed.

Matching process and criteria		
Stage 1	Stage 2	Stage 3
Review the 11 matching criteria points for preferences	Review the free text boxes for any additional preferences and supporting information	Review of mentee and mentor preferences, conflicts of interest and specific requirements before confirming the match

Figure 27.1: Matching process and criteria.

Attendance at orientation training is compulsory for all mentees and mentors. It is delivered via an online interactive webinar, facilitated by the Programme Manager and external Mentoring Consultant. The orientation covers the following key topics:

■ the programme team and their roles;
■ an overview of the aim and objectives of the programme;

- the role of the mentor and mentee;
- ethics and confidentiality;
- the mentoring platform;
- the professional development offer;
- the programme evaluation approach, phases and methods; and
- Support documentation.

Following the mentoring programme orientation, mentees and mentors are invited to attend a broad range of continuing professional development (CPD) optional interactive workshops. The purpose of the CPD workshops is to provide ongoing support at key transition points in the mentoring relationship, focusing on knowledge, skills and behaviours. The overall objective of the CPD workshops is to enable participants to achieve satisfactory and successful mentoring relationships. The core CPD topics include:

- developing an effective mentoring relationship;
- beginning the mentoring relationship;
- the roles of the mentor and mentee;
- EMCC Global Mentoring core competencies;
- purpose, direction and goals;
- the phases of the mentoring relationship;
- maintaining momentum in the relationship; and
- reviewing and closing the mentoring relationship.

The programme team have developed additional workshops, based on interim feedback from mentees and mentors, to support specific topic areas such as work–life balance, resilience and transitioning from mentee to mentor. Furthermore, mentees and mentors are able to attend 'drop-in' sessions to meet the programme team on a monthly basis to address any aspect of their mentoring practice. In line with EMCC Global ISMCP requirements, mentors are also provided with ongoing monthly reflective practice support with peer-mentoring workshops, facilitated by a suitability qualified and experienced external mentoring consultant.

The mentoring programme has a robust evaluation framework in place which supports the continuous improvement of the programme, the collation of evidence of achievement against the programme's aim and objectives to share with stakeholders, and identification of lessons learned to inform the potential future programmes and wider audiences. The evaluation consists of two phases. Phase one takes place at four to five months and comprises a light-touch temperature check survey for all participants, providing a feedback opportunity and to address any issues which may arise. At the end of programme, participants are invited to complete an in-depth survey, focusing on their mentoring relationship experience and outcomes. Four matched pairs attend semi-structured interviews with an external mentoring consultant, providing the opportunity to create in-depth case study exemplars.

The mentoring programme and team are supported by the NIHR Academy Mentoring Programme Steering Group which includes representatives from a broad range of NIHR's research infrastructure and disciplines. The Steering Group is chaired by

Professor Anne-Maree Keenan, one of the NIHR Academy's Associate Deans. The role of the Steering Group is to support the development of the programme. They were instrumental in the development of the aims and objectives of the programme. All decisions about the programme are discussed at the Steering Group meetings and decisions are made through a consensus approach. They review and discuss any continuous improvements and evaluation activities, as well as providing insight from their respective professions and disciplines. The Steering Group meets on a regular basis; when the programme was in development the meetings were monthly, this changed to bimonthly meetings when the first cohort was launched, quarterly after the first year and twice yearly following the completion of the first year of the programme. This is due to the programme running 'business as usual' from this stage onwards.

Programme impact and participant experience

NIHR is committed to the ongoing formative and summative evaluation of the mentoring programme. This second evaluation focuses on the summative interview analysis of the first mentoring programme cohort. Cohort 1 interviews were conducted between 7 June and 8 July 2022. The interviews were conducted online over Zoom by an external mentoring consultant. The approved transcriber produced ninety-nine pages of transcription across five matched pair interviews, ranging between seven and fourteen pages per interview. The external mentoring consultant prepared initial matched pair case studies. Each case study summarized the transcript content, including mentor and mentee profile, relationship focus, reflections on the mentoring relationship and perceived value. A second external mentoring consultant prepared matched pair interview summaries and the internal evaluation report.

Drivers for joining the programme

The *mentees* viewed the NIHR mentoring programme as an opportunity to learn from a researcher within their field of practice, an opportunity to experience formal mentoring, consider career progression and transition, and improve work–life balance. The *mentors* viewed the NIHR mentoring programme as an opportunity to share experience and expertise, and support colleagues who are keen to progress their research careers in the field of health and social care.

Mentoring relationship focus

Through the programme evaluation mentees and mentors described the overall focus of their mentoring relationship as career planning and progression, building capacity for fellowship applications, research funding and outputs, networking and building relationships, navigating the academic environment including politics and self-presentation, managing work–life balance and leadership development.

Perceived value of the mentoring programme

The NIHR mentoring programme has had significant impact on the mentees at both personal and professional levels. Professional: as early career professionals, the mentoring conversation with experienced senior practitioners has helped mentees to explore career options and seek guidance on the next stage of their careers. Some mentees expressed that they felt hugely supported in their career transition and learnt ways of networking, applying for research grants, managing the work environment, and building collaborative relationships and leadership capacity. Personal: at a personal level, the mentoring increased their self-confidence, awareness of self-care and ability to manage work–life balance practices.

Mentees have described how the mentoring has supported them in both the career and psychosocial space:

- *'My mentoring experience has been fantastic. My mentor has helped me to recognize my worth and has gently encouraged me to stretch outside of my comfort zone.'*
- *'Having the opportunity to discuss my career with an experienced academic has been very valuable. I appreciated the time given and the support received so far. Having a mentor outside my institution has been very beneficial as it created a safe space for me to open up about various concerns.'*
- *'My mentor connected me with other Clinical Academics in my clinical community. They also shared their experience of other colleagues who have crafted a career similar to the one I am aiming for.'*
- *'A perspective from someone who is neither in my area nor my institution with whom I can discuss things that I can't talk about with my immediate work colleagues.'*

The NIHR mentoring programme has enabled mentors to build their emotional intelligence and develop their own self-insight around the holistic practice of mentoring, supporting their mentees' personal and professional development, including confidence building, leadership positioning and self-presentation, and successfully navigating a postdoctoral career. The formalization of the mentoring relationships and the accompanying training and CPD workshops were viewed as effective learning and reflective spaces by several mentors. As most of the mentor–mentee matches are across interdisciplinary health research areas, mentors also widened their knowledge and gained further insights into new areas of work.

For mentors the benefits have been broad, encompassing a sense of personal satisfaction, development of key mentoring skills and connectivity:

- *'Keeps me grounded within the wider clinical academic community.'*
- *'Supporting someone else in a more junior research career position.'*
- *'Exposure to diverse scenarios that collectively contribute to my mentoring approach.'*
- *'Helps me to improve my people skills and active listening.'*
- *'Feels positive that I can help someone struggling with issues.'*
- *'Interesting to see what barriers exist in career progression and how others view/ react to them.'*
- *'I think it has been useful to reflect on my own mentoring practice and experiences. The relationship provides a useful mirror as well!'*

The survey and matched pair interview evaluation data highlights that the mentoring programme and the mentoring relationships are having a significant impact on *both* mentee and mentor learning and growth, and addressing key topics.

Lessons learned for others and future intentions

With any mentoring programme, particularly in the early phases, there are numerous lessons learned. The learnings fall into three categories: 1) the application of a mentoring platform and its practical usage; 2) the design of action learning sets for mentors to support their reflective practice; and 3) the ability to attend CPD sessions in the current climate and work pressures. To address the issues raised by programme participants, the programme team reviewed the use of the mentoring platform and its application.

Key changes in relation to the content and delivery of the CPD provision include:

- the inclusion of in-person training events, in addition to the ongoing provision of online CPD sessions for mentees and mentors;
- the addition of topic-specific CPD sessions for work–life balance, resilience, reflective practice, ethics, diversity and inclusion, and transitioning from mentee to mentor;
- the creation of a peer-mentoring group for mentees to meet and network;
- the adaptation of action learning to peer mentoring for all participants; and
- the provision of a greater variation of formats and timings to support access to CPD for mentors and mentees.

The NIHR mentoring programme team will be looking to further develop and continually improve the programme in the financial year 2023–2024 to ensure that it supports the strategic goals of the organization.

References

Åkerlind, G. S. (2005). *Postdoctoral researchers: Roles, functions and career prospects. Higher Education Research & Development*, **24**(1), 21–40.

Hafsteinsdóttir, T. B., van der Zwaag, A. M., & Schuurmans, M. J. (2017). *Leadership mentoring in nursing research, career development and scholarly productivity: A systematic review. International Journal of Nursing Studies*, **75**, 21–34.

Hafsteinsdóttir, T. B., Schoonhoven, L., Hamers, J., & Schuurmans, M. J. (2020). *The leadership mentoring in nursing research program for postdoctoral nurses: A development paper. Journal of Nursing Scholarship*, **52**(4), 435–445.

Omary, M. B., Shah, Y. M., Schnell, S., Subramanian, S., Swanson, M. S., & O'Riordan, M. X. (2019). *Enhancing career development of postdoctoral trainees: Act locally and beyond. The Journal of Physiology*, **597**(9), 2317–2322.

Ranieri, V., Barratt, H., Fulop, N., & Rees, G. (2015). *Clinical academics' postdoctoral career development. BMJ*, **351**.

Ranieri, V., Barratt, H., Fulop, N., & Rees, G. (2016). *Factors that influence career progression among postdoctoral clinical academics: A scoping review of the literature. BMJ Open*, **6**(10), e013523.

van der Weijden, I., Teelken, C., de Boer, M., & Drost, M. (2016). *Career satisfaction of postdoctoral researchers in relation to their expectations for the future. Higher Education*, **72**(1), pp.25–40.

Chapter 28
Cherie Blair Foundation for Women: Mentoring Women in Business Programme

Efe Olokpa

Introduction

The Cherie Blair Foundation for Women works with women entrepreneurs in low- and middle-income countries to enable them to reach their potential. We are committed to eliminating the global gender gap in entrepreneurship and creating a future where women entrepreneurs thrive.

Training, mentoring and partnerships are at the heart of the Foundation's work, deploying technology innovatively to reach and connect with women entrepreneurs. Since our inception in 2008, we have supported more than 200,000 women to start, grow and sustain successful micro-, small- and medium-sized businesses in more than one hundred countries.

The Foundation's Mentoring Women in Business (MWIB) programme is a gold accredited,[17] global, cross-border mentoring programme open to women in low- or middle-income countries running a business at any stage – or about to launch one – in any industry. It matches women entrepreneur mentees with business professional mentors anywhere in the world. Over the last decade we have continued to hone, innovate and adapt our mentoring programme and it can be tailored to reach groups of women in specific sectors, geographies or value chains, and to earlier or later stages of business development.

Why mentoring?

The MWIB programme was born from a belief in the power of mentoring and the role technology can have in building connections and networks. We believe that mentoring plays an important role in supporting women entrepreneurs to overcome the challenges they face in business environments that are too often biased against women's full participation. For an individual, mentoring can be empowering and transform the success of a business. At a global scale, we believe that mentoring is a crucial part of closing the gender gap in entrepreneurship.

---

17   https://cherieblairfoundation.org/news-list/mentoring-accreditation/

The gender gap in entrepreneurship is part of the wider global inequality in women's economic empowerment and participation. The World Economic Forum estimates that it will take another 268 years to close the economic gender gap[18] and, shamefully, that this number is going in the wrong direction with the challenges exacerbated by the COVID-19 pandemic.

In entrepreneurship, the gender gap includes inequalities in investment, skills and business development opportunities, access to technology and the internet, and access to markets and networks. The gap is evident from what women say about their experiences as entrepreneurs and the tiny proportion of investment flowing to women-owned enterprises – globally this is 2–10% of commercial bank finance and just 2% of venture capital. In the Foundation's 2021 research into how gender stereotypes affect women entrepreneurs, 61% said that they negatively impact their business growth and 49% say they affect profitability[19]. Our impact data shows that mentoring can help to shift the dial on many of these factors for individual women entrepreneurs; notwithstanding that wider, systems-level change is needed to support all women entrepreneurs to have equal opportunities.

In over a decade since its launch in 2010, the MWIB programme has supported almost 6,000 women entrepreneurs as mentees from more than 100 countries and our impact data tells a compelling story. Women entrepreneurs who have successfully participated in the programme report increased knowledge, skills, confidence and networks. Of those who graduated from the mentoring programme in 2021, 98% reported increased business skills, 68% saw an improvement in their business performance, 72% reported improved confidence and 78% had increased their personal networks.

Mentors provide a diversity of insights, advice, wisdom and guidance. Freda, from Ghana, an entrepreneur and recent graduate of the mentoring programme said, *'I gained new leadership insights, expanded my network and I'm in the process of entering new markets all because of the mentoring programme. My mentor's support and her availability to listen allowed me to gain confidence in the decisions I made.'*

Mentors benefit as well. Of mentors who graduated in 2021, 90% reported that they had learned new skills during the programme that they would be able to use in their work environment, 89% gained knowledge of new cultures, 69% improved their listening skills and 60% learnt about doing business in a new sector or market.

The Foundation's approach to mentoring

Mentoring is a long-standing form of training, learning and development, and an increasingly popular tool for supporting personal development. It's a collaborative learning relationship between two individuals that leads to insights, decisions, planning and action that facilitate professional and personal development.

Our approach to mentoring ensures the mentor acts as a guide and facilitates learning moments in the conversation. The mentor–mentee relationship requires a high level of trust, safety and vulnerability with the intention of creating an experience where the

---

18   World Economic Forum
19   Cherie Blair Foundation for Women (2021). *Gender stereotypes and their impact on women entrepreneurs.*

mentee learns about self-reflection and different approaches to various situations. We know that mentoring relationships are most successful when driven by the mentee. The role of the mentor is to create a safe and trusted environment so that the mentee feels comfortable asking the questions that are considered obstacles to the mentee's career and or personal and professional growth.

The MWIB programme is unlike other mentoring services offered in the Women's Economic Empowerment sector because it facilitates more than a one-to-one connection between mentees and mentors. It offers personalized support across the mentoring journey through a clear programme cycle and access to business and personal development resources and tools, such as live webinars and training materials. It also supports women's network development through an online community.

As well as running their businesses, women in any part of the world are more likely than men to hold a greater share of the responsibility for unpaid care and domestic labour. The flexibility of the programme means that participants can meet around work and family commitments, to find a time that suits them.

The programme model

The MWIB programme is a carefully structured and closely managed programme (Figure 28.1). The recruitment, selection, training and matching of mentoring pairs is rigorous to ensure that the right people can participate in the programme at a time that is right for them.

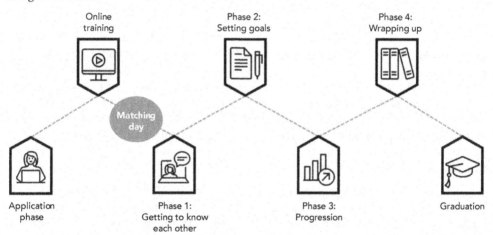

Figure 28.1: The MWIB programme.

Recruitment

The Foundation recruits mentees through non-profit or social enterprise organizations in low- and middle-income countries who work directly with women entrepreneurs. These partners refer outstanding women entrepreneurs from their programmes to become mentees, providing a useful additional element to their own programming and a way to offer cross-border mentorship support without the accompanying expenditures to the women they are working with.

The majority of our mentors are recruited through collaboration with our corporate partners, who make financial contributions to cover the cost of their workforce participating as mentors. Additionally, individuals can apply independently as a self-funded mentor where they have to self-fund their own participation and that of their mentee. Most recently, the Foundation launched a scholarship fund to offer former mentees the opportunity to become a mentor for free. Offering scholarships has meant that we can further support the talented and experienced women entrepreneurs in our alumni community and enable them to continue their professional growth while reaching even more women as their mentees.

Selection

Through the onboarding process, potential mentors and mentees complete a carefully constructed application form that aims to ensure participant suitability for the programme. To be eligible, a mentee needs to be a woman entrepreneur from and currently living in a low- or middle-income country. They can either be running or due to launch their business within the next three months and must have at least 51% ownership (decision-making capabilities). Mentors must have a minimum of seven years of work experience and be able to commit to speaking with their mentees for a minimum of two hours each month for one year. The programme currently runs in English language, but we're actively exploring routes to facilitate the programme in more languages in the future.

Training

Following careful review of each application form, successful applicants are invited to complete the Foundation's online pre-matching training. The training has been developed with the purpose of providing participants with the skills and knowledge needed to build successful mentoring relationships. Both mentors and mentees are required to complete the same training. We take time to outline our approach to mentoring and the roles of a mentee and mentor very clearly so both mentees and mentors enter the programme with the same expectations. Using a mix of short videos and documents, participants are able to watch and read through the training materials at their own pace. Key topics covered include the structure of the mentoring programme; programme competencies; the role of the mentee and mentor and how they can best fulfil those roles.

As a global, cross-border programme, we understand potential challenges can arise due to cultural differences. The training takes this into account and provides useful guidance to participants on how they can best navigate around potential challenges, as well as how they can access support from the programme team at any stage.

At the end of the training, participants can reflect and check their understanding of the learning through a brief test. They can also share feedback with us through a short survey, which enables us to continue to make necessary improvements to the training.

After completing the training, mentees are invited to have a 15-minute phone call with one of our support team members. We use the opportunity to make sure that mentees understand all elements of the programme and confirm their English language skills.

Matching

We take special care in getting to know our mentees and mentors to find them the best possible match. Using a person-centred approach, we review each of our participant's profiles, their priorities and what they hope to achieve through mentoring. We then take the information provided and run it through our bespoke algorithm that pinpoints potential matches, focusing on an alignment of topics and skills. When matching, we can consider other factors such as preferences for time zone, business stage, sector or industry. However, we've found that matching based on the mentee's needs and mentor's expertise is preferable over matching by sector, as the support that mentors provide is more relevant to the specific needs of the mentee. This has led to stronger outcomes for mentees and mentors, who have gone on to work together on a range of business and professional development needs that include planning, finance and accounting, leadership and management, marketing, and communications.

The mentoring journey

To ensure participants get the most out of their time together, the relationship is broken down into four key phases (Figure 28.2). The set phases aim to enable pairs to build mutually beneficial mentoring relationships, where they are encouraged to work together on developing an action plan tailored to the mentee's needs and the mentor's interests. At the start of each phase, the mentoring team are on hand to share information about how pairs will work together during that phase.

Figure 28.2: The four phases of the mentoring journey.

In **Phase 1**, pairs will spend time getting to know each other and building trust. At the start of the mentoring relationship, we invite all newly matched mentees and mentors to a welcome webinar hosted by the Foundation team where they are welcomed into the programme and receive important information about the upcoming year.

In **Phase 2**, pairs collaboratively set SMART goals for the mentee to work toward.

Phase 3 is the progression stage and this is where most of the great work in the mentoring relationship takes place. Pairs work together to make progress against the agreed goals.

In **Phase 4**, pairs wrap up their mentoring relationship and come to the end of the programme. During this phase, pairs will use the remaining time on the programme to look back on what they have learnt and achieved together, review any outstanding objectives and chart out next steps. There is also a celebratory 'graduation' event for both mentees and mentors to share and enjoy the achievements of their mentoring relationship.

Supporting the journey

The tailor-made mentoring platform

The one-to-one mentoring connection is at the heart of the programme and it's conducted entirely through our custom-built online mentoring platform[20]. The platform was designed to help our mentoring pairs build cross-border relationships, find solutions to problems, collaborate on projects and celebrate achievements. Because everything is done online, we've found that people often express themselves more openly using online technologies, as it takes away some of the fear or reservations and helps to create an open, safe space for sharing and reflection. It also provides excellent flexibility, enables cross-border learning connections, helps save on travel costs whilst opening a whole new pool of expertise, and facilitates peer-to-peer learning.

Through the platform, pairs can conduct video calls and share direct messages, track goals, upload and review files and documents, monitor and analyse their progress, easily track their individual learning, and stay in touch with the MWIB programme support team.

Relationship support

The MWIB programme takes great care in offering dedicated relationship support to each mentor and mentee. This consists of providing individualized, attentive support to improve their ability to engage with the programme and build a productive mentoring relationship.

Throughout the duration of the programme, we remain in regular contact with our mentoring pairs using scheduled messages, surveys and calls. We have also developed a suite of learning materials, that we share with pairs as they progress through the different phases of the programme. This continuous support throughout the mentoring cycle, is one of the most valued services we provide and is key to the success of the programme. The support mechanisms play a critical role in assisting participants in meeting and connecting, resulting in the development of relationships that yield the greatest potential outcomes. Feedback from a recent graduate mentee from Nigeria highlights the importance of this support: *'I appreciate the constant check-ups and feedback given by the support team. Through this, I knew I wasn't alone in the journey.'*

Wider business and personal development

Building on the rich learning experience of the one-to-one mentoring relationships, the programme also facilitates a variety of skills and knowledge development activities. Monthly webinars are delivered by expert mentors for mentees, mentors and programme alumni. These monthly webinars cover a series of business and personal development subject matters. Previous examples include protecting your business from cybercrime, communicating with confidence, balancing life and work duties, and business-to-business (b2b) selling. The monthly theme of the webinar also informs the curated learning resources that the mentoring team share with all current and previous participants in our LinkedIn community.

---

20   The MWIB team has collaborated with software provider Mentorloop (https://mentorloop.com) to develop a bespoke online mentoring platform.

Supporting women's networks

To supplement the one-to-one mentoring relationships and learning materials, the MWIB programme also runs an online networking community on LinkedIn. This LinkedIn community was created so mentees and mentors can share challenges, experiences, encouragement and advice, and connect with a growing worldwide community of forward-thinking entrepreneurs and professionals. Feedback shows that this networking facility is beneficial for participants; of the mentees who graduated in 2020, 88% increased their professional network.

Monitoring, evaluation and learning

The Foundation has implemented a systematic monitoring, evaluation and learning (MEL) process, to track, document and monitor the programme's progress and record the participants' achievements. Our MEL structure helps ensure that we can continue strengthening the programme design and implementation. Using surveys, we can collect data from participating mentors and mentees at key points in the programme. The application form, embedded in our mentoring platform, serves as the baseline for the programme. A pre-matching training survey captures whether the training is and continues to be fit for purpose; a mid-point survey encourages participants to reflect on whether the training and other materials well prepared them for their mentoring relationship, and what progress they have made so far; and an endline survey allows us to compare data to the application form to report on the impact of the programme.

In addition to the above surveys, our mentoring software also facilitates the collection of feedback through post-meeting surveys which are emailed to participants to enable them to rate the meeting and or add a comment. Thirty days after getting matched, and every ninety days after that, participants are asked to rate their mentoring relationship and add comments in a mentoring quality score survey.

All our surveys gather both qualitative and quantitative data and we analyse the results of these surveys on an intake-by-intake basis as well as annually. We draw out data that helps us to assess the extent to which mentors' and mentees' participation on the programme has had a positive impact on the mentee's business, such as acquiring new clients, setting up new processes and an increase in revenue, and their own personal development, including acquiring new knowledge, skills, attitudes and confidence.

Learning and looking ahead

At the Foundation, we know how the benefits of mentoring can have a tremendous impact on both mentees and mentors. From building new skills and rejuvenating interest in their work, making new contacts, to forging bonds with individuals in another part of the world. Since its launch in 2010, we have continuously worked to develop a programme that places value on using mentoring best practice, providing excellent service, and utilizing technology in an innovative way to manage an extensive global network.

In 2021, the MWIB programme was awarded gold-level accreditation in the International Standards for Mentoring and Coaching Programmes (ISMCP) by the European Mentoring and Coaching Council (EMCC). This globally recognized accreditation showed that our programme met the highest industry standards, meeting 98% of the ISMCP's rigorous criteria: clear clarity of purpose, strong stakeholder training and briefing, meticulous selection and matching of participants, robust measurement and review, a high standard of ethics, and excellent administration and support.

The Foundation is committed to the process of reviewing and developing the programme to ensure that we continue to deliver a thoughtfully designed and systematically managed programme. Looking ahead, we have a clear vision of how we can continue to differentiate the programme, which includes offering the mentoring programme in multiple languages, alongside developing additional learning and training resources based on mentees' and mentors' needs. We will also continue to place importance on the monitoring and evaluation of results and impact on all our stakeholders, to ensure that we continue to deliver a programme that significantly contributes to providing reciprocal benefits for both mentees and mentors.

Chapter 29
Leadership Mentoring for Ethnic Minorities: The Development of the RISE Mentoring Programme

Sabinah Janally, Masuma Rahim, Amra Saleem Rao & Surinder Johore

Mentoring for ethnic minorities

In recent years, increasing attention has been given to the factors which prevent ethnically minoritized professionals from progressing in their careers. One method of ameliorating this, mentoring, was highlighted in a report by the Chartered Institute of Personnel and Development (CIPD) in 2017. The report found that ethnic minority individuals were more likely to perceive mentoring to be effective in helping their career and personal development than White employees (CIPD, 2017). In 2018, the UK government recommended that companies should offer mentoring specifically for ethnic minority employees to improve workplace diversity (Mooney, 2018). This recommendation followed evidence of significant pay gaps between white and ethnic minority employees (Mooney, 2018). Unsurprisingly, such racial disparities also affect the career progression in the psychological professions (Kline, 2014; CIPD, 2017)).

Although mentoring has been long-established in UK psychology, it has rarely been offered systematically or formally. In the British Psychological Society (BPS) Practice Guidelines (BPS, 2017), mentoring is discussed in relation to a psychologist seeking *'a mentoring relationship with colleagues in order to focus their attention on skills to add to their competencies. Psychologists taking on the role of mentor often support the psychologist with their career path. Early career psychologists may find it beneficial to be mentored by a more experienced psychologist.'* Official mentoring programmes have been established by the Leadership and Management Faculty of the Division of Clinical Psychology (DCP) (https://www.bps.org.uk/member-networks/dcp-faculty-leadership-and-management). Other than the Valued Voices Mentoring Programme (Alcock, 2021 for aspiring ethnic minority clinical psychologists, to the authors' knowledge, there has not been a scheme specifically created to support the development of ethnic minority psychologists and psychological therapists.

Given this, research into mentoring for ethnic minorities within psychology in the UK is limited and possibly non-existent, whereas, in the US, it has received significantly more interest due to the under-representation of ethnic minorities in psychology doctorate programmes (American Psychological Association (APA) Office of Minority Affairs, 2008). Mentoring has been recommended as one approach to attract and retain ethnic minority psychology students (Rogers & Molina, 2006; Evans & Cokley, 2008). In 2015, Chan and colleagues completed a grounded theory study aimed at understanding the mentoring needs of American ethnic minority doctoral counselling and clinical psychology students, shedding light on the impact of race, ethnicity and culture on the mentoring relationship. They propose a five-factor, multicultural, ecological model of ethnic minority mentoring, identifying the following themes:

- Culturally sensitive career guidance, support and fostering a sense of belonging and unity with the profession: this involves the mentee being coached on managing racially oriented criticism.

- Creating psychological trust within a mentor–mentee relationship requires a mentor to foster a sincere connection with the mentee, helping them feel heard. Mentors need to take a compassionate approach in listening and validating mentees' experiences of race-related issues with attention to multiculturalism, race and diversity.

- Consideration of the systemic and contextual factors in the mentoring dyad: Chan et al., (2015) argue for divergence from traditional mentoring models to take the process of reflection beyond the individual.

- Awareness of the interconnectedness of the contexts and how they interact: this helps mentees develop a sense of safety to discuss incidents of racial biases that may have occurred in one context but infiltrated others and acknowledges the existence of racial biases within the profession.

- Recognition of the significance of the reciprocal relationship of mentoring: acknowledging that mentee and mentor have equal influence on one another, and demonstrating an awareness of 'how the mentee's culture affects him/her, builds trust and rapport, along with helping to identify the mentee's specific needs. In turn, mentees feel supported, affirmed, and empowered (Chan, 2008, p. 263).

The model provides direction on how mentoring for ethnic minority psychological professionals in the UK could be established, with the caveat that mentors need to have the courage to engage in brave discussions to recognize the personal, professional and social challenges presented to ethnic minority individuals (Schlosser et al., 2011; Janally, 2020).

Leadership mentoring

Since the launch of the National Health Service (NHS) in 1948, effective leadership has remained an organizational and national priority (Rowling, 2011). However, work by Roger Kline (2014) aimed at understanding the impact of the Race Equality Action Plan (Department of Health, 2004) on the racial compositions of NHS leaders in London uncovered the difficulties faced by the organization in achieving the goals of the plan (Janally, 2021). The study found that only 8% of the Trust board members were from an ethnic minority background, which was lower than in 2006 (9.6%) (Janally, 2021). The findings suggested that those occupying lead roles within the NHS in London were not representative of the workforce or the London population. Since leaders play a significant role in shaping organizational culture, discrimination may occur because of the limited representation of diversity within strategic levels of the organization (Kulich et al., 2014). The DCP Leadership and Management Faculty preliminary unpublished survey (2019) on challenges faced by minoritized groups highlighted a number of further barriers, including a lack of senior posts/development roles within the profession, lack of organizational support to development, discrimination against minorities, personal circumstances impacting on leadership opportunities, political climate, lack of relevant training, confidence and ethical concerns about leadership roles.

There are ongoing concerns about ethnic minority NHS staff experiencing discrimination at work. The Workforce Race Equality Standard (WRES) (NHS England, 2021) report showed the percentage of ethnic minority staff that had personally experienced discrimination at work from a manager, team leader or other colleagues had increased markedly since 2015. Minority ethnic staff are still more likely to enter formal disciplinary processes and less likely to be appointed from shortlisting when applying for jobs. The WRES report notes, *'Improving the inclusivity of recruitment and promotion is essential for a more diverse workforce and more diversity of senior leadership which we know is a key factor in driving culture transformation, embedding sustainable change and improving patient outcomes.'*

The RISE mentoring programme: The social and political context

The murder of George Floyd and racial and social inequalities in times of the COVID-19 pandemic has brought into sharp focus the collective and individual racism that continues to exist. The growing influence of the Black Lives Matter movement encouraged many of us to have difficult conversations around issues of race, whiteness and systemic oppression. Importantly, it was the first time that many people felt able to acknowledge the existence of racial trauma openly and try to make sense of their lived experiences.

Racism and hostility can be overt or more nuanced, it can be direct or indirect, consciously or unconsciously transmitted. Thinking about race and racism arouses strong feelings such as anxiety, guilt, shame and anger (Lowe, 2013). There is a need for safe spaces to promote reflection and authentic dialogue about diversity issues in psychotherapy and beyond and an exploration of the conscious and unconscious thoughts and feelings around the difference of others.

Systemic inequalities continue to exist within health care. It is clear within the psychological professions that more needs to be done in relation to accessing services and why particular minority groups might be under-represented. As part of the NHS long-term plan to create a better workforce to meet the needs of the community it serves, various initiatives have been set up to try and address this. A recent Health Education England (HEE) initiative on improving equity and inclusion for people to access psychological professions training is underway, with an increase in funded places for Clinical Psychology and Child and Adolescent Psychotherapy training. There is also recognition there can be more barriers to career progression for those from minority ethnic backgrounds once qualified, with an aim of developing leadership coaching and mentoring opportunities to support minority ethnic psychological professionals to reach their full potential and take on senior and leadership roles. The rationale for such approaches is clear: a motivated, included and valued workforce helps deliver better quality patient care.

Development and implementation of RISE

In response to these issues, there were calls for the psychological professions to redress the ongoing inequities. In autumn 2020, HEE announced funding for a number of initiatives designed to improve the representation of minoritized people within those professions. One initiative focused on the provision of twelve hours of mentoring to more than one hundred ethnic minority NHS psychological professionals in England. Unusually, mentors – who typically did this work for free and in their own time – were to be offered payment for their services.

The funding announcement was made in December 2020, with the caveat that the funds had to be disbursed by April 2021. As such, an operational team comprised of representatives from all the professional bodies involved – spanning psychotherapists, applied psychologists, systemic psychotherapists, psychoanalysts, counsellors, and CBT therapists – was formed to deliver the programme in the required time. It was decided that members of all psychological professions involved in the scheme should be invited to express an interest in becoming mentors, and that those people should be offered training in providing leadership-focused mentoring. The scheme was named the RISE Ethnic Minority Leadership Mentoring Programme.

Some one hundred and twenty responses were received from potential mentors, and respondents were then invited to complete a more in-depth form outlining their experiences, their motivation to be part of the scheme, and what they felt they could offer mentees. Ninety completed questionnaires were returned. The respondents were invited to attend one of two whole-day training events focused on outlining the context and aims of the scheme, the experience of being an ethnic minority within and beyond working in the NHS, the impact of racial minoritization and racial trauma, the mentoring process and leadership models. Reflective spaces were embedded throughout the training to explore the impact of racism in various work roles, to think about leadership within a systemic lens, to consider how mentoring may help personal and professional development as well as discussing the potential challenges that may be faced by both mentees and mentors. Mentors were also encouraged to organize informal peer-support groups.

Simultaneously, mentees were recruited via all NHS Trusts in England, with the support of HEE regional offices. The NHS Trusts were invited to express an interest in being part of the scheme and identifying employees from ethnic minority backgrounds to be put forward as mentees. Once mentees had been confirmed to have funding for the programme, they were asked to submit a form outlining their interests, experiences and goals for the programme. Mentees were provided basic demographic details for all mentors and were able to request fuller details for those they wished to contact. They were then encouraged to choose their preferred mentors and to establish relationships with them independently. Once these relationships had been established, mentors could invoice the mentee's employing NHS Trust. Approximately one hundred and twenty mentees were offered mentoring. Mentors and mentees were advised to begin their relationships in March 2020. It was anticipated that most mentoring relationships would come to end after the twelve sessions had been delivered.

Evaluation

For quality assurance, a systematic evaluation was developed alongside the implementation of the mentoring scheme. Questionnaires were created to explore the aims of the scheme which included gaining feedback on the mentees' leadership development, experiences of systemic and structural racism within the workplace and the management of this in the mentoring relationship, as well as the impact of mentoring on the personal and professional development of both the mentors and mentees. The questionnaires were sent out after six months and twelve months from when the scheme began. Focus groups were also held with the mentors and mentees in December 2020. Key findings from the six months review and from the focus groups are presented below. Analysis on the twelve-month evaluation is underway.

The main findings from the six months review:

- 93% of respondents rated overall quality of the mentoring they were receiving as high or very high;
- 90% said the mentors met their expectations;
- 96% of mentees reported they had established a relationship with their mentor based on trust;
- 91% reported the mentors were skilled or very skilled at holding discussions related to the oppressive challenges that they (mentees) were facing;
- 94% reported the mentors were very or extremely skilled at building their confidence; and
- 75% reported that the mentors were very skilled or extremely skilled at helping them to set leadership goals.

As part of the evaluation of the RISE Ethnic Minority Leadership Mentoring Programme, focus groups were carried out with the mentors and mentees. The sessions aimed to draw upon the participants' perspectives and experiences of mentorship. Discussion centred on what had worked well and what could be done differently, the existence of oppression and discrimination within the workplace and how this was addressed in the mentoring relationship.

Mentors found that many of their mentees presented with low confidence and observed that a significant part of their role was to help their mentees to recognize their worth and to validate their skills and competence. Mentors reflected on their mentees' feelings of *'stuckness'* and *'shame'*, and how these impacted on their understanding of progression and leadership. Mentees recognized that leadership meant more than moving up to a higher band; many began to see how they could develop confidence in their leadership skills within their current position. They began to understand how to create opportunities within their existing contexts, such as by leading service evaluations or establishing regular discussions on racial (in)equity in psychological practice. Mentees spoke of finding their mentors inspirational, and that they acted as role models, being someone to aspire to with the knowledge that they have become a leader within the discipline despite facing oppressive challenges. Mentees commented on feeling empowered after engaging in the mentoring sessions. For some, mentoring helped them to move to the next steps on the career ladder such as promotion, secondment and/or a move to a senior band.

The mentoring relationship helped mentees to openly acknowledge feelings of shame related to the barriers they had faced in progressing to senior roles. For some, mentoring enabled them to explore the vulnerability caused by multiple experiences of discrimination over the course of many years. Mentoring helped many to see that they did not have to carry the burden of systemic racism and that it was the NHS which had to change rather than them. Mentees felt liberated by finally having a space for themselves. Some said that for the first time, they felt validated and heard. They also spoke of feeling safe to bring their whole self without fear and judgment. Some mentees described their experience of mentoring to be enriching and holistic, which enabled them to connect with mentors on a professional, cultural and familial level.

A focus on discrimination became central for some. Mentors recognized how difficult but important it was to hear their stories and acknowledge the existence of racial trauma. Mentees spoke of having a space to reflect with someone (their mentors) about oppression, and the effects and emotional impact this can have. Mentors and mentees reflected on acknowledging the frustration of ethnic minorities *needing* a mentoring scheme. Mentors wondered, *'how must this feel for mentees?'* Both highlighted that mentoring continues to locate the *problem* within the individual, leaving the organization taking little or no responsibility when it came to addressing systemic racial discrimination. Mentors acknowledged a sense of feeling powerless when hearing these stories; one mentor said, *'I felt that I had no impact or power – how do we help to make a change?'*

For mentees, being able to reflect on intersectionality was important. Mentors spoke of needing to notice and own their personal assumptions and biases. Mentors reflected on how to manage DNAs, disengagement and ruptures. Self-critical thoughts relating to disengagement occurred for some; a space to reflect on these thoughts with other mentors was highlighted as an improvement to the scheme.

Mentees and mentors relished that the scheme celebrated difference – and that the learning was reciprocal. Mentors noticed that mentees held strong values pertaining to social justice and inclusive leadership. Many mentees spoke of applying for new roles, seeking opportunities with greater responsibility, appreciating their self-worth and wanting to develop a network with other mentees to drive the changes they want to see within the psychological professions.

Conclusions and recommendations

There is value in mentoring schemes, but there is still the question of scarcity of resources. By paying mentors, RISE stands out as the exception to the rule rather than the default. And although the scheme was set up in response to unprecedented global events, the true test is whether the scheme is still being funded and promoted once those events have receded in our collective memories.

The scheme has demonstrated that mentoring can help in enabling conversations on how work experiences and career progression can be impacted by discrimination, microaggression and racism. As authors, we felt moved and inspired by many stories of resilience and commitment shared by mentors and mentees. The work, nevertheless, is challenging due to the context around discrimination and systemic racism, which impacts both mentors and mentees requiring particular attention to mentoring relationship and processes, as well as the limits of mentoring. Such mentoring schemes need to be carefully designed, facilitating an ethos of learning and reflection with enabling support networks for mentors and organizers. We need to acknowledge that mentoring is only a part of the solution. It is important to acknowledge that mentoring centres the 'problems' attached to being an ethnic minority within the individual/ mentee. Experiences from such initiatives need to be a part of a learning cycle incorporating a systemic view with feedback loops into the organizations and leadership development matrices. Racial equity needs to be considered as integral within the therapeutic and psychological professions. A fuller evaluation report is underway for the HEE, which, alongside the findings, will be highlighting the above themes as well as the need for coordinated system-based strategy to support professional development of psychological practitioners from ethnic minorities. Mentoring has a great role to play as demonstrated by this scheme. However, learning from the scheme needs to be taken on board, as well as mentoring to be embedded within a wider strategy around overcoming barriers to equity and inclusivity.

Furthermore, systemic work is needed to support the leadership development of ethnic minority professionals. Organizational cultural transformation must take place at every level in the NHS and societal systems so that marginalized groups feel valued and supported to thrive. Our professions must acknowledge our flawed histories and start to hold open and honest conversations about the mistakes we have made. We need to acknowledge our ongoing struggles to embrace the issue meaningfully. This will require rising beyond the reactive and enacting change to address the barriers preventing the progression of ethnic minority psychological professionals and therapists.

References

Alcock, K. (2021). *Valued Voices Mentoring Scheme.* The British Psychology Society. Integrated Service Model project ECT GB DCP Research Grant application Oct 2017 Final.doc (bps.org.uk).

American Psychological Association (APA) Office of Minority Affairs (2008). *2008 Annual Report: APA Committee on Ethnic Minority Affairs.* https://www.apa.org/pi/oema/committee/annual-report-2008.pdf

British Psychological Society (BPS) (2017). *BPS Practice Guidelines.* https://www.bps.org.uk/guideline/bps-practice-guidelines-2017-0

Chan, A. W. (2008). *Mentoring ethnic minority, pre-doctoral students: An analysis of key mentor practices.* Mentoring & Tutoring: Partnership in Learning, **16**(3), 263–277.

Chan, A. W., Yeh, C. J., & Krumboltz, J. D. (2015). *Mentoring ethnic minority counseling and clinical psychology students: A multicultural, ecological, and relational model.* Journal of Counseling Psychology, **62**(4), 1–16.

Charted Institute of Personnel and Development (CIPD) (2017). *Addressing the Barriers to BAME Employee Career Progression to the Top.* https://www.cipd.org/globalassets/media/knowledge/knowledge-hub/reports/addressing-the-barriers-to-BAME-employee-career-progression-to-the-top_tcm18-33336.pdf

Department of Health (2004). *Race Equality Action Plan.* http://webarchive.nationalarchives.gov.uk/ + /http://www.dh.gov.uk/en/Publicationsandstatistics/Bulletins/DH_4072494

Evans, G. L., & Cokley, K. O. (2008). *African American women and the academy: Using career mentoring to increase research productivity. Training and Education in Professional Psychology*, 2(1), 50–57.

Janally, S. (2020). *Addressing the unmet needs of BAME trainees through a system of mentoring. Clinical Psychology Forum*, 331, 6–13.

Janally, S. (2021). *Still I rise – clinical psychologists' journey as leaders from ethnic minority backgrounds: A reflective piece. Clinical Psychology Forum*, 339, 24–31.

Kline, R. (2014). *The 'Snowy White Peaks' of the NHS: A Survey of Discrimination in Governance and Leadership and the Potential Impact on Patient Care in London and England.* Middlesex University Research Repository. https://www.mdx.ac.uk/__data/assets/pdf_file/0015/50190/The-snowy-white-peaks-of-the-NHS.pdf.pdf

Kulich, C., Ryan, M. K., & Haslam, S. A. (2014). *The political glass cliff: understanding how seat selection contributes to the underperformance of ethnic minority candidates. Political Research Quarterly*, 67(1), 84–95.

Lowe, F. (2013). *Thinking Space: Promoting Thinking about Race, Culture and Diversity in Psychotherapy and Beyond.* Karnac Books.

Mooney, A. (2018, April 12). *UK board directors told to mentor women and BAME employees. Financial Times.* https://www.ft.com/content/4e26fcb8-3d9a-11e8-b7e0-52972418fec4

NHS England (2021). *Workforce Race Equality Standard (WRES) Report.* https://www.england.nhs.uk/about/equality/equality-hub/workforce-equality-data-standards/equality-standard/

Rogers, M. R., & Molina, L. E. (2006). *Exemplary efforts in psychology to recruit and retain graduate students of colour. American Psychologist*, 61, 143–156.

Rowling, E. (Ed.) (2011). *The Future of Leadership and Management in the NHS, No More Heroes.* The King's Fund. https://www.kingsfund.org.uk/sites/default/files/future-of-leadership-and-management-nhs-may-2011-kings-fund.pdf

Schlosser, L. Z., Lyons, H. Z., Talleyrand, R. M., Kim, B. S., & Johnson, W. B. (2011). *Advisor–advisee relationships in graduate training programs. Journal of Career Development*, 38(1), 3–18.

Chapter 30
Reciprocal Mentoring for Inclusion: An Enabler for Systemic Transformation

Charmaine Kwame

> *The NHS Constitution for England: It is there to improve our health and well-being, supporting us to keep mentally and physically well, to get better when we are ill and, when we cannot fully recover, to stay as well as we can to the end of our lives. It works at the limits of science – bringing the highest levels of human knowledge and skill to save lives and improve health. It touches our lives at times of basic human need, when care and compassion are what matter most.*

(Department of Health and Social Care, 2015)

We face a significant challenge in translating the NHS Constitution into a reality, through the backdrop of a rapidly changing NHS England architecture, establishment of Integrated Care Systems, recovery and reset through a global pandemic, an active social justice movement for equality and the negative impact of health inequalities on vulnerable groups combined with the continued challenge to deliver more with less. The *NHS People Plan 2020/21* (NHS England, 2020), and more recently the *NHS Long Term Workforce Plan* (NHS England, 2023), recognize that tackling inequalities within the NHS system is critical and high-quality, timely, accessible, inclusive leadership development for the workforce, can enable a positive impact on the quality and experience of health care services to our communities. Coaching and mentoring can play a big part in equipping leaders with these leadership skills in the face of existing challenges. This chapter draws upon my personal experience of designing and delivering a programme of *reciprocal mentoring* with a particular focus on inclusion to enhance transformational change.

A personal journey to reciprocal mentoring for inclusion

Working as an executive coach for sixteen years with over twenty-three years of industry knowledge within private and public sectors, including investment banking, financial regulation, government and health care, the most rewarding aspect of my career to date has been applying coaching and mentoring to some of the most challenging issues faced by the NHS. This work has contributed to enabling an inclusive culture to begin proactively dismantling the systems and behaviours that discriminate from within.

As a biracial, neurodivergent woman, who is a single mother of a daughter with a disability and an active foster carer of looked after children within London, I'm very aware of how discrimination shows up within systems for marginalized people and am familiar with experiences of racial discrimination, powerlessness and navigating systems that are not designed with difference in mind. Born in the diverse melting pot of East London to working class parents of very different racial cultures (white mother and black father), I have directly faced discrimination in what should have been safe places such as public transport, school, hospitals, supermarkets, work and even sometimes from the very people who were part of my own family system. My parents divorce during childhood, and conflicting sense of identity, also compounded my confusion around sense of belonging – where did I actually fit when I wasn't fully part of one aspect of my culture, or the other? In my adult years, my lived experience of navigating systems that were not designed with difference in mind, trying to advocate on behalf of family and young people in my care, was complex, frustrating and challenging. At times the very people holding the processes I was stumbling over were only too aware of the issues and were equally frustrated but felt powerless to challenge.

Professionally, I have encountered the realness of race and disability discrimination, getting stuck within the career trajectory as a senior leader equipped with the right professional skills, knowledge and experience, compared to white peers who seemed to progress past my 'stuckness' at speed, even when starting out in less senior positions than me. It took many years to admit this reality. I avoided recognizing what was happening, afraid of what it would mean to accept this truth. To survive, I often adapted my behaviour to fit the professional environment so I could blend with the status quo, network with the perceived movers and shakers, adopt the personality traits of colleagues I saw as successful, respected and accepted, even if some of those behaviours directly conflicted my own values system. This worked for a while but over time, added to the trauma. Such lived experience accumulated over the years, taking a massive toll on my health and well-being. I turned inwards, creating a conflicting internal narrative that suggested it was me – I was the lowest common denominator. I wasn't good enough, smart enough, normal enough, personable enough, ambitious enough, white enough, to ever fit. At other times I would actively challenge the system for equity. This came at a cost of being seen as 'the problem', 'the agitator', passed over for professional opportunities, ignored, feared, ridiculed and even bullied. At one point I was lost and didn't understand who I was anymore.

To survive and heal, I focused on my passion and the space I did fit – within the coaching and mentoring community. I took a deep interest and desire to help shape programmes that could help leaders thrive who faced systemic barriers to their development because of their difference. Ironically, in leading the work to affect change I faced the same barriers and inequities as our programme participants but learned awareness of my responses, extending compassion to myself and others, and building this wisdom into my practice.

The birth of reciprocal mentoring for inclusion

Early in 2019, after co-designing and delivering well-evaluated coaching programmes centred on inclusive coaching, I was asked to consider developing a reverse mentoring programme to tackle systemic barriers specifically faced by colleagues from black and minority ethnic backgrounds. Unfair discrimination exists and negatively impacts the lives of people in the workforce and wider communities, with previous attempts at reducing inequity not having taken the NHS far enough. All leaders have a responsibility to develop their ability to be more effective leaders of Equality, Diversity and Inclusion (ED&I) and drivers of social justice and to use that ability to practically bring about change. I hadn't seen any real transformational change within the system coming from the impact of reverse mentoring.

After some deep thought, I wanted to do something radically different. An approach with impact, that adopted the trusted, well-established mentoring models but took it a step further toward system change. I brought together a faculty of brilliant people with insight, expertise and lived experience on the subject matter – mentoring, leadership development, culture change and ED&I. The next eight months was spent going out into the system, collaborating with colleagues from under-represented groups to understand their lived experiences and views, and blending these insights with ED&I evidence, data and the perspectives of the wider coaching and mentoring community. Through the co-design process, we underpinned the programme with content based on the latest research, thinking and innovation within leadership development and aligned with our system learning during the scoping phase.

We wanted Boards to fully subscribe and meaningfully participate, allowing room for learning from experience to combat against this becoming a tick-box exercise. We felt it was important to work through the complex dynamics of fear, not getting it right, saying the wrong thing, guilt, helplessness and shame, which senior leaders had bravely expressed in their attempts to drive equity. We were all learning and making mistakes on this journey as part of our development. Following our engagement work, three keen and ready organizations were identified to be early adopter pilot sites to test out the concept while we evaluated early impact.

The programme vision

This section elaborates on the programme vision, key principles and developmental approach, as well as how reciprocal mentoring was incorporated in the programme design.

The programme relied on creating a safe and brave space where every senior executive director entered into a reciprocal mentoring partnership with a colleague from an under-represented group within their own organization. The relationship is intended to enable a social change where those from under-represented groups are able to take the opportunity to become 'partners in change' with more senior allies in the system, utilizing their shared wisdom, intelligence, knowledge, experience, leadership and courage to dismantle systemic barriers which marginalize those from under-represented groups. The aim is to shift the underlying culture to one where the power of difference is respected and valued, and where prejudice and unconscious biases are challenged to benefit the system.

The intended benefits of the programme were to:

- contribute to achieving organizations that are antiracist, equitable, diverse, inclusive, compassionate and able to provide the highest quality of care for our communities;

- develop leaders with knowledge, skills and behaviours that embody and sustain cultures of compassion and inclusion while challenging discriminatory practice and actively dismantling systemic barriers;

- support the development and retention of leaders who are from under-represented groups by enabling them to thrive professionally and progress into those hard-to-reach senior leadership roles; and

- enable systemic transformation by addressing the critically important challenges faced by society through changing constructs such as whiteness, privilege, power and heteronormativity that negatively affect the lives of the most vulnerable and marginalized.

The key principles underlying the programme are stated as below:

- **Change and transformation**

  A high-impact systemic change approach underpinned by evidence-based theories of change which provide skills for taking action beyond and beneath the superficial.

- **Reciprocal mentoring**

  Skills for building strong reciprocal mentoring partnerships founded on human connection, which seals their commitment as equal partners for change.

- **Equality, diversity and inclusion**

  Developing ED&I subject matter expertise includes awareness of unconscious as well as conscious forces at play in systems, to develop understanding of the complexities and contradictions that exist around disability, race, gender, class, sexuality, sexual identity and other areas of exclusion.

How this approach builds on other mentoring models

Traditional mentoring	Reverse mentoring	Reciprocal mentoring for inclusion
Mentor is typically more experienced and holds more positional power than the Mentee.	The mentoring model role is reversed with inversion of existing positional power. The Mentee becomes the Reverse Mentor.	The pair both take on the role of Mentor and Mentee with learning, expertise and lived experience reciprocated both ways, challenging the traditional norms of exercising hierarchy that can work against equity.
The Mentor opens the doors to their world, connecting the Mentee to opportunities, experiences and networks to benefit the development of the Mentee.	The Reverse Mentor opens the doors to their world, connecting the Reverse Mentee to their learning and insight through their lived experience to benefit the development of the Reverse Mentee.	The pair both open doors of knowledge, insight and lived experience to benefit individual and collective learning. Risk of vulnerability is shared equally leading to greater levels of trust and human connection, which is important for how they work as 'partners for change'.
The power lies with the Mentor.	The power lies with the Reverse Mentor.	Power and accountability are shared equally.
Expertise, knowledge and insight sits with the Mentor.	Expertise, knowledge and insight sits with the Reverse Mentor.	Expertise and knowledge sit with both parties and is co-developed through the learning process – neither can help the other transform if they are not prepared to transform themselves.
Approach to addressing ED&I varies with little evidence to demonstrate systemic change.	When applied to address ED&I, the Reverse Mentee develops understanding of their personal biases and impact on the system.	Both develop understanding of their personal biases and the ways in which the system works against greater equity. Crucially, they also develop their ability to make transformational interventions together.

Table 30.1: Comparison of reciprocal mentoring for inclusion with other models (adapted Charles, 2021).

The programme pedagogy and approach

The twelve to eighteen-month programme was designed to be flexible so organizations could scale the programme components according to budget, resources and specific ED&I objectives. Some aspects of the programme content were fixed to ensure the core curriculum was delivered to meet overall strategic objectives, while other aspects could be personalized during the planning and preparation phase. Each organization would recruit a cohort of up to thirty participants consisting of the entire Executive Board paired with colleagues from unrepresented groups.

Initially, the programme was centrally coordinated and delivered with facilitated aspects managed through a central pool of faculty and subject matter experts, with delivery a combination of both face-to-face and virtual sessions. Later, we adapted the model so it could be entirely locally coordinated through a digital platform, allowing greater flexibility, accessibility and ownership at a local level.

To ensure a well-run programme, it was split it into three phases:

Phase 1: Programme preparation

- programme marketing and expressions of interest
- Executive Board commitment to participate for programme duration
- initial shortlisting against programme criteria
- administering Readiness Assessment Tool to proceed to Phase 2.

Phase 2: Programme governance and onboarding

- clarifying organizational objectives and evaluation measures
- exploratory design work to personalize aspects of the programme
- organization set up of local Implementation Board
- recruiting of programme participants and matching mentoring pairs
- programme participants complete pre-work
- pastoral care, arrangements to support staff emotional well-being outside of the programme environment.

Phase 3: Programme delivery and evaluation

- delivery of 12–18 months of development through five learning modules which include reciprocal mentoring sessions between mentoring pairs, supervision and cohort action learning sets spaced out over 8–12-week intervals
- quarterly check-ins with local Implementation Board to co-design the next tranche of development activities against the programme blueprint and assess impact against organizational objectives
- evaluation of impact throughout each stage of programme delivery using the four levels of The New World Kirkpatrick Model; Reaction, Learning, Behaviour and Results (Kirkpatrick Partners, n.d.).

Learning modules

The programme contained five learning modules with a focus on the following topics:

- self-awareness and reflexivity exploring, what you do and how you do it;
- practical and transferable skills of application through structured activities aimed at transformational systemic change, including theories and models of change, the emotional cycle of change, models of learning, and organizational development;
- core reciprocal mentoring skills, psychological safety, and developing and deepening the mentoring alliance;
- intersectionality, power and privilege, the social determinants of health, allyship and trauma-informed practice, triggers and racialized trauma; and
- sharing of the learning journey and impact as an individual, in pairs and Action Learning Impact Groups, building networks, influencing and negotiating.

The modules were designed to be delivered through a blended learning approach with a module delivered approximately every 8–12 weeks to ensure sufficient time to embed the learning locally. The approach included:

- facilitated intensive onboarding at programme start up;
- knowledge builder self-guided online study modules with videos, podcasts, reading and virtual campus content;
- specific subject matter expert masterclasses and workshops;
- reciprocal mentoring meetings between mentoring pairs and supervision;
- learning journals and participant assignments;
- Action Learning Impact Groups organized within each organization cohort;
- sessions with actor facilitators to test learning;
- group coaching;
- joint learning events to spread impact between cohorts;
- 'learning in action phases' between each module of development to apply learning within the system;
- references and bibliography citing the literature, with suggested further optional reading; and
- a paired, structured activity at the end of each module to demonstrate application of learning to practice and action, leading to influence and impact within the organization.

As mentioned earlier, three organizations were identified to be early adopter pilot sites to test out the concept while we evaluated early impact. A case study is provided below:

A Case Study

One organization recruited twenty-four programme participants, including all Executive Board Members, to lead as a community and champion a culture of community and inclusiveness where everyone can thrive. The focus was to dismantle structural inequalities for staff and patients through the lens of race and disability, utilizing the Workforce Race Equality Standard (WRES) data as a starting point for improvement. The programme resulted in the formation of a powerful staff alliance and the development of a change framework with clear objectives and key performance indicators (KPIs) for the next three years toward transformation.

Through the three early adopter organizations, we captured the following learning:

- Ensure Executive Board commitment and participation is in place from the start for credibility, organizational buy-in and trust of the programme participants.
- Onboarding and preparation are key – use a readiness tool to assess where an organization is at and support them toward embarking on the programme when they are ready.
- Programme participants drawn from the diverse spectrum of under-represented groups is critical – match mentoring pairs for diversity and stretch, using insight around individual participant learning objectives to 'intelligently match'.
- Have clear and specific objectives in the short, medium, and longer term for how the programme will serve ED&I transformation – manage expectations that transformational change takes time and this programme is for long-term change as well as short-term gain.

- Have a robust communications and marketing strategy and engage closely with inclusion networks/leads – seek out and engage in spaces where voices are not being heard, rather than reverting to the usual suspects.

- Select programme participants who are prepared to learn about themselves and others, work on self and be vulnerable – as well as being prepared to embrace their power, wisdom and ability to influence change.

- Keep the programme content relevant and up to date so participants can connect with what matters now – ensure content and delivery is accessible and inclusive for all programme participants.

- Setting up the early workshop sessions properly is key – contracting and creating a psychologically brave space lends itself to developing successful reciprocal mentoring pairs, who go on to lead and influence system change.

- Be honest about the journey and challenges participants will face in developing their reciprocal mentoring partnerships – they will make mistakes (we expect that) and can feel challenged, worried, clumsy, awkward and not initially feel it is 'working'. This is normal and not necessarily a sign of the relationship breaking down.

- Pastoral support, advice and signposting is critical and non-negotiable – resurfaced trauma does occur, and we need to ensure the well-being of programme participants.

- Diversity in the representation of facilitators is critical and must include people of colour – ensure facilitators are equipped with the right skills to hold the space for ED&I-focused work.

Progress of the reciprocal mentoring for inclusion programme

Early in 2020, we were faced with a global pandemic which had devastating consequences worldwide. In response, we were asked to scale up the programme to support system leadership. During the process, through 2020–2021, from three earlier adopter sites, we recruited in excess of forty Boards across the country with a wait list. Organizations saw the value of embarking on the programme and its benefit in supporting the system through a global crisis.

At points, our early adopter sites and delivery teams had to pause and restart delivery of the programme multiple times due to staff redeployment in response to the pandemic, which was challenging and impacted on evaluation and programme delivery timescales. These organizations still persisted in such a difficult climate to keep the programme running, showing commitment and energy each time, so we resumed delivery. They valued having this programme to support the organizational response to pandemic-related challenges, through recovery and eventually into reset.

Early signs showed the programme was having a very positive impact and making a clear difference to leadership during very uncertain and challenging times when ED&I was even more critical than ever. Work in the three early adopter organizations is still in progress. The section below provides comments from the early feedback:

- *'We felt engaged, challenged for the better, uncomfortable at times (expected) but very safe, everything we hoped for and more.'*
- *'The programme has helped us work closer with marginalized members of our communities during the pandemic, having brave and uncomfortable but very required conversations about the vaccination programme, the myths and mistrust. I never understood this before and I am prepared to get more uncomfortable in service of all members of our community.'*
- *'I have felt braver to challenge where I see direct discrimination from service users to our staff and where I sense inequity in the service we provide.'*
- *'When you understand what's happening you can't unsee what's happening – we then have a responsibility to change it for the better.'*
- *'This has triggered the formation of a powerful alliance of staff who are passionate about a fair and equitable inclusive place to work.'*
- *'This programme has given me hope that our value, contribution, and knowledge will be seen and heard by those in power, I'm finding my voice.'*
- *'Our board are committed to spreading this programme across the entire footprint of our remit over the next three years.'*

The programme sparked the interest of other parts of the health and care sector and we also sharing learning with colleagues in the police, military, prison service and higher education institutions. In addition, we had the opportunity of sharing our programme and learning at the European Mentoring and Coaching Council (EMCC) Global Conference (2020), Coaching at Work Global Conference (2021), and the West Midlands Employers Conference (2020).

By Spring 2021, NHS budgets were significantly decreased as a result of COVID-19 spending and our programme funding was negatively impacted to reflect the reduction in funding across the entire system. Our team and programme stakeholders had to think differently about how programme delivery could still be made possible with much less resource, increasing system demand, and existing in-progress cohorts waiting for development, while still providing the transformational impact of the programme. Through a co-design group, we considered blending the programme with other established strategic programmes of work and how the digital space could assist in developing a flexible, scalable product that could complement other tools and interventions within a smaller budget. During this period, NHS England announced an organizational restructure which created uncertainty about where existing structures would fit, so sustainability was a key factor in the redesign process. Building on the learning from the original programme blueprint, we developed a new digital product, at a fraction of the cost, that can be tailored to fit and be scaled to any budget.

At the time of writing this chapter, this newly developed product was being tested with existing cohorts. While it takes away the centralized function of onboarding, facilitation, and coordination, it does allow local organizations to design a blueprint that fits their needs, underpinned by expert online digital content. The programme has been responsive to organizational contextual changes. We hope that early implementer sites will continue to deliver the programme objectives and that its impact will continue to be measured and evaluated through the longer term. We believe that skeleton framework, with its core values and key principles, offers potential to respond and adapt to the local needs.

Final reflections

I have not only witnessed strength, resilience, beauty, wisdom, hope and courage from programme participants and programme faculty, but also noticed my own bubbling well of silent anger, shame, resentment and sadness, which stemmed from my own emergent learning and surfacing of repressed racialized trauma. The last four years have been healing, stretching, emotional and, at times, very hard but the creativity, hope, collaboration and determination from everyone to design and mobilize this work has been like nothing else I have experienced – an absolute privilege. Programme participants have spoken of finding their voice, feeling validated, feeling heard, feeling understood, feeling connected, ready to challenge, ready to change, ready to heal, ready to stand up to injustice, and ready to put the hard work in, collectively. We all stood for a common purpose; to make the NHS a place for everyone. I witnessed the early impact of the programme and the positive evidence that reciprocal mentoring, set out in a carefully designed systemwide programme, can collectively enable systemic change through a coordinated and joined up change approach, spreading learning across the entire system while retaining the beauty of human connectedness and difference each mentoring pair has at its core.

Over the last five years, with so many brilliant people contributing to the collective wisdom of our programme, to acknowledge them all, I would have run out of word count before I even started! Some have moved on, some remain to deliver this work in the new NHS England, very sadly some are no longer with us but remembered every single day through our work, the lives it touches and the very words you are reading. Through these beautiful people, I have learned the true nature of humanity, compassion, healing and forgiveness, finally finding my voice and 'fit' in this world. I am forever grateful to all of you.

The NHS is changing and … we still have much work to do!

In memory of Alan J. Nobbs, Andrew Foster, and Ben Fuchs, who all contributed towards the development of the Reciprocal Mentoring for Inclusion Programme.

References

Charles, E. (2021). Reciprocal mentoring model comparison [unpublished]. People Opportunities Limited.

Department of Health and Social Care (2015). *The NHS Constitution for England.* https://www.gov.uk/government/publications/the-nhs-constitution-for-england/the-nhs-constitution-for-england

Kirkpatrick Partners (n.d.). *The New World Kirkpatrick Model.* https://www.kirkpatrickpartners.com/the-kirkpatrick-model/

NHS England (2020). *We are the NHS: People Plan 2020/21 – Action for Us All.* https://www.england.nhs.uk/wp-content/uploads/2020/07/We-Are-The-NHS-Action-For-All-Of-Us-FINAL-March-21.pdf

NHS England (2023). *NHS Long Term Workforce Plan.* https://www.england.nhs.uk/publication/nhs-long-term-workforce-plan/

Chapter 31
Mentoring in the US

Interview with Lisa Fain

What would you most like to share with us for the Handbook chapter about your perspectives and experiences of mentoring, particularly in the US? Why do you feel this is important?

My perspective on mentoring comes from working with organizations on creating mentoring programmes and seeking to build mentoring cultures. I'm seeing mentoring on the 'uptick'. By that I mean that there is an increased organizational appetite for mentoring. With so much work being done with remote teams and in virtual meetings, there is no longer any question that mentoring across distance can be effective. As the younger generations are entering the workforce and rising within their organizations, they are expecting and requesting mentoring. Indeed, the availability of mentoring has become a criterion in choosing employment. The viewpoint has changed from mentoring that has been earned to mentoring that is expected. Organizations are using it both as a tool for attraction and retention.

As I understand it, in the US, mentoring is far more organizational than in Europe. One of the distinctions here is that we don't have a lot of people who are professionally paid as individual mentors. Mentoring is viewed as something that is unpaid, voluntary and provided through either an organizational or institutional structure, or is sought informally on an individual basis. Certainly, individuals are seeking out mentors on an informal basis, but it is rare that mentors are paid for this work. The structure of an individual as a paid mentor seeking business is mostly reserved for coaches.

Organizations are looking more and more to mentoring as a tool to create inclusion in the workplace and to leverage the diversity within their workforce. So, whether it is intentionally finding mentors and mentees and matching them across difference, whether it is complementary mentoring where a more senior person is being mentored by someone more junior, or some other modality, it is used more and more as a tool to create inclusion and cross-cultural understanding in workplaces. Often, these initiatives are led by the Diversity, Equity and Inclusion team or the Human Resources team within organizations.

Why is it particularly important in America?

I don't know that it is necessarily any more important in America than in other parts of the world. Here in America, we have such terrible problems with inequity and under-representation of traditionally marginalized populations at the management and executive levels. One of the very few effective ways of addressing this, if you mentor correctly, is to foster meaningful relationships with people across difference in the workplace that provide access and exposure to positions of power for people who haven't traditionally had access.

Also, as the generational makeup of our workforce is changing, mentoring is a great way to attract, retain and engage younger talent. The flip side of the expectation of mentoring of the younger generation of professionals is the willingness to leave the organization to find a place that has the attributes they seek. So there is not the same loyalty to organizations or patience for growth over the long term. It is a very healthy impatience as it forces organizations to really invest in professional development. If we want the best young talent and the wisdom of a younger generation in our various industries, mentoring is critical.

Can you tell us a little more about how mentoring works in the US, particularly in health and social care professions?

Mentoring is sorely needed in health and social care professions. I don't have any deep expertise in those industries in particular, but I can tell you anecdotally in the medical field, for physicians, nurses, health care assistants and those in direct patient care, it is go, go, go all the time. Most European countries have a very different system when it comes to health care insurance, billing and reimbursement. Here, the financial margins are really tight in the patient service professions. That puts a lot of pressure on the professionals in patient care fields to spend time on patient care rather than spending time on their own development and learning. What's more, in those fields, mentoring is often not mentoring at all but knowledge transfer. Of course knowledge transfer is critical, but career mobility, satisfaction and self-care often suffers as a result. In health care, there is a dire need for true mentoring and the kind of connection that mentoring breeds. It is important for health care professionals to be able to pause and reflect, particularly now when there is so much emergency and burnout, which needs to be balanced with the pressure for health care professionals to see patients. There is a tension there. There is a real case of burnout and a frustration that there is no time at the end of the day to focus on their own growth, other than CLE –continuous learning and education courses – where you make sure you are up to date on technical skills. How do we encourage medical and administrative professionals in health care to pause, think about professional development and what it means for the future of health care?

My suspicion is that social care is as dire as health care, if not more. People in both health and social care are suffering. It is presumptuous of me to speak on behalf of the whole of health care and social services in the US, given it is an enormous industry with complex and disparate needs, and is not an area in which I specialize, so I will only share what I observe or know directly. In the Pacific Northwest, where I am, there are huge issues with homelessness, with the economy right now. This is no surprise. Social services organizations here are providing a lot of services and are very stretched. So, there is a need to pause and reflect through mentoring on professional development, and for self-care.

What would you consider to be the current achievements and 'cutting-edge' developments that are happening in mentoring in the US?

I am seeing a greater understanding that mentoring is a tool to achieve more diverse, equitable and inclusive work environments, with organizations dedicating more resources toward that goal. There is a lot more interest now in complementary mentoring (where the mentor is more junior to the mentee). This mentoring is a powerful way to achieve several objectives, including cross-cultural understanding, exposure for younger mentors, the creation of valuable learning relationships in the workplace, intergenerational perspectives and succession planning. We are seeing more mentoring circles of peer mentors. These are more topical than individual mentoring relationships and perhaps therefore there is more interest in diversity, equity and inclusion issues, and influencing leaders. A group of colleagues will get together, talk about their own goals and development, review an article and/or have someone come and speak.

Another exciting thing I expect we will be seeing more of as organizations start to prioritize mentoring, is holding leaders accountable for investing in their own learning and the learning of people who report to them. One way to do this is to require all leaders to have a mentor and to be a leader as a condition of their performance. I don't see it that often, but I think that is going to be a game changer, to see mentoring more organizationally.

What organizations are using intergenerational perspectives and mentoring circles?

All mentoring can create greater intergenerational connections. Recently, I've seen complementary mentoring used at a major global bank, a transportation industry company, and a research institution. Peer circles are used widely but especially by larger companies and can be a great solution when you have more mentees available than mentors. There are a couple of Fortune 500 companies who are using them, where you have the population and space. I have not seen them with health care clients yet, though there may be some who are using them that I am not aware of. I suspect that most are still in the traditional mentoring space and tiptoeing round it for the reasons I outlined earlier.

What do you think has changed in the field of mentoring in the US?

Certainly, generational expectations and assumptions about mentoring have changed. I think about the Traditionalist generation (people in the workforce who were born before 1946 when there really weren't formal mentoring programmes.) It was much more about knowledge transfer, to the extent that it existed, and it was always informal. The Baby Boomer generation ethos was more 'you earn it', and the Generation X (birth years 1965–1980) which followed, is much more likely to view mentoring as something that is nice to have, but that you get over time. Now, there are mentoring programmes and, as I've already noted, availability of mentoring is a criterion for making choices about whether to take or stay at a particular job. To me this change is exciting because mentoring creates access and inclusion.

An informal mentoring culture is terrific, but this increased demand is compelling organizations to consider formal programmes that create matching, structure and accountability around mentoring.

There are three big problems with relying solely on informal mentoring:

1. If mentoring is only informal, you can't harness mentoring as a strategic tool because you don't know who has the relationships.
2. It's hard to measure results where you only have an informal mentoring culture. You won't be able to show causality, or monitor the quality of the mentoring relationships.
3. Organizations that rely solely on informal mentoring perpetuate inequity. People from marginalized populations rarely have the same access to mentors. With formal mentoring you can match across difference, and/or target mentoring to specific groups of employees.

How do you characterize a mentoring culture?

Because mentoring is ultimately a learning relationship, a mentoring culture is one that is committed to and which holds its people accountable for, always learning and growing, and which makes time for, and dedicates resources to, professional development. It's exciting when organizations start to commit to being learning cultures. When it comes down to it, a mentoring culture is a learning culture. Mentoring cultures start to hold their leaders accountable for investing in their learning and the learning of others, with mentoring at the heart of it.

What are they key opportunities and threats for mentoring now and in the future in the US?

Key opportunities include, as I mentioned above, a new generation entering the workforce that appreciates, and demands, mentoring. One of the most exciting opportunities is already underway, and that is the globalization of mentoring. We have many global clients that have implemented mentoring programmes where mentee and mentor are on different continents. Not only does this create greater cultural dexterity, competency and awareness, but it also connects organizations with disparate offices. Additionally, organizations using mentoring as a tool for creating inclusive work environments, and utilizing complementary mentoring to create cross-cultural and intergenerational relationships in the workplace. Of course, there is also the opportunity for the certification and professionalization of mentoring on an individual basis, which is a trend you are already seeing in Europe.

Threats include lack of budget, time and economic issues. A lot of the factors that are contributing to this crisis in social care are continuing to be threats. What's going to happen in terms of the pandemic, and so on; any uncertainty prevents progress organizationally and impacts on the budget as well.

What has to happen is that we have to have growth of both formal and informal mentoring. Informal mentoring is incredibly important – there is something amazing that happens when mentoring grows out of organic interpersonal connection, but the problem with it is that sometimes it is not truly mentoring. Sometimes it's a 'drive by' conversation or just a lunch. It's not that those connections aren't valuable, but they don't have the same kind of deep learning and development that mentoring does. Additionally, when you rely solely on informal mentoring, you don't have the ability to track results, and more importantly, often individuals who feel marginalized in the workplace don't end up in these relationships. Formalizing mentoring allows for greater equity, tracking and accountability to make sure that mentoring is successful and accessible to all.

Lack of strategy and resources around mentoring is another real threat. We often tell clients, don't implement a mentoring programme if you are not going to have the institutional support for it, or integrate it with your overall learning strategy. If you are not going to have accountability around mentoring, it will just be 'castles in the air'.

Finally, I am curious to learn more about the impact of the rise of artificial intelligence on mentoring. It may be an opportunity, a threat, or a combination of both. We don't know what that is going to look like but I do think that it is going to have an effect on the economy, on knowledge transfer, jobs that are available for human beings and on professional development.

In the absence of organizational strategy, isn't it important to just get started on mentoring on an individual basis?

Of course. Individuals must take ownership for their own learning, so it is important to form your own mentoring relationships when a mentoring programme isn't otherwise available. Also, sometimes we use a 'beachhead' approach, by anchoring mentoring in a part of the organization where there is interest and strategy, rather than waiting for it to be adopted more globally. When this happens, we often find that the success in the area that has adopted mentoring will generate interest and enthusiasm for bringing mentoring to a wider audience.

In some of the health and social care settings that you describe, where they are under pressure all the time, we have seen the 'why' to do with recruitment and retention. Some of those organizations have a good mentoring programme which can keep staff from burning out.

A podcast I was listening to focused on the mental health epidemic. As you think of health and social care organizations, it's about all the things you just mentioned plus the mental health of providers as well. With all this pressure, with lives on the line and pressure to bill, it has to have an impact on the well-being of the provider. Mentoring can be a tool to help alleviate all that.

In terms of this chapter, what would be the key things you would want to get across to readers?

The need for mentoring is universal, and I suspect it is more similar in Europe and the US than it is different. The increased demand for mentoring among younger generations and the use of mentoring as a tool to create inclusive work environments are real bright spots. It is exciting to see new modalities like complementary mentoring and peer mentoring being more widely embraced, and to see organizations increasingly buy-in to the reality that having structure and accountability around mentoring will create business and programmatic results. All of this underscores the importance of building competency for mentors and mentees in terms of how to create meaningful mentoring relationships. They can determine the level of structure they want, or the level of formality. But understanding what good mentoring is will help build those relationships.

Do you think that will come about by developing training programmes nationally, locally and within organizations to facilitate that? What are the 'hows' of that?

Organizations must set expectations that their employees at all levels invest in their own learning and in the learning of others, and they must provide the training so that mentors and mentees understand the fundamentals of mentoring. Of course, there are also plenty of people who don't work in organizations that provide such training, but who want to engage in mentoring. For those people, it will be important to seek out training as well. There are a few independent organizations (I'm part of one) that offer training and certification to individuals. To really hone your skills, it is great to find forums for people to connect and share best practices, create community and exchange resources.

There is a view from one of the leads in the coaching world, that mentoring has fallen behind coaching and that coaching is developing a strong evidence base and research that mentoring hasn't, particularly in Europe. He may be right about the European picture he was giving. We felt there is something about mentoring which is really valuable but slightly informal. It's usually unpaid and generative in that sense. Can mentoring develop some of the same strengths as coaching in terms of evidence base but without having to become too tightly constrained by a particular model? This is uplifting because it's saying that there is development going on in mentoring. It tends to be more informal and often driven by the people who need it, rather than coaching, which tends to be driven by a top-down approach.

I think we are already at a place where there is evidence about mentoring in the formal and informal contexts, and that it isn't constrained to a particular model. I disagree that there is not a strong research base in mentoring. In fact, mentoring has been widely researched in various contexts. Here are just a few examples. There is an annual conference at the University of New Mexico called the Mentoring Institute, where people share the research and practices they are doing. My mentoring colleague Christine Pfund is doing some great work in this area at the University of Wisconsin-Madison's *National Research Mentoring Network Coordination Center*. Lillian Eby, at the University of Georgia, has been doing research on mentoring for many years, as has Kathy Kram at Boston University. There is wonderful research coming from other countries as well. Many of my colleagues at the International Mentoring Association are engaged in research around mentoring, and we offer an award at our biennial conference for research in mentoring. The Chronicle of Evidence-Based Mentoring shares ongoing research about the power of mentoring, particularly youth-mentoring.

Are there any other key things you would want written in this chapter about mentoring in the US?

We have talked about organizational mentoring; there is a whole industry around youth mentoring that is thriving here. A lot of organizations are doing some powerful work around mentoring youth. See, for example, Mentor at www.mentoring.org . When you start mentoring youth widely, when the young people become adults they value mentoring widely and begin to pass it on. This is very hopeful for mentoring. When you are talking about mentoring an 11-year-old in the inner city, it's a slow drip to that youth passing it on. The beauty of a slow drip is that eventually the bucket gets filled.

As an example, January is National Mentoring Month. To honour that month, at the Center for Mentoring Excellence, we did a series of interviews with long-standing mentoring pairs. One of the mentors was Briauna Wills, an African American woman in her early 20s who grew up in inner city Baltimore, Maryland. She started an afterschool mentoring programme called Young Queens in Training to provide supportive services to girls ages 8–18 years. I interviewed Briauna and her mentee, Brooke Woods. They had a really nurturing relationship while Brooke was in high school and she is now entering a profession of her own. I have no doubt Brooke will pay it forward to another young woman. You can imagine the ripple effect on mentoring with programmes like these. Here's a link to that interview.

Is there anything else you would like to add that you want to include in the chapter?

Mentoring is happening in all sorts of contexts here in the US. As part of our National Mentoring Month interview series, in addition to Briauna and Brooke, whom I mentioned earlier, we interviewed several other long-standing mentoring pairs. One was Judge Walter Rice, and his mentee, Bishop Mark McGuire. Mark, by his own admission, had made some bad choices as a youth and ended up appearing in Judge Rice's courtroom in Ohio for sentencing. Judge Rice knew Mark was a good person who had made some bad choices, and when he sentenced him, he told Mark that when he was done serving his time, he would owe the community. Mark never forgot Judge Rice and several years later, started a non-profit organization and began creating real positive change in his community. He sought out the Judge as his mentor and they have stayed in contact over many decades, each learning from the other and gaining a lot from the relationship, despite difference in education, religion and generation. Mark has since been a mentor to many others. This was one of the most inspirational examples of the power of mentoring I have seen. You can watch that interview here.

Another example is Chevy Cook and Jim Perkins, two amazing leaders who met at West Point Military Academy. They developed a relationship after Chevy offered to be available as a resource for any cadet who needed him, and Jim took him up on that offer. What resulted is a friendship, reciprocal mentorship and a non-profit called Military Mentors that Jim and Chevy founded and Chevy now leads. This is a terrific example of the importance of creating your own learning relationships and offering up mentorship in a genuine way. You can watch that interview here.

As I dig deeper into this work, I am learning how mentoring appears in many contexts and it is exciting to see it pervading all aspects of society. It is exciting to see it play out in all sorts of ways that will make a big difference for the next generation.

What is it about mentoring that it is taken forward in some areas but in other areas it is stalling, and what is needed to change that?

There are some industries where formal mentoring hasn't taken hold in the same way. I haven't seen it as effectively in the legal profession or, as we discussed earlier, in health care and the social services. When people are compensated (and profits are measured) by hours worked, it can be difficult to prioritize mentoring. Often in high-pressure fields, such as health care, there is a tension between investing time and energy into mentoring and meeting whatever the objectives of your job are in terms of financial incentive or patient care. That can be really difficult. Sometimes you have to slow down to speed up. People will be more effective if they set aside that time. How to change it? Rely on informal mentoring and mentoring moments. Create your own learning relationships and invest in learning what it takes to create successful mentoring relationships, and then celebrate and share the successes. Eventually, others will see the benefits and it will take hold more widely.

Chapter 32
Toward a Developmental Mentoring Approach for China

Tony Dickel & Michelle Chan

Summary

Failure to set powerful, inspiring goals and then measure progress while understanding and working with 'interference' is one of the most common causes of corporate coaching and mentoring failure. This is particularly true in China where complexities relating to individuals' surrounding cultural, social and family systems tend to have a more profound impact on development than in the West.

This chapter addresses how working toward a 'well-formed goal' (WFG), taking into account cultural, familial, social, mental, emotional, behavioural and a broad range of other factors, provides a strong image of desired outcomes and can anticipate the various waypoints in the journey toward these outcomes. This structured yet highly flexible process supports both mentees and mentors to keep their goals, desired outcomes and resources available to the mind in the very moments when obstacles and interference occur (the 'Moments of Choice', or MoCs), providing a strong beacon to guide action in the midst of the tumultuous change and systemic complexity that typifies modern China.

Background: Retrieving 'lost' mentoring in China

Mentoring is seen by many in China as a Western innovation, which had been imported to China in recent years. This not entirely true. Studies suggest that Western models of mentoring theory and practice, with Chinese characteristics, have been successfully adapted to and work well in China (Yang et al., 2011).

Giving a little historical context, mentoring in China flourished at the time of the Spring and Autumn period (770–476 BCE). Emperor Wu (156–87 BCE) of the Han dynasty later implemented policies dismissing all but Confucianism to consolidate the authority of the government. Mentors thereby lost their standing in the culture with hierarchical and paternalistic leadership styles dominating the country until the current generation.

Leaders born during the 1980s and 1990s, have grown up in an era of reform and opening. As more and more of these individuals step into leadership roles, older Chinese leaders have needed to become more responsive to their demands for more accommodating leadership styles within the framework of culturally determined ground rules.

Complexity

China is experiencing profound, simultaneous and accelerating shifts in economic, political, social, technological, environmental and demographic conditions. This is creating a high degree of overwhelm and demand upon the attention of leaders and their teams. This overwhelm distracts leaders from being able to keep their eye on the prize and remember what they really care about, resulting in aspirations, outcomes, goals and necessary actions being lost to the mind at the MoC.

The second dimension of complexity to consider is the impact of the social/family systems environment. Any mentoring or coaching programme which does not respect and consider these factors is doomed to either fail or at least be less effective than would be the case if the mentoring journey includes these factors!

It is our view that success in mentoring and coaching against this backdrop of complexity implies being unhurried with goal setting, instead allowing for liminality and emergence as unconscious and systemic factors become more known. Being too hurried with this part of the process risks missing developmental opportunity, creating stress and negatively impacting -efficacy. The process set out below is paradoxical. It puts more emphasis on the goal-setting phase, yet allows for continuous refinement and change as self-awareness improves.

Introduction to the 'well-formed goal' process

Moving on personal change or improvement goals in the midst of such profound overwhelm depends on being able to create a strong image of the desired outcome state linked to a 'felt' positive emotional prediction. Also necessary is an 'in the moment' awareness of potential interference, together with a mentally rehearsed response strategy to such interference. The WFG process makes all the above 'available to the mind' in MoCs, even when life, in all its busyness, gets in the way. This in turn provides a strong beacon to inspire/guide action in the moment (Pally, 2007)! Given the systemic complexity partly driven by cultural drivers, this is especially so in the East.

It has been noted by other authors that successful mentoring relationships in China are constructed with awareness of the impact of systemic, including cultural, issues. In particular, with awareness of the pervasive influence that the legacy of China's Confucian roots continues to wield (Zhou, Lapointe, & Zhou, 2019), both in terms of the programmes as a whole and the individual mentor–mentee relationships. This chapter deals primarily with an approach to help create the conditions for success inside an individual mentor–mentee programme.

Moving on a developmental goal may need us to bring awareness to subconsciously held hidden goals (Kegan & Lahey, 2009, pp. 35-42) so that conscious choices of action can be made at the MoC. Such hidden goals are often based upon individual interpretations of social constructs operating within a culture. We call this cultivating 'actionable self-awareness'. This means awareness that one can actually apply at the MoC.

The approach is highly developmental in nature and is best suited to situations where desired behavioural changes require development in the form of increasing maturity, wisdom, or, as Robert Kegan calls it 'mental complexity' (Kegan & Lahey, 2009, pp. 13-20).

We have set out some extensively field-tested questions which you can ask mentees to get them thinking about their goals and aspirations, rather than only problems or remedies (Lawley & Tompkins, 2012), and to have the consequences of movement toward the goal 'sink into the bones'. The WFG process is synthesized from the traditions of neuro-linguistic programming (NLP) (Knight, 2020), Integral Theory (Wilber, 2005), and behavioural and cognitive neuroscience (Barrett, 2017; Berkman, 2018; Boyatzis, Rochford, & Taylor, 2015; Compton, 2003; Pally, 2007), together with many other influences from the mindfulness, positive psychology and third wave cognitive behavioural traditions.

Where does WFG fit?

The WFG process is one of a number of ways that we help a mentee to work steadily toward a clear goal that is capable of inspiring the necessary action/behaviour in what we call the MoC. Note that the fact that the goal is 'well-formed' doesn't mean it will not change over time. Goals are often liminal and elusive early on in the process and if they *do* change, it is often due to the increasing clarity of what's needed, what might interfere and what's needed to meet interference, at the MoC. It may be that the mentee has become aware that there is something else that needs attention before the mentee can move forward with desired behaviours or actions. There may be a cognitive or emotional process blocking desired behaviour. A common example in China is where a mentee needs to learn to speak their truth in important meetings but keeps being derailed by the *perceived* need to respect the authority of others or to protect the relational field. The WFG process helps a mentee anticipate and rehearse a response to such anxieties.

Characteristics of a WFG

The essence of a WFG

In essence, a WFG has four main characteristics:

Succinct and concise

While we often say that it is emotion that drives behaviour not language, language is important because it points to and can recall emotion which, once recalled, underpins behaviour. As such, we encourage mentees to articulate their goals using concise and clear language which is easy to remember. But this isn't the real point. The real point is that remembering the goal…

…brings up a (positive) emotional charge

The idea is that when a goal is brought to mind, there is a cascade of 'remembering'. Resources, mind-states and, most importantly, a predicted emotional experience that serve to power the necessary behaviours in the moment.

In essence, the mentee is creating a memory of an emotional prediction which sinks into the mind, making it meaningful and more accessible in those key moments of choice (Pally, 2007).

The case of Richard

Let's consider the case of someone we will call Richard. He was receiving mentoring related to his ability to manage performance within his team (his mentor was the previous leader of the team, whom Richard respected greatly). The challenge was that his mentoring goals did not connect with him emotionally. He hadn't resolved the real dilemma of how to show up when faced with underperformance in his team, given his interpretation of the cultural imperative to preserve relationships at all costs. He had been on performance management training but his mindset was not supportive! At the MoC, he made unconscious predictions about how he would feel if others were upset with him, driving avoidance behaviour (see Hayes, Strosahl, and Wilson (2011) for more on this).

Includes awareness of interference

Given the complexity described above it has become very difficult for there to be immediate clarity on what might enable or interfere with progress towards mentoring outcomes. In **Richard's case**, interference was primarily motivational in nature. He, theoretically, had the skill, and the will, to do better with this area but in the moment was hijacked by worries about what might happen if such performance management were not taken well by the manager. WFGs anticipate what might get in the way, not only physically and structurally, but also behaviourally, emotionally, culturally and mentally. And then...

Includes anticipated response to interference

...when such interference arises, the mentee develops response strategies that can be executed at the MoC.

Note that the 'immediate' response strategy may simply be the recognition of the need to practice recognizing and managing the limiting stories running in the moment.

Getting to a WFG

Once a mentoring goal is genuinely well-formed then movement occurs smoothly and (relatively) easily as interference is mentally rehearsed and then dealt with in the moment. In this way, the mentee is less likely to be hijacked by old 'reactive' patterns, keeping them stuck in mental (and therefore behavioural) habits (Macdonald & Muran, 2021).

Initial goals will likely change along the way as mentees become more aware of what is most important to them as they deal with the interference that inevitably arises on the journey, or as mentees realise that there are preconditions to the achievement of the original goal(s). Resolving such preconditions may become goals in themselves (Gollwitzer & Oettingen, 2020).

The case of Jane

An example of this is leader, Jane, who was working toward the outcome of improving empowerment, delegation and communication. It wasn't that she didn't want to change, but more that she felt unsafe experimenting with new behaviour. She was intolerant of the risk of something going wrong if she didn't manage situations closely. She carried around a psychological immune system that kept her stuck in her old patterns of thinking, feeling and doing in the moment (Kegan & Lahey, 2009)! She also had a secondary interfering belief that she had to look after her people and prevent them from tripping up. These stories defeated her best attempts to change.

Jane later realised that the initial goal was to build awareness of the pattern that was driving her existing behaviour and to remember that she was 'safe to practice' using her skills at the MoCs.

The SCRIP process

The SCRIP (Specificity, Context, Resources, Impact, Possibility) process is a way to ensure that a change goal is well formed yet allows for emergence and liminality. The process comprises a number of elements (Figure 32.1):

Figure 32.1: The SCRIP model.

1. The core of the process is to elicit **Specificity** and succinctness, as far as possible, so a mentee can easily bring to mind 'the what and the why' of what's needed in an MoC.

2. What, indeed, are the key moments where there is an opportunity to practice new behaviours (**Context**)?

3. What positive outcomes might happen (and what negatives are less likely to) (**Impact**)?

4. What might help/interfere as I try to make the changes needed (**Resources**)?

5. What will it be like when this (change) occurs (**Specificity** and **Impact** connecting with emotional predictions)?

6. The required actions are actually doable by the mentee themself (**'Possible?'**).

If a change/improvement goal is not clear and well-articulated it will likely not be actioned in the MoC. This isn't in itself a problem, it's simply an opportunity to make the goal 'better formed'. This is important as failure to achieve change goals may otherwise create a sense of hopelessness or a feeling that the person cannot change or achieve goals (Bandura, 1997; Gollwitzer & Oettingen, 2020). Check that the goal has enough specificity so that it can be remembered easily in the MoC. Examples of goals that are not specific enough are *'I want to be happier'*, *'I want others to respect me'* or *'I want to be less emotional around others'.* Examples of more specific goals might be *'I want to become better at managing my own sales call reluctance with clients whom I assess to be resistant* (improvement goal) *so that I might to earn enough money over 5 years to buy a spacious and comfortable home for my family, send my daughter to a great school and take a trip around the world* (outcome). *Then I will feel as if I have done something meaningful in my life* (impact).' Another example might be, *'I want to show up with others in fair but appropriately tough way* (improvement goal) *that is likely to engender respect* (outcome).'

Further work may associate the goal with sensory anchors (What will an envisioned future look/feel sound like?; What will the mentee be doing, and with whom?; How might others be feeling and behaving?) so that the goal is likely to be remembered in those, key MoCs.

Specificity

- What is the goal, **specifically?**
- How will progress be measured?
- How will you remember what you need to do to progress this (in the MoC)?

If an individual session goal is NOT in line with the programme goal (which does happen) then a more exhaustive SCRIP questioning process MAY be appropriate. Mentors need to be sure that the mentee is actually working on the thing that is *genuinely* the most important thing for them for that session. Failure to do this will undermine the programme. Of course, if other things 'keep coming up', then it may be necessary to re-examine commitment to or attainability of the original programme goals.

Context

Meaning is often defined by context. In broad terms, this is the 'when?', 'by when?', 'where?', 'how?', and 'with whom?' of the goal. The mentor should have the mentee talk about the various contexts that surround their goal.

There are four main kinds of contexts (REST):

- relational – with whom?
- emotional – when I am feeling...
- situational – where?/what?/in which 'role' that I play in my life...?
- time.

Consideration of the various applicable contexts makes the goal more specific and motivational as the image of its attainment becomes better anchored.

Note: There can often be many relevant contexts. For example, *'I would like to be more patient with my staff* (relational) *when I feel frustrated* (emotional) *due to poor performance on important projects* (situational).'

Resources

This is a check on the various resources available which will enable movement on the goal, or interference which will inhibit. It is here where cultural factors can be explored in depth to tease out areas of potential support or interference and is best done early to ensure mentee awareness of skills, knowledge, time, mindsets, relationships, systems, and other internal and external resources being available or missing. It can be useful to use a model such as Wilber's Integral Model (Wilber, 2000) to help ensure that 'everything and everyone' that may enable or interfere with progress is considered.

Note that mentors may need also to check in with their own resources. The mentor's own view of the relationship and the systems in which it exists will impact on how the mentor shows up, particularly under agitation driven by subconscious drivers, and 'hidden' goals (e.g., the need to take responsibility for the progress of the mentee).

Some ideas

Some questions the mentor can ask related to resources are set out in Figure 32.2 in an adapted integral format, which ensures coverage of 'everyone and everything' that may support of interfere. The point is that holding this framework in mind can help the mentor develop questions from first principles to support the growth of the mentee.

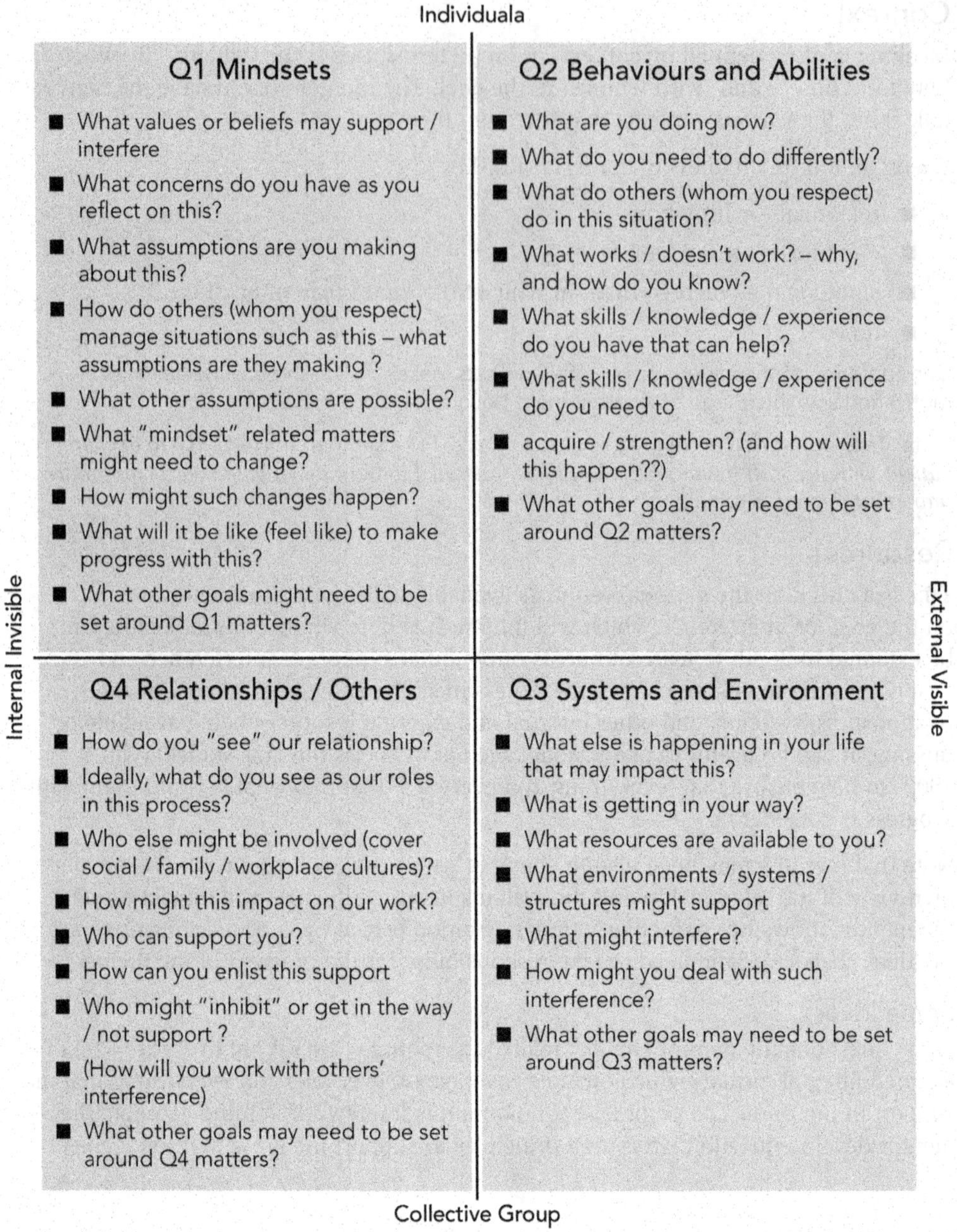

Individuala

Q1 Mindsets	Q2 Behaviours and Abilities
■ What values or beliefs may support / interfere ■ What concerns do you have as you reflect on this? ■ What assumptions are you making about this? ■ How do others (whom you respect) manage situations such as this – what assumptions are they making ? ■ What other assumptions are possible? ■ What "mindset" related matters might need to change? ■ How might such changes happen? ■ What will it be like (feel like) to make progress with this? ■ What other goals might need to be set around Q1 matters?	■ What are you doing now? ■ What do you need to do differently? ■ What do others (whom you respect) do in this situation? ■ What works / doesn't work? – why, and how do you know? ■ What skills / knowledge / experience do you have that can help? ■ What skills / knowledge / experience do you need to ■ acquire / strengthen? (and how will this happen??) ■ What other goals may need to be set around Q2 matters?
Q4 Relationships / Others	Q3 Systems and Environment
■ How do you "see" our relationship? ■ Ideally, what do you see as our roles in this process? ■ Who else might be involved (cover social / family / workplace cultures)? ■ How might this impact on our work? ■ Who can support you? ■ How can you enlist this support ■ Who might "inhibit" or get in the way / not support ? ■ (How will you work with others' interference) ■ What other goals may need to be set around Q4 matters?	■ What else is happening in your life that may impact this? ■ What is getting in your way? ■ What resources are available to you? ■ What environments / systems / structures might support ■ What might interfere? ■ How might you deal with such interference? ■ What other goals may need to be set around Q3 matters?

Internal Invisible — *External Visible*

Collective Group

Figure 32.2: Integral exploration ideas (adapted from Wilber's integral model).

Questions:

■ What are you learning about your situation/your goal/yourself as you reflect on this exploration?

■ What do you want do with this learning (pointing to any goals, actions, practices or thinking that might be useful)?

It is when exploring resources and interference that it is often discovered that original goals need to be modified or further clarified, or that the original goal is, in fact, an outcome of movement on other goals that in themselves need to be further explored.

In the case of Richard, he realised through this exploration that he was being blocked by the narrative that was creating 'experiential avoidance'. He realised that working with this narrative and creating a reframed, alternative narrative was on the critical path to his being able to bring appropriate behaviour to his performance management conversations.

Impact

A WFG includes awareness of its impact for the mentee's life or the lives of others, connecting to a (positive) emotional prediction. A strong awareness or 'remembering', in the MoC, of this prediction provides the fuel to power the mentee past their personal 'immunity to change' (Markus, 2016), thereby making behavioural change more likely. The exploration of impact also deals with an exploration of what the mentee might need to let go of and what this might cost them, often manifesting as a need to tolerate a moment of discomfort, now, in order to have the chance for some benefit in the longer term.

It can be useful to look at this systemically using a simple framework which we have created called the 'matrix of wise attention' (Figure 32.3). This begs the question: *'What is for the best, not just for me, now, but for us, longer term?'* With such awareness, the mentee can then zoom out and practice orienting the mind to a longer-term, us-focused, mode of attention, motivating constructive behaviour in the direction of what is 'wise'.

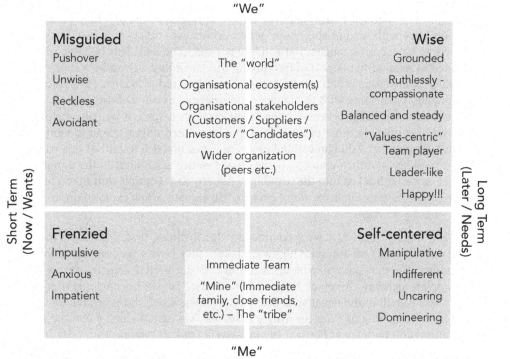

Figure 32.3: Matrix of wise attention.

> ## The case of Amy
>
> Amy, head of the social media business unit of a major Chinese tech company, had received feedback that she 'needs to grow her people through better delegation and empowerment', thereby enabling her to focus on more strategic matters. She is assigned a mentor who is a new general manager from their network security business unit. However, this desired outcome was requested by Amy's manager, rather than by Amy herself. Although she seemed to agree with her manager on desired outcomes, the mentor has many of the qualities that Amy's manager wants her to cultivate, and she had been well trained in the skills of delegation and empowerment, the mentoring ultimately failed as she was unable to envision positive outcomes for the 'system', instead being overcome by the short-term discomfort of empowering others to act.

At the MoCs, she was stuck because she felt unsafe letting go of her need to overmanage situations and do everything herself. Her 'immunity to change' was creating intolerance to the risk that something might go wrong if she changed behaviour. She was telling herself that if something went wrong then she would be held accountable and, forever unable to recover, would be fired, not be able to find another job and then 'look bad' in front of family, friends and others (often a dreaded outcome in the Chinese cultural context). In the MoCs, she failed to see the longer-term picture, i.e., that her bosses would likely appreciate her attention to the practice of empowerment/delegation, thereby seeing her as having high potential for future development, and that the worst-case outcomes she was predicting were either highly unlikely or could be mitigated if and when they arose. As a result of not seeing impact clearly in the MoC, she travelled down the same path again and again, on an 'autopilot highway' that leads her to drive off a cliff!

Applying this to **Richard's case**, his avoidance was related to the prediction that he couldn't live with the possibility that relationships with others may be damaged if he were to have conversations that actually needed to be had. This behaviour is misguided in relation to his goal of developing this capability, driven by a short-term intolerance of upsetting others, and creating discomfort and avoidance behaviour. Exploring and connecting with the longer-term systemic benefits of the desired behaviour and reminding/rehearsing the language skills helped. It was also helpful to allow him to connect to those of his values that he wanted to practice in the moment. One such aspirational value he wanted to develop and practice as part of this was the value of presence and then courage; being able to notice discomfort in the moment, how he was being hooked into the avoidance pattern and working with this. The mentor used a *'what's the worst thing about…'* downward arrow exploration to help 'install' this awareness!

Looking at impact in the way we recommend helps mentees, first, to see, and then, to take the exit roads off autopilot highways before they have gone past the point of no return. The new path may be unclear, but taking it is NOT actually unsafe. The autopilot highway, driven by 'immunity to change', creates behaviours that are actually less safe than the negative predicted outcomes which those behaviours are meant to be protecting us from (in **Amy's case**, she was actually being blocked from future promotion because of her fear of empowering and delegating)!!

The big idea behind the exploration of impact is to help create congruence between desires, values and needs, a mental rehearsal of response(s) to 'interference' (Table 32.1).

Table 32.1: Sample impact enquiry.

Question	Comment
On a scale of 1-10, how important is this to you?	If below 7/10, may need to make further enquiries. Progress may be unlikely.
What happens if there is no change (feelings, relationships, outcomes etc.)?	Instills commitment to the change needed. Explore comprehensively – what will be the outcomes for you and for others, and how will this feel?
What's the best thing about making progress with this?	Use the 'upward ladder'. Repeat question until mentee can no longer answer or says something like "I don't know but I just know it will feel good"!
What's the worst thing about not progressing this?	Again, instills a sense of motivation.
Is it worth what it might take for you to make the changes that you require?	Mentally rehearsing the things that may interfere in the moment and checking if they can live with the cost of overcoming this interference.
What might you have to give up or 'let go of' to do this?	Often relates to a belief that has been tightly held for some time which creates 'experiential avoidance'.
What about others? (Gains or losses in the short, medium and long term – see 'matrix of wise attention').	Helps mentee to see into a longer term focused view of outcomes.
What else will happen? What won't happen?	Widening the view further.
In what way is this meaningful for you?	
Again, how committed are you to making this change (on a scale of 1-10)?	Double check at the end of exploration of impact.

Possibility

This is simply about ensuring that the change goal is under the control of the mentee – in other words, that they can feasibly do something about it!

For example, if a stated goal is *'I want my direct reports to support me better'*, then this, as stated, is not under the mentee's control, whereas *'I want to find ways to better coach, mentor, train and support my direct reports so that they are in a position to take on more responsibility'* may be.

One thing to watch here is the time context. Mentees have different relationships with time. Many want everything to happen tomorrow! Others realise that, given time and patience, more is potentially under their influence. The 'matrix of wise attention' can help structure skilful enquiry about this area.

Some ideas for possibility are shown in Table 32.2.

Table 32.2: Enquiry of possibility.

Question	Comment
What needs to happen so that that might happen? (keep asking the question until you get to a first step the mentee can take)... or	We call tis technique "backwards laddering" and brings the mentee quickly to what they, themselves, need to do.
What might you need to do differently so that might happen?	Again, establishes ownership for the practice goals that are being contemplated.
What part of this is this under your control or influence	Again, creates a sense of personal accountability.
Can this happen?	Begins to get to real challenges that the mentee needs to overcome if movement is to occur.
What is the first step you can take which might lead to this?	Points towards an initial behavioural experiment to "test" the goal.
If you **can** do this, then what's been holding you back (this question points to both impact (see similar question under impact) and also points to the fact that there may be something else getting in the way (such as the goal not being under the mentees spere of possibility).	When asking this question, if the mentee is self-aware enough (as apposed to being entangled in their cultural narrative), they may tell you a story that points towards some of their interpretations of cultural norms. If they are entangled in the story, rather than able to "see" the story, they may find this question difficult to answer in which case one can share stories or observations from own or others' experience.

Final questions: – Where the 'rubber meets the road'

The idea with this form of questioning is that the mentee may realise that they are not prepared to give up that which is preventing them from making the changes they need in order to be happier or more successful in their work or lives.

Challenge the mentee by asking:

- 'If you could remember the complete content of our conversation in every moment, would you make the necessary choices of action in the direction of your goals?';
- 'What is it that you would need to bring back to mind in future 'moments of choice'?; and...
- '...so, how might you remember?'

The final three questions often point toward revised goals (for example, cultivation or strengthening of such core mental qualities or values as patience, presence, curiosity, acceptance, courage, etc.).

Final summarization

Finally, see if the mentee is able to articulate the goal as a sentence or two that incorporates what they want, together with what happens when they 'get' it ... for example, *'I want to learn to allow others, where appropriate, to fully express themselves without interruption so I can become a more empowering leader'*.

Remember, it isn't language that moves us to action, it is emotion. The goal of the WFG process is to define mentoring goals in such a way as to help the mentee bring back the feelings they had at the point of setting the goal. In this way, they are more likely to take the required actions, at the right time.

Conclusion

Mentoring with Chinese characteristics has great potential as a developmental intervention in China, if done well, using processes that allow the mentee to explore the gamut of their concerns, and navigate the dilemmas thrown up by the need to integrate cultural imperatives into the need for organizational performance.

Further study designed to explore how the psychological needs of younger Chinese leaders can integrate with their economic ambitions would, we are sure, fascinate!

References

Bandura, A. (1997). *Self-efficacy. Harvard Mental Health Letter*, **13**, 4–6.

Barrett, L. F. (2017). *How Emotions are Made: The Secret Life of the Brain*: Pan Macmillan.

Berkman, E. T. (2018). *The neuroscience of goals and behavior change. Consulting Psychology Journal: Practice and Research*, **70**(1), 28.

Boyatzis, R. E., Rochford, K., & Taylor, S. N. (2015). *The role of the positive emotional attractor in vision and shared vision: Toward effective leadership, relationships, and engagement. Frontiers in Psychology*, **6**, 670.

Compton, R. J. (2003). *The interface between emotion and attention: A review of evidence from psychology and neuroscience. Behavioral and Cognitive Neuroscience Reviews*, **2**(2), 115–129.

Gollwitzer, P. M., & Oettingen, G. (2020). *Implementation intentions*. In M. D. Gellman (Ed.), *Encyclopedia of Behavioral Medicine* (pp. 1159–1164). Springer.

Hayes, S. C., Strosahl, K. D., & Wilson, K. G. (2011). *Acceptance and Commitment Therapy: The Process and Practice of Mindful Change*: Guilford Press.

Kegan, R., & Lahey, L. L. (2009). *Immunity to Change: How to Overcome It and Unlock Potential in Yourself and Your Organization*. Harvard Business Press.

Knight, S. (2020). *NLP at Work: The Difference that Makes the Difference*: Hachette UK.

Lawley, J., & Tompkins, P. (2012). *REPROCess: Modelling attention. Neuro Linguistic Programming*, **5**.

Macdonald, J., & Muran, C. J. (2021). *The reactive therapist: The problem of interpersonal reactivity in psychological therapy and the potential for a mindfulness-based program focused on 'mindfulness-in-relationship' skills for therapists. Journal of Psychotherapy Integration*, **31**(4), 452–467.

Markus, I. (2016). *Efficacy of immunity-to-change coaching for leadership development. The Journal of Applied Behavioral Science*, **52**(2), 215–230.

Pally, R. (2007). *The predicting brain: Unconscious repetition, conscious reflection and therapeutic change. The International Journal of Psychoanalysis*, **88**(4), 861–881.

Wilber, K. (2000). *Integral Psychology*. Shambhala Publications.

Wilber, K. (2005). *Introduction to integral theory and practice. AQAL: Journal of Integral Theory and Practice*, **1**(1).

Yang, L.-Q., Xu, X., Allen, T. D., Shi, K., Zhang, X., & Lou, Z. (2011). *Mentoring in China: Enhanced understanding and association with occupational stress. Journal of Business and Psychology*, **26**(4), 485–499.

Zhou, A. J., Lapointe, É., & Zhou, S. S. (2019). *Understanding mentoring relationships in China: Towards a Confucian model. Asia Pacific Journal of Management*, **36**(2), 415–444.

Chapter 33
Mentoring in the Middle East: Research and Findings

Clare Beckett-McInroy

This chapter presents research on the format, experience, types and volume of mentoring across the Middle East to ascertain a picture of cultural, religious and other nuances at play. It addresses both public and private sector experiences. The importance of mentors is shared in al-Qur'an (surah al-Tawbah 9:71) where mentors play important roles in helping and guiding people to do what is moral and to avoid negative thoughts and activities (Fariza, 2005). In general, research in the Middle East is limited across research areas, and especially research related to health care and mentoring, compared to other geographical locations – a thorough literature review was unavailable. Noteworthy research includes:

- Aderibigbe et al. (2015) examined peer mentoring for undergraduate students in a private university in the United Arab Emirates, stating that peer mentoring can be strengthened with recognition, more training and clarification of expectations.

- Alhadlaq et al. (2019) considered the nuances of e-mentoring teenagers and found that co-design with the mentor and the mentee in the initial stages of mentoring increased impact. It was also noted that mentoring programmes can help to further develop and fine-tune professional identity formation.

- Alkhatnai's (2021) research in Saudi Arabia on mentoring in higher education identified that mentees benefited only when trust was established and that mentors sometimes confused their mentorship role with that of supervising, rather than guiding, their mentees.

- Alqahtani et al. (2021) conducted a large-scale survey with College of Medicine Bachelor of Medicine and Bachelor of Surgery students at King Khalid University, in Saudi Arabia, from June 2018 to May 2019 with the research question, *'To what extent are medical students benefitting from mentoring?'* Both mentors and mentees shared that meeting times, time pressures, mentor/mentee disinterest, non-commitment and lack of awareness of the programme inhibited effective mentoring. 67% of students (mentees) stated that they benefited from mentoring. One-on-one mentoring was preferred by most students (82.5%). Only 68.6% of students had satisfactory contact with their tutors. The research concluded that, *'An essential instrument in the career development of a medical student is mentoring. A goal-oriented and well-planned mentoring program is not only beneficial for mentees but also the mentors. Strategies should be planned, especially in the developing countries, to motivate the students and the teacher equally for the success of such programs.'*

- Mishkin and Johnson (2020) explored group mentoring in international development projects in the Middle East and found that '...*mentors used approaches that applied transformational leadership concepts in the form of idealised influence, inspirational motivation, individualised consideration and intellectual stimulation'.*

- Pattisson (2020), from The British University of Egypt, explored teacher trainees' understandings of mentoring within a Middle Eastern Bachelor of Education programme, with particular reference to Arab women. There were clear overlaps with findings from other geographical and cultural contexts related to perceptions of mentoring. It was also noted that an understanding of the nature and influence of social assumptions is needed. This helps to avoid misinterpretation related to trainees' unwillingness to engage with the mentoring process fully. Examples of this include: more listening than speaking to a mentor; lifting one's chin up in disapproval as well as discomfort in asking for support (Qatar Foundation International, 2023); and mentoring by non-mahram men (people with whom marriage is prohibited) with Arab women in public places (Mentor Global Consultants, 2022), which also has implications in health care relations.

- Toner (2004) conducted a Middle East-wide study where trained mentoring facilitators were hired to support English as a Foreign Language teachers in promoting effective collaboration. *'Peer mentoring appears to shift the emphasis from a defined body of subject knowledge and one specific training to skill sharing in the workplace and to balancing pedagogic knowledge with subject knowledge and combining strengths offered by non-native-speaking and native-speaking teachers...'.*

Defining mentoring

The present author used the European Mentoring and Coaching Council (EMCC) definition of mentoring as a frame of reference:

> *Mentoring is a learning relationship, involving the sharing of skills, knowledge, and expertise between a mentor and mentee through developmental conversations, experience sharing, and role modelling. The relationship may cover a wide variety of contexts and is an inclusive two-way partnership for mutual learning that values differences.*

(EMCC, 2022)

Mentors act as role models and sounding boards for their mentees, offering guidance to help them reach their goals (Association of Talent Development, 2022).

The following definitions, in terms of types of mentoring, were shared with respondents for alignment and classification:

- **One-on-one mentoring:** This type of mentoring is the most traditional of all. Only the mentor and mentee are involved, and it is usually a more experienced individual paired with a less experienced or much younger mentee.

- **Group mentoring:** In this model, one or several mentors work with a group of mentees. Schools and youth programmes often apply this model because there may not be enough time or resources to have one mentor for each participant.

- **Peer mentoring:** Participants in this model are from the same role or department or have shared or similar experiences, whether in their professional or personal lives. These peers pair up to offer support to each other. This can be a group or a one-on-one mentoring relationship.

- **Distance or e-mentoring:** With our current technology, the mentorship relationship no longer has to be face-to-face. Using online software or even email, participants in this type of mentoring can connect virtually without losing their personal touch.

- **Reverse mentoring:** This mentoring relationship is flipped from the traditional model. Instead of a senior professional mentoring a more junior employee, the junior employee mentors a more senior professional. This relationship is usually for the younger or more junior professional to teach the skills, a new application or technology to the more senior one.

- **Speed mentoring:** This type of mentoring is a play on speed dating and usually occurs as part of a corporate event or conference. The mentee has a series of one-on-one conversations with different mentors and usually moves from one mentor to the next after a brief meeting. The mentee should come prepared with questions for advice from the senior-level professionals.

- **Informal mentoring:** Informal mentoring may take place among professionals and with families and communities. In an informal environment, mentees may set goals, yet measurement may be looser. Relationships and processes tend to be unstructured.

- **Formal mentoring:** Formal mentoring relationships include actionable and measurable goals, defined and set with determined requirements.

Research method

Data was gathered through a survey using snowball sampling over four months where existing connections of the author provided referrals to 'recruit' further respondents – namely those that have lived and worked or presently live and work in the Middle East (Kirchherr & Charles, 2018). Data was collected from fifty professionals, thirty-six presently working in private sector organizations and fourteen working in the public sector. The data provided ten themes for analysis and sentiment analysis, with a dictionary of negative, neutral or positive words used for examination. Further semi-structured interviews and email correspondence was completed with two senior health professionals, specifically in Qatar, who showed particular interest in the research.

Findings

Theme One: Experiences of mentoring received by respondents

The respondents shared a range of mentoring experiences, and many found that it was '...*very helpful...*', with informal mentoring being more prevalent than formal mentoring in the public sector. Informal mentoring programmes are often implemented to complement and strengthen formal mentoring programmes in order to achieve organizational strategies and goals (Hansford & Ehrich, 2006).

It was noted that some of the respondents were unclear about the differences between mentoring and coaching as they shared that, for example, they had received '... *coaching [and] academic coaching...*'. This was more evident from respondents working in the public sector (N = 9 out of 14) than the private sector (N = 3 out of 36).

> *Coaching/executive coaching/academic research supervisor...*

> *There has also been an impact on me, whether I am the mentor or mentee, which I consider to be positive...*

Interview data identified time spent beneficially in the service of the mentee's development for their job role as 'positive'.

> *Through career advice, education, five years as a mentor...*

> *One year, with a CFO, finance sector the impact was more confidence and [to] broaden ideas...*

> *...academic mentoring for fourteen years through postgraduate studies...*

> *I am a mentor currently to three colleagues through a work-related scheme, and informally assisting three others on a personal basis (from prior friendships – mainly offspring of friends seeking similar career options). I have also used two informal mentors to assist and evaluate my career development options over many years, one of whom has now left us, and the other is a former colleague...*

> *I had amazing informal mentors in my job who guided me through the many difficulties related to local and corporate culture. The impact of having mentors was absolutely vital to understand how to navigate the complexity of the workplace, understand my role, my areas for improvement and my strengths, and unlock my potential. Thanks to mentoring, I reached a high level in the corporate ladder and became more confident and aware of the contribution I bring to the decision-making table...*

One public sector respondent shared that:

> *I have been mentored and I have mentored a large number of young people over the past twenty years – in educational and informal settings....*

Mentoring took place for personal and professional topics *'...informally and more formally from senior colleagues [in the private sector] in the financial sector...'*. It was considered *'...very useful and thought-provoking...'*.

A Middle East Public Relations Association (MEPRA) member shared that their mental health survey conducted in April 2020 revealed that *'...more than a third of our industry's professionals felt they were not well supported by companies with regards to their health and well-being...'* and this is one reason why this association, among others, provides formal mentoring.

Theme Two: Awareness of mentoring that other people have participated in

Subtheme: By seniors

Being mentored by 'seniors' and managers was mentioned considerably, *'I was mentored by an experienced manager who was supportive to me and I really benefited a lot from that...'*. Training for mentors was mentioned on three occasions, *'I have witnessed professionals in the HR, Procurement, IT, and project management functions on training mentors teaching and mentoring new arrivals to the company...'*. Again, confusion in relation to the terminology and clarity of the mentoring roles was evident in terms of data around where mentors operate *'...[in] teaching, education, software engineering, coaching and business sectors...'*. From both public and private sector respondents, the word 'senior' or similar was used by twenty-seven at least once when referring to a mentor.

Subtheme: Impact

Impact was described as being *'... difficult to assess...'* to *'...immensely beneficial and impactful...'* where *'All friends and colleagues who received mentoring benefitted immensely from the support provided to them, which also they consider crucial for their career development...'*. The latter quote was taken from a private sector respondent.

Another perspective was that *'As in any mentoring situation, all factors can impact the result – gender, location, age, cultural and educational background, family and work expectations. The ME [Middle East] is no different – dynamics across genders are just one example where societal aspects may prevent (for example) a woman consulting and being open to a male mentor or mentee...'*.

Subtheme: Informal mentoring

Under informal mentoring, family members, religious advisors or guides, and friends were noted to provide such a service.

> *Most major organisations that I know of [in the Middle East] have some sort of mentoring options, which LinkedIn also promotes regularly...*

Larger and global organizations were also considered to be '...*better...*' at development, such as mentoring, from the interview data. The survey data also revealed that informal mentoring was evident in both public and private sector organizations. However, more formal mentoring with trained mentors was only referred to by one public sector respondent.

Theme Three: Proving mentoring to others

Subtheme: Knowledge-share

A subtheme emerged relating to knowledge-share from expatriates working in the Middle East. For example, it was shared that '...*[in] Saudi Arabia, United Arab Emirates, Qatar, and so on ... by nature of these gulf states being rich in resources, they've always attracted expatriates as professionals ... whilst indigenous people, such as Saudis, Qatari, and Emiratis, have ... been in need of learning new skills in order to catch up with the [foreign] professionals in the skills and knowledge areas.*' This skill and knowledge share was identified as taking place through formal training as well as mentoring.

Mentoring is also provided informally in a variety of ways including from colleagues, friends and family, '*I provide [mentoring] to my team members and also to my youngest brothers...*', '*I have personally provided mentoring and guidance to my colleagues throughout my twenty years that had passed just by virtue of being with high experience and a positive attitude to share my knowledge and skills. This went on for twenty years. And again in the oil and gas sector...*', '*I have mentored junior staff members in admin and academic research ... for seven years now...*', with some relationships lasting long term '*I am still in touch with a fair number of mentees, and I am in touch with my mentor of over thirty years ago...*'.

Mentees share the impact of mentoring with their mentors, '*I am very committed to mentor others, at all levels, not necessarily colleagues working in my department. Those who I mentor are grateful for the impact it has on their self-confidence, self-awareness as well as their career development.*'

From interview data it was found that '*A culture of mentoring...*' is being worked on across residency and fellowship training programmes in Hamad Medical Corporation, the main teaching tertiary care facility in Qatar. Developing structured mentoring programmes and training both faculty and trainees in mentoring is recommended to improve the current practice of mentoring within the training programmes. Mentoring is also advocated, for example, for any Clinical Nurse Specialist who '*Pursues and participates in educational and mentoring opportunities to increase effectiveness as a change agent*' (Hamad Medical Corporation, 2023).

Subtheme: Formal programmes

A number of respondents shared that they have mentored informally and as part of their job roles. For example, '*Being a senior professional for the past 20 years, I have mentored tens of younger professionals in an informal capacity, as I was seen as the subject matter expert and guiding mentor just by seniority at several companies I served ... I established the mentorship program as a trend for two years, so I've seen formal mentors mentoring ... That program lasted for two years, and it was quite successful. Twenty years prior to this within the oil and gas sector, I was in the learning mode more than the mentoring mode, so I sought seniors to ... teach me the many skills that I have been exposed to...'.*

Theme Four: Nuances of mentoring in the Middle East

Subtheme: Understanding mentoring

Worded in numerous ways, the survey showed that *'...the power of mentoring is not yet fully understood and sometimes the relationship may be affected by gender: for a male, being mentored by a female may still be difficult in the Middle East? I have not experienced formal mentoring programs or processes.'* In terms of relationship *'...the establishment of mentoring relationships is left to the individuals rather than being formalised'.* This correlates with the research of Alqahtani et al. (2021) where the process, setting up of sessions and relationship development between the mentor and the mentee affected the impact positively and negatively.

One private sector respondent shared that understanding of mentoring and *'...what we call professional is organization specific ... [there are] no global rules ... mostly constructs...'* and yet patterns emerge in organizations. This prompted my curiosity around patterns in other collectivist, as opposed to individualist, cultures which would be a further area of research interest.

Subtheme: Trust

Trust appeared as a subtheme of mentoring nuances where *'People here trust the experienced people and listen carefully to eldest ones'*, *'...mentoring, in the Middle East as well as in any other countries, is based on trust which I find even more important here. In my experience, mentoring relationships help people to increase the trust among them, creating opportunities to build friendship and long-term relationships that go beyond the mentoring one...'* while lack of trust in a *'...different culture...'* as seeking help through speaking to others can feel shameful *'...as word gets around...'*, other people may hear that this is taking place, and so *'trust [is an] issues...'.* What also emerged was *'The traditional culture causes the coach or mentor to be viewed as much higher/senior than the mentee or coachee...'.*

Psychosocial state, self-efficacy, transfer of knowledge, skills and ability, positive change, and career help should be considered because they have received a lot of attention in mentoring programme research literature (Hansford & Ehrich, 2006; Fox et al., 2010; Ismail & Ridzuan, 2012).

Subtheme: Amount of mentoring

There is a perception of a lack of mentoring and especially little exposure to professional mentoring (Abdalla, 2015):

> *...not a great deal [of mentoring] takes place in the medical field...*

It is interesting to note that ten of the respondents shared that the amount of time required for mentoring may be underestimated both in relation to arranging mutually convenient session times, within sessions and in terms of the number of sessions for impact to happen. Furthermore, four respondents mentioned that other priorities may take precedence when mentoring is not formal. *'Coaching is taking off in the Middle East but there isn't much mentoring, yet. Mentoring may take place informally in Majlis and through friends, family and colleagues. However, power dynamics and possibly a collectivist society means that sometimes difficult conversations and 'telling' are avoided...'.* A *Majlis* is an Arabic term meaning 'sitting room' where special gatherings, usually of men who share common interests, take place.

Theme Five: Mentoring process

Megginson et al. (2006) suggest in their book *Mentoring in Action,* that developmental relationships transition through five phases: rapport building, direction setting, progress making, winding down and moving on. Mutual respect, alignment of values and purpose, as well as shared expectations of roles and responsibilities support rapport building. Next, direction setting, giving the relationship a sense of purpose, and working out what the short-, medium- and long-term direction might be, needs to take place.

The amount of learning for both the mentee and mentor is greatest during the middle period of the relationship (progress making) while both communication and support enable mentee learning (Ismail & Ridzuan, 2012). Effective mentors respond to the needs of mentees as they focus on developing solutions through ensuring a relaxed, yet business-like atmosphere, gaining consensus on purpose, exploring issues from the mentee perspective, clarifying, challenging assumptions, drawing on experience, building the confidence the mentee, recapping and facilitating the mutual agreement of actions by both partners, and offering an outline for the agenda of the next meeting. That said, graduate students from the Middle East, where high-context cultures emphasize indirect communication and respect for authority, may tend to avoid making direct requests for help. Instead, they are more inclined to seek support through subtle hints or suggestions.

A high-context culture refers to a cultural environment where communication relies heavily on implicit messages, non-verbal cues, and the context of the situation to convey meaning. In high-context cultures, people place a significant emphasis on relationships, trust and shared understanding within their social groups. This means that much of the information and meaning is embedded in the context of the interaction or relationship, rather than explicitly stated in the words spoken.

Conversely, low-context cultures rely more on explicit verbal communication, where messages are conveyed directly and explicitly. In these cultures, people tend to value clarity, precision and directness in communication.

Understanding whether a culture is high-context or low-context can be crucial for effective communication and interaction, especially in multicultural settings or when working with individuals from different cultural backgrounds (Brandt, 2014).

Since the culture is found to be less direct (Klopf, 1995) and *'...mentors need training to enable effective listening beyond words...'* shared one interviewee. It may be that mentees from countries that are more polychronic are more flexible in terms of planning, yet a mentee may be more deferential to the 'experienced/older mentor' where culturally the relationship is less flexible. In a monochronic culture it may be more acceptable to challenge a more senior colleague or a mentor, providing more flexibility in that respect, whilst meeting times are respected.

When winding down, the mentee and mentor plan to close the relationship by reviewing and celebrating what has been achieved, while moving on involves closing the formal mentoring relationship to become, for example, friends and/or colleagues. It was found that *'Formal closing of mentoring relationships is important to support future interactions...'.*

There was significant resonance in terms of views on the structure of mentoring in the Middle East where it was believed *'We still lack the structured mentoring with specific objectives...'*, where it is *'...rarely clear cut scheduled, usually upon demand, collective or informal settings...'* and *'It is more like an obligation because it is usually one way: expatriates mentoring and teaching local people.'* Mentoring is seen as having a *'... basic process...'* in the public sector and this is not different in *'...major companies...'.* It was also shared that *'...I have not known it to be part of, for example, learning and development, in organisations'.* Additionally, it was felt that *'...[mentoring] is more available in the collective rather than one on one mentoring...'.*

Theme Six: Gender and age

There were some references in the data to the significance of gender and age across the answers to the questions. For example, *'...in our culture, it is not always welcomed to have a mentor from another gender ... ladies feel more comfortable to talk to lady mentor...'*, *'...mostly same gender...'*, and *'...mostly [they are the] same gender...'* One respondent living in Saudi Arabia stated an important factor that *'...there are much less women in the workplace...'.* It was also felt that with *'Women and mentoring, a lot more can be done!'*

Subtheme: Client expects advice and answers

> *As said before, gender may have an impact as male colleagues may feel embarrassed being mentored by a female. With regard to age, I found reverse mentoring from younger colleagues (GenZ and Millennials) supporting baby boomers in the digital transition very interesting...*

Diving deeper into this in interviews and triangulating data, it surfaced that this is an atypical power relation in a Middle Eastern workplace and general culture.

'Sometimes people do want to support and mentor ... they are nervous about how it will be received. So, more education and understanding of its benefits would help mentoring to grow and have impact....' In this light, Todd's research (1997) may stand also for mentors who are Middle Eastern nationals, *'Students often come from an environment where they are not allowed to criticize teachers, raise questions that could embarrass the teacher or even to correct them if they make a mistake. It is therefore not surprising that they find it hard to put forward their own ideas.'*

In relation to career: *'Context is everything – and mentoring is not a common thing since the family and extended family play a more significant role in young people's lives...'*

Theme Seven: Shifts in mentoring practices

Professional experiences working with organizations and survey data showed that *'People are becoming more aware of mentoring…'*. It was also highlighted that *'…in the past five years organizations are much more aware of the need for mentoring as a necessity for sustainability of the company'*. Mentoring in the health and wellness fields is more accepted *'When the government encourages it on society level in KSA* [the Kingdom of Saudi Arabia] *for example…'* balanced with *'A greater understanding of coaching and mentoring roles…'*. Interestingly, it was also noted that there is now *'…more accepting of women in power in a mentoring position…'*, clarified as mentees are more accepting of mentors when they are women, if they are in higher power positions. There is still clarity needed about the distinction between mentoring and coaching as *'…coaching is now more accepted as a tool…'* and, in this case, the respondent used coaching and mentoring interchangeably through comments such as *'In my experience, when our organization hired an executive coach, everything changed and the coaching culture began to positively influence all work relationships, fostering informal mentoring across the entire organization.'* There is a need for mentoring to be further understood (Mentor Global Consultants, 2022).

It was recognised that there is *'…more acceptance [with] non-Middle Eastern residents [who] might have experience and ideas to contribute to the region, but [there is] push-back from Middle Eastern colleagues who want to go their own way or short-circuit the development loop…'*.

'It is not something I have seen in the public sector, and yet some telecoms, for example, do it…' while, contrary to this, development for mentors takes place at Qatar Foundation, a large not-for-profit, as well as through voluntary societies in Bahrain, such as the Bahrain Society for Training and Development (BSTD).

Theme Eight: Impact of mentoring (general)

Developing individuals for leadership positions was identified significantly as the most impactful use of mentoring. Personal development *'…in an increasingly complicated workplace…'* was specifically highlighted in one response. This was followed by mentoring for organizations, teams and succession planning, mentioned equally as a way mentoring can create impact. Next, knowledge-share, health/well-being and the wider system were noted where mentoring can have a positive impact. Mentoring groups and mentoring for technical content were seen as the least impactful categories shared.

From the interview and email correspondence one specific positive experience of mentoring was shared by Ian Kenneth Pople MD FRCS, Chief, Division of Neurosurgery, Sidra Medicine, an international biomedical institute of excellence created in 2015 by *Qatar Foundation*, and Associate Professor of Clinical Neurological Surgery, Weil Cornell Medicine, Qatar, *'My main observation when I first arrived from the UK as a senior physician at Sidra Medicine in Qatar is that the Arabic cultural norm of strict deference to higher ranks in the medical community was leading to a lack of decision-making and initiative within my team, so the first step in mentorship was to reassure the team that initiative and delegated decisions were highly valued and should be encouraged. This led to improved morale, confidence and efficiency in my particular team with a healthy ongoing freedom to discuss and debate the best treatment strategies for our patients in order to achieve the better outcomes.'*

Theme Nine: Increasing the impact of mentoring in the Middle East

A significant number of respondents felt that mentoring needs '...*to be more structured...*', that '...*measurable tools are needed to reveal impact so people accept it a lot more...*', that '...*More exposure and certified practitioners...*' are important.

Subtheme: Rewards

A theme of rewards showed up in the data across sections. For example, it was shared that *'Due to the nature of mentoring being a one-way sort of [relationship] between expatriates and locals, enticing organizations to reward mentors can lead to impressive results...', 'Companies and government should include mentoring as a compulsory training for all its staff, to increase awareness of employees of how to be mentors and mentees and ultimately to increase knowledge sharing between its staff. Also, to cope with the knowledge management economy...'* and *'better rewards for mentors: mentees generally get their own benefit, if the process is working properly...'.* It was felt that *'More community leaders modelling* [mentoring]...' provides younger professionals with an advantage. Systemic changes are also noted such as *'Promotion of a mentoring culture within the organisations but also at a school level, would in my view be very beneficial to normalise mentoring as an important tool for human development.'* This is also reiterated here *'Good mentoring cannot solely be a tick-box exercise by major companies. It's worth highlighting what the mentoring relationship is meant to achieve for all parties, to avoid a mismatch of expectations.'*

A range of positive benefits to mentoring were mentioned, such as *'I believe building awareness is very essential; especially in the very roots of understanding, the needs for learning, I guess for continual learning as well as the need to preserve knowledge that is knowledge management and knowledge sharing...',* and *'...mentoring overlaps with "telling the rules" for some. It is a promising area for investment until defined in the cultural mindset of people, though...'* and *'Mentoring also facilitates peer-to-peer knowledge sharing, which is vital for the development of a knowledge-economy.'*

Summary, conclusions and recommendations

Despite the relatively small sample size (N = 48) it was clear that when respondents addressed mentoring provisions in private sector organizations, an increased amount of structure, organization in relation to set-up of mentoring services and formality was prevalent. Mentoring appeared to be less available in the public sector, especially in relation to formal mentoring. This also raises questions about the theme of access within certain organizations and sectors. That the many different types of mentoring were not evident in the public sector as explained by one public sector worker, '...*there would be a great deal of benefit to those mentored and to organisations if it was part of organisational culture. Relationships here are influenced by age and yet a mentor doesn't have to be older, just wiser, so I have never known reverse mentoring to be a 'thing' in the Middle East...'.*

Awareness-raising was identified as a key element to creating individual professional and systemic impact from mentoring. *'It needs to be fully understood, more formal, and have impact measures in place.'* Further research into impact measures for formal, compared to informal, mentoring may be relevant. Similarities and differences in relationships and other nuances also need further research when mentoring is being provided by a Middle Eastern professional or an expatriate. Alkhatnai (2021) shares that there is lack of research into the implications of gender on mentoring relationships and impact. Interestingly, gender differences did not show significantly in the data and group mentoring was not mentioned at all.

Mentoring was identified as a positive development tool by thirty-four of the fifty respondents and it is felt that a specific survey question on this topic may have increased this number further. At present, mentoring in the Middle East is perceived as a positive influence on improving skills and working relationships and, as demonstrated by the evidence currently available, many have already benefited from mentoring. However, more research is needed to identify existing types of mentoring, how it is expressed in different types of organizations and the various groups of participants involved. If mentoring is to have impact, significant work is needed to grow the capacity of the mentor and the mentee for optimum effect. The importance of trust in the relationship was noted by almost half the respondents, '...*although many ingrained habits and elements are changing, the mentoring process relies on the openness, goodwill and wish to succeed...*'. It is indicated that psychological safety sustains impact in mentoring relationships.

Power relations, age gaps, and other cultural-related issues were identified as relevant factors affecting access, understanding and the impact of mentoring in the Middle East. There was no mention of mentors and mentees needing to speak the sample language; however, it may have been implied. Reverse mentoring appears to be in its infancy, if practiced at all.

The role of mentoring needs to be developed further and this could include: defining mentoring and its role in an organization; mentor training; clarifying the role and expectations of mentor/mentee; distinguishing mentoring from coaching/training; formalizing the who/what/when/why of mentoring; and removing barriers to effective mentoring. Aligning around the purpose or desired results of the mentoring, as well as what commitment looks like from both the mentor's and mentee's perspectives, may support mentoring in being effective. Furthermore, in the Middle East, it may be beneficial for mentors to gain recognition for their mentoring work in some way, such as a certificate of appreciation from organizations. Likewise, mentees may enjoy the same acknowledgement for their time and effort, or may appreciate credit hours for mentoring if they are students. Offering examples or demonstrations of mentoring sessions, sharing of behavioural competencies, success case stories and clear processes should be considered.

References

Abdalla, I. (2015). *Being and becoming a leader: Arabian Gulf women managers' perspectives. International Journal of Business Management*, **10**(1), 25–39. https://www.ccsenet.org/journal/index.php/ijbm/article/view/41237

Aderibigbe, S. A., Antiado, D. F. A., & Sta Anna, A. (2015). *Issues in peer mentoring for undergraduate students in a private university in the United Arab Emirates. International Journal of Evidence Based Coaching and Mentoring*, **13**(2), 64–80.

Alhadlaq, A., Kharrufa, A., & Oliver, P. (2019). *Exploring e-mentoring: Co-designing and un-platforming. Behaviour and Information Technology.* **38**(**11**), 1122–1142.

Alkhatnai, M. (2021). *Mentoring in Saudi higher education: Considering the role of culture in academic development. International Journal of Academic Development,* **28**(**1**), 20–30.

Alqahtani, S. S., Al-Samghan, A., Alshahrani, A., Almalki, Y., Ghazwani, E., Amanullah, M., Shati, I. A. (2021). *To what extent are medical students benefiting from mentoring, Middle East Journal of Family Medicine,* **19**(**1**), 124–132.

Association of Talent Development (2022). *What is Mentoring?* https://www.td.org/talent-development-glossary-terms/what-is-mentoring

Brandt, K. (2014). *Discussion and Contrast of High- and Low-Context Cultures as Defined by E. T. Hall.* Seminar paper.

EMCC (2022). *Thought Leadership and Development: Mentoring.* https://www.emccglobal.org/leadership-development/leadership-development-mentoring/

Fariza, M. S. (2005). *Tekanan emosi remaja. Jurnal Islamiyyat,* **27**(**1**), 3–24.

Fox, A., Stevenson, L., Connelly, P., Duff, A., & Dunlop, A., (2010). *Peer-mentoring undergraduate accounting students: The influence on approaches to learning and academic performance. Active Learning in Higher Education,* **11**(**2**), 145–156.

Hamad Medical Corporation (2023). *Education, Learning and Development.* https://www.hamad.qa/EN/Hospitals-and-services/Nursing/Nursing-Strategy/Nurse-Scope-of-Practice/Clinical-Nurse-Specialist-Scope-of-Practice/Pages/Education,-Learning-and-Development.aspx

Hansford, B., & Ehrich, L. C., (2006). *The principalship: How significant is mentoring? Journal of Educational Administration,* **44**(**1**), 36–52.

Ismail, A., & Ridzuan, A. A. (2012). *Relationship between mentoring program and academic performance. The mediating effect of self-efficacy. The Proceeding of the 3rd International Conference on Business and Economics Research (ICBER).*

Kirchherr, J., & Charles, K. (2018). *Enhancing the sample diversity of snowball samples: Recommendations from a research project on anti-dam movements in Southeast Asia. PlosOne,* **13**(**8**), e0201710.

Klopf, D., (1995). *Intercultural encounters.* Morton Publishing.

Mentor Global Consultants (2022). *Running Corporate Mentoring Programs in the Middle East.* https://mentor-gc.com/insights/running-corporate-mentoring-programs-in-the-middle-east

Megginson, D., Clutterbuck, D., Garvey, B., Stokes, P., & Garrett-Harris, R. (2006). *Mentoring in Action: A Practical Guide* (**2nd ed.**). Kogan Page.

Mishkin, K., & Johnson, S. (2020). *Evaluating participatory group mentoring in international development projects in the Middle East, Development in Practice,* **30**,(**4**), 423–436.

Pattisson, J. (2020). *Teacher trainees' understandings of mentoring within a Middle Eastern BEd program. International Journal of Mentoring and Coaching in Education,* **9**(**4**), 325–339.

Qatar Foundation International (2023). https://www.bartleby.com/essay/Nonverbal-Communication-in-Arabs-Culture-FKG82AXHKG4Y#: ~ :text = Arabs %20touch %20more %20between %20the,close %20friends %2C %20 accepted %20and %20honored.&text = Contact %20between %20the %20opposite %20sexes %20in %20public %20 is %20considered %20close %20to %20obscene.&text = Women %20tend %20to %20speak %20higher %20and %20 more %20softly %20than %20men

Todd, L. (1997). *Supervising postgraduate students: Problem or opportunity?* In D. McNamara, & R. Harris, (Eds.) *Overseas Students in Higher Education: Issues in Teaching and Learning.* Routledge.

Toner, S. V. (2004). *Peer Mentoring and Professional Development: A Study of EFL Teaching in the Middle East* [EdD thesis]. The Open University.

Chapter 34
Médecins Sans Frontières Mentoring and Coaching Hub, Norway Mentoring Programme

Julie Haddock-Millar, Agnese Pinto, Chandana Sanyal & Neil Kaye

Introducing the humanitarian sector and mentoring

The international humanitarian sector comprises a network of governmental and non-governmental organizations that are engaged at a global and/or local scale in providing humanitarian assistance to people affected by conflict, epidemics or disasters. It employs more than 250,000 aid workers worldwide (James, 2016), many of whom work in highly volatile and high-risk environments.

There is a consensus that the humanitarian environment can be physically and psychologically demanding due to differing institutional structures, economic and political instability, ethnic and religious rivalries, political complexities, insecurity and high-risk situations (Katz et al., 2012). Over the last twenty years, there has been increased recognition that humanitarian workers are subject to stressors that can negatively impact on mental health if individuals are not effectively supported. In the short term, continued exposure to stressors can result in anxiety and depression; in the long term, without sufficient support, exposure to stressors can result in burnout.

Stressors include, among others, difficult living conditions, increasing work demands, work conditions, team dysfunction and conflict. There are clear links to the retention and high turnover rates associated with the sector. These issues can be addressed in several ways, such as: enabling humanitarian workers to stay connected with their personal networks through the telephone or Internet for personal communications, encouraging workers to try and separate work and social time, actively engaging in social activities, limiting work hours and providing conflict resolution support in teams. The support of a mentor to a newly appointed humanitarian worker can provide much needed professional friendship, reassurance and comfort, where more experienced mentors share their knowledge or wisdom with the less experienced mentee (Kram, 1985; Ragins & Cotton, 1999; Wanberg et al., 2003, Bozeman & Feeney, 2007).

Introducing the MSF mentoring programme

Médecins Sans Frontières (MSF), referred to in English as Doctors Without Borders, is an international humanitarian medical non-governmental organization. Staff work in extraordinary circumstances within varying contexts, performing functions within roles, which often stretch them personally and professionally. Optimizing performance in any national, regional or organizational context can often be an elusive ideal. In the humanitarian environment, workers are particularly disposed to a number of challenges and barriers to optimizing performance. This includes the professionalization of the humanitarian sector, aligning individual and organizational values with the local context and culture. Coping in these highly pressurized environments requires sustaining resilience and energy to maintain physical and mental health in order to avoid staff burnout and retention problems.

In 2010, MSF Operational Centre Brussels (OCB) took the strategic decision to move towards a Human Resource Development (HRD) approach based on competencies. The main objective was to develop the competencies of individual positions within the Operations Centres. This strategy was partly in response to one of MSF's major challenges of finding, selecting and developing future Project Coordinators and Heads of Mission. This challenge prompted the need for developing new HR tools and programmes to support these growing needs. OCB requested a review, starting in 2010, which determined that mentoring in the first six months of a new management position is associated with greater career success and progression within the organization in question. As a part of the HR Development Strategy, the mentoring pilot was initiated in mid-2011. This pilot phase continued until 2013. Initially, support was focused on two roles: first-time Field Coordinators and Heads of Mission.

As the programme grew from 2014 to 2016, the decision was made to apply for funding in late 2016. At the same time, a secondary partnership was initiated between MSF Norway and Operational Centre Barcelona and Athens (OCBA) in order to share expertise and resources, and, most importantly, to launch a number of coaching pilots. MSF Transformational Investment Capacity (TIC) funding was received in 2017 for a period of three years. At the end of 2013/beginning of 2014, the following mentoring programme objectives were developed:

- Provide mentoring support to first-time coordinators, to improve and strengthen key competencies.
- Support the mentee in building his/her own resilience capacity.
- Create more space and enable more knowledge transfer inside the organization through dialogue and sharing of experience.

The Mentoring and Coaching Hub (M&C Hub) team developed their context-specific definition of mentoring:

- It is a process of learning from a senior colleague.
- The mentor provides advice when appropriate, shares knowledge and experiences, and supports the development of the mentee using a self-discovery approach.
- The mentoring relationship accompanies the mentees while they address issues in their work environment.
- The mentor does not 'fix' issues in the project/mission; rather helps the mentee to identify his/her own solutions and remains out of the mentee's management line.

The focus of the mentoring support is the development of the mentee's competencies, at the same time providing the space and time to reflect and vent. The M&C Hub created a visual of their approach to mentoring and shared it with both mentors and mentees prior to commencing their mentoring relationships (Figure 34.1).

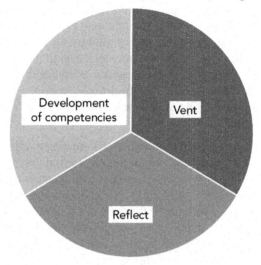

Figure 34.1: M&C hub mentoring model.

The *Development of competencies* focuses on the role of specific competencies relevant to each mentee, typically including leadership- and management-related areas. *Vent* provides the space where mentees can be honest about their experiences, thoughts and feelings, without fear or judgement. *Reflect* provides the opportunity for mentees to step back from their role and their day-to-day responsibilities to unravel their thoughts, make sense of their experiences and generate new insights.

Mentoring programme framework

MSF M&C Hub adopted the European Mentoring and Coaching Council (EMCC) Global International Standards for Mentoring and Coaching Programmes (ISMCP) as an overarching framework for the design, implementation and evaluation of the programme in 2016. The mentoring programme was accredited by EMCC Global at the GOLD standard, the highest level.

The official MSF mentoring programme website offers all required information for applicants. The programme has been widened to more international and national staff positions for both mentees and mentors since the beginning of 2020. The mentor application process and the mentee self-assessment provide a robust basis to assess and match the mentors' experiences/qualities and mentees' needs and preferences. In most cases, the mentee is put in touch with more than one mentor and can have an initial meeting or meetings to make a final matching decision. Mentors and mentees describe the matching as mainly successful.

Mentors are usually experienced in the role the mentee is presently in, and may or may not have experience in the same context (country, type of mission/intervention). While the focus on the relationship is not on the mentor sharing their experiences, this information is readily accessible should the mentee ask for it. Mentors are independent of the management line of the mentee and adhere to non-interference with operations. This means that mentors guide mentees in their analysis of the situations they face in their work, but the clear responsibility for decisions rests with mentees and their line managers. For mentees to make the most of this developmental support, confidentiality between the mentor and the mentee is a foundational principle. Additionally, participating in the mentoring programmes is voluntary for mentees and mentors. From the mentee perspective, this means that the mentoring relationship is a chosen part of their development pathway and they themselves recognize the value in this type of professional relationship. For mentors, this means MSF is able to access a dedicated pool of senior staff who are looking to engage in developmental relationships and commit to the programmes.

Mentors and mentees are supported with initial and ongoing training. The M&C Hub achieved the EMCC Global Quality Award for the mentor training programme in 2017 and this programme continues to evolve as the needs of mentors develop. The mentor training programme has been reviewed and now includes additional practice activities, including role play, diversity issues and reflections. A set of mentor competencies have been added and a post-mentor training talk with mentors has been put in place. Mentors are offered continuing professional development (CPD) activities and new initiatives, such as group supervision, the mentor café (informal online meeting room) and the community of practice, which highlights the commitment to supporting mentors on the programme. Mentees are offered a one-to-one online induction to provide the required understanding and knowledge prior to commencing a mentoring relationship.

The mentoring programme has a robust evaluation framework in place, which supports the continuous improvement of the programme, the collation of evidence of achievement against the programme's aims and objectives to share with stakeholders, and identification of lessons learned to inform the potential future programmes and wider audiences. In addition, an extensive impact evaluation research study was commissioned and conducted between 2017–2019 to further strengthen and enhance the key aspects of the mentoring programme, including ongoing review and formal evaluation.

The research team adopted a two-phased, mixed-method, longitudinal approach, encompassing the views of mentees, mentors and key stakeholders. The research engaged participants involved in the mentoring programme since the beginning of 2014, with tremendous participation results. Mixed methods included an online survey for mentees and mentors, and semi-structured interviews with matched mentees and mentors, in addition to non-matched participants and key stakeholders. Participants also provided visual representations as metaphor to demonstrate the impact of mentoring. Phase 1 involved an online survey, followed by matched pair interviews and visual metaphor. Phase 2 was a repeat of Phase 1, and the same participants were invited to take part in a follow-up survey, interview and updated visual metaphor. The continued participant engagement from Phase 1 to Phase 2 was outstanding: 76% of mentees and 91% mentors took part in Phase 1 and Phase 2 interviews and 65% of mentees and 86% of mentors took part in Phase 1 and Phase 2 of the survey. Overall, the research team conducted 86 interviews; 45 interviews in Phase 1 and 41 in Phase 2; these included 14 matched pair interviews in Phase 1 and 10 matched pair interviews in Phase 2.

Programme impact and participant experience

The results show that the mentoring programme is having a significant positive impact on mentees, mentors *and* MSF more broadly. Mentoring supports mentees' personal and professional development. Participant impact can be grouped into two overarching themes: career-related and psychosocial. Career-related outcomes include leadership and management capability, teamworking, decision-making and negotiation. Psychosocial-related outcomes include well-being, resilience, stress management and preventing burnout. The most valuable outcomes relate to increased self-esteem, confidence, leadership and management capability. Evidence shows that mentors are supporting mentees to build their resilience capability, and this in turn is having a positive impact on retention, demonstrated in their intention to stay with MSF on the completion of their mission. We know that resilience can be developed through the process of dialogue, enquiry and deliberate practice and that mentors work to create a psychologically safe space where work–life balance issues can be addressed, helping mentees to adapt and thrive even in volatile, uncertain, difficult times. Mentoring positively impacts the mentees' ability to bounce back and cope with challenges. The mentor is able to provide a metaphorical resting place for their mentee. This allows mentees to pause, breath, unravel the chaos in their head and take a different view of the situation they find themselves in.

Mentoring is a vital resource, supporting mentees to successfully transition into their role, complete their mission and commit to further missions. Mentoring has a positive impact on participants' intention to stay with MSF at the end of their mission. Indeed, one of the most significant areas of operational impact for any organization, regardless of the context is retention and succession planning. The negative impact of staff leaving mid-appointment or at the end of an appointment not only affects the mission but also the longer-term succession planning. A statistic that features in a number of interviews in Phase 1 is that at least 50% of first-time field workers leave MSF either during their mission or at the end. It is clear to see why this is an area of enquiry in this study. When commissioning this research, the M&C Hub were interested in exploring retention for both the mentoring programme and MSF – for example, mentors volunteer again to continue to mentor, mentees become mentors.

For a number of mentees and mentors in Phase 1, the impact of mentoring on staff retention across the MSF movement is clear:

> *I am a better Field Coordinator as a result of my relationship,*
> *the team dynamic is strong, the project runs smoother. If*
> *this year had not been positive, this for me was the make*
> *or break of whether I wanted to stay in this sector. As a*
> *consequence of the mentoring relationship MSF will get me*
> *for another year, another project.*

(A9 Mentee)

> *I am convinced that mentoring has an operational impact. I think my wife would have left the mission much earlier if she did not have a mentor.*
>
> (A4 Mentee)

> *I do not feel comfortable as a Field Coordinator, but I would go back because I know that my situation was not normal.*
>
> (A4 Mentee)

Taking it one step further, evidence suggest that mentees are able to positively influence others in the field that make their intention to leave known.

One mentor describes a situation where his mentee was able to support a staff member which prevented early departure:

> *Dealing with another first missionary, who was lost in her position. She felt overloaded, overwhelmed, she was struggling with strong national staff. The potential early departure of the female, would have made disruption, left a gap, left MSF – the impact would have been higher rather than the temporary impact.*
>
> (B2 Mentor)

Retention extends beyond mentees completing their first missions, to consider retention of mentors and mentees on the mentoring programme. We consider whether mentors wish to continue to support mentees and if mentees wish to become mentors. Evidence suggests that all mentors in Phase 1 are willing to work with new mentees and that, regardless of their previous mentoring experience, all are willing to continue to mentor. In at least two cases, mentors were previously mentees, and several mentees would consider becoming a mentor in the future.

In Phase 2, the positive impact of mentoring in relation to retention of mentees is evident in the interview transcripts of mentees and mentors, illustrated by the following comments:

> *One of my mentees would have left his mission if it was not for the mentoring. Ultimately it was a positive mission; he said without the mentoring it would have ended badly and the mentoring was a turning point.*
>
> (Mentor B2)

*My mentee completed her mission, and the relationship
is now closed ... she needed emotional and operational
support. My mentee became emotionally fragile and heading
towards burnout within a few weeks, she was about to resign
... I needed to strengthen her resilience to be able to cope
with the situation ... I had to support her ... it worked out
well because she stayed in the mission and finished it.*

(Mentor, B25)

In Phase 1 *and* Phase 2, mentees and mentors are acutely aware of the operational
impact of mentoring, both the immediate and longer-term impact. This is illustrated by
the following comments:

*During my mentoring, I was a Field Co, managing a project
with XX expatriates and XXX national staff. The success of
this mission was influenced by the quality of the mentoring
I received, and it remained markedly so in my operational
work.*

(Mentee, A8)

*The experience of mentoring was very positive for me.
It is important for first appointment Field Managers to
have a mentor. The transition involves an increase in the
management and leadership role. It is a big shift from
managing the daily technical, operational activities. Two
things happen – one is burnout because they are outside their
comfort zone and pushed beyond their limits. Second, they
are fired from the mission because they are not experienced
enough. Their career ends with MSF.*

(Mentee, A16)

Mentees recognized the intense pace of their role, the challenges associated with their
project, and the high-risk – in some cases – volatile and violent environmental context.
Mentors were able to provide a safe space for mentees to vent, reflect, gain perspective
and recognize their strengths and needs. As a result of the mentoring, the majority
of mentees were able to shift from a constant state of panic to a stretch zone, where
mentees felt a sense of empowerment, greater confidence and self-esteem, alongside
an enhanced ability to see and understand their development areas and access
resources to support their needs

A key aspect of the impact evaluation is the degree to which reciprocal learning is
evident in the mentoring relationships, in particular, the extent to which mentors
learn from the experience. There is clear evidence that mentors also benefit from
the relationship, developing their knowledge, understanding and skills, which are

then utilized in a variety of roles. For mentors, the mentoring relationship keeps them connected to the field and to the issues field workers are facing, applying their knowledge and skills to listen, question and, in many cases, guide their mentee through the myriad situations and issues. Mentoring therefore flexes their knowledge, understanding and skills in relation to learning and development more broadly, but specifically regarding the dynamic role of the mentor. This is particularly evident in the context of supporting female field workers. The following comments from Phase 2 participants illustrate reciprocal learning:

> I am not a soft person; I can be strong and firm but mentoring provides the listening ear which is of huge help. It is simple and small, but I do learn from it, asking questions, listening evaluating etc. When I need to recruit, assess, evaluate on my missions I am able to utilize the skills that I develop in my mentoring role. It helps me in my role.
>
> (Mentor, B15)

> I am constantly identifying with issues of the mentees in relation to my own practice. I am learning to flex my mentoring muscles.
>
> (Mentor, B6)

> The mentoring experienced has influenced my ideas around development, identifying people's needs and develop them. Mentoring has increased my competence to support people in the field.
>
> (Mentor, A23)

> I receive a lot of knowledge from my mentees; therefore, I am able to improve my performance … sharing knowledge impacts on performance, therefore it positively impacts on the mission. I have seen how the increase in confidence and the development of rapport, mutual understanding all helps towards building teams and improving team working.
>
> (Mentor, B3)

The impact of mentoring reverberates throughout MSF, at all levels in the organization, as individuals question the institutional, cultural and political environment in relation to the degree to which learning, development, management and leadership are effectively supported.

Lessons learned for others and future intentions

Opportunities for improvement include the alignment between mentoring and other developmental interventions, including individual and team coaching, participant recognition and engagement, ongoing CPD and specific training and tools to address mentees' needs in the field. There is a clear opportunity for the MSF M&C Hub to continue to work with Operational Centres and Partner Sections to continue to develop and enhance mentoring practice; in addition to developing an external facing role, contributing to the mentoring community across the globe.

Recommendations include the opportunity to strategically align mentoring with other learning and development activities within MSF and ensure mentoring is recognized, supported and advocated. This will involve clarity around where mentoring is *currently* strategically positioned within MSF, in addition to identifying where and how mentoring might be strategically positioned in the future. Alongside field workers developing into the role as a leader and manager, their greatest challenge is well-being, stress management and burnout. Ensuring field workers are adequately supported prior to going into the field and to 'self-care' during their mission, recognizing the early signs of stress and burnout, and identifying and implementing coping strategies are vital if MSF wish to support field workers to successfully support themselves, their teams and their beneficiaries. In the humanitarian context, caring for field workers so that they can effectively care for others is an imperative.

References

Bozeman, B., & Feeney, M. K. (2007). *Toward a useful theory of mentoring: A conceptual analysis and critique.* *Administration & Society,* **39**(**6**), 719–739.

James, E. (2016). *The professional humanitarian and the downsides of professionalization. Disasters,* **40**(**2**), 185–206.

Katz, J., Nguyen, D., Lacerda, C., & Daly, G., (2012). *Voices from the field: Optimising performance for humanitarian workers. Development in Practice,* **22**(**2**), 256–266.

Kram, K. E. (1985). *Mentoring at Work: Developmental Relationship in Organizational Life.* Scott, Foresman and Company.

Ragins, B. R., & Cotton, J. L. (1999). *Mentor functions and outcomes: A comparison of men and women in formal and informal mentoring relationships. Journal of Applied Psychology,* **84**(**4**), 529–550.

Wanberg, C. R., Welsh, E. T., & Hezlett, S. A. (2003). *Mentoring research: A review and dynamic process model.* In J. J. Martocchio, & G. R. Ferris (Eds.), *Research in Personnel and Human Resources Management* (**Vol. 22**, pp. 39–124). Elsevier Science.

Section 4:
Future Directions for Mentoring – Where to From Here?

Chapter 35
Spiritual Mentoring

Peter Hawkins

Introduction

Spiritual mentoring is a collaborative inquiry, in service of helping a seeker/mentee journey further on the spiritual path.

As such, it is different to other forms of mentoring that may be supporting a person with their studies and qualifications, or their role or career, all of which are in the service of furthering their worldly success.

It is also different from psychotherapy, where the purpose is to heal trauma, pain, mental distress and dis-ease, so the patient or client can have a more fulfilled life.

However, both of the above can shade into the domain of spiritual mentoring. Mentoring on studies or work roles can bring the mentee to ask the question: 'What is worthwhile and what is truly meaningful in what I study or practice?' In psychotherapy, a deep inquiry into one's 'self' may lead the patient or client beyond the personal self, to awareness of the transpersonal and collective self. In the Koran, it is written that *'he who truly knows himself knows their Lord'* and in many forms of Hindu, Buddhist and Taoist practice, the path of the pilgrim starts, as did Gautama Buddha's journey, with contemplating oneself, and one's own mind.

Inquiry process

I asked a number of good friends and colleagues, who practice as spiritual mentors from many different traditions, including Buddhist, Christian, Quaker, Unitarian and Sufi, how they would describe spiritual mentoring. Their replies are illuminating and when their lights stand alongside each other they provide even richer wisdom through their interconnections. Please listen and notice the patterns made by these threads as they run through these wonderful sharings.

The first question was asking them to complete the sentence: 'I would define spiritual mentoring as…'. Here is a medley of their responses:

> *…walking alongside someone on their journey through life.*
>
> *…being alongside a fellow seeker and giving indications of possible directions of travel/areas of investigation in a person's life.*

...a collaborative inquiry into the great matter of life and death, to signal openness in a shared way to questions that emerge from the opening of the heart's path, to be able to value and sit with vulnerability, not-knowing, to acknowledge failure, to feel things responsively with the whole of one's body and sensibility, to be encouraging and generous in one's disposition.

...accompanying the mentee as s/he finds their way to incorporate an explicit, a conscious, loving and courageous way of living and working in Right Relationship with themselves, with others, with the environment, and with all that is beyond themselves, however they conceive that.

...one of the ways love shares itself, one of the ways presence shares itself, one of the ways we care for each other by bringing a person to a point at which they allow the recognition of their own love-presence, or awareness-presence, to be revealed. The mentor helps to create the conditions for this revelation to occur but cannot transmit it or make it happen. That revelation, if it happens, is a matter of ripeness and grace.

The role of the mentor

I also asked my generous inquiry group of spiritual mentors to complete the sentence: *'The role of the spiritual mentor or guide is...'.* Here are some of their answers:

...to provide a safe space. To be a companion on the journey. Listening, exploring and open to everything. Discussing and offering experience.

...to assist the mentee to discern how the Holy Spirit may be leading her/him into greater awareness of the Mystery, and greater surrender to Love.

...to provide a mutually understood focus, to be emotionally courageous, to be open-minded; to offer containment and validation when required.

...to not [be] different from a friend. She does her best not to walk ahead and call back to the seeker, 'This way! This way!' but to walk beside her friend and in that companionship develop a trust and ease between them that allows honest inquiry into the seeker's self-image, fears, hopes, and avoidances. As the seeker's trust grows, he or she may be able to risk releasing their grip on their self-story and habitual points of view, and to see what is afresh.

...to be present to, to be willing to accompany, the mentee, and to listen with an open heart as the mentee finds their way to awareness and clarity about ways of being in relationship with themselves, with others, and with all that is beyond these.

(See Lushwala, (2012), p. 127).

The practices that the mentor uses

When asked about how the spiritual mentor fulfils this role, there was a strong consensus around four key practices (as far as possible I have used a mixture of their own words):

- Listening with an open, loving heart, and a willingness to receive, without judgement, all that comes. Listening purely, without judgement, without validating or invalidating what the seeker says.
- Asking questions to help the mentee identify areas of life, inner and outer, that need attention/reflection/changed awareness/changed ways of living.
- Using intuitive attention to discern what is not being said/is not yet in awareness.
- Bringing focus to what emerges – returning, again and again, to the present moment, to what the seeker is experiencing in the here and now.

The practice of spiritual mentoring

Reflecting on these sharings, reminds me that the spiritual path goes beyond Maslow's 'self-actualization' or self-realization. For us Ravindra (2014, p. 25) writes: *'as long as self-realization is myself-realization, the demon of "mine" does not leave us.'* In this he echoes the teachings of Buddha, the Bhagavad Gita, the Christian Gospels and many Sufi poets, as well as the teachings of the Prophet Muhammed.

The spiritual mentor is paradoxically not doing the mentoring. They are the friend, the listening ear, the companion on the journey. The mentor may open the window, but it is the winds and rains of life that blow in and provide the development. The mentor then supports the mentee to learn from life's challenges.

It is life that provides the learning agenda. Life is constantly there as a teacher, showing us that which is beyond our current understanding, providing us with new lessons and daily new challenges. But it depends on whether we/the mentee can relate to what happens in our lives in this manner.

Yet we cannot make the journey by our self. Because our self gets in the way. We cannot fully see ourselves, as our seeing is clouded by how we have been enculturated and educated. It is clouded by our beliefs and ways of seeing the world and clouded by our wants, desires and emotional reactions.

So, how does the mentor support the mentee's journey? Let me outline just a few of the ways I am aware of, from having been blessed by being helped on my journey by many spiritual mentors from diverse traditions, as well as sitting and walking with spiritual mentees. I will also draw on the answers from those who contributed to the inquiry I mentioned in the earlier section on the Inquiry Process.

I will outline:

- how the spiritual mentor listens differently from many other mentors;
- how the mentor is equal and alongside their mentees, and holds a wider perspective;
- how they might interrupt the mentee's interruptions of themselves by using stories, humour, paradox, etc.;
- how they walk the mentee to their learning edge;
- how the spiritual mentor might provide paradoxical challenges that take the mentee beyond their current way of being; and
- how an ethical spiritual mentor is a channel to a rich lineage of 'the spirit of guidance'.

How the spiritual mentor listens differently

Elsewhere, I have written about levels of listening required for the coach (Hawkins & Smith, 2013), the systemic coach (Hawkins & Turner, 2020), the psychotherapist (Hawkins & Ryde, 2019) and the team coach (Hawkins, 2021). The spiritual mentor needs these and more:

1. being fully present and focused on the other *(attending)*;
2. listening to the facts and the story being told and being able to play these back *(accurate listening)*;
3. listening not just with ears and cognitive mind, but in and through one's body with sympathetic resonance *(empathic Listening)*;
4. listening with and through the story of the other – recognizing it is a story – listening with compassion and empathy to everyone in their life and story *(wide-angled empathic listening)*;
5. listening through and with the person to all the nested systems they are part of – discovering what life is requiring from them *(eco-systemic or generative listening)*; and
6. listening from deep emptiness without reaction, attachment or judgement, allowing what needs to emerge to arrive and be present *(pure listening)*.

This sixth level takes much practice, as Ravindra (2014, p. 105) writes:

> *This tuning in to the subtler dimensions is possible only by cleansing our ordinary perceptions and quieting the mind. The requirement … is to be present with stillness and a silence of the body, the mind, and the emotions so that one might hear a rose petal fall, the sound of thoughts arising, and the silence between thoughts. The arising of thoughts and emotions is part of the play of nature, and watching this play with complete equanimity, without being disturbed, belongs to the spirit.*

My good friend and spiritual mentor Elias Amidon also talks of 'pure listening' about which he says:

> *With pure listening, one is neither validating nor invalidating the person who is speaking. Rather, one strives to listen wholly and with clarity, and in a way that is devoid of any positive or negative value judgments. As one engages in this form of listening with another, something interesting happens: if I am the speaker, and you're listening to me purely, the result is that I then dive much deeper into what I am saying because I sense you are truly present.*

(Whidbey Institute, 2012)

Both Elias and Ravi Ravindra are speaking of listening from emptiness and with non-attachment. Being non-invested in the other, or their story, or in oneself or one's thoughts, but just being fully present to what arises.

How the mentor is equal and alongside their mentees, and holds a wider perspective

The spiritual mentor walks alongside the seeker, where they are, not being better or different, not knowing better or first, but discovering together with them through collaborative inquiry. At the same time, they need to hold a wider perspective, garnered from their own rich spiritual journey. One goes to a spiritual teacher not for their words and teaching alone, but to be in the presence of the quality of their being. One goes to the spiritual mentor as a companion who one can sense knows the road, but helps you find it for yourself, and at the same time helps you wait for life to show it to you.

The spiritual mentor helps you pay attention, not to the contents of your story, but how you, and the culture you are marinaded in, are together creating the story. They are helping you to unpick the story and to let go of your attachment to a fixed perspective and seeing your story as the only reality. They are allowing you to be more fully with what is, and what is emerging.

How a spiritual mentor can interrupt our interruptions of ourself

The spiritual mentor interrupts our own mental and emotional interruptions of ourselves. I have never forgotten when still in my teens, going with some other young spiritual seekers to visit a wise old monk. We were full of questions, which he interrupted by saying:

> *You young people are in such a rush to be enlightened. Just remember when you are enlightened, 'You' are not there.*

The spiritual mentor may offer a story, some humour or even a surprising piece of behaviour that shakes you out of the fixity of your thinking. This is the paradoxical tradition of spiritual mentorship, that can be found most strongly in Zen, Sufi and other mystical lineages, and which is different from both most psychotherapeutic and Western religious direction traditions.

I have illustrated this paradoxical tradition in a modern version of an old Nasrudin story (Hawkins 2005, p. 68). For those of you not familiar with the Nasrudin tradition, he was the wise fool who teaches wisdom through his own foolishness. The original Nasrudin lived in what is now eastern Turkey nearly 1,000 years ago, but his teaching lives on and nearly every taxi driver from Istanbul to Jakarta will willingly tell you their favourite Nasrudin story.

THE CUP IS TOO FULL

One day an eminent consultant and author came and asked Nasrudin whether he would be willing to be his mentor.

'There is nothing I can teach you,' responded Nasrudin.

'Don't be so modest,' replied the eminent consultant. 'I am told that you are the best teacher for somebody like myself who is already an expert in their field.'

Nasrudin shrugged and invited the consultant for some tea. He carefully laid the table, brought out his best china and warmed the teapot. When the tea was made he began to pour and kept pouring until the tea was flowing over the edge of the cup and all over the table. Eventually the consultant jumped to his feet and said:

'Stop pouring you fool, can't you see the cup is too full to have any more tea in it?'

'Ah!" said Nasrudin, "I can see that I must empty the cup before I pour any more in, but cups are easier to empty than successful consultants.'

How spiritual mentors walk with you to your learning edge

Spiritual mentors gently and supportively walk with us to our learning edge. To the cliff where all our grounded learning runs out, and then they stay with us at that edge, looking into the foggy abyss and listening to the waves. They do not teach or coach but enable us as mentees to learn from life. Arkan Lushwala, who is a spiritual guide from the Peruvian Indigenous tradition and an acknowledged teacher by the Lakota people of North America, describes this beautifully:

> *Elders ... never tried to be the intermediaries between me and the truth. They always encourage me to discover the truth on my own, with my own heart. Those who instructed me did not try and educate me; they left me alone on a hill, they gave me medicine, they played tricks on my ego, and mostly, they touched my little heart with their big heart.*
>
> *When I was ready to learn something, they put me in situations where they knew I would learn by myself.*
>
> (Lushwala, 2012, p. 127)

Spiritual mentors give you paradoxical challenges that take you beyond yourself

Spiritual mentors or elders help provide new experiences that don't just add another item to our very full bank of what we have done, but put us into 'paradoxical seizure' (Hawkins & Smith, 2013), where our current ways of thinking, doing and being are of no help, and something new is needed, something from beyond our current self-limitations.

A good example of this is the practice of the spiritual mentor providing the seeker with either a koan or a Sufi chilla. I will now explore both.

A *koan* is a question that has no factual objective answer. Its essence is a paradox. Yet the person receiving it must use all their mental and emotional resources in trying to answer it. That is until they exhaust their current mental thinking and emotional being and a moment of 'metanoia' comes by grace. A classic Zen koan is 'What is the sound of one hand clapping?'. More modern varieties in spiritual mentoring might include: 'What is worthwhile?' 'What is love?'

A *chilla* is like a Zen koan in action – a task the seeker is given, which they can accept or say no to. If they accept, they have to commit themselves fully to achieving the task, but it is a task that cannot be fully achieved without a self-transformation. It is the journey not the goal that is transformative. I was once asked by my spiritual teacher to arrange for my parents to invite him to tea, so they could discuss me, without me being there. I was horrified, I had never told my parents I had been in psychotherapy, let alone was meeting with a strange, part-Indian Sufi teacher. Their world was tidy, ordered, Protestant and suburban. Through their eyes he would seem wild and foreign and an unwanted intrusion. This meeting could never happen, particularly if I was not there to translate and control what happened in the vast chasm between their two worlds! My parents would never agree. My mentor saw my frozen fear and gently said: *'If you ask them from your heart they will say yes.'* His gentleness cut like a sword through all my defences. I knew he was right, I had no way out, other than cowardice. It took several sleepless nights to find the courage to ask from my heart and allow these two worlds, both parts of me, to meet beyond my illusory control. This meeting led to a surprising transformation in my father and also our relationship.

The chilla and the koan lead you to a place beyond your current ways of being. But they are not ends in themselves. They are just aids to letting life more fully transform you. A sentiment beautifully caught by Cavafy (1975) in his poem *Ithaka*, here abridged:

> As you set out for Ithaka
>
> hope your road is a long one,
>
> full of adventure, full of discovery.
>
> ....
>
> Hope your road is a long one.
>
> May there be many summer mornings when,
>
> with what pleasure, what joy,
>
> you enter harbours you're seeing for the first time;
>
> ....
>
> Keep Ithaka always in your mind.
>
> Arriving there is what you're destined for.
>
> But don't hurry the journey at all.
>
> Better if it lasts for years,
>
> so you're old by the time you reach the island,
>
> wealthy with all you've gained on the way,
>
> not expecting Ithaka to make you rich.
>
> Ithaka gave you the marvellous journey.
>
> Without her you wouldn't have set out.
>
> She has nothing left to give you now.
>
> And if you find her poor, Ithaka won't have fooled you.
>
> Wise as you will have become, so full of experience,
>
> you'll have understood by then what these Ithakas mean.

(C. P. Cavafy: Collected Poems. (1975).
Reproduced with permission of Princeton University Press)

The ethical spiritual mentor is a channel to a rich lineage of 'the spirit of guidance'

Beware spiritual teachers who are self-appointed and self-benefiting. All spiritual guides, mentors and teachers need to be held by, and accountable to, a community and a lineage. There are many recent stories of charismatic spiritual teachers becoming abusive of followers and using their power for self-advancement. The spiritual mentor does not need to be perfect, for none of us are. But they need others who can challenge their behaviour and blind spots. A spiritual mentor is not trading on their personal wisdom, but is one who can open the door to a rich heritage and living stream of wisdom that flows down the generations. A perennial wisdom that is both ever-changing and yet always carries the same truth, albeit in new forms. An ethical spiritual mentor does not have fixed competencies and certifications but is accountable to both their tradition and their community of practice.

Practicing as a spiritual mentor

In my life I have been a counsellor, a psychotherapist, executive coach, systemic team coach and a consultant, and also a supervisor and trainer of all the above. Through all my life I have been a spiritual seeker, who has been constantly blessed by the unexpected arrival in my life of spiritual mentors and guides. In more recent years, I have been initiated as a spiritual guide and mentor and as a universal celebrant, conducting weddings, funerals, child blessings and life transition ceremonies. So, now some people come to me as a spiritual mentor, while others come in one of my other roles, but our work together is informed by, and at times shades into, spiritual mentoring.

To give one example of the former, a young single man who taught music in schools and was a skilled musician came to see me for spiritual mentoring. When he first came, his life was turbulent and unsettled and I offered him some simple breathing and centring practices, so he could find his silence and place of rest and source. It was several years before he came back, now ready to deepen his journey. When he was self-isolating in the countryside, in COVID-19 lockdown times, he would do long walks along the river valley. I encouraged him to follow the river to its source and then contemplate the source beyond the source. The next stage was for him to go and find a part of the river that was singing to him and listen to the song it was singing and ask the river if he could take the song and play it on one of his instruments. He later sent me the recording of the song he learnt from the river, played with such sensitivity on his guitar.

When I am in the role of psychotherapist or coach or supervisor, my listening may start with empathically hearing their story and the challenges they are facing in their work and wider life. But part of me is always listening through the immediate issues, to their life's journey and the lessons that life is presenting them through these life events. I may ask: *'Tell me the story of your life from your birth, to what has brought you right here, right now in just two minutes?'* or: *'Tell me what makes your heart sing? When are you most fully alive?'*

Once I have made a heart connection with the person, I will then move to the approach Eve Turner and I have outlined in Chapter 36 on eco-systemic mentoring and ask: '*Who and what does your work/life serve?*' and then '*Who and what else? Who beyond your family, beyond your organization, beyond your community? What beyond the human world?*', opening the wider eco-systemic levels that flow through and beyond the individual, and helping them see themselves and their issues in a much wider and deeper context. I invite those stakeholders and wider levels into the room and ask if those people were here, including your ancestors and future generations and the ecology, what would they be telling us is the work you and I need to be doing together. We may also walk together through nature, listening together to what nature and other beings are able to teach us concerning the challenges the mentee has brought.

How spiritual mentoring then becomes more central is by listening without any judgement or attachment to the person's whole life journey as it has unfolded and helping them to discover what is now emerging, and what is calling them to their next stage of becoming.

Conclusion

Every mentor, whether or not they have a spiritual interest or their own spiritual path, needs to be aware of how they address the aspects of their mentee's spiritual and transpersonal life. This includes the mentor being willing to explore the mentee's religious and spiritual background and experience, whatever culture or religion or belief system it comes from, with real non-judgemental interest.

It also includes helping the individual explore what gives meaning and creates lasting value in their lives, beyond material and personal success. In recent years, there has been a great deal of interest in *vertical development* (Kegan, 1982; Rooke & Torbert, 2005;Barrett, 2010; Hawkins & Smith, 2013, Chapter 2) and all the key writers point to how the higher stages of individual adult development include a transpersonal and spiritual aspect. Other writers, such as Wilber (1993; 1996; 2006)and Rohr (2009), more specifically describe the stages of spiritual maturity. Thus, to mentor a person on all stages of their life's journey requires helping them transition from one way of perceiving and being in the world (what Torbert calls their 'action logic') to one that is more inclusive and less 'self-centred'. Enabling step changes in a person's mindset requires an aspect of spiritual mentoring and this is particularly true when mentoring individuals in the later stages of their career or life, when the focus moves from building a strong 'authentic self' and a successful career and life, and moves to letting go of self – what the Sufis describe as the path of 'Fana', or unselfing.

My hope is that this chapter has helped you and your mentees discover more fully the beauty of widening perspectives, and to be able to join the great poet Rilke (1905) in saying:

I live my life in ever widening circles,

each superseding all the previous ones.

Perhaps I never shall succeed in reaching the final circle,

but attempt I will.

And to join in the beautiful prayer of the Lakota, Sioux, first nations Americans 'Aho Mitakuye Oyasin All My Relations'.

> *You are all my relations, my relatives, without whom I would not live. We are in the circle of life together, co-existing, co-dependent, co-creating our destiny. One, not more important than the other. One nation evolving from the other and yet each dependent upon the one above and the one below. All of us a part of the Great Mystery.*

(In Lushwala, 2012)

A practice to take away: From greed to the need of life

Every time you find yourself considering what you want, experiment with turning your personal 'I want' or 'I need' around to asking *'What does life need from me right now?'* – what Coleridge termed *'The one life in me and abroad.'*

With grateful acknowledgement of Elias Amidon, Elizabeth Birtles, Catherine Todd, Jeremy Woodcock, and Jeremy Young who all responded to my short inquiry on 'Spiritual Mentoring'.

Recommended reading

Amidon, E. (2012). *The Open Path: Recognizing Nondual Awareness*. Sentient Publications.

Hawkins, P. (2019). *Resourcing: The neglected third leg of supervision*. In E. Turner, & J. Passmore (Eds.), *The Heart of Coaching Supervision: Working with Reflection and Self-Care*. Routledge.

Wilber, K. (2006). *Integral Spirituality: A Startling New Role for Religion in the Modern and Postmodern World*. Shambhala.

References

Barrett, R. (2010). *The New Leadership Paradigm*. Richard Barrett. https://www.barrettacademy.com/books/the-new-leadership-paradigm

Cavafy, C. P. (Translation Copyright © 1975, 1992). *The City*. In *C.P. Cavafy: Collected Poems*, trans. by E. Keeley, & P. Sherrard, G. Savidis (Ed.). Princeton University Press.

Hawkins, P. (2005). *The Wise Fool's Guide to Leadership*. O Books.

Hawkins, P. (2021) Leadership Team Coaching: Developing Collective Transformational Leadership, Kogan Page.

Hawkins, P., & Ryde, J. (2019). *Integrative Psychotherapy: A Relational, Systemic and Ecological Approach*. Jessica Kingsley.

Hawkins, P., & Smith, N. (2013). *Coaching, Mentoring and Organisational Consultancy*. McGraw Hill Education.

Hawkins, P., & Turner, E. (2020). *Systemic Coaching: Delivering Value Beyond the Individual*. Routledge.

Kegan, R. (1982). *The Evolving Self: Problem and Process in Human Development*. Harvard University Press.

Lushwala, A. (2012). *The Time of the Black Jaguar: An Offering of Indigenous Wisdom for the Continuity of Life on Earth*. Arkan Lushwala.

Ravindra, R. (2014). *The Pilgrim Soul: A Path to the Sacred*. Quest Books.

Rilke, R. M. (1905). *Das Stunden-buch [Book of Hours]*. Trans. by A. E. Flemming. Insel-Verlag.

Rohr, R. (2009). *The Naked Now: Learning to See How the Mystics See*. The Crossroad Publishing Company.

Rooke, D., & Torbert, W. (2005, April). *Seven transformations of leadership. Harvard Business Review*, 67–76.

Whidbey Institute (2012). *Traveling the Open Path: An Interview with Elias Amidon*. https://whidbeyinstitute.org/elias-amidon/

Wilber, K. (1993). *The Spectrum of Consciousness*. Theosophical Publishing House.

Wilber, K. (1996). *Up from Eden: A Transpersonal View of Human Evolution*. Routledge & Kegan Paul.

Wilber, K. (2006). *Integral Spirituality: A Startling New Role for Religion in the Modern and Postmodern World*. Shambhala.

Chapter 36
Eco-Systemic Mentoring: Growing our Ecological Capacity to Create a Sustainable Future – An Urgent Priority

Peter Hawkins & Eve Turner

Introduction

This chapter considers how mentoring can help people make a greater contribution to addressing the ecological and climate crisis, by focusing not on what the individual wants to achieve, but what they can uniquely do that the world of tomorrow needs.

It provides an eco-systemic process, that starts with an enquiry process that connects both mentor and mentee more fully with ourselves, our immediate community, the world of our wider stakeholders and then the 'more-than-human' world of our shared Earth.

In the next phase after this enquiry process, the mentoring helps the mentee discover new perspectives and new possibilities for action. The final stage of the eco-systemic process is to turn these new insights into embodied action.

Engagement exercise

Let us start with an exercise (with gratitude to Krznaric, 2020, pp. 66–68) which we invite you to participate in.

Think of someone you mentor or someone who would benefit from your mentoring, perhaps a young person you know, a peer/colleague who is keen to develop a new skill or someone who simply needs encouragement. Try to bring to mind their face, their voice, their expressions. Consider what you know of their hopes, their dreams and their aspirations. What do you imagine is the help and support they most need from you? How do they need you to be alongside them?

Now go forward many years into the future, and imagine it is that person's work leaving party. You are listening in and you hear them looking back over their career, over the good and more challenging times, over their hopes met and perhaps of some left unfulfilled. And they are talking about the people who made a difference to them during their career and why. Some reflections are told with real warmth and gratitude, others are spoken of with some regret, as opportunities never quite realised.

And now the mentee mentions you as someone who made a difference – what are they saying about the difference that your mentoring made and what it opened up for them in their lives?

Now come back to the present. Considering those reflections, how might this inspire you in your mentoring moving forward? What might you need to learn and develop today, to help your capacity as an effective mentor? What are your next steps?

Introduction

Paul Hawken writes in his book *Regeneration: Ending the Climate Crisis in One Generation*:

> *Vital connections have been severed between human beings and nature...*

> *This disconnection is the origin of the climate crisis, it is the very root – and it is where we discover solutions and actions that can engage all people, regardless of income, race, gender or belief.*

> (Hawken, 2021, p. 9)

Our work is to heal this deep and dangerous separation.

'*Humanity is in peril, and we need to change our ways*' (Whybrow et al., 2023, p. 1). In recent millennia, humans have focused on how they can better the lot of their own species and they have become very good at this. We have now reached a point where we have dominated the rest of the Earth and created the Anthropocene, a geological period of time that describes how human activity has become predominant on our planet's climate, earth, biodiversity and ecosystems. So, our success has come at enormous cost to all other species we share this earth with, and the wider biosphere, lithosphere, hydrosphere and atmosphere. As a species, we have extracted and exploited every aspect of our wider ecology; the carbon and minerals we have mined and burnt, the topsoil we have poisoned, up to a million species facing extinction through our actions (United Nation, 2019) and the air we have polluted. The cost is now so overwhelming it is threatening every aspect of this planet and having an increasingly destructive impact on human life.

The most recent Intergovernmental Panel on Climate Change (IPCC) report (IPCC, 2022) makes clear the task facing us. It points to the average annual greenhouse gas emissions being at their highest levels in human history. Limiting a global temperature rise to 1.5°C is almost out of reach without immediate and deep emissions reductions across all sectors. The impacts include our warmer oceans, rising water levels, degraded habitats – including those for humans – leading to more mass migration (Watson, 2022), and the loss of species and biodiversity. Yet, as reported by Dewan and Ramirez (2022), '*we already have the solutions – the only thing preventing us from taking advantage of them is political will and status-quo interests in fossil fuels ... renewable energy sources like wind and solar are now economically viable and becoming cheaper by the day.*'

In her book on Indigenous wisdom, Kimmerer shows how all beings are bound by:

> '...a covenant of reciprocity: plant breath for animal breath, winter and summer, predator and prey, grass and fire, night and day, living and dying' with water, clouds, soil and rocks dancing in a 'continual giveaway of making, unmaking and making again the earth ... In the dance of the giveaway, remember that the earth is a gift we must pass on, just as it came to us. When we forget, the dances we'll need will be for mourning. For the passing of polar bears, the silence of cranes, for the death of rivers and the memory of snow.
>
> (Kimmerer, 2020, p. 383)

Many of us know this intuitively but may find it hard, personally and professionally, to face up to the consequences of what is happening, expressing emotions from grief, to anger, to guilt, to hopelessness. Yet, if we need to transform as a species, then all we do, including our mentoring, is simply part of that.

So, practically, how can we move forward and how can we be collaborators, communicators and connectors for the changes we need? We can move to a place where we take responsibility, not in a disabling, overwhelming sense, but feeling enabled, for example, to question policies, politicians and business leaders, to make different purchasing decisions and to collaborate with others for change. We can do self-work and work with others, deepening and widening our human consciousness – acting and speaking from our heart and drawing on Active Hope, which we will discuss in the next section. We can ask ourselves, 'How do we collaborate with our mentees, and develop our focus so it moves beyond what our mentees might want to be, their individual hopes, their aspirations, and extends into who the world needs them to be, to develop ourselves around a collective and lasting vision for a sustainable future?

As part of this, we will consider not what humans want from the world, but what is needed to heal the deep split between the human and the 'more-than-human' world. We may be at a point of crisis, or of transformation, but we need to recognize that the behaviour of our species has been responsible for this global crisis and unless we do so, we cannot be part of the solution. We need to fundamentally change how we individually and collectively think and perceive the world, and therefore how we act in it (Whybrow et al., 2023).

As mentors we are in such a good position to do this work. As Whybrow et al. (2023, p. 147) describe: 'our most fundamental gift is that of listening ... We may hold big questions, yet at the heart of our work as practitioners our most important role remains – creating and holding a safe space, being a 'container' that allows the exploration of our feelings, our thoughts, our concerns, and doing this with love and compassion, free of judgement, expectation, or a pre-defined action plan.' And Whybrow et al. (2023) note that this is also true for us, not just our mentees.

Three key features of eco-systemic mentoring

An early working definition of mentoring was offered by Eric Parsloe (University of Glasgow, 2022):

> *Mentoring is to support and encourage people to manage their own learning in order that they may maximise their potential, develop their skills, improve their performance and become the person they want to be.*

This was further developed by Hawkins and Smith (2006; 2013) but 'eco--systemic mentoring' takes both much further by focusing on what the world needs us to be, as opposed to what our individual ego wants. It starts from the awareness of our total interconnectedness, not just as one human family, but with all beings and life with whom we share this planet. The individual is nested from birth in a family, within a community and a culture, within the human species, within an ecology. A systemic perspective also recognizes that all the systemic levels we are nested within are also nested within us. When an individual comes to mentoring, their family system, culture and the wider ecology all arrive within them, from the way they perceive and view the world, the air they breathe, the food they eat, etc. (Hawkins & Turner, 2020).

Eco-systemic mentoring addresses the ecological and climate crisis by its focus on deepening and widening human consciousness and, in particular, that of the mentee. It does this by helping them explore the many worlds they are part of, and which are therefore part of them.

There are three key aspects of this practice as shown in Figure 36.1 and we will explore each of them.

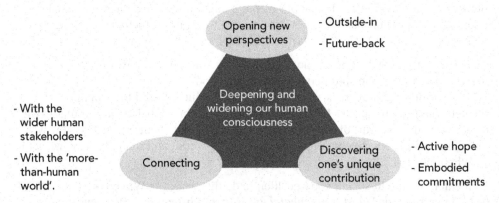

Figure 36.1: Eco-systemic mentoring '(reproduced with permission of Renewal Associates, 2022).

Connecting

> Only connect! *That was the whole of her sermon.* Only
> connect *the prose and the passion, and both will be exalted,*
> *and human love will be seen at its height.*

(E. M. Forster, *Howards End*, 1910)

Eco-systemic mentoring is helping the individual connect with all that is within them and all that they are part of. To experience how their life is a constant flow between all the systemic levels of the many living elements within them, the flow of air, food, water, blood and hormones in, through and out of them. To connect to the many systems they are nested within; the family and teams they are part of; the communities and organizations that these groupings are nested within; the wider cultures and one human family which is intricately interconnected; and the one Earth we share with so many complex ecosystems and other living beings. All are in constant ever-changing flow, and who they are is constantly changing at the crossroads of these many tides.

Salmon (2000), an Indigenous American writer and academic, has coined the phrase 'kincentric ecology' and would encourage us to see ourselves in the widest possible context and connections:

> *Indigenous people view both themselves and nature as part*
> *of an extended ecological family that shares ancestry and*
> *origins. It is an awareness that life in any environment is*
> *viable only when humans view the life surrounding them as*
> *kin. The kin, or relatives, include all the natural elements*
> *of an ecosystem.*

(Salmon, 2000, p. 1327)

Mentoring provides a space where the individual can connect more fully with the people they work with, with the work they do, with their purpose and passion, and to bring their whole selves and their connections. So, it offers a space where the individual can connect the prose of their current concerns with the poetry of their dreams, and connect the prose of their challenges with the poetry of beauty that calls to them from beyond themselves.

Opening new perspectives

The major barriers to any human fulfilling their potential, lie not in the world round them but in the limitations of their ways of perceiving and understanding the world. The great Sufi poet Mevlana Jalaludin Rumi asks, '*Why in the plenitude of the Universe have you chosen to fall asleep in such a small dark prison?*', and the prison he is referring to is the limiting assumptions and restrictive frames through which we engage with life. However, the mentor's role is not to try and change anyone's mind, but to provide ways by which the mentee can discover new perspectives, open up new windows. This is done by thinking 'outside-in' – by inviting the mentee to step into the shoes of all their stakeholders and view their life and development from many different perspectives. Also, to think 'future-back', as in the opening exercise in this chapter, bringing in the voice of the future self, or the voices of future generations. So, as a mentor we might ask, 'Thinking of the world/ community/organization you would like to be part of in 2030, what's the work you will appreciate us doing today, and even regret us not doing?'

Active Hope (Macy & Johnston, 2012) encourages this reflection, suggesting that we can choose our response to what we face. Macy and Johnstone (2012, p. 3) see Active Hope as a three-step practice: first, taking a clear view of reality; second, identifying what we hope for regarding the direction we'd like things to move in or the values expressed; and third, we actively take steps to move ourselves or our situation in that direction. By doing this we focus on our intention and the confidence that we can take action, and then embody these commitments.

Discovering one's unique contribution

All evolution is co-created, between an organism or a species and it its ecological niche. Spencer's reductive phrase of Darwin's evolutionary theory into the *'survival of the fittest'* has for too long, and for too many people, been misunderstood and seen as survival of the strongest. Darwin was highlighting the importance of the 'fit' between a species and its wider ecology, the ability of the species to adapt, change and most importantly, co-create with and within its ecological niche. All success is also co-created between an individual, team, organization or community, and the needs of the context in which it lives and operates. We are all born with and develop different skills, aptitudes, attitudes and strengths. To be successful we have to find the right fit between what the world of tomorrow needs, and what we uniquely have to offer; to discover our own unique contribution to the web of interconnections of which we are just one extremely small part.

How do we fully occupy our unique niche? We do not try and be someone else, for all other spaces are already taken. That is why Peter, many years ago, alighted on the question: 'What can you uniquely do that the world of tomorrow needs?' The wording is very precise, to guard against chasing after what made your mentor, mentee or role models successful yesterday and in the past, but consider instead what the world of tomorrow is calling forth, that you are in the best possible position to respond to. People often say of the successful, *'they were lucky as they were in the right place at the right time'*, while others say, *'you make your own luck'*. Both we believe are half-truths, for the right place and right time come from finding the right connection between your potential offering and the emerging needs of the world around you.

Successful entrepreneurs and business leaders are those who can anticipate future needs and are ready to ride the next wave of change as it arrives. To do this they need to be unattached to short-term demands and targets and able to *'think long-term in a short-term world'* (Krznaric, 2020). They also need to be an environmental scanner who is attentive to the changing trends and patterns in the world about them. In addition, they are hungry learners, who look to engage fully with the world in ways that disconfirm what they currently believe, rather than seeking out confirmation of their past beliefs and assumptions.

What does this mean for mentoring?

To become an eco-systemic mentor, particularly within healthcare, we need to start by deepening and broadening our work – connecting both with ourselves and our wider purpose. Only when we have done the work for ourselves, can we then facilitate the work in our mentees. This requires us to each work through the five stages of the Hawkins Eco-Phase model as outlined in Whybrow et al. (2023) and in Figure 36.2.

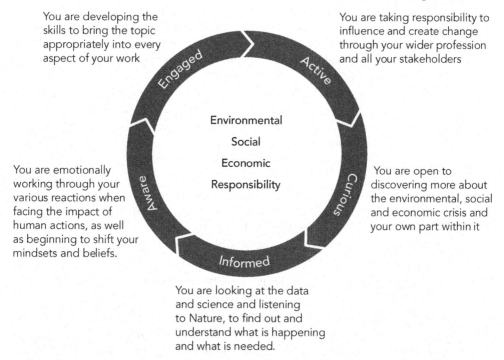

You are developing the skills to bring the topic appropriately into every aspect of your work

You are taking responsibility to influence and create change through your wider profession and all your stakeholders

Environmental

Social

Economic

Responsibility

You are emotionally working through your various reactions when facing the impact of human actions, as well as beginning to shift your mindsets and beliefs.

You are open to discovering more about the environmental, social and economic crisis and your own part within it

You are looking at the data and science and listening to Nature, to find out and understand what is happening and what is needed.

Figure 36.2: The Eco-Phase model (Renewal Associates and the Climate Coaching Alliance).

We need to be constantly **'eco-curious'** and enquiring about the wider environment and the rapid changes that are happening in all aspects of Earth's ecology, so we become more and more **'eco-informed'**. With this learning process comes waves of emotional reactions and responses, which we need to both listen to and work through so we can become **'eco-aware'** and realise the ecological crisis is not a problem out there, but deeply rooted in each and every one of us. Only then are we needed to mentor others in a way that is **'eco-engaged'**, where the ecology becomes a partner in every mentoring conversation. However, just changing our mentoring conversations is not enough and the final stage is to become **'eco-active'**, helping to transform our professional bodies, organizations and communities. The journey as shown is not linear and requires constantly going around the cycle, both in ourselves and in our mentoring work, so that we are constantly healing the split in us and contributing to healing the split between the human and 'more-than-human' worlds.

To mentor in an eco-engaged way will require us first to be curious, to be open to exploration and to own our own feelings about what is going on in the world, and to be connected to ourselves and to others, mirroring what Salmon (2000) described as kincentric ecology. Just by being, and allowing, indeed encouraging, a breadth of dialogue, free of judgement or expectation, we may allow wider perspectives to emerge.

We can start by opening up conversations

1. We begin, shoulder to shoulder, in partnership, both discovering through a dialogical enquiry the work the wider world needs us to explore. We might go outside and while walking draw natural elements into our conversation – this can be done in person and virtually, where both of us walk simultaneously and draw on what we are each seeing, hearing and feeling.

2. We ensure our reflection has breadth and well as depth as we consider how we connect with others, for example, through our leadership. We may ask questions such as 'Who and what is your life in service of?' and 'What most matters in your life?' And we develop our ability to 'play witness', to stand back and not get drawn into our reactions to the emotions and hopes, the concerns and challenges raised.

3. We draw on our essential gifts of deep listening and really hearing, avoiding unnecessary interruptions, and do so with both compassion and reflective enquiry. Sometimes, the simplest word can be enough – someone makes a statement such as *'I worry I won't be enough...'* and you offer the one word 'for...' or 'to do...' so that they continue their own exploration.

4. To open up the enquiry to a wider perspective we can also draw on a variety of tools, as well as on poetry, music, our own writing, etc. Some examples are:

    a. Neil's Wheel (2022; see also Whybrow et al., 2023, pp. 176–178), which has seven named segments (financial, human, environmental, legacy, valued/calling/meaning/purpose, whole-life fulfilment, enabling the greatness in others) and one left blank to complete as needed. It allows the mentee to consider, with openness, the areas that matter to them in the way they interpret them. An example is that, for some mentees, 'environmental' is about their work culture, for others it is about what is facing the planet.

    b. Linda Aspey's systemic framework 'With the earth in mind' (Aspey, 2022) also looks at areas like purpose, values and emotions as a way to explore critical issues and bring potential for meaningful change.

Another step is to create new perspectives

Here we suggest just a few ideas for our work with mentees. More can be found in Chapters 10–15 in Whybrow et al. (2023).

- It is easy for us all to be insular in our thinking, focusing on our own team, our own piece of work, the now, and forgetting broader and longer contexts. So, we begin by listing all the other parties to our work, our so-called 'stakeholders'. Some will be obvious, like the organization, the team, the division, but who and what else? Can we keep going? Maybe now you/your mentee have some that are slightly less obvious, like taxpayers, or patients/clients/customers, their families, the wider community, friends, our banking and insurance systems.

And then being 'kincentric' and ask again, who and what else? Does that open up more exploration? Did you include future generations (including future staff, customers, family), our ancestors and the 'more-than-human' world)?

- And we must never forget the 'thirteenth fairy'. When Grimbleshanks wasn't invited to Sleeping Beauty's royal christening she was 'hopping mad' (Umansky, 2014, p. 1). Her spell that Sleeping Beauty would prick her finger on her sixteenth birthday and die was turned into sleeping for a hundred years, but the moral is who/what have we forgotten to invite to the party, at our peril?

- Now we can 'invite' the views of these other parties to our work. We can also invite mentees to use differing time frames. We might ask, 'In two years (or five, etc.), what is the work you will be pleased we did today? What might you regret not considering?'

- To help us in this, we might employ techniques such as 'the empty chair' where we invite our mentee to 'bring someone, or some being, into the room' and sit in the chair and speak as them. What views would they offer? What suggestions might they make? What challenge could they bring?

- And we can shift deliberately. Heifetz and Linsky (2002) suggest we move from the dance floor to the balcony and use that metaphor to watch the dance we are part of from a different perspective.

And next we consider how might we do this in a way to find our unique place

The approaches above are a good place to start. Sometimes, though, we come up against our own, or our mentee's resistance, or 'stuckness'. Here we can use joining words or a reframe. If a mentee is doubting their own ability and suggesting they cannot make a difference, you might gently offer, *'And if you could make a difference your first step might be…?'* Or when a mentee says, *'they wouldn't choose someone like me'* we might simply say (sometimes more than once) *'…because…'* with a slight question in our tone. Or our mentee says, *'The people in charge will never do this…'* And you offer *'yet'.*

We can also be playful. In Whybrow et al. (2023), the Council of Beings (pp. 87–89) requires us to speak from the perspective of another 'more-than-human-being', an animal, a tree, a plant, a rock, a mountain or the sea, and then understand what insight that perspective offers and how we might respond. We might use drawing here, putting in key stakeholders and the bridges and barriers that connect us or keep us apart. We could use figures, cards, objects, videos, blogs, podcasts, metaphors, reading and so on to expand our thinking and understanding and creatively connect with the diverse elements of our world. Then we might use the question from our exercise at the start, and pause, considering what is the difference the world needs us to make, and what we would like to hear someone say about us at their retirement, or at the end of their life.

And when, as we do, we revert to our polarity thinking, those lovely contrasts that grab our attention and lock us into 'right' or 'wrong', or 'good' or 'bad' ways of thinking – *'…is it ok to do this?', '…am I good enough?', '…do I know enough?'* and so on, we can just have a quick laugh at ourselves and notice the danger. And as Portia Nelson (1993) suggests, avoid the 'hole' and go down another street.

A case example

Rather than tell you a story about someone else's mentoring, we are going to offer this part of the chapter as a free mentoring session, just for you. You will need a paper and pen to capture your responses and a quiet space to engage with your full being. The ***** indicate places for you to stop reading and find your own response.

Welcome to your mentoring session.

Please imagine you have come to one of us authors for a mentoring session. What would be the focus of the enquiry, personally and in your work in health care, you would like to explore? Please take some time to note down the core aspects of your enquiry and the questions and concerns that are engaging you.

*****

Now pause and lay aside those questions and tell me about you and what is most important to you in your life and work. Where are you most alive and vital, and what makes your heart sing?

*****

Now pause again and consider and write down who and what does your life and work serve. Try and write names of individuals, then groups of stakeholders and then the wider human and ecological communities. Any 'thirteenth fairies'?

*****

If you invite all these different stakeholders into your imagination, ask them for their response to your core enquiry questions that you wrote down earlier. Now capture some of the key messages that emerged from these 'outside-in' perspectives.

*****

In your imagination, travel forward in time to the you of ten years from now. Imagine how life has changed for you, your stakeholders and the wider ecology. What might this older you advise on your enquiry questions? What would they be encouraging you to do right now?

*****

Now return to the present and write down how your enquiry has changed with the help of these 'future-back' perspectives.

*****

Based on what has emerged from connecting with these perspectives, complete the sentence 'What I can uniquely do that the world of tomorrow needs from me now is.......?'

*****

Now stand up and step into an embodied version of you, living to your full potential, and speak out loud your commitment to the first steps you need to take on this next adventure.

*****

Thank you for the difference you are going to make in our world.

Conclusion

Traditionally, mentoring has been like mission statements – starting from what the individual wants to achieve in the world. In contrast, eco-systemic mentoring is purpose-led starting 'outside-in' and 'future-back' – what the wider world needs from the unique place that the individual occupies in the wider, interconnected ecosystem. We each need to discover the fuller part that the greatly challenged Earth, that we are blessed to inhabit, requires from us, and this is very hard to do without friends, coaches and mentors who are willing to fully challenge and support us, to discover and commit to fully becoming who we are needed to be, and mentors who are committed to their own journey of purpose driven discovery.

Recommended reading

Kimmerer, R. (2020). *Braiding Sweetgrass: Indigenous Wisdom, Scientific Knowledge and the Teachings of Plants*. Penguin Books.

Hawkins, P., & Turner, E. (2020). *Systemic Coaching: Delivering Value Beyond the Individual*. Routledge.

Whybrow, A., Turner, E., McLean, J., with Hawkins, P. (2023). *Ecological and Climate-Conscious Coaching: A Companion Guide to Evolving Coaching Practice*. Routledge.

References

Aspey, L. (2022). *With the Earth in Mind*. Aspey Associates. https://www.aspey.com/with-the-earth-in-mind

Dewan, A., & Ramirez, R. (2022, April 4). *UN report on climate crisis confirms the world already has solutions -- but politics are getting in the way*. CNN. https://edition.cnn.com/2022/04/04/world/un-ipcc-climate-report-mitigation-fossil-fuels/index.html

Forster, E. M. (1910). *Howards End*. Penguin Books. 2012

Hawken, P. (2021). *Regeneration: Ending the Climate Crisis in One Generation*. Penguin.

Hawkins, P., & Smith, N. (2006). *Coaching, Mentoring and Organizational Consultancy: Supervision and Development* (**1st ed.**). McGraw Hill

Hawkins, P., & Smith, N. (2013). *Coaching, Mentoring and Organizational Consultancy: Supervision, Skills and Development* (**2nd ed.**). Open University Press.

Hawkins, P., & Turner, E. (2020). *Systemic Coaching: Delivering Value Beyond the Individual*. Routledge.

Heifetz, R., & Linsky, M. (2002, June). *A survival guide for leaders*. Harvard Business Review. https://hbr.org/2002/06/a-survival-guide-for-leaders

Intergovernmental Panel on Climate Change (IPCC) (2022). *Climate Change 2022: Mitigation of Climate Change*. https://www.ipcc.ch/report/sixth-assessment-report-working-group-3/

Kimmerer, R. (2020). *Braiding Sweetgrass: Indigenous Wisdom, Scientific Knowledge and the Teachings of Plants*. Penguin Books.

Krznaric, R. (2020). *The Good Ancestor: How to Think Long Term in a Short-Term World*. W H Allen.

Macy, J., & Johnstone, C. (2012). *Active Hope: How to Face the Mess We're in Without Going Crazy*. New World Library.

Neil's Wheel (2022). *One Life, One World, One Humanity, One Future: Making Something Good Happen*. https://neilswheel.org/

Nelson, P. (1993). *There's a Hole in My Sidewalk: The Romance of Self-Discovery*. Beyond Words/Atria Books.

Salmon, E. (2000). *Kincentric ecology: Indigenous perceptions of the human nature relationship*. Ecological Applications, **10**(5), 1327–1332. http://dx.doi.org/10.2307/2641288

Umansky, K. (2014). *The 13th Fairy*. Barrington Stoke.

United Nations (2019). *UN Report: Nature's Dangerous Decline 'Unprecedented'; Species Extinction Rates 'Accelerating.'* https://www.un.org/sustainabledevelopment/blog/2019/05/nature-decline-unprecedented-report/
University of Glasgow (2022). *Mentoring*. https://www.gla.ac.uk/media/Media_415574_smxx.pdf

Watson, J. (2022). *Climate change is already fueling global migration. The world isn't ready to meet people's changing needs, experts say*. PBS News Hour. https://www.pbs.org/newshour/world/climate-change-is-already-fueling-global-migration-the-world-isnt-ready-to-meet-peoples-needs-experts-say

Whybrow, A., Turner, E., McLean, J., with Hawkins, P. (2023). *Ecological and Climate-Conscious Coaching: A Companion Guide to Evolving Coaching Practice*. Routledge.

Chapter 37
The Evolution of Mentoring Theory and Practice: A Personal Reflection

Interview with Kathy Kram

What would you most like to share with us, for this Handbook chapter, about your perspectives on and experiences in the field of mentoring research that you feel are significant and groundbreaking? Why do you feel this is so important?

I'd like to start with my earliest interests in mentoring. When I started my first full time job after college, I noticed several individuals who took an active interest in my success as a newcomer to the business world and the field of Human Resources Management (HRM). As I reflected on this, I recognized the significant and positive impact that others' interest in me [had on] my growth and development. This was in the context of a time in our history of heightened awareness of how men and women were treated differently in the workplace, stemming from the [US Equal Employment Opportunity Commission] (EEOC) legislation. As I pursued my quest to understand the dynamics of these relationships, I began to read early publications in the popular press on mentorship. I first became aware of the practice of mentoring in the 1970s, when publications related it to the advancement of professionals in their chosen careers and addressed the question: What's the role of more experienced people in a field in helping young people get established in professional roles?

The overlay of affirmative action for equal employment opportunities then started to shape the agenda for research. By the 1980s, the questions were, for example, starting to look at comparing the employment experiences of women and men. One of the reasons that mentoring first started off as focusing on the development of younger adults came from Dan Levinson's research captured in his book *Seasons of a Man's Life* – he studied the development of the lives of adult men, and in particular, the role of mentoring in a young man's life (Levinson et al., 1978). As I started off working in a male-dominated work environment, I became interested in how this idea related to women's experiences.

After several years working in industry, I pursued my doctoral studies in Organizational Behaviour. I have been rooted in the world of mentoring scholarship and practice ever since. During the 1980s and 1990s, there was a big research focus on the outcomes of mentoring, exploring questions such as: Did it lead to career advancement, higher self-esteem, higher job satisfaction? There was also a focus on preconditions such as 'What does it take to be an effective mentor or mentee?'

I've always been interested in the *process* of mentoring, and today that is embraced as absolutely critical to understanding developmental relationships. By 'the process' I mean the interaction of mentor and mentee and what they each bring to the relationship with promise for learning and growth. As this took hold in the 1990s, there was a burgeoning of research in this area – what helps a healthy learning process and what causes dysfunction? There is a fair amount of research now, too, on the 'dark side' of mentoring (e.g., Scandura, 1998; Eby, 2007). I became interested and wrote a paper with Monica Higgins in 2001 where we talked about reconceptualizing mentoring not as a dyadic relationship but as a developmental network, which one might define as a group of relationships which focus on the learning and development of a focal person (Higgins & Kram, 2001).

If I am advising someone now about starting a mentoring programme, I always emphasize the limitations of conceptualizing mentoring as simply a one-on-one relationship – it can be that, but individuals are going to have more developmental opportunities if they conceptualize mentoring as a small group of people whom they can enlist into their lives to help them grow and develop. This is the framework that makes the most sense, and that's where the research is heading in the US. There has been work on peer mentoring, group mentoring – a lot of different variations on the theme of mentoring – which creates a lot of challenge conceptually, but actually reflects a lot more of what goes on in people's lives. (e.g., Murphy & Kram, 2014; Parker et al., 2018)

Do you think that because many work cultures have evolved to be more efficiency-based and performance-managed the opportunities that existed twenty or thirty years ago for accessing a network of informal mentoring are increasingly scarce, making formal mentoring programmes more important?

I hadn't thought of it like that, but that makes a lot of sense. I once went through a period of thinking that formally assigned mentoring was not as effective as informal mentoring, but as the cultures of professions and organizations have changed it may be a necessary approach, just to create the opportunities that are no longer as readily available to informally interact with potential mentors.

Employee resource groups have formed here in the US where, for example, women meet to discuss the unique challenges faced by women in a male-dominated setting and this could be reframed as peer mentoring – it's creating an opportunity to get the support and development that you don't get if you don't create the space for it. These kinds of groups have emerged for a range of non-dominant groups in White, male-dominated settings, and they are often launched by HRM and diversity initiatives (Murrell & Blake-Beard, 2017).

We also have to look at the context in which a mentoring relationship is unfolding – we have to look at macro factors, such as the politics and social norms and economics, to understand what's unfolding at the level of the mentoring relationship. An open systems perspective, as outlined by Bronfenbrenner (1994), is an important 'macro' perspective that informs my research, even though it's more at the 'micro' level of dyadic or small group relationships. The context in which mentoring occurs is crucial.

In the UK, mentoring in the nursing professions has historically been a part of a formal supervision and monitoring context, which has given it a very different meaning.

When a supervisory role is combined with a mentoring role it's difficult because there are conflicting purposes there that might undermine the developmental nature of the relationship.

Can you tell us any more about research that has been done into group approaches to mentoring?

I wrote a paper with Monica Higgins in 2001 on developmental networks (Higgins & Kram, 2001), and since then people have increasingly done research not just on the single dyadic relationship but also into what happens when people create a robust developmental network where you can get different kinds of developmental support and mentoring from different individuals. There have been some articles, such as that by Elana Feldman – one of my former students – and Bill Kahn, and it's about wrestling with different advice that you get from different developers (Feldman & Kahn, 2019). That's a new complexity. If you see yourself as having multiple developers – how do you reconcile the conflicting advice? How people handle this depends on their stage of cognitive and emotional development – are they able to handle conflicting advice and see this as an opportunity to pave a unique pathway for themselves – or do they get stuck in 'should I go with A or B?'

This is an interesting example of how life stage and cognitive and emotional development impact on what people experience in mentoring relationships.

What do you feel are key messages to share for your chapter about research and practice in mentoring, from both a mentee and mentor perspective, for leaders of organizations and those setting up mentoring programmes?

My view is that one needs to look at the nature of the context in which the mentoring is happening, what each individual brings to the relationship, and also the emotional competencies that the individuals need in order to build a growth-enhancing relationship. I've co-authored a book with Polly Parker, Tim Hall and Ilene Wasserman on peer coaching, and in that we talk about how, in order to be effective peer coaches, people need to know themselves well in terms of what they have to offer to a peer and also in terms of what they might need from a peer (Parker et al., 2018).

We conceptualize peer coaching as a two-way process, where both parties have the potential to learn – maybe on different issues – but if they have the listening skills and the self-awareness, they can develop mutuality and reciprocity in their relationship that leads to learning on both sides.

How do you view the relationship between mentoring and coaching?

I view coaching as more narrowly focused on work-related performance, and mentoring is broader and deeper, may take into account other life contexts and is usually longer term. So, actually, in my original research I found coaching to be part of mentoring, that is all the mentors that I spoke with were doing some form of coaching but they were also doing a lot of other things, including counselling, role modelling and offering friendship at a deeper level that were not within the scope of coaching.

I am aware that the terms coaching and mentoring are used in a whole range of different ways by different people, and so after doing research into developmental networks I began to feel more comfortable using the term developmental relationship to avoid the ongoing debate about coaching vs mentoring. But it's necessary to advise organizations and professions to come up with a shared understanding of what you mean by mentoring and let it be contextually defined, rather than defined by 'an expert'. Just here in the US, you can go to five different organizations and get five different definitions.

What do you make of that Kathy, that there are so many definitions of mentoring and a blurring between definitions of coaching and mentoring?

I think it reflects the fact that relationships are embedded in a larger system and that the larger system defines what the relationship is like, how it's understood by its members – so it's really the idea of a systemic perspective – no relationship exists out of context really.

If you think about a marriage, there are many opportunities for partners to mentor each other and coach each other, but they rarely talk about it that way unless they're psychologists! But it's part of the relationship.

I don't know – there's been a lot written on coaching in the last twenty years and it seems to me there are a lot of different definitions of coaching around. Again, it's hard to choose one definition. I think it's about being explicit about how you're defining it for your purposes. This is not a very satisfying answer, and then the critics of this approach will say how do you distinguish mentoring from helping relationships, which is a good question isn't it?

It's a good question – I was just going to ask how you would define that for yourself Kathy?

I think [there are] some helping relationships I could call mentoring or coaching, I think helping relationships are a broader category yet that could include mentoring, and coaching. Edgar Schein has done a lot of groundbreaking work on how to apply a process approach to organizational dynamics at individual and group levels, and he wrote a book called *Helping* which is very relevant to understanding both mentoring and coaching relationships (Schein, 2009). The Center for Positive Organizations, founded at the University of Michigan by Jane Dutton and colleagues, is forging an understanding of 'high-quality connections' (e.g., Dutton & Heaphy, 2003); many years ago, she and I realised we had a lot in common in terms of what we were trying to understand and we were going about it in very similar and different ways. There's a whole line of research that she's been involved in with her colleagues which looks at trust, rapport, mutuality and reciprocity, and these are dimensions of dyadic interactions that foster and hold up mentoring. These areas of research bring new lenses to understanding what's going on between two people (Dutton & Ragins, 2007).

What do you think about the evidence base for mentoring as compared to coaching, which often appears to be developing clearer evidence bases?

My first reaction to that is that I was more certain about the nature of mentoring back in the early 1980s than I am now, because I see more of its complexities. I have a colleague, Belle Rose Ragins, who has done a lot of work on mentoring and, in particular, high-quality mentoring (Ragins & Verbos, 2007). And within that context she will talk about mentoring episodes which are short-term interactions – it may not lead to a longer-term mentoring relationship but in that particular episode something transpires that has a big impact on one or both people. There are episodic events that can produce 'catapults of learning' – insights which didn't evolve over the course of a year or two but which happened in a moment (Fletcher & Ragins, 2007, pp. 273–299). I'm not sure that's something you would want to address.

That is powerful in relation to looking at whether work environments that have become more managed for a certain kind of efficiency are still able to provide as many naturally occurring episodes of learning and mentoring as they once did.

How workplace diversity has impacted the role of mentoring also adds complexity in terms of building effective mentoring relationships (e.g., Ragins, 1999). There are a number of scholars across the world who are focused on the impact of globalization – how is mentoring different in India, the US and Europe (e.g., Murrell & Blake-Beard, 2017)? *All* of these broader cultural issues very much affect the mentoring relationship, so in writing a book on mentoring it's hard to have a consistent view because there are so many variations.

Our book has been an emerging journey – we have authors from Europe, the US, Australia, South Africa and many other countries – and we're realising there aren't really that many books out there on coaching and mentoring that show and share those differences.

Yes, and there is a hunger for it – for this kind of approach. More recent work includes explicit attention to how both societal and organizational cultures shape the nature of mentoring, coaching and developmental relationships more generally (e.g., Murrell & Blake-Beard, 2017; Ghosh & Hutchins, 2022).

What do you feel has/might have hindered effective mentoring theory and research from your perspective? What needs to be done to change this?

This may be more of a US-based problem, but I think the biggest hindrance is the focus on quantitative empirical evidence, which tends to privilege tangible outcomes, such as salary increases and promotion, and does not really illuminate the range of experiences and developmental outcomes as much as extrinsic outcomes.

The other hindrance is the focus on what the mentee gets out of the relationship, rather than recognizing that, in my view, the highest quality mentoring occurs when both individuals are actually learning and growing. That idea of mutuality and reciprocity is very much part of the Positive Organizational Scholarship literature (e.g., Dutton & Heaphy, 2003; Cameron & Spreitzer, 2011; Stephens et al., 2011). Still, to this day, people tend to look at one person's learning rather than recognizing that it is an opportunity for both people to learn.

When people start thinking about starting a programme of any kind for a group, such as nurses, in order to engage people to be effective mentors they need to feel as though there is something that's going to come to them for investing time in efforts to create high-quality relationships (e.g., Ragins & Verbos, 2007). If they haven't experienced being a mentor before they might not be able to conceptualize how they, too, might learn from it.

As editors for this Handbook, we have discussed whether it may be that the fuzzier and more open-minded approach of mentoring is one of its strengths in that it provides people some space to explore things that they can't yet clearly articulate regarding their role and their development needs?

I do think measures such as advancement rates, promotion rates and salary increases are only a small part of a larger story. So, whenever I've designed an assessment or evaluation, I've always invited qualitative feedback from participants – both mentors and mentees – regarding how they experienced these developmental relationships along the way, and how they perceive changes in life satisfaction, identity and aspirations for the future.

We set up some research for our British Psychological Society (BPS) mentoring programmes for clinical psychologists using qualitative measures, which we put a scale to, and health and well-being were a really strong indicators of positive impact – as well as confidence in leadership, and management skills.

Were those acceptable as evidence for the value of the programme?

Yes, it was a pilot study and the BPS have set up a steering group to extend mentoring based on the outcomes of programmes such as the one for clinical psychologists – and also as it's been a key request from members across all of the different sections of the organization.

Is there anything you haven't said that you feel should/you would want to be included in your chapter?

It will be useful for readers to have a sense of the evolution of the field that started with the focus of one dyadic relationship targeted on helping young adults entering the world of work (Kram, 1988), and now it is considered a developmental relationship or a developmental network that is an important potential resource at every life transition. That's how we've travelled collectively over the years (e.g., Higgins & Kram, 2001).

Also, the context has changed so much – you've mentioned how in health care contexts there may be less opportunity for informal mentoring. It's also true that in the [COVID-19] pandemic people [have not been] running into each other so much in the office. With hybrid work, the opportunities for relational learning are quite different – we've all spent two years on online meetings and perhaps we are all developing ways of connecting more meaningfully online (e.g., Ghosh & Hutchins, 2022).

I've developed mentoring for women in leadership positions all over the world and although online work hasn't got all of the same micro cues that you might need in therapy, you learn to attune in a different way.

Mentoring will, undoubtedly, be different ten years from now compared to today, because the context will continue to change. We have to keep updating our understanding and continue our enquiry because the contextual influences keep changing. For example, consider how the nature of mentoring has changed since the beginning of the pandemic. Undoubtedly, opportunities for informal interaction leading to ongoing dyadic mentoring relationships have diminished. And, at the same time, online communication, Zoom gatherings, and other online communities have become major sources of mentoring and coaching, perhaps yet to be documented.

This conversation has been exciting to me and also humbling because there is so much we don't know, which is maybe one of the reasons why it's such a fascinating topic.

Non-specific relationship factors continue to be one of the most powerful factors in psychological therapies, and in mentoring the relational connection – and the context – also seem really important.

Yes. My colleagues, Professors Teresa Amabile, Douglas (T.) Hall, Laura Crary, Lotte Bailyn and I are now looking at how relationships with spouses, adult children, friends and community members may provide to support people who are retiring and constructing new identities and new life structure without work as a central organizing context in their lives. I like the term *relational learning* as it covers a whole range of relational supports including mentoring and coaching, as well as family, friendship and community relationships. It is clear that at every major life transition, individuals can benefit from growth-enhancing relationships with multiple developers, just as those in early career years seek to do.

And, I think it is critical to be mindful of the ways in which structural inequalities may continue to limit the range of relational support – whether it be mentoring, coaching or developmental relationships more generally. In instances of limited resources and social inequities, formal programmes that bring individuals together who wouldn't otherwise meet and facilitate relationship building across differences, will ultimately lead to more accessible sources of relational learning for everyone.

In the future developing accessible sources of relational learning might be quite an integrative way forward for those with limited resources and help facilitate social equity. What you are saying also seems to me to bring the coaching and mentoring fields together rather than polarizing them – relational learning is the heart or essence of growth and evolution.

References

Bronfenbrenner, U. (1994). *Ecological models of human development*. International Encyclopedia of Education (**2nd ed., Vol. 3**, pp. 1643–1647). Elsevier Sciences.

Cameron, K. S., & Spreitzer, G. M. (Eds.) (2011) *The Oxford Handbook of Positive Organizational Scholarship*. Oxford University Press.

Dutton, J. E., & Heaphy, E. D. (2003). *The power of high-quality connections*. In K. S. Cameron, J. E. Dutton, & R. E. Quinn (Eds.), *Positive Organizational Scholarship: Foundations of a New Discipline* (pp. 263–278). Berrett-Koehler Publishers.

Dutton, J., & Ragins, B. R. (2007). *Exploring Positive Relationships at Work: Building a Theoretical and Research Foundation*. Lawrence Erlbaum Associates, Publishers.

Eby, L. T. (2007). *Understanding relational problems in mentoring: A review and proposed investment model*. In B. R. Ragins, & K. E. Kram (Eds.), *The Handbook of Mentoring at Work: Theory, Research, and Practice* (pp. 323–344. SAGE Publications.

Feldman, E., & Kahn, W. (2019). *When developers disagree: Divergent advice as a potential catalyst for protégé growth*. Organization Science, 509–537.

Fletcher, J. & Ragins, B. R. (2007). *Stone Center relational cultural theory: A window on relational mentoring*. In Ragins, B. R. & Kram, K. E. (Eds.) Handbook of Mentoring at Work: Theory, Research, and Practice. SAGE Publications.

Ghosh, R., & Hutchins, H. M. (Eds.) (2022). *HRD Perspectives on Developmental Relationships: Connecting and Relating at Work*. Palgrave Macmillan.

Higgins, M. C., & Kram, K. E. (2001). *Reconceptualizing mentoring at work: A developmental network perspective*. Academy of Management Review, **26(2)**, 264–288.

Kram, K. E. (1988). *Mentoring at Work: Developmental Relationships in Organizational Life*. University Press of America.

Levinson, D. J., Darrow, C. N., Klein, E. B., Levinson, M. H., & McKee, B. (1978). *The Seasons of a Man's Life*. Ballantine of Random House Publishing.

Murphy, W., & Kram, K.E. (2014). *Strategic Relationships at Work: Creating Your Circle of Mentors, Sponsors and Peers in Business and in Life*. McGraw Hill.

Murrell, A. J., & Blake-Beard, S. (2017). *Mentoring Diverse Leaders: Creating Change for People, Processes, and Paradigms*. Routledge.

Parker, P., Hall, D. T., Kram, K. E., & Wasserman, I. (2018). *Peer Coaching at Work: Principles and Practices*. Stanford University Press.

Ragins, B. R. (1999). *Gender and mentoring relationships: A review and research agenda for the next decade*. In G. N. Powell (Ed.), *Handbook of Gender and Work* (pp. 347–370). SAGE Publications.

Ragins. B. R., & Kram, K. E. (Eds.) (2007). *The Handbook of Mentoring at Work: Theory, Research and Practice*. SAGE Publications.

Ragins, B. R., & Verbos, A. (2007). *Relational mentoring and mentoring schemas in the workplace*. In J. Dutton, & B. R. Ragins (Eds.), *Exploring Positive Relationships at Work: Building a Theoretical and Research Foundation* (pp. 91–116). Lawrence Erlbaum Associates, Publishers.

Scandura, T. A. (1998). *Dysfunctional mentoring relationships and outcomes*. Journal of Management, **24(3)**, 449–467.

Schein, E. (2009). *Helping: How to Offer, Give, and Receive Help*. Berrett-Koehler Publishers.

Stephens, J. P., Heaphy, E., & Dutton, J. E. (2011). *High-quality connections*. In K. S. Cameron, & G. M. Spreitzer (Eds.), *The Oxford Handbook of Positive Organizational Scholarship* (pp. 385–399). Oxford University Press.

Chapter 38
The Boundary Between Coaching and Mentoring: A Practitioner Perspective

Jonathan Passmore

The differences between coaching and mentoring

In the 1990s, coaching and mentoring were viewed as similar practices because they were vaguely defined, and the differences between them weren't clearly articulated – if anything mentoring was seen as the more dominant approach. Over the last twenty years, however, we've seen the progressive professionalization of coaching with the creation of a number of professional bodies.

These professional bodies, such as the International Coaching Federation (ICF), and the European Mentoring and Coaching Council (EMCC), have been largely practitioner-oriented. While some, such as the EMCC, started as mentoring bodies, they have increasingly shifted toward coaching, reflecting the faster-paced growth in that area of practice.

We've also seen, over the same period, a growth in the number of coaching psychology bodies. This started in Australia and the UK with the formation of networks, which subsequently developed into more formal Special Interest Groups and the achievement in the UK of Divisional status within the British Psychological Society (BPS). There are equivalent groups within a number of psychological associations internationally including Australia, South Africa, New Zealand and many other countries.

Since 2000, we have seen continued evolution, where coaching has become more clearly defined, and more clearly differentiated from mentoring. The skills to deliver coaching too have been more clearly defined (Passmore, 2021a). As this process of differentiation has gathered pace, so coaching has become the more dominant of the two approaches. I would argue that over the next decade we are going to see the continued separation of coaching and mentoring. Coaching will be seen as something that everybody in the workplace should have, with perhaps a leader or manager providing the coaching, or an external partner. While mentoring will continue to be seen more as long-term career guidance from an older, wiser, more experienced colleague.

Of course, the two approaches have much in common with their styles of engagement, – both are conversational approaches, and both are predominantly future-focused. But while mentoring often includes as much advice and guidance as questions, coaching's focus is very much toward open questions which stimulate reflection and personal insight and awareness.

There is a danger that as coaching grows among individuals (leaders or managers) and through professional bodies, this may be perceived as denigrating the role of mentoring, which could see its further decline in popularity. I would argue that there is a really important role for mentoring, and that mentors shouldn't be neglected. Mentors need training, they need support and they need professional standards. There is a role for mentoring in every HR strategy. But to achieve this, mentors need to develop a higher level of professionalism, and organizations, as well as mentors, need to recognize the role that mentoring can play and the contribution that it can make to individuals.

The changing mode of delivery of coaching and mentoring

For the last twenty years, up until about 2019, most coaching and mentoring was delivered face to face; often you would meet up informally for a coffee, either inside or outside work, and engage in a coaching or mentoring session. This has been changing.

Around 2010, migration started toward online delivery, but the majority of sessions were still face to face – individuals meeting in offices or hotel lobbies. This was facilitated by the emergence of Skype and later Zoom or Google Meet as digital spaces to connect. But the Spring of 2020 changed all of that with the need to minimise personal contact as a result of the COVID-19 pandemic. Face to face flipped to online almost overnight in most developed economies, demonstrating the power of digital. From a research study (Passmore, 2021b) about future trends in coaching, the results indicated that not only had most coaches switched to online, but they also intended to continue with this approach. The main reason stated was that although coaches recognized that the process was more distant, it was much more convenient – meaning that they could connect to several people in a day, with less associated travel costs and time.

A second trend that has been accelerated by the pandemic is the scale of delivery. Up until 2019, the majority of coaching had been delivered by sole practitioners or small organizations with between two and two hundred coaches working together, usually in a single city, region or country. Since 2020, online digital providers such as Coach Up (who I work for), Better Up, and EZRA (part of LHH) have grown significantly, with growth paths which will take them from small start-ups pre-2020 to global organizations by 2025.

Many organizations had tried coaching in smaller doses, and these digital platforms have allowed organizations to scale up from coaching maybe twenty-five managers to two hundred and fifty, and from one or two locations to fifty locations across the globe, making it an easier implementation for enterprise-size organizations with global footprints. For coaches, the benefits of coaching online have included being able to offer more sessions per day, and with zero travel time and costs, the overall price of coaching has been reducing over the past few years. In consequence, access to coaching has now extended more widely across organizations, from elite or senior leaders to middle managers, and this trend is likely to continue with the development of AI Coach bots, further reducing costs and improving accessibility.

Evidence suggests that this pattern will continue, with more people training as coaches, growth in providers and increasing popular awareness of coaching and its benefits. The result will be that everyone (or practically all employees) will be able to request coaching to support their development.

Where does this leave mentoring? One initial observation is that it leaves a gap in the market for mentoring to follow the same path, maybe at a smaller scale, but on a tech-delivered mentoring platform, where people from across the world can connect, pay a registration fee and be matched with someone in their sector, with the knowledge and experience they are seeking to help support their personal career journey.

But to make this transition, mentoring may need to move away from a personal service model, where delivery is typically free, to one where there are some transaction costs involved. While these costs may only be to cover registration costs for a connection licence, mentors can still offer their sage advice for free, and mentees can access at a low cost a relationship to help them move forward. For public sector areas, such as the NHS, local government and not-for-profits, this model can offer a new way forward in a changing and technology-driven world.

The research

In terms of research, coaching has gone from practically nothing twenty years ago to being a substantial field of research activity. In 2000, one could count on two hands the number of research papers, some dating back to the 1920s when coaching was used by university debating societies, spreading through two or three papers in the 1930s, when coaching was an 'experiment' used to help training in manufacturing, to its explosion in the late 1990s. Coaching research has accelerated from a few case studies in these early years to a substantial body of RCTs (randomised controlled trials), qualitative research and systematic reviews which demonstrate effectiveness.

In contrast, mentoring research has continued on its steady path, with excellent research demonstrating its value, but not the rocket trajectory that coaching has witnessed. There has been some great work from Kathy Kram in the US and David Clutterbuck in the UK, but overall, the interest remains low and the total number of mentoring studies has remained stable over this period.

This growth in coaching has seen a parallel growth in the number of university programmes available, such as those at Oxford Brookes University, University of East London, Henley Business School, Sydney University and Columbia University, all of which have emerged since 2000.

For mentoring to prosper we need to enhance our efforts to increase the legitimacy of mentoring as an effective intervention for individuals and organizations alongside coaching, training and other forms of staff development. This needs to be echoed in research and university-level training, and by the promotion of the identity of mentors alongside those of coaches.

Mentoring's greatest strength is the long-term nature of the relationship; from personal experience, this can run on for five or even ten years, providing support for individuals and helping them think through issues and 'chew the fat' with a wiser guide. Mentoring also has an important role to play in addressing the challenges of under-representation, which the work of Kram and others has emphasized (Tong & Kram, 2012).

Conclusion

It's worth celebrating the fact that coaching has developed so significantly with high-quality university-based programmes and a research agenda, but maybe it is time for mentoring to step up. It has a really important part to play. So, if you're the director of a charity, a local authority director, or a clinician, then a mentoring relationship will no doubt be of benefit, helping you think through your ongoing development, your career and the challenges you face.

References

Passmore, J. (2021a). *The Coaches' Handbook: The Complete Practitioner Guide to Professional Coaches.* Routledge.

Passmore, J. (2021b). *Future Trends in Coaching: Executive Report 2021.* Henley Business School, EMCC. https://assets.henley.ac.uk/v3/fileUploads/Future-Trends-in-Coaching.pdf

Tong, C., & Kram, K. (2012). *The efficacy of mentoring.* In J. Passmore, D. Peterson, & T. Freire (Eds.), *The Wiley Blackwell Handbook of the Psychology of Coaching and Mentoring* (pp. 217–242). Wiley Blackwell.

Chapter 39
Connecting the Strands of Mentoring Research

Interview with Lillian Eby

The Blackwell Handbook of Mentoring (2007) stated 'Although the concept of mentoring is often traced back to the early Greeks, relative to other areas of scientific inquiry the study of mentoring is still in the early stages … We hope we have woven the beginning strands of connective fibre that will continue to grow into a network of interconnections between the research domains of mentoring.'

We hope we are continuing to grow those connections with this Handbook. To start, we wondered what would you most like to share with readers of this Handbook chapter about your perspectives on, and experiences in, the field of mentoring research that you feel are important, significant or groundbreaking?

Our 2010 *Blackwell Handbook of Mentoring* was pretty unusual as we were really trying to take an interdisciplinary approach by integrating organizational mentoring with educational mentoring (which covers a really wide range from children to PhD students), and with mentoring to underserved populations of youths.

Key research for integrating our understanding of mentoring includes Kathy Kram's initial qualitative work, which was incredibly important – although it's interesting that many of the findings from her qualitative study have not been the subject of much empirical enquiry since. So, going back and reading those original works is what I would encourage people to do, in order to find out what are the key findings and ideas that have not been tested. Kathy's work has been incredibly influential for me and for all mentoring researchers.

I would also point to Brad Johnson's work (Johnson & Huwe, 2003; Johnson et al., 2007; Johnson, 2015) in the more educational domain. He's done incredibly important work, particularly around gender and mentoring. He's really become a powerful advocate for mentoring for women and under-represented minorities, but particularly for women in helping us understand how gender intersects with mentoring (Johnson & Smith, 2016). He provides really practical advice for men who want to mentor women. I really respect him tremendously because he is really bridging the science and practice gap.

Rose Ragins (Ragins & Cotto, 1999; Ragins & Scandura, 1999; Ragins et al., 2000) has also had an enormous and long-standing programme of research into mentoring, which has helped us understand different types of mentoring support, and gender and mentoring from an empirical perspective. She conducted a lot of the foundational quantitative empirical work on mentoring.

My long-term collaborator and friend Tammy Allen has also done a lot of work to help understand aspects of formal mentoring that are particularly important (Allen et al., 2006a; 2006b), as well as important meta-analytic work (Allen et al., 2004). Her work has shaped the way we think about mentoring, by integrating these different bodies of research from organizational, under-represented youth and educational mentoring (Allen & Eby, 2007.)

I would also point to work that has just come out of the National Academies of Science, Engineering and Medicine recently in the United States (Byars-Winston & Dahlberg, 2019), which has had a consensus panel that was really interesting. They did a wonderful job in distilling evidence-based recommendations for mentoring, with a strong emphasis on mentoring in STEMM (Science, Technology, Engineering, Mathematics and Medicine). This work focuses on understanding the unique issues facing under-represented minorities to help prepare the next generation of scientists.

Those are what I would see as the foundational pieces of work that have shaped the field of mentoring.

What do you think has changed, developed and moved on in the field of mentoring and research since you first co-edited *The Blackwell Handbook of Mentoring* in 2007?

I think in the field of management and organizational psychology there is a lot of stagnation right now. There aren't a lot of researchers studying issues of mentoring at work or in organizational contexts. I think part of that is because, as in other areas of study, once you answer a lot of questions you can struggle with what next, what would be the next questions to ask.

Having said that I am continuing to work in this space and younger researchers are also developing. One area in particular that is developing is mentoring in relation to issues of diversity, especially outside of organizational psychology. I tend to focus on United States research. There is a big response here to Black Lives Matter and a lot of critical reflection that has happened in US institutions, including higher education. Professional institutions, such as the American Psychological Association, are also coming to terms with the role that they have played with promoting, perpetuating and failing to challenge race issues in psychology. This has led to an increase in interest in what we can do to rectify racial inequality. There has also been an increasing and heightened interest in this topic, particularly as it relates to preparing people for faculty jobs and the importance of having diverse faculties for mentoring and role modelling. This heightened emphasis on diversity is definitely something that is new. A lot of it has been more discussion and practical programming than it has been empirical research. Another place that you see a lot of this development is in mentoring in medicine and health care, because we know that there has been a lot of under-representation in those areas.

The other thing I would say is I do see more of an emphasis on what competencies mentors need to have, particularly interpersonal and cross-cultural competencies. Where we used to focus a lot more on the protégée perspective, I think there is increasing recognition that we need to focus more on the need to prepare people for entering into these mentoring roles, particularly related to diversity.'

Are there any other key things you would like to see from research, theory and practice perspectives or from multiple perspectives?

I would want to see practical recommendations, particularly around designing and delivering mentoring programmes, and also encouraging informal mentoring because we know that is important too. One of the things I do find worrying is that often you do find recommendations that are not really evidence-based. So, I would like to see educators and practitioners drawing on the empirical research that is out there. Also, drawing on the literature that may be more experimental, or social psychology-oriented research on relationships and friendships. I don't think that literature often gets integrated into the study of mentoring but it holds a lot of promise. We definitely need more research on diversity in mentoring because there is very little research that has looked at these issues in a really systematic way.

Our psychological bulletin (Eby et al., 2013) looked across hundreds of primary studies in community, workplace and educational settings. We found that demographic differences between the mentor and the protégée were largely unrelated to the amount of support and satisfaction that protégées reported. That is very different from what you hear about if you look at the popular press on diversity and mentoring. Even if you look at a lot of more evidence-based recommendations on mentoring you see lots of suggestions for making sure you match people on certain demographics, but empirical support for this recommendation is lacking.

So, there are some myths out there about mentoring which it would be really nice to debunk. One of them is that you have to have demographic similarity, when what you have to have is *some* similarity, but people can be similar in lots of different ways. If we can think about ways to enhance perceptions of similarity, enhance trust and belongingness, this would help. It would get us away from the more distal factors, like gender or race similarity, that are often believed to enhance relationship quality, and which it's often not even possible to match people on. For example, it's not always possible to match people on racial similarity and efforts to do so can put a tremendous burden on diverse mentors, who often have a lot of demands on their time.

We can also think of ways of enhancing mentoring relationships, by using findings from social psychology on enhancing relationships more broadly, from the psychology of inclusion, positive psychology, the psychology of attachment. These areas of work can offer fresh perspectives for thinking about mentoring.

That is really refreshing to hear and gives some real pointers for research into mentoring over the next decade. It'll be very interesting to see if that unfolds when another mentoring handbook comes out in ten years. Are there any ways that the mentoring field and the research findings have changed over the last few decades?

I think there have been some milestones along the way, such as the challenge to the assumption that mentoring is always a good thing. Research that I did in the early 2000s (Eby et al., 2004; 2008), and Terri Scandura's conceptual work (Scandura, 1998), discussed the potential downsides of mentoring. This work is important because, like all relationships, there are going to be high points and low points.

Particularly with formal mentoring, we are putting people together and constraining the way they can interact. For example, in an organizational context there are norms about how close people can get and how they can interact, particularly if there is a power difference. So, we need to find a way of destigmatizing the negative and recognizing that it's a part of all relationships. I have seen this shift in the popular press in talking about mentoring in more realistic ways.

I have often heard mentors say that they don't think they have much to offer, or they don't really feel equipped to be a mentor. We need to find ways to help mentors feel efficacious in their role, and this speaks to the way that these relationships can be hard, particularly at the beginning. We can't set up an expectation that two people will just come together and it will be life-changing – sometimes it is, but more often than not, it's not.

We are also recognizing that formal mentoring is not necessarily a poor cousin to informal. You can have a really high-quality formal relationship, just as you can have a really poor informal one. We really need more research on formal mentoring because often we throw it all together in a bucket as if it's one thing, whereas there are lots of aspects of formality – How long is the relationship? Is there a contract? How much training do you have? Are there expectations for frequency of meeting? And all these different aspects can be researched to find out what optimizes effectiveness.

There is also more recognition that mentoring is not a panacea or a cure-all for your career – that it's one of many experiences that may or may not have a positive effect. There is still a lot of rhetoric suggesting that you have to have a mentor, or that women have to have mentors, as if it's essential, when in reality the effect sizes can be pretty modest. Mentors do matter, but they're not everything. Mentors can only do so much for people.

If assumptions are being made that everybody needs a mentor then it seems to be putting a lot of pressure on mentors, and we really need to be realistic.

The Blackwell Handbook suggests that imposing overly specific and excessively rigid definitions doesn't acknowledge the complexities of mentoring as a relationship embedded in real-world difficulties – so having core concepts, being informed about the field and explicit about the aims, goals and intentions of your mentoring and what context it is embedded in is key to being able to evaluate outcomes and to progressing the field. Does this still hold as the best approach to progressing the field of mentoring?

That is a great question because yes, it's complicated. On the one hand mentoring relationships are really idiosyncratic – they're going to look different for different people, different dyads, different contexts – but on the other hand we need to study it. To do this we need to develop some kind of systematic measurement, so this does create a bit of a rub. As psychologists, we want to find patterns of behaviour, so we're looking for those key antecedents of relationship quality that would hold across different kinds of relationships. We also need to recognize that in different contexts different kinds of relational features may be more or less important. For example, in diverse mentoring relationships with under-represented and majority group participants I would expect things like authenticity and trust would be particularly important. These features would also be important in other mentoring relationships, but the predictive power might be different.

Research does need to place some boundaries on these variables but in practice we need to consider what are the goals of the programme, what are we hoping that mentoring will affect. Those outcomes might look very different in a faculty mentoring programme, a youth mentoring programme or a programme for succession planning in an organization.

I think we've got to find that sweet spot between trying to identify systematic factors but differences in expected outcomes. In a lot of mentoring programmes the expected outcomes aren't all that clear – so sometimes a mentee's expectations can be that this is going to help me get a promotion, when really that is not at all what the programme is designed for, it's designed to get you better integrated into the organization. This can lead to people being dissatisfied with the programme.

What I would recommend for formal programmes is to be very clear for both the mentor and mentee about what the programme is designed to do. This comes from the study of relationships in general – when people have unclear expectations, it will probably lead to disappointment.

People can bring loaded and implicit expectations whereas when expectations are made explicit it allows clarity and evaluation. We've been exploring how coaching and mentoring have developed quite differently, with mentoring having less of a direct relationship to performance of a skill set important to a job or role, and more of a relationship to supporting reflective thinking about one's role or job. What are your thoughts about this?

We sometimes can lose sight of what it is that mentoring can do, and that it is a relationship. I think mentoring is completely different from coaching. Mentoring is a long-term, mutually committed relationship and that is not coaching. I also think compensating mentors is misguided too, personally. This is more opinion, but there is some evidence that paying people for things means that intrinsic motivation for performing the role goes down (Deci & Ryan, 2012). It may change the dynamic, so now, as a mentee, am I wondering *'is the only reason that Sarajane is mentoring me is that she's getting paid for it?'*, rather than that she cares about me, or that she really believes in me.

I find that really problematic – turning these communal relationships into something that is transactional. I think it goes against the corpus of what we know about mentoring. I would argue that it no longer becomes a mentoring relationship – maybe that is a bit too strong but these relationships are supposed to be based on wanting to help, so payment may change the mentor's motivational frame. I think it could also hinder closeness. I don't know, it's an interesting empirical question.

I often get asked, how is mentoring different from coaching or supervision, and I think it is because it's entered into more voluntarily – even formal mentoring relationships are entered into more voluntarily by the mentor. It's still about wanting to help others rather than to get a thousand dollars or whatever it is. I'm curious to see how that dynamic might redefine things – I could be wrong.

It sounds as though the payment issue is a key area for future evaluation and for thinking about possible impacts on the motivational frame for mentoring.

There are some mentoring programmes in the UK that are offering payment to mentors – particularly to help promote inclusivity in diverse populations – and these are being evaluated. So, this issue will be explored and evaluated.

Yes, and I am also worried and concerned that programmes such as this also need to be careful in terms of how they frame the overall programme, so you can make sure you don't create a backlash effect. You don't want to create a backlash amongst those who aren't eligible for the programme, and you also want to make sure that it doesn't inadvertently look like a 'charity' for the diverse protégé. Mentoring programmes for women concern me because unless they're marketed and promoted in the right kind of way and in context, it can make it look as though women need something special. In other words, people may make attributions that women need some kind of special treatment, or that they need this help because they weren't as competent to start with. This sort of accusation has been levelled for decades at training that targets women. Similar issues apply with programmes to support inclusivity. Some people from diverse backgrounds have very positive reactions to affirmative action approaches, and some have very negative reactions. There are also individual differences in whether people want to participate in these programmes or not, and how they think it will affect how they are viewed by others.

There is a real responsibility for mentoring programme directors to communicate that it's not a remedial programme or a special measure, but that it's an attempt to help deal with systematic inequities. I'm also not sure that mentoring is the solution to such systematic inequities given the relatively small effect sizes for mentoring, particular on career outcomes such as pay or promotion rates. I think it can be viewed as a quick fix that can make it look as though we're trying to do something, when there are really much bigger societal things going on that we need to focus on.

What do you feel might have hindered effective mentoring theory and research, and what could be done to change this?

I don't see a lot of new theorizing or a lot of new empirical perspectives. I'm not quite sure why that is. There is so much potential for mentoring to inform areas like diversity and inclusion, or leadership, and yet those areas of literature are not well integrated. I think there is a lot of opportunity for integration.

I hope that younger scholars step up and study mentoring. I do see some of this happening, but I think we need some fresh perspectives and some different methodologies. We know very little about what actually happens during mentoring relationships. We know something about average experiences, but if we could better understand the episodic experiences of mentoring and how those unfold over time, or use textual analysis to determine conversational patterns that occur between mentors and mentees, then we could figure out what really determines positive outcomes or reciprocal exchanges.

Those are some of the things we are trying to do in our lab. They're very difficult to study and very time intensive. But I think we need fresh perspectives or new approaches, methodologically too, rather than just looking at the typical correlational design where we're just measuring average mentoring. I'm hopeful that people will start to move in those directions and certainly there is a good bit of intervention-based research that is happening in the higher education field of mentoring which is really helpful (e.g., Byars-Winston et al., 2018). There has been very little programmatic evaluation work in my area.

The other thing we know almost nothing about is how to match people effectively, and that is the million-dollar question. What do you match people on, how do you do it, and what matters most? We still know very little about that. Organizations do all kinds of different things. I don't know what happens in educational contexts, but in an organizational context we've looked at Fortune 500 companies and tried to figure out what they are matching on. They're either not telling us, or it's not clear, or the matching process is random. Nobody really knows what is important. I think if we could know that, we could do a much better job matching people. I really hope it's not just basic demographics because that would really constrain our ability to maximize the people who want to give back to their field.

It's interesting that the clinical psychologists mentoring programme didn't use matching, but gave mentees a list of mentors, with the choice of selecting a mentor from that list. This appears to have worked well. It's also really interesting that you use the word 'stagnating' and that might be something really important to learn from to help the field move forward.

Some of the contributors to this Handbook may be bringing fresh perspectives to researching and thinking about mentoring. As mentoring starts to develop within the public sector field, and particularly within the professions who are trained in psychosocial approaches and psychological therapies, people are starting to bring approaches that have helped us understand what the active ingredients are within a therapeutic relationship to understanding what happens in a mentoring relationship. Even though the two kinds of relationship are different, there are some interesting overlaps and ways of studying both.

There are certainly a lot of overlaps and similarities between mentoring relationships and the therapeutic alliance. There are clearly differences too – therapeutic relationships tend to be more time limited, tend to involve therapists or counsellors who are paid for their services, and tend to be focused on different things – but there is some overlap in terms of thinking about the active ingredients of supportive relationships. We know quite a lot about that, and some of the measures of therapeutic alliance look a lot like psychosocial mentoring and even career-related mentoring, if you strip off the context. So, I think that literature could be really informative. I don't follow that literature closely but we discussed its relevance to mentoring in a recent article (Eby & Robertson, 2020).

Similarly, the literature around clinical supervision for professionals in clinical contexts – that looks a lot like mentoring. In fact, you could say it is mentoring of a kind – a formal supervisory kind of mentoring. Some have argued that supervisory mentoring can be highly effective because there are more interaction opportunities in supervisory mentoring relationships. Also, supervisory mentors really understand mentees' jobs and are already engaged with helping them to develop competencies to be successful.

Is there anything more you would like to add that we haven't covered?

I think this has been a great conversation and I really do hope that this book sparks different ways of thinking about mentoring and particularly that it encourages different methodological and empirical studies. I think the practice side of mentoring is pretty well developed, but it's something that should be informed by the science. I do hope that this book will spur people to study things in different ways and explore different theories. I think we've had a really fruitful conversation that I hope will be helpful for people.

We are in need of building on some of the fresh avenues of research that are just starting to develop. I wonder what your vision is of the field in ten years' time?

It depends on who is studying mentoring and what they bring to the field to help it move forward. I would hope we would see new theories being brought to bear in understanding the perspectives of both the mentors and mentees. I would hope that we would see more microbehavioural research on what is really happening in mentoring relationships, and I would hope we would see more studies using episodic and experience-based sampling (Gabriel et al., 2019). Also, I would hope that we would see more integration across different areas – we tried to do this with our handbook and also we had a special issue of the *Journal of Vocational Behaviour* that was multidisciplinary. But I don't see a lot of multidisciplinary approaches to mentoring right now, so I would hope that people would step back and start looking outside their own comfort areas of scholarship to think about what other theories or perspectives could really inform what we do.

One thing that we haven't really talked about, which I think is really important but very hard to study, is that we know that mentoring is not just about one mentor. There are usually a series of mentors across a lifespan and/or multiple mentors at the same time. Kathy Kram and Monica Higgins did some work on developmental networks, but there has been very little follow up and empirical work on that because it's really complicated to study. But now we have methods such as social network analysis that are much more well established, and which we could possibly bring to bear on some of those questions.

We could also use retrospective qualitative accounts for people to reflect on their history of mentoring relationships and how that has shaped them, because it's really that culmination of different relationships that constitute the distal impacts that we're interested in. It's not usually about this one mentor I had at this one point in time, so I do think that's really important and probably why research in our field yields pretty modest effect sizes for the average amount of mentoring you receive from a particular person. Yet when people reflect on what has been important in their career they talk about mentors in the plural.

For me, it's not just one person but many people who have shaped and influenced me, but if you asked me on a survey to think about one mentor and how much career support I received, then that is just one part, one person. So, thinking about those relationship constellations or networks and studying them empirically is tricky and time consuming, which is probably why there is limited research in this area.

The [COVID-19] pandemic has certainly influenced progress in the field. For example, here we have had to delay some of our research into relational processes but we are now hoping to be able to publish some of the results soon. The pandemic has certainly also made us aware of how important relationships are. We've had to review so many different ways to look at work relationships and online relationships and this could spark people to think about these things differently.

References

Allen T. D., & Eby L. T. (2007). The *Blackwell Handbook of Mentoring*. Blackwell Publishing.

Allen, T. D., Eby, L. T., & Lentz, E. (2006a). *Mentorship behaviors and mentorship quality associated with formal mentoring programs: Closing the gap between research and practice*. Journal of Applied Psychology, **91**(3), 567–578.

Allen T. D., Eby, L. T., & Lentz, E. (2006b). *The relationship between formal mentoring program characteristics and perceived program effectiveness*. Personnel Psychology, **59**(1), 125–153.

Allen, T. D., Eby, L. T., Poteet, M., Lima, L., & Lentz, E. (2004). *Career benefits associated with mentoring for protégés: A meta-analysis*. Journal of Applied Psychology, **89**(1), 127–136.

Byars-Winston, A., & Dahlberg, M. L. (2019). *The science of effective mentorship in STEMM: A consensus report*. National Academies of Science, Engineering and Medicine. National Academies Press.

Byars-Winston, A., Womack, V. Y., Butz, A. R., McGee, R., Quinn, S. C., Utzerath, E., Saetermoe, C. L., & Thomas, S. B. (2018). *Pilot study of an intervention to increase cultural awareness in research mentoring: Implications for diversifying the scientific workforce*. Journal of Clinical and Translational Science, **2**(2), 86–94. https://www. cambridge.org/core/journals/journal-of-clinical-and-translational-science/article/pilot-study-of-an-intervention-to-increase-cultural-awareness-in-research-mentoring-implications-for-diversifying-the-scientific-workforce/DD84DDF876B187BD902A110234A39C1C

Deci, E. L., & Ryan, R. M. (2012). *Self-determination theory*. In P. A. M. Van Lange, A. W. Kruglanski, & E. T. Higgins (Eds.), *Handbook of Theories of Social Psychology* (pp. 416–436). SAGE Publications.

Eby, L. T., Allen, T. D, Hoffman, B. J., Baranik, L. E., Sauer, J. B., Baldwin, S., Morrison, M. A., Kinkade, K. M., Maher, C. P., Curtis, S., & Evans, S. C. (2013). *An interdisciplinary meta-analysis of the potential antecedents, correlates, and consequences of protégé perceptions of mentoring*. Psychological Bulletin, **139**(2), 441–476.

Eby, L. T., Butts, M., Lockwood, A., & Simon, S. A. (2004). *Protégés' negative mentoring experiences: Construct development and nomological validation*. Personnel Psychology, **57**(2), 411–447.

Eby, L. T., Durley, J., Evans, S. C., & Ragins, B. R. (2008). *Mentors' perceptions of negative mentoring experiences: Scale development and nomological validation*. Journal of Applied Psychology, **93**(2), 358–373.

Eby, L. T. & Robertson, M. M. (2020). *The psychology of workplace mentoring relationships*. Annual Review of Organizational Psychology and Organizational Behavior, **7**, 75–100.

Gabriel, A. S., Podsakoff, N. P., Beal, D. J., Scott, B. A., Sonnentag, S., Trougakos, J. P., & Butts, M. M. (2019). *Experience sampling methods: A discussion of critical trends and considerations for scholarly advancement*. Organizational Research Methods, **22**(4), 969–1006.

Johnson, W. B. (2015). *On Being a Mentor: A Guide for Higher Education Faculty* **(2nd ed.)**. Routledge.

Johnson, W. B., & Huwe, J. M. (2003). *Getting Mentored in Graduate School*. American Psychological Association.

Johnson, W. B., Rose, G., & Schlosser, L. Z. (2007). *Student-faculty mentoring: Theoretical and methodological issues*. In T. D. Allen, & L. T. Eby (Eds.), *The Blackwell Handbook of Mentoring* (pp. 49–69). Blackwell Publishing.

Johnson, W. B., & Smith, D. (2016). *Athena Rising: How and Why Men Should Mentor Women*. Bibliomotion.

Ragins, B. R., & Cotton, J. L. (1999). *Mentor functions and outcomes: A comparison of men and women in formal and informal mentoring relationships*. Journal of Applied Psychology, **84**(4), 529–550.

Ragins, B. R., Cotton, J. L., & Miller, J. S. (2000). *Marginal mentoring: The effects of type of mentor, quality of relationship, and program design on work and career attitudes*. Academy of Management Journal, **43**(6), 1177–1194.

Ragins, B. R., & Scandura, T. A. (1999). *Burden or blessing? Expected costs and benefits of being a mentor*. Journal of Organizational Behavior, **20**(4), 493–509.

Scandura, T. A. (1998). *Dysfunctional mentoring relationships and outcomes*. Journal of Management, **24**(3), 449–467. https://doi.org/10.1177/014920639802400307

Scott, J. (1988). *Social network analysis*. Sociology, **22**(1), 109–127. https://doi.org/10.1177/0038038588022001007

Epilogue

*There was once a wise Zen master. People travelled from
far and wide to seek his help, and to learn the way to
enlightenment. One day, a scholar visited and asked the master
to teach him. Soon, though, it became obvious that the scholar
was full of his own opinions and knowledge. So, the master
suggested that they have tea. He poured tea into the guest's cup
until it was full – then kept pouring until the cup overflowed
onto the table. "You are like this cup," he said, "so full of ideas
that no more will fit. Come back to me with an empty cup."*

The Empty Cup is a parable that highlights the importance of having an open
mind, humility and receptivity to new ideas and experiences. In this spirit, we
have attempted to approach the rich field of mentoring in a manner that seeks out
cutting-edge ideas and new insights. We have invited diverse writers to build up a
rich tapestry of perspectives and experiences, in order to help the field grow and
evolve. And through the process of editing and writing, we have noticed a key thread
that weaves continuously through the processes, aims and purpose of mentoring – a
relationship of mutuality, humility and openness focused on learning and development
to enable the growth and development of individuals, teams, and organizations.

Through this thread, and through its ability to work creatively with relational
dynamics and complexities, mentoring has been shown to have tremendous potential
and broad reach across a wide spectrum of areas. It has reached through various
stages of the life cycle and in different forms across groups such as vocational
mentoring, workplace mentoring, leadership mentoring, eco mentoring and spiritual
mentoring. The chapters in this book take the reader on a journey through the diverse
landscape of mentoring – across the terrain of models, approaches, perspectives and
diverse applications – demonstrating cutting-edge innovation and critical thinking to
embrace the challenges of our increasingly conflictual globalised world.

Summary of key themes

Below, we briefly outline some of the key themes of the Handbook – themes that stand
out for us across the different sections of the book. The list is not exhaustive, and the
themes described are often interconnecting. There are many more that the reader may
have identified through their associations while navigating through various chapters.

1. **The evolution of mentoring and emerging paradigms**

   Definitions and scope. Mentoring has evolved from a single dyadic
   relationship between a senior individual and a protégé, and has spread
   its wings into new formats, areas and contexts. While there remains no
   consensus on a tight definition, for our purposes mentoring today can be
   seen as referring to a range of approaches to developmental relationships

that enable people to reflect on their personal goals and to develop their own way of responding to their environments. There may be slightly different definitions of mentorship reflecting its aims, expected outcomes and development in particular contexts. In many places mentoring has evolved into formats such as group mentoring, reverse and reciprocal mentoring, and the explicit establishment of mentoring networks rather than a single mentoring relationship. We have noted many innovations in the types of mentoring taking place. Its application has become richer across professional groups over the course of time, and key themes such as how gender, diversity, cultural identity, spirituality, parenthood and work roles intersect with mentoring are now being widely explored.

Mentoring, coaching, and supervising. Readers will have noted this theme emerging across some chapters. While there are overlaps in terms of the roles that mentoring, coaching and supervision play in professional development, there are also clear distinctions. In some places where mentoring has not evolved to an advanced form, it is often squeezed into supervision or line management relationships which involve management and evaluation of the mentee. This runs the risk of mentoring not being driven by mentee needs, but instead becoming diluted into another 'top down' relationship driven by organizational needs. In some contexts, mentoring and coaching are virtually indistinguishable; but overall, across many contexts, coaching tends to be a paid-for relationship whereas mentoring tends to be a free, altruistic relationship. Also, at a general level mentoring tends to have a broader life context, whereas coaching tends to be about enhancing a skill set in a particular context.

Informal and formal mentoring programmes. Public sector culture now includes more business and competitive elements in the management of services. This makes informal mentoring increasingly difficult to achieve, which has in many areas led to the evolution of formal mentoring programmes akin to those that have existed in business for some time. These formal programmes need to mix 'bottom-up' and 'top-down' support to enable healthy development for individuals, and to support them to challenge their environmental context.

Paid-for and free mentoring. The move towards programmes of mentoring is raising the issue of paid-for versus free mentoring. There are strong opinions on both sides of this debate. The key issue is whether paid-for mentoring can maintain the generous 'giving' relationship that is the heart of good mentoring. There is a growing movement towards the 'professional mentor'. This is driven by senior executives wanting to pursue a post-retirement career helping others but not wanting to become coaches, which they perceive as undervaluing their accumulated experience. The Mentoring Academy concept, pioneered in Poland, equips these mentors with skills and qualifications at least equivalent to coaches. This may be a future focus for research and evaluation.

Mentoring in the digital world. Online mentoring has grown, fuelled by the COVID-19 pandemic, and has become a common way to deliver mentoring. Whether this affects the nature of the mentoring relationship would be a fruitful avenue for future research.

Mentoring as a resource for organizational development. Mentoring impacts on areas of personal development such as the enhancement of resilience, leadership skills and professional roles. As mentorship programmes develop, so too does the opportunity for organizational development through increased organizational awareness about the impact of mentoring on recruitment and retention, staff well-being, resilience and career development.

Ownership. Mentoring can be an initiative within an organization such as a Health Trust, or it can be offered by an external agency such as a national professional body. It may often start informally without any organizational backing, and then develop into a programme with organizational support. Ownership and authority for mentoring are vital to its development and evaluation outcomes. A careful analysis of organizational culture, plans and needs is important to establish links with other developmental initiatives that may complement and support mentoring to achieve specified objectives with an evaluation strategy.

Cultivating a strategic mindset. It is essential to be strategic in setting up mentoring services. We have highlighted this in several illustrations. Strategic thinking has contributed to the evolution of mentoring in offering learning and developmental support across a range of areas such as growing talent, developing leadership skills, managing change and transition, supporting resilience at challenging times, and working with diversity and intersectionality.

2. Factors contributing to effective mentoring

Clear goals. Research continues to shed light on what contributes to effective mentoring. An operational definition of mentoring and clarity of the goals of mentoring are key to success, as these factors ensure that mentors and mentees have a clear shared framework in mind.

Quality of relationships. The quality of mentoring relationships and alignment of relational processes with developmental needs is a key factor for effective mentoring. Recent research is beginning to look in more detail at relationship factors and processes to identify core skills that characterise effective mentoring relationships. Some of the vital factors identified include clear goal setting within the relationship, as well as compassion, connection with the context, and working with personal and professional boundaries. Often there is also attention to well-being, work-life balance and diversity challenges.

Support systems. Effective mentoring programmes often support mentors and mentees with evidence-based resources such as guidelines for mentoring and training for mentors. There are also sometimes meetings with peers or programme leads to discuss any issues involved in the mentoring process. Evaluation by mentors and mentees of the outcomes of mentoring, and access during mentoring to identified programme leads, can support the effectiveness and governance of a programme.

3. Governance and assurance

Quantitative and qualitative evaluation. The move towards delivering mentoring as part of a formal programme has opened the door to governance and assurance systems. For instance, if mentoring is focused on developing leadership skills, then along with an evaluation of mentee and mentor satisfaction, an evidence-based questionnaire from the leadership field can be given to mentees before and after mentoring in order to determine specific outcomes in this area. Qualitative data can also be gathered to learn from mentees and mentors what their experience of the programme has been.

Standards and governance. While the surge of mentoring initiatives is encouraging, there are questions around quality, ethical practice and governance. The European Mentoring and Coaching Council (EMCC) has produced evidence-based standards that can be used across programmes to establish good practice and to facilitate communication and learning between different programmes. Such organizations also promote ethical standards. Governance can be supported by having identified programme leads who are easily contacted so that any problems within the mentoring relationship can be addressed early on. We have included examples of evaluation strategies across a range of settings to demonstrate the importance of governance and assurance; however, this is an area that requires further progression.

4. Challenging structural inequalities

Mentoring is being used to help challenge structural inequalities and to enhance diversity and inclusivity. While mentoring on its own cannot be expected to change these structural issues, it can be an important tool among a broader range of methods. A mentoring relationship provides a safe space to unpack complex dynamics and the interplay between individual, group and organizational factors. Attention to how these factors and dynamics might play out in the mentoring relationship is an important aspect to consider.

Gaps and perspectives not covered

We believe that this is the first mentoring handbook to focus primarily within the field of health and social care. As such, we have covered mentoring for medics, nurses, social workers and psychologists; however, there are many more professions within the field of mentoring that due to space restrictions we have not been able to cover in any detail.

Educational and business contexts. We have given some examples from outside health and social care to enable exploration of how mentoring can evolve in different national and organizational contexts. However, this has not been an exhaustive exploration, and volumes exist that cover mentoring in educational and business fields in a more comprehensive way.

Research. Mentoring is an evolving field that requires significant further research and evaluation. Although we have included some chapters dealing with research and evaluation, it has not been a key focus of this work – and therefore it may appear to be a gap.

Looking to the future

Connecting past, present, and future is an important element of learning and growth. Through the tapestry of its chapters, this book offers a space to reflect upon roads travelled and less travelled in the field of mentoring. It is heartening to see innovation and creativity across cultures, and in a multitude of settings, that aims to develop mentoring relationships with a deep spirit of enabling growth, development and transformation. The journey so far offers hope to both current and future generations of mentors and mentees to explore new areas alongside taking up work to solidify its foundation. As we near the end of this Epilogue, we have highlighted a few key areas with potential for further growth in the coming years.

New approaches to research. With a good enough operational definition of mentoring in each context, the differences in approach can be contained, integrated and supported by research looking at outcomes and effectiveness. New directions are evolving around the intersection of mentoring with health and social care professions. For example, professionals in mental health are looking at mentoring processes in more detail, as well as exploring specific skills for promoting generative cognitive change and enabling compassion, leadership competence and organizational development. The mentoring relationship is different to a therapeutic relationship, but mentoring research can learn and benefit from evidence-based research into the relational skills required in mental health contexts.

New theories. While the mentoring field has grown rapidly, there has not been as much theorising linked to empirical research. Cross-fertilisation across professional groups and nations can be a helpful way forward to consider what might enhance mentoring relationships, and what evidence there is for competencies in specialist areas such as eco mentoring, leadership development and diversity across cultures.

Challenging organizational structures. Mentoring and coaching, although distinct from each other, are likely to play an increasing part in optimising organizational health by supporting preparation for lifelong learning and ongoing development. Mentoring can help to challenge and change organizational structures, particularly those preventing inclusivity and diversity. Having said this, it is also clear that mentoring alone cannot be seen as a quick fix for structural problems; however, it can play an important catalytic role now and in the future.

Recruitment and retention. Mentoring offers a way to support people's continuing professional development (CPD) and thereby to enhance recruitment, retention and an enabling organizational culture. This depends on a positive and supportive approach to staff development, and on the organization seeing the development of assertive staff able to challenge the status quo as healthy and in the organization's long-term interests.

Questions and reflections

Increasing effectiveness.

Can the relatively recent growth of mentoring in health and social care spark some new areas of research into the relational skills that enhance outcomes for mentees and mentors? Can the growth in mentoring training and mentoring programmes also lead to the development of more robust research and evaluation?

Drawing together strands of research.

Can bodies such as the European Mentoring and Coaching Council (EMCC) act to draw together and integrate different strands of research in different contexts, and to support the accreditation of key skills that are common across different settings? Can such action balance the diversity of mentoring approaches while also enabling evaluation of the core skills and processes that different forms of mentoring share?

Compassion, spirituality and ecological factors.

Mentoring is developing ways to integrate issues such as compassion, spirituality and ecological factors into the frame of working. Each of these is a potential growth area for future practice and research.

Continuing to thrive.

Can mentoring maintain its generous and generative stance as it moves towards more formal, and sometimes paid-for, programmes? We believe that the growth of developmental relationships suggests a healthy future in which mentoring will thrive.